Java™ 2 Certification

New
Riders

201 West 103rd Street, Indianapolis, Indiana 46290

Jamie Jaworski

Java™ 2 Certification Training Guide

International Standard Book Number: 1-56205-950-5

Library of Congress Catalog Card Number: 99-63309

Printed in the United States of America

First Printing: July 1999

01   00   99   4   3   2   1

Trademarks

Warning and Disclaimer

EXECUTIVE EDITOR
Tim Ryan

DEVELOPMENT EDITOR
Jon Steever

MANAGING EDITOR
Jodi Jensen

SENIOR EDITOR
Susan Ross Moore

COPY EDITOR
Mary Lagu

INDEXER
Cheryl Landes

PROOFREADER
Mona Brown

TECHNICAL EDITOR
Alexandre Calsavara

SOFTWARE DEVELOPMENT SPECIALIST
Bill Eland

INTERIOR DESIGN
Nathan Clement

COVER DESIGN
Sandra Schroeder

COPY WRITER
Eric Borgert

LAYOUT TECHNICIANS
Brian Borders
Susan Geiselman
Mark Walchle

Contents at a Glance

PART III   Becoming a Sun Certified Java 2 Developer

PART IV   Appendixes

Table of Contents

5 Flow Control and Exception Handling   103

6 Overloading, Overriding, Runtime Type, and Object Orientation 131

PART II: Becoming a Sun Certified Java 2 Architect

PART IV: Appendixes

About the Author

Jamie Jaworski

Jamie Jaworski is a professional Java developer and Sun certified Java programmer, developer, and architect who works for the U.S. Department of Defense. Mr. Jaworski has been a Java consultant to Sun and has written several best-selling books on Java and JavaScript, including *Java 2 Platform Unleashed* and *Mastering JavaScript and JScript*. He also writes the SuperScripter column for CNET's popular Web site for Webmasters, `Builder.com`.

Dedication

This book is dedicated to my lovely wife, Lisa Jaworski.

Acknowledgments

I'd like to thank everyone who helped to see this book to completion. In particular, I'd like to thank Margo Maley Hutchison of Waterside Productions for making the book possible; Tim Ryan, Jon Steever, Susan Moore, Mary Lagu, and Katie Robinson of Macmillan Computer Publishing for their numerous suggestions that improved the overall quality of the book; and Alexandre Calsavara for his excellent technical input. Alexandre's keen technical insights made this a better book. I'd also like to thank George Stones for helping with the book's Web site and for providing online support for this book. Finally, I'd like to thank Lisa, Jason, and Emily for their patience, love, and understanding.

Tell Us What You Think!

As the reader of this book, *you* are our most important critic and commentator. We value your opinion and want to know what we're doing right, what we could do better, what areas you'd like to see us publish in, and any other words of wisdom you're willing to pass our way.

As an Executive Editor for New Riders, I welcome your comments. You can fax, email, or write me directly to let me know what you did or didn't like about this book—as well as what we can do to make our books stronger.

When you write, please be sure to include this book's title and author as well as your name and phone or fax number. I will carefully review your comments and share them with the author and editors who worked on the book.

Fax: 317-581-4770

Email: java@mcp.com

Mail: Tim Ryan
         Macmillan Computer Publishing
         201 West 103rd Street
         Indianapolis, IN 46290 USA

Introduction

Java 2 Certification

In just a few years, Java has become one of the world's most popular programming languages. Java's initial popularity stemmed from its association with the Web and its capability to deliver executable content to Web pages. This popularity increased as programmers discovered Java's power, simplicity, and rich APIs. Java's popularity increased further as both large and small companies invested in building Java-based information infrastructures.

One of the results of Java's popularity is that there is a high demand for skilled Java programmers and system architects. However, due to Java's brief existence, experienced Java programmers are hard to find. Hardly anyone in the field has more than a few years experience in developing Java applications. This is a problem for both employers and programmers. Employers cannot rely on the traditional number of years of experience in selecting senior-level Java programmers and software engineers. Star Java programmers have a hard time differentiating themselves from entry-level Java programmers.

The Java certification exams provide a solution for both employers and programmers. Employers can identify skilled Java programmers by their certification level. Programmers and software engineers can attest to their knowledge of Java by pointing to their certification credentials.

The Java certification program is not new—it has been around since version 1.02 of the Java Developer's Kit. However, a new certification exam—the Java Architect exam—was introduced with Java 2. The differences between the three exams are as follows:

◆ Programmer exam—The Programmer exam tests the candidate's knowledge of the Java language and basic API packages. Programmer certification is a prerequisite to Developer certification.

◆ Developer exam—The Developer exam tests the candidate's ability to complete an extended programming assignment and answer questions concerning the issues and tradeoffs involved in the assignment's completion.

◆ Architect exam—The Architect exam tests a candidate's familiarity with the technologies used to build Java-based enterprise applications and the candidate's ability to resolve issues in Java application design. This exam focuses on much higher-level software and system engineering skills than the Programmer and Developer exams.

Being a Java evangelist since its initial alpha release in 1995 and having written several books on Java, I was intrigued about how Sun would go about testing programmers. When I finally took the JDK 1.1 Programmer's exam back in 1998, I was amazed at the great job that Sun's testers had done at selecting a challenging and highly appropriate set of questions for the test. When I was invited in December of 1998 to visit Sun's Broomfield, Colorado campus to select the questions for the Java 2 Programmer's exam, I jumped at the chance. Since then, I've been actively involved in all aspects of Java certification, taking and passing each of the three exams and developing an online training course for DigitalThink. I am confident that this book will help you in your quest to attain Java certification, no matter which certification exam you take.

Attaining Java certification is not easy. The most basic certification exam the Programmer exam is very difficult, even for an experienced Java programmer. This exam covers every aspect of the Java language and many of the core classes and interfaces of the basic API packages. In order to pass this exam you must acquire both a breadth and depth of experience with the Java language and selected API packages. This book is organized to help you to prepare for the Programmer, Architect, and Developer exams as follows:

◆ Part I of this book is dedicated to the Programmer exam and is organized according to Sun's published exam topics and objectives. It contains a detailed and focused description of the topics that are covered by the exam, numerous questions that review your understanding of these topics, and even more questions that you can use to measure your progress and determine when you're ready to take the exam.

◆ Part II prepares you for the Java Architect exam. It introduces the technologies that are covered by the exam and describes the issues and tradeoffs involved in building Java-based distributed applications. It also provides review and sample exam questions that you can use to assess your mastery of the exam topics.

◆ Part III covers the Java Developer exam. It provides you with background information on what to expect and provides a number of tips that will help you to successfully complete your assignment. The essay part of the Developer exam is also covered. Approaches to preparing for and answering the essay questions are described. Sample exam questions are examined and answers to these questions are provided.

WHO SHOULD READ THIS BOOK

This book is for anyone who wants to take and pass any of the three Java 2 Platform certification exams. If you are an experienced Java programmer and you want to pass the Programmer exam, this book will show you how. It will fill any gaps that you might have in your knowledge of the Java language or fundamental API packages. It will cover all that you need to know to do well on the exam and help you to assess your test readiness through hundreds of review and sample exam questions. If you study the material presented in each chapter, use the review questions to identify areas that you need to improve in, and continue your study until you get high grades in the sample exam questions. Then you'll be on a direct path to passing the exam.

If you are not an experienced Java programmer, you'll need to learn how to program in Java before taking the Programmer exam. I suggest that you start with Sun's online Java tutorial at `http://www.javasoft.com/docs/books/tutorial/index.html` and work your way through an intermediate to advanced Java book, such as *Java 1.2 Unleashed*.

If you are an experienced software or system engineer and you want to take and pass the Java Architect exam, this book will point you to the information that you need to know in order to pass the exam. While you won't be an experienced architect after reading six chapters, you will have covered the Architect exam topics and learned about the salient issues faced by the architects of Java-based applications. Moreover, the review and exam questions of these chapters will help you to determine whether you need more study or are ready to take the exam. You don't need to take the Java Programmer exam to take the Java Architect exam. However, as you can probably guess, knowledge of Java programming is extremely helpful for anyone who wants to design Java-based applications.

If you successfully pass the Java Programmer exam, you may want to achieve a higher level of certification by taking and passing the Java Developer exam. The Java Developer exam is a two-part exam that consists of a programming assignment and an essay exam. The programming assignment requires you to complete a partially developed Java application according to a list of very specific instructions. The essay exam consists of a small number (5–10) of short-answer essay questions. In order to take the Java Developer exam you must take and pass the Programmer exam. If you haven't taken the Programmer exam, then you should definitely start with that. Don't worry about the Developer exam until you have the Programmer exam

under your belt. Once you've taken the Programmer exam, I recommend that you take (or at least study for) the Architect exam. The object-oriented design principles that you cover in preparing for the Architect exam will help you to do better on the programming assignment part of the Developer exam and also help you to answer the essay questions with a better understanding of the design tradeoffs they address.

GETTING STARTED

To use this book, you'll need a computer and operating system that support the Java 2 Platform. There are a wide variety of operating systems that support the Java 2 Platform, including Windows 2000, NT, 98, and 95, Linux, and Solaris. Ports of the Java 2 Platform to many other operating systems are in the works. The examples used in this book were developed under Windows 98. However, they are pure Java and will run under all Java 2 Platform implementations.

The CD-ROM that accompanies this book contains all the source and compiled code for all examples presented in this book. The CD-ROM is a hybrid that works on Windows, Linux, UNIX, and Macintosh platforms. In addition, it contains an Exam Preparation program that helps you to review the material presented in each chapter and a Simulated Exam program that tests your knowledge of this material. Appendixes A and B show you how to install and run these programs.

HOW TO USE THIS BOOK

No matter which exam you are studying for, I recommend that you start with Chapter 1 and proceed through each chapter of the book in order, working through all review and exam questions. Passing the

Programmer exam is a prerequisite to taking the Developer exam. However, I believe that the refined understanding of the Java language and basic API that you need to pass the Programmer exam is also an important asset to a Java Architect. I also believe that the object-oriented software engineering skills that you need to pass the Java Architect exam will help you to do better on the Java Developer exam.

CONVENTIONS USED IN THIS BOOK

This book follows certain conventions that make it easier for you to use.

◆ List of Objectives—Each chapter begins with a list of objectives that identify areas you should focus on in studying the material presented in the chapter.

◆ Chapter Outline—The chapter's outline is presented after the list of objectives, enabling you to get a quick overview of the chapter's organization.

◆ Study Strategies—Study strategies that identify ways to prepare for the certification exam are provided, following the chapter outline.

◆ Chapter Introduction/Summary—In order for you to understand where you are going and where you have been, each chapter begins with a short description of the information that will be presented and ends with a summary of the material that was covered.

◆ Key Terms—A list of key terms are provided at the end of each chapter. You should review each term and make sure that you are familiar with how the term applies to the material that you studied in the chapter.

◆ Review Questions—Review questions are short-answer questions that test your comprehension of the material that was presented in the chapter. I recommend that you write down your answers to these questions to increase your retention of the information you've studied.

◆ Exam Questions—Exam questions are multiple-choice questions that are modeled after questions that appear in the certification exams. These questions are used to test your knowledge of the material covered in the chapter and determine whether you need further study before going on to the next chapter or taking the certification exam.

◆ Answers and Explanations—The answers to each of the review and exam questions are provided along with short explanations as to why each answer is correct.

◆ Suggested Readings and Resources—Each chapter ends with a reference to additional information that you can use to learn more about the information that you just studied.

A monospaced font is used to identify program code. An *italic monospaced font* is used to identify any placeholders used in Java syntax descriptions.

In addition, the following visual cues will help draw your attention to important information.

> NOTE   Notes like this are used to call your attention to information that is important to understanding and using Java or doing well on the certification exams.

E X A M T I P	Tips like this are used to identify ways that you can use Java more efficiently or prepare yourself for the certification exams.

W A R N I N G	Warnings like this are used to help you to avoid common problems encountered when using Java and when answering exam questions.

THE BOOK'S WEB SITE

To help you with your certification studies, I've put together a Java certification Web site that supplements the information presented in this book. It provides a forum for feedback on the certification exams and contains any corrections for errors that are discovered after the book's printing. The URL for this Web site is `http://www.jaworski.com/java/certification/`. If you have any questions, comments, or suggestions concerning the book, its Web site, or the certification exams, please direct them to `support@jaworski.com`

BECOMING A SUN CERTIFIED JAVA 2 PROGRAMMER

This chapter helps you to prepare for the exam by covering the following objectives:

Know what topics are covered in the certification exam and what technologies are addressed by these topics.

▶ The skills required to pass the Java 2 programmer certification exam are many. You must be familiar with all aspects of the Java programming language. You must be familiar with the core packages of the Java 2 API. You must also be able to write both console and AWT programs. These areas cover a very wide range of potential topics. By knowing the exact topics covered by the exam, you'll be able to focus on sharpening the programming skills you need to pass the exam.

Know how the exam is given.

▶ The more that you know about the certification exam before going in to take it, the fewer surprises you'll have, and the better off you'll be.

Know how to prepare for the certification exam.

▶ Given limited time and resources, you'll want to get the best return for the time that you put into studying. This chapter will give you study tips that can help you to maximize the benefits of your study efforts.

Know how to take the certification exam.

▶ Some people take tests better than others. This doesn't necessarily mean that they are smarter or better prepared. Sometimes it means that they use a better test-taking approach. This chapter covers a test-taking approach that can help you improve your overall exam score.

CHAPTER 1

Overview of the Java Programmer Exam

Outline

CHAPTER INTRODUCTION

This chapter introduces you to the Sun Certified Programmer for Java 2 Platform Examination. It identifies the topics that the exam covers, discusses how the exam is given, and provides you with tips and other information on how to take the exam.

This chapter kicks off Part I of this book. Part I prepares you with the information that you need to pass the Java 2 programmer certification exam. Although all the information is covered, some information is more important than the rest. By reading this chapter carefully before going on to other chapters in Part I, you'll have a better feel for the information to focus on in order to successfully pass the exam.

WHAT THE EXAM COVERS

The Java 2 programmer exam covers a wide range of topics related to the Java programming language, core API packages, and console and AWT program development. It contains 59 questions on programming topics that a well-versed Java programmer is be expected to know. These questions are organized according to the following topics (supplied by Sun):

1. Declarations and Access Control

    -   Write code that declares constructs and initializes arrays of any base type, using any of the permitted forms both for declaration and for initialization.

    -   Declare classes, inner classes, methods, instance variables, `static` variables, and `automatic` (method local) variables, making appropriate use of all permitted modifiers (such as `public`, `final`, `static`, `abstract`, and so forth). State the significance of each of these modifiers, both singly and in combination, and state the effect of package relationships on declared items qualified by these modifiers.

    -   For a given class, determine if a default constructor will be created, and if so, state the prototype of that constructor.

    -   State the legal return types for any method, given the declarations of all related methods in this or the parent classes.

2. Flow Control and Exception Handling

   • Write code using `if` and `switch` statements, and identify legal argument types for these statements.

   • Write code using all forms of loops, including labeled and unlabeled use of `break` and `continue`, and state the values taken by loop counter variables during and after loop execution.

   • Write code that makes proper use of exceptions and exception-handling clauses (`try`, `catch`, `finally`) and declares methods and overriding methods that throw exceptions.

3. Garbage Collection

   • State the behavior that is guaranteed by the garbage collection system and write code that explicitly makes objects eligible for collection.

4. Language Fundamentals

   • Identify correctly constructed package declarations, import statements, class declarations (of all forms including inner classes), interface declarations, and implementations (for `java.lang.Runnable` or other interface described in the test), method declarations (including the `main()` method that is used to start execution of a class), variable declarations, and identifiers.

   • State the correspondence between index values in the argument array passed to a main method and command-line arguments.

   • Identify all Java programming language keywords.

   • State the effect of using a variable or array element of any kind when no explicit assignment has been made to it.

   • State the range of all primitive data types, and declare literal values for `String` and all primitive types, using all permitted formats bases and representations.

   • Write code to implement listener classes and methods, and in listener methods, extract information from the event to determine the affected component, mouse position, nature, and time of the event. State the event class name for any specified event listener interface in the `java.awt.event` package.

5. Operators and Assignments

- Determine the result of applying any operator, including assignment operators and `instanceof`, to operands of any type, class, scope, accessibility, or any combination of these.

- Determine the result of applying the `boolean equals()` (`Object`) method to objects of any combination of the classes `java.lang.String`, `java.lang.Boolean`, and `java.lang.Object`.

- In an expression involving the operators &, ¦, &&, ¦¦, and variables of known values, state which operands are evaluated and the value of the expression.

- Determine the effect upon objects and primitive values of passing variables into methods and performing assignments or other modifying operations in that method.

6. Overloading Overriding Runtime Type and Object Orientation

- State the benefits of encapsulation in object-oriented design, and write code that implements tightly encapsulated classes and the relationships "is a" and "has a".

- Write code to invoke overridden or overloaded methods and parental or overloaded constructors. Describe the effect of invoking these methods.

- Write code to construct instances of any concrete class, including normal top level classes, inner classes, static inner classes, and anonymous inner classes.

7. Threads

- Write code to define, instantiate, and start new threads using both `java.lang.Thread` and `java.lang.Runnable`.

- Recognize conditions that might prevent a thread from executing.

- Write code using synchronized wait(), notify(), and notifyAll(), to protect against concurrent access problems and to communicate between threads. Define the interaction between threads, and between threads and object locks, when executing synchronized wait(), notify(), or notifyAll().

8. The java.awt package—Layout

    - Write code to implement listener classes and methods and, in listener methods, extract information from the event to determine the affected component, mouse position, nature, and time of the event. State the event class name for any specified event listener interface in the java.awt.event package.

    - Write code using component container and layout manager classes of the java.awt package to present a GUI with specified appearance. Resize the behavior and distinguish the responsibilities of layout managers from those of containers.

9. The java.lang package

    - Determine the result of applying any operator, including assignment operators and instanceof, to operands of any type, class, scope, accessibility, or any combination of these.

    - Write code using the following methods of the java.lang.Math class: abs(), ceil(), floor(), max(), min(), random(), round(), sin(), cos(), tan(), and sqrt().

    - Describe the significance of the immutability of String objects.

10. The java.util package

    - Make appropriate selection of collection classes/interfaces to suit specified behavior requirements.

The above topics and exam objectives are very concrete and can help you to focus your study in preparation for the exam. The chapters of Part I are organized according to these topics and objectives, as shown in Table 1.1.

```
TABLE 1.1
```

CHAPTER TO EXAM TOPIC MAPPING

Chapter	Title	Exam Topic
2	Language Fundamentals	Language Fundamentals
3	Operators and Assignments	Operators and Assignments
4	Declarations and Access Control	Declarations and Access Control
5	Flow Control and Exception Handling	Flow Control and Exception Handling
6	Overloading, Overriding, Runtime Type, and Object Orientation	Overloading, Overriding, Runtime Type, and Object Orientation
7	Garbage Collection	Garbage Collection
8	Threads	Threads
9	The java.lang Package	The java.lang Package
10	The java.util Package	The java.util Package
11	The java.awt Package: Components and Facilities	The java.awt Package: Layout
12	The java.awt Package: Layout	The java.awt Package: Layout
13	The java.awt Package: Event Handling	The java.awt Package: Layout
14	The java.awt Package: Painting	The java.awt Package: Layout
15	The java.io Package	Input/Output-related questions

As you can see from the above table, Chapters 2 through 10 map directly to the exam topics. Chapters 11 through 14 cover the java.awt exam topic. Because there is a tremendous amount of background information required to write AWT programs, I've broken it out into four separate chapters.

Although no specific exam topic on java.io is listed, there are several exam questions that require knowledge of the java.io package.

How the Exam Is Given

The exam consists of a computer-based test consisting of 59 multiple-choice and short-answer questions. The tests are given at Sylvan Prometric Testing Centers. You'll have 90 minutes to take the test.

The multiple-choice questions are either single-answer questions or multiple-answer questions. Single-answer questions are indicated by radio buttons. Multiple-answer questions have check boxes.

The short-answer questions ask you to enter a word or line of text. These questions comprise less than 10% of the exam questions. The short-answer questions are usually very succinct because the answer verification software cannot handle a large number of alternative answers.

The exam questions appear on the computer screen one at a time. You can skip a question and return to it later. You can also move backward and forward between the questions you've answered and those you have yet to answer.

Being a Great Programmer Is Not Enough

One word of caution on the programmer certification exam. You may consider yourself the world's greatest Java programmer and you may be right. However, your great programming skills will not necessarily result in a high exam score. Being a great programmer will only get you part of the way there.

The certification exam requires that you be a good Java programmer and know a great deal about the Java programming language and Core API. Certainly, being a great programmer implies that you know a lot about the Java language and API. However, there are lesser-used details of the language and API that you might not use in your programs which could show up on the certification exam. For example, you may be a window application programmer and not use the numerical shift operators. Likewise, you may write multithreaded servers and not really get into the details of AWT programming.

NOTE

Java 2 programmer exam URL   The URL `http://suned.sun.com/usa/cert_progs.html?content=scpj2_details` is the place to start if you want to sign up for the Java 2 programmer exam.

The Java 2 certification exam tests you on the breadth and depth of your programming knowledge. More important, it tests you on your ability to apply that knowledge by forcing you to carefully think through many exam questions.

So if you are a great programmer, do yourself a favor and be a great student. Read through all the chapters and answer all the practice questions before taking the exam. By doing so, you'll be able to save time, money, and face.

HOW TO PREPARE FOR THE EXAM

By deciding to study this part of the book, you've taken the best first step to preparing for the exam. The chapters in this part will provide you with the background information that you need to take the test. Thoroughly read through each chapter, even if you think that you know the material cold. Sometimes an additional bit of information or a different slant on how a technology is used can make the difference when you must select the correct answer.

After reading through each chapter, answer the review and exam questions. These questions will test your knowledge of the material covered and give you an idea of what you can expect on the exam.

After completing all the chapters of this part, use the exam preparation and simulation programs contained on this book's CD to test and retest your knowledge. The tests are randomized, so they'll be different each time you take them. When you answer a test question incorrectly, go back and restudy the material. Keep on doing this until your exam scores are in the high 90s. At this point, you should be able to easily pass the Java 2 programmer certification exam.

HOW TO TAKE THE EXAM

By working through the approach described in the previous section, you'll have the knowledge required to pass the certification exam. However, by adopting the right test taking approach, you should be able to improve your test score even further.

The way that test questions are scored is simple. You receive one point for each correct answer. You need 42 correct answers to pass the test. Based on this, your test taking strategy should aim at getting the most correct answers. I suggest that you go through the exam and answer all the questions that you are reasonably sure you can answer correctly. DON'T WASTE TIME DWELLING ON QUESTIONS THAT YOU ARE HAVING A HARD TIME ANSWERING.

After you've made a first pass through the questions, go back and try to answer the questions that you were stuck on. At this point, you should try to answer all the exam questions. If you don't know the answer to a question, take your best guess. You won't be penalized for wrong answers and any correct guess will improve your overall score.

After answering all the exam questions, if you still have time left, go back and check your answers. However, don't try to second guess yourself. Instead, reread each question and each answer to make sure that you haven't misunderstood any questions or incorrectly read an answer.

CHAPTER SUMMARY

This chapter introduced you to the Sun Certified Programmer for Java 2 Platform Examination. It identified the topics that the exam covers, discussed how the exam is given, and provided you with tips and other information on how to take the exam. You should now be able to go on to study the remaining chapters of Part I. But before going on, take a look at the following exam questions. These questions are provided by Sun to give you an idea of what kinds of questions to expect in the certification exam. Don't worry if you don't know the answers to these questions. The information you need to answer will be presented in the remaining chapters of Part I.

APPLY YOUR KNOWLEDGE

Exam Questions (from Sun)

1. What would be the result of attempting to compile and run the following piece of code?

```
public class Test {
 static int x;
 public static void main (String args—]) {
  System.out.println("Value is " + x);
 }
}
```

   A. The output "Value is 0" is printed.

   B. An object of type NullPointerException is thrown.

   C. An "illegal array declaration syntax" compiler error occurs.

   D. A "possible reference before assignment" compiler error occurs.

   E. An object of type ArrayIndexOutOfBoundsException is thrown.

2. What should you use to position a Button within an application Frame so that the size of the Button is NOT affected by the Frame size?

   A. A FlowLayout

   B. A GridLayout

   C. The center area of a BorderLayout

   D. The East or West area of a BorderLayout

   E. The North or South area of a BorderLayout

3. Which is the advantage of encapsulation?

   A. Only public methods are needed.

   B. No exceptions need to be thrown from any method.

   C. Making the class final causes no consequential changes to other code.

   D. It changes the implementation without changing the interface and causes no consequential changes to other code.

   E. It changes the interface without changing the implementation and causes no consequential changes to other code.

4. What can contain objects that have a unique key field of String type, if it is required to retrieve the objects using that key field as an index?

   A. Map

   B. Set

   C. List

   D. Collection

   E. Enumeration

5. Which statement is true about a non-static inner class?

   A. It must implement an interface.

   B. It is accessible from any other class.

   C. It can only be instantiated in the enclosing class.

   D. It must be final, if it is declared in a method scope.

   E. It can access private instance variables in the enclosing object.

APPLY YOUR KNOWLEDGE

6. Which are keywords in Java?

   A. NULL

   B. sizeof

   C. friend

   D. extends

   E. synchronized

7. Which declares an abstract method in an abstract Java class?

   A. public abstract method();

   B. public abstract void method();

   C. public void abstract Method();

   D. public void method() {abstract;}

   E. public abstract void method() {}

Answers to Exam Questions

1. A The program compiles without error. The default value of an uninitialized int variable is 0.

2. A The size of a component that is laid out via a BorderLayout or GridLayout is affected by the Frame size. This is not the case with a FlowLayout.

3. D When a class is properly encapsulated, it is possible to change the class's implementation without changing its interface. Implementation changes do not affect other classes which abide by this interface.

4. A The Map interface provides the capability to retrieve objects by their keys. The others do not.

5. E An object of a non-static inner class is able to access private variables of objects of the outer class in which it is defined.

6. D and E The words, extends and synchronized, are Java keywords. The others are not.

7. B The abstract keyword must precede the method's return type.

Suggested Readings and Resources

Details of the Sun Certified Architect for Java Technologies (http://suned.sun.com/usa/cert_progs.html?content=scpj2_details).

This chapter helps you to prepare for the exam by covering the following objectives:

Know how to identify correctly constructed package declarations, import statements, and program main() methods.

▶ To be a Java programmer, you must know how to create packages, import classes and interfaces from other packages, and create a program's main() method. The certification exam will definitely test your knowledge of these.

Be able to state the correspondence between index values in the argument array passed to a main() method and command-line arguments.

▶ The indexing of command-line arguments differs from C and C++ to Java. Exam questions in this area are designed to trip up C and C++ programmers.

Know how to identify all Java programming language keywords.

▶ You must know which keywords are reserved by Java so that you don't use them as identifiers in your programs. You can count on seeing an exam question that will test your knowledge of Java's keywords.

Know how to identify valid Java identifiers.

▶ Creating a simple identifier is basic to Java programming. You are very likely to see an exam question that tests your ability to distinguish valid identifiers from invalid identifiers.

CHAPTER 2

Language Fundamentals

Be able to state the effect of using a variable or array element of any kind, when no explicit assignment has been made to it.

▶ Java automatically initializes field variables and arrays. This is important to know when developing Java programs. You'll see questions on initialization on the certification exam.

Be able to state the range of all primitive data types, and declare literal values for String and all primitive types using all permitted formats, bases, and representations.

▶ You must know the range of a type to determine when a value is out of range. You also must know how to create primitive values for each type. This is another rich area for exam questions.

STUDY STRATEGIES

As you read through this chapter, you should concentrate on the following key items:

▶ How to identify a Java package

▶ How to import classes and interfaces from other packages

▶ How to create a program's main() method

▶ How to access command-line arguments

▶ How to create valid identifiers

▶ How field variables and arrays are initialized

▶ What the range of each primitive type is

▶ How to create literal values of each primitive type

▶ How to create String literal values

CHAPTER INTRODUCTION

This chapter covers the fundamentals of the Java programming language. If you've written Java programs, you should be familiar with most of the material in this chapter. However, odds are there are a few things that you might not be sure of. The questions on the certification exam will exploit this uncertainty—so pay careful attention to the material that's presented. Make sure that you read through each section, even if you think that you know it cold. The review questions and exam questions will let you know how well you know this material and will give you an idea of how well you will do in exam-related questions.

THE STRUCTURE OF JAVA PROGRAMS

Java programs are composed of declarations of *classes* and *interfaces*. Classes define *variables*, which provide named access to data, *methods*, which perform actions consisting of operations on the data, and *constructors*, which create instances of classes, referred to as *objects*. Data items consist of primitive data values—such as byte, char, and int values—and objects—such as arrays, I/O streams, and GUI elements.

Interfaces define collections of methods that are implemented by classes. They are also used to define *constants*, which are data values that cannot be changed.

Java programs are written using one or more *compilation units*, which are Java source code files. Every source code file consists of the name of a class or interface followed by the .java extension. Since Java identifiers are case-sensitive, source code filenames are also case-sensitive.

Each source code file may contain at most one public class or interface. If a class or interface is declared as public, the source code filename must be the name of the class or interface (followed by the .java extension). If a source code file does not contain a public class or interface, it may take on a name that is different from its classes and interfaces.

IDENTIFYING PACKAGES

Java classes and interfaces are organized into *packages*. Packages provide a naming context for classes and interfaces. In other words, packages enable different programmers (or even the same programmer) to create classes and interfaces with the same name. For example, if you and I both create a class named Cool and then use the two different versions of Cool in the same program, the compiler and runtime system won't know which version to use. But, if I put my Cool class in the My package, and you put your Cool class in the You package, the compiler and runtime system will have no problem, as long as we refer to Cool using its package name.

Packages are identified by the package statement. It must appear as the first statement in a source code file

```
package packageName;
```

If a package statement is omitted, the classes and interfaces declared within the package are put into the default no name package. In the Java 2 Platform Software Development Kit (SDK), the package name and the CLASSPATH environment variable are used to find a class or interface that is located in another package.

> **NOTE**
>
> **Use of Packages** In addition to being used as a naming context, packages are used to organize related classes and interfaces into a single API unit to which access may be controlled.

IMPORTING CLASSES AND INTERFACES FROM OTHER PACKAGES

The import statement is used to reference classes and interfaces that are declared in other packages (without having to specify their names each time they are referenced). There are three forms of the import statement:

```
import packageName.className;

import packageName.interfaceName;

import packageName.*;
```

The first and second forms enable the identified classes and interfaces to be referenced without specifying the name of their package. The third form allows all classes and interfaces in the specified package to be referenced without specifying the name of their package.

NOTE

Importing `java.lang` The `java.lang` package is always imported by default and does not need to be imported by an `import` statement.

THE `main()` METHOD

The `main()` method is used as the entry point for a Java application program. All programs must have a `main()` method or they cannot be run. The `main()` method is a method of the class that is executed to run the program.

For example, if your program's name is `MyProgram`, then the `MyProgram` class must be defined in a file named `MyProgram.java`. The `MyProgram` class must have a correctly defined `main()` method.

A correctly defined `main()` method has the following form:

```
public static void main(String[] args) {
  // Statements go here
}
```

The `main()` method must be declared as `public`, `static`, and `void`. The `void` keyword must appear immediately before `main()`. The `public` and `static` keywords may be interchanged. The `main()` method has one argument—an array of `String` arguments. This argument may be defined as `String[] args` or `String []args` or `String args[]`. The `args` argument may use any valid identifier. For example, you can use `arg`, `myArgs`, or `parms`. However, `args` is standard, and you should probably stick with it. As a convention, when I refer to `args`, I'm referring to the argument to a program's `main()` method.

NOTE

Applets Applets are not required to have a `main()` method.

The `args` array is used to access a program's *command-line arguments*. These arguments are passed to a program when it is invoked. They are passed as part of the command that is used to invoke the program.

For example, to run the `MyProgram` program, you would enter

```
java MyProgram
```

Suppose that you wanted to pass the arguments 2 and 3 to `MyProgram`. You would invoke it as follows:

```
java MyProgram 2 3
```

The `String` object `"2"` would be accessed as `args[0]`, and the `String` object `"3"` would be accessed as `args[1]`. If you are a C or C++ programmer—pay attention. Java accesses command-line arguments using different indices than do C and C++ programs.

The `ArgsTest` program of Listing 2.1 shows how command-line arguments are accessed using the args array. When you run the program using the following command line

```
java ArgsTest this is a test
```

it displays the following results

```
args[0] = this
args[1] = is

args[2] = a
args[3] = test
```

LISTING 2.1

THE ArgsTest PROGRAM

```
class ArgsTest {
 public static  void  main(String[] args) {
  for(int i=0;i<args.length;++i) {
   System.out.println("args["+i+"] = "+args[i]);
  }
 }
}
```

COMMENTS

Java provides three styles of comments:

```
/* This is a
   multiline comment. */

// This is a single-line comment.

/** This is a
    multiline javadoc comment */
```

The first comment style supports traditional C-language comments. All text appearing between /* and */ is treated as a comment. Comments of this style can span multiple lines.

The second comment style supports single line C++ comments. All text following the // until the end of the line is treated as a comment.

The third comment style is used by the javadoc documentation generation tool. All text between the /** and */ is treated as a javadoc comment. javadoc comments may span multiple lines. You don't need to know about javadoc on the certification exam. However, if you are interested, it is described in the tools section of the Java 2 platform documentation.

Comments cannot be nested. If comments appear within a String or character literal, they are treated as part of the String or literal.

IDENTIFIERS AND KEYWORDS

Identifiers are used to name Java language entities. They begin with a Unicode letter, underscore character (_), or dollar sign ($). Subsequent characters consist of these characters and the digits 0–9. Identifiers are case sensitive and cannot be the same as a reserved word or the boolean values True or False or the null value. Avoid using the dollar sign character; it is intended for use by compiler-generated identifiers.

The following are examples of valid Java identifiers:

◆ myIdentifier

◆ $my_identifier

◆ $123

The following are invalid Java identifiers:

◆ 1badIdentifier

◆ bad-too

◆ %badID

The following words are reserved by the Java language and cannot be used as identifiers:

abstract	do	import	return	void
boolean	double	instanceof	short	volatile
break	else	int	static	while
byte	extends	interface	super	
case	final	long	switch	
catch	finally	native	synchronized	
char	float	new	this	
class	for	package	throw	

```
const      goto        private    throws
continue   if          protected  transient
default    implements  public     try
```

Although you don't necessarily need to memorize the above list, it's a good idea to familiarize yourself with it because you are very likely to see at least one exam-related question that requires knowledge of the preceding keywords.

PRIMITIVE TYPES AND LITERAL VALUES

Java defines eight primitive types. Variables that are declared as a primitive type are not references to objects. They are only place-holders to store primitive values. The eight primitive types are byte, short, int, long, float, double, char, and boolean.

The byte, short, int, and long types represent 8-, 16-, 32-, and 64-bit signed integer values. The char type represents an unsigned 16-bit value. The float and double types represent 32- and 64-bit floating point values. The ranges of the primitive types are shown in Table 2.1.

TABLE 2.1

RANGES OF NUMERIC TYPES

Type	Range
boolean	true and false
byte	$-(2^7)$ to $2^7 - 1$
char	0 to $2^{16} - 1$
short	$-(2^{15})$ to $2^{15} - 1$
int	$-(2^{31})$ to $2^{31} - 1$
long	$-(2^{63})$ to $2^{63} - 1$
float	Float.MIN_VALUE to Float.MAX_VALUE, Float.NaN, Float.NEGATIVE_INFINITY, Float.POSITIVE_INFINITYdoubleDouble.MIN_VALUE to Double.MAX_VALUE, Double.NaN, Double.NEGATIVE_INFINITY, Double.POSITIVE_INFINITY

The literal values of these integer types are written using positive or negative decimal, hexadecimal, or octal integers. Hexadecimal values are preceded by 0x or 0X and use the letters a through f (uppercase or lowercase) to represent the digits 10 through 15. Octal numbers are preceded by 0. Long decimal values have an l or L appended to the end of the number. Examples of conversions between decimal, hexadecimal, and octal values are shown in Table 2.2.

TABLE 2.2

DECIMAL, HEXADECIMAL, AND OCTAL VALUES

Decimal Value	Hexadecimal Value	Octal Value
14	0x0E	020
123	0x7B	0173
4567	0x11D7	010727

The float and double types represent 32- and 64-bit IEEE 754 floating-point numbers. Float numbers have the f or F suffix. Double numbers have d or D. If no suffix is provided, the default double type is assumed. Floating-point numbers may be written using any of the following forms:

```
digits . optionalDigits optionalExponentPart suffix

. digits optionalExponentPart suffix

digits optionalExponentPart suffix
```

The suffix is optional. It consists of f, F, d, or D, as described previously.

The exponent part is optional. It consists of an e or E followed by a signed integer. It is used to identify the exponent of 10 of the number written in scientific notation. For example, 1000000.0 could be represented as 1.0E6. If a floating-point literal does not contain a decimal point, then it needs to have either the exponent part or the suffix to be recognized as a floating-point literal (as opposed to an integer literal).

The Float and Double classes define three special float and double constants. The special value NaN is used to represent the value for "not a number" that occurs as the result of undefined mathematical operations. The values, POSITIVE_INFINITY and NEGATIVE_INFINITY, represent infinite values in the positive and negative directions.

The char type represents 16-bit Unicode characters. Unicode is a 16-bit superset of the ASCII character set that provides many foreign-language characters. A single character is specified by putting the character within single quotes ('). There are three exceptions: single quote ('), double quote ("), and backslash (\). The backslash character (\) is used as an escape code to represent special character values. For example, a single quote would be represented by '\''. The character escape codes are shown in Table 2.3.

TABLE 2.3
CHARACTER ESCAPE CODES

Escape Code	Character
\b	backspace
\t	tab
\n	linefeed
\f	form feed
\r	carriage return
\"	double quote
\'	single quote
\\	backslash

The backslash can also be followed by an 8-bit octal value (\000 through \377) or by a u or U followed by a four-digit, hexadecimal value (\u0000 through \uffff). The four-digit value can be used to specify the full range of Unicode characters.

The boolean type represents the logical values true and false.

String literals are also supported by Java. String literals are not primitive values. They are a shorthand notation for representing String objects. Strings consist of characters enclosed by double quotes ("). The character escape codes may be used within String literals to represent special characters within the string.

The literal value `null` is used to identify the fact that an object is not assigned to a variable. It may be used with any variable that is not of a primitive data type.

Class literals were introduced with Java 1.1. A class literal is formed by appending `.class` to the name of a primitive or reference type. It evaluates to the class descriptor of the reference type or class descriptor of the primitive type's wrapper class. The expression `void.class` evaluates to the class descriptor of the `Void` class. For example, suppose `Test` is a class that you've declared. The following statement displays the output `class Test`:

```
System.out.println(Test.class);
```

Automatic Initialization

Field variables and the elements of arrays are automatically initialized to default values. Local variables are not automatically initialized. Failure to initialize a local variable results in a compilation error. Table 2.4 identifies the default values of each primitive type.

NOTE

Field Variables and Local Variables
Field variables are variables that are declared as members of classes. *Local variables*, also referred to as *automatic variables*, are declared relative to (or local to) a method or constructor.

TABLE 2.4

DEFAULT VALUES FOR PRIMITIVE TYPES

Type	Default Value
boolean	false
byte	0
char	\u0000
short	0
int	0
long	0l
float	0.0f
double	0.0d

Field variables of object types and the elements of arrays of object types are automatically initialized to the `null` value.

The Initialization program (Listing 2.2) illustrates the use of the automatic initialization of field variables and arrays. It displays the following output:

```
boolean: false
byte: 0
char:
short: 0
int: 0
long: 0
float: 0.0
double: 0.0
Object: null
int[2]: 0 0
Object[2]: null null
```

> **Declaring Arrays and Objects** The declaration and use of arrays and objects are covered in Chapter 4, "Declarations and Access Control."

LISTING 2.2

THE Initialization PROGRAM

```
class Initialization {
 boolean bo;
 byte by;
 char c;
 short s;
 int i;
 long l;
 float f;
 double d;
 Object o;
 public static void main(String[] args) {
  Initialization app = new Initialization();
  app.run();
 }
 void run() {
  int[] intArray = new int[2];
  Object[] objectArray = new Object[2];
  System.out.println("boolean: "+bo);
  System.out.println("byte: "+by);
  System.out.println("char: "+c);
  System.out.println("short: "+s);
  System.out.println("int: "+i);
  System.out.println("long: "+l);
  System.out.println("float: "+f);
  System.out.println("double: "+d);
  System.out.println("Object: "+o);
  System.out.println("int[2]: "+intArray[0]+" "+intArray[1]);
  System.out.println("Object[2]: "+objectArray[0]+"
"+objectArray[1]);
 }
}
```

CHAPTER SUMMARY

KEY TERMS

- Interface
- Class
- Field Variable
- Local Variable
- Automatic Variable
- Constant
- Object
- Method
- Constructor
- Compilation Unit
- Source Code File
- Package
- Naming Context
- Import
- Command-Line Argument
- Comment
- Keyword
- Primitive Type

This chapter reviewed the basics of Java programming. You learned how to create packages, import classes and interfaces from other packages, and create a program's main() method. You also learned how command-line variables are accessed, identifiers are formed, and which keywords are reserved by the Java language. You were introduced to each primitive type, learned its range of values, and learned how to create literal values of each type (and also the String type). You should now be prepared to test your knowledge of these subjects. The following review questions and exam questions will let you know how well you understand this material and will give you an idea of how you'll do in related exam questions. They'll also indicate which material you need to study further.

APPLY YOUR KNOWLEDGE

Review Questions

1. What is a Java package and how is it used?

2. What is a compilation unit?

3. How are Java source code files named?

4. What restrictions are placed on the location of a `package` statement within a source code file?

5. Which package is always imported by default?

6. What is the return type of a program's `main()` method?

7. What is the argument type of a program's `main()` method?

8. Which non-Unicode letter characters may be used as the first character of an identifier?

9. Which characters may be used as the second character of an identifier, but not as the first character of an identifier?

10. Are `true` and `false` keywords?

11. Is `null` a keyword?

12. Is `sizeof` a keyword?

13. Name the eight primitive Java types.

14. What is the range of the `short` type?

15. What is the range of the `char` type?

16. Is `"abc"` a primitive value?

17. To what value is a variable of the `boolean` type automatically initialized?

18. To what value is a variable of the `String` type automatically initialized?

Exam Questions

1. In order for the `public class MyClass` to successfully compile, which of the following are true?

   A. `MyClass` must have a correctly formed `main()` method.

   B. `MyClass` must be defined in the file `MyClass.java`.

   C. `MyClass` must be defined in the `MyClass` package.

   D. `MyClass` must be imported.

2. In order for a source code file, containing the `public class Test`, to successfully compile, which of the following must be true?

   A. It must import `java.lang`.

   B. It must declare a `public` class named `Test`.

   C. It must be named `Test.java`.

   D. It must have a `package` statement.

3. In order for the `MyProgram` program to be compiled and run, which of the following must be true?

   A. The `MyProgram` class must be defined in `MyProgram.java`.

   B. `MyProgram` must be declared `public`.

   C. `MyProgram` must have a correctly formed `main()` method.

   D. `MyProgram` must import `java.lang`.

APPLY YOUR KNOWLEDGE

4. Which of the following are true?

   A. If a `package` statement is included in a source code file, it must appear as the first non-blank line.

   B. If an `import` statement is included in a source code file, it must appear as the first non-blank line.

   C. If a `main()` method is included in a source code file, it must appear as the first non-blank line.

   D. If a `public` interface is declared in a source code file, it must have the same name as the source code file.

5. Which of the following are valid `main()` methods?

   A. `public static void main() {     }`

   B. `public static void main(String[] argc)`
   `   {   }`

   C. `void main(String[] args) {    }`

   D. `public static void main(String []args)`
   `   {    }`

6. What is the output of the following program when it is invoked using the command line `java Test this is a test`?

   ```
   class Test {
   public static void main(String[] args) {
     System.out.println(args[1]);
    }
   }
   ```

   A. `this`

   B. `is`

   C. `a`

   D. `test`

7. Which of the following are valid Java comments?

   A. `\\ This is a comment.`

   B. `/* This is a comment. */`

   C. `/** This is a comment. */`

   D. `\* This is a comment *\`

8. Which of the following are valid Java identifiers?

   A. `%id`

   B. `$id`

   C. `_id`

   D. `#id`

9. Which of the following are valid Java identifiers?

   A. my-id

   B. my_id

   C. 101ids

   D. id101

10. Which of the following are Java keywords?

    A. `interface`

    B. `sizeof`

    C. `super`

    D. `volatile`

11. Which of the following are Java keywords?

    A. `NULL`

    B. `null`

    C. `extends`

    D. `main`

APPLY YOUR KNOWLEDGE

12. Which of the following are primitive types?

    A. byte

    B. String

    C. integer

    D. Float

13. What is the range of the short type?

    A. 0 to 2^{16}

    B. $-(2^{16})$ to 2^{16}

    C. $-(2^{15})$ to 2^{15}

    D. $-(2^{15})$ to $2^{15}- 1$

14. What is the range of the char type?

    A. 0 to 2^{16}

    B. 0 to $2^{16} - 1$

    C. 0 to 2^{15}

    D. 0 to $2^{15}- 1$

15. What is the octal equivalent of the decimal value 123?

    A. 0173

    B. 123

    C. 0x123

    D. 0x173

16. What is the hexadecimal equivalent of decimal 123?

    A. 0x173

    B. 0x123

    C. 0x7B

    D. 173

17. What output is displayed as the result of executing the following statement?

    ```
    System.out.println("// Looks like a
    comment.");
    ```

    A. // Looks like a comment.

    B. / Looks like a comment.

    C. No output is displayed.

    D. The statement results in a compilation error.

18. Which of the following are valid double literals?

    A. 1D

    B. 1E-5D

    C. e2d

    D. 1ed

19. What is the output of the following program?

    ```
    public class Question {
     public static void main(String args[]){
      boolean[] b = new boolean[2];
      double[] d = new double[2];
      System.out.print(b[0]);
      System.out.println(d[1]);
     }
    }
    ```

    A. true0.0

    B. true0

    C. false0.0

    D. false0

20. What is the output of the following program?

    ```
    public class Question {
     public static void main(String args[]){
      Object[] o = new Object[2];
      byte[] b = new byte[2];
      System.out.print(o[0]);
      System.out.println(b[1]);
     }
    }
    ```

APPLY YOUR KNOWLEDGE

A. 0

B. o0

C. A `NullPointerException` is thrown

D. null0

Answers to Review Questions

1. A Java package is a naming context for classes and interfaces. A package is used to create a separate name space for groups of classes and interfaces. Packages are also used to organize related classes and interfaces into a single API unit and to control accessibility to these classes and interfaces.

2. A compilation unit is a Java source code file.

3. A Java source code file takes the name of a `public` class or interface that is defined within the file. A source code file may contain at most one `public` class or interface. If a `public` class or interface is defined within a source code file, then the source code file must take the name of the `public` class or interface. If no `public` class or interface is defined within a source code file, then the file must take on a name that is different than its classes and interfaces. Source code files use the `.java` extension.

4. A `package` statement must appear as the first line in a source code file (excluding blank lines and comments).

5. The `java.lang` package is always imported by default.

6. A program's `main()` method has a `void` return type.

7. A program's `main()` method takes an argument of the `String[]` type.

8. The non-Unicode letter characters $ and _ may appear as the first character of an identifier.

9. The digits 0 through 9 may not be used as the first character of an identifier but they may be used after the first character of an identifier.

10. The values `true` and `false` are not keywords.

11. The `null` value is not a keyword.12. The `sizeof` operator is not a keyword.

13. The eight primitive types are `byte`, `char`, `short`, `int`, `long`, `float`, `double`, and `boolean`.

14. The range of the `short` type is $-(2^{15})$ to $2^{15} - 1$.

15. The range of the `char` type is 0 to $2^{16} - 1$.

16. The `String` literal `"abc"` is not a primitive value.

17. The default value of the `boolean` type is `false`.

18. The default value of an `String` type is `null`.

Answers to Exam Questions

1. B   A class does not need a `main()` method to compile. Nor does it need to be defined in a package or imported. However, a `public` class needs to be defined in a source code file of the same name.

2. C   A source code file must take the same name as any `public` class or interface that it declares.

3. C   For a class to be compiled and run, it must have a correctly formed `main()` method. It does not need to be declared `public`.

APPLY YOUR KNOWLEDGE

4. A and D   Package statements must appear as the first non-blank line of a source code file (if they appear at all). If a public class or interface is declared in a source code file, then the source code file must take the name of the public class or interface.

5. B and D   The main() method of answer A is missing an argument. The main() method of answer C is missing the public and static modifiers.

6. B   The String "is" is assigned to args[1].

7. B and C   Comments use slashes and not backslashes.

8. B and C   The only special characters that may appear in an identifier are _ and $.

9. B and D   The only special characters that may appear in an identifier are _ and $. Digits may not be used as the first character of an identifier.

10. A, C, and D   The sizeof operator is not a Java keyword.

11. C   NULL, null, and main are not Java keywords.

12. A   Neither String, integer, nor Float are primitive types.

13. D   The range of the short type is $-(2^{15})$ to $2^{15} - 1$.

14. B   The range of the char type is 0 to $2^{16} - 1$.

15. A   The octal value 0173 is equivalent to the decimal value 123.

16. C   The hexadecimal value 0x7B is equivalent to the decimal value 123.

17. A   Comments may not appear in a String literal.

18. A and B   Since the value e2d begins with a letter, it is treated as an identifier. Since there is no signed integer value after the e in 1ed, it is an invalid double literal.

19. C   The default value of a boolean is false and the default value of a double is 0.0.

20. D   The default value of an Object is null and the default value of a byte is 0.

Suggested Readings and Resources

Gosling, James, Joy, Bill, and Steele, Guy, *The Java Language Specification*. Addison Wesley, 1996.

This chapter helps you to prepare for the exam by covering the following objectives:

Be able to determine the result of applying any operator, including assignment operators and `instanceof`, to operands of any type class scope or accessibility or any combination of these.

▶ You must know how to use Java operators to be able to evaluate expressions and determine the results of Java statements. Many of the test questions involve analysis of sample code.

Know how to evaluate Java expressions according to operator precedence and associativity rules.

▶ The rules of operator precedence and associativity are key to determining the order in which expressions are evaluated. You must become familiar with these rules and be able to apply them to the evaluation of complex expressions.

Know when and how values of one type are converted to values of another type during expression evaluation.

▶ Many operators require that their operands be of a specific type. In some cases, operands of other types are automatically converted to the required type during expression evaluation. Knowing when and how this occurs is critical to answering some exam questions.

In an expression involving the operators &, ¦, &&, ¦¦, and variables of known values, be able to state which operands are evaluated and the value of the expression.

▶ A few exam questions focus on the differences between these operators. By knowing which operators operate in a "short-circuit" fashion you'll be able to correctly answer these questions.

CHAPTER 3

Operators and Assignments

Know how to determine the result of applying the `boolean equals(Object)` method to objects of any combination of the classes `java.lang.String`, `java.lang.Boolean`, and `java.lang.Object`.

▶ The `equals()` method of `Object` differs from the `==` operator in that it is used to determine if two objects have equal values (as opposed to equal object references). Knowledge of the uses of `equals()` and `==` is required to answer several exam questions.

Java Operators include the following:

As you read through this chapter, you should concentrate on the following key items:

▶ How the / and % operators are used

▶ The difference between ++i, i++, --i, and i--

▶ How the instanceof and cast operators are used

▶ The difference between logical and logical short-circuit operators

▶ The use of the bitwise and shift operators

▶ How each of the assignment operators work

▶ How the ternary operator works

▶ The operator precedence hierarchy

▶ How operator precedence and associativity affects the evaluation of expressions

▶ When and how automatic type conversion takes place

CHAPTER INTRODUCTION

This chapter is an easy chapter to master. It is also an important one to know. Operators are a basic building block from which Java expressions and statements are built. You should already be pretty familiar with the use of many of the operators covered in this chapter. On the other hand, there may be a handful of operators that you've seen before, but you are not quite familiar with. It's up to you to identify which ones they are and firm up your knowledge of how they work. This is essential to doing well on the exam. There are a number of operator-specific and operator-related questions. These are some of the easier questions on the test. You should answer all of them correctly. If you don't learn operators well, not only will you miss some of the operator-specific questions, you may also miss some of the more complex questions that assume knowledge of basic operators.

This chapter reviews all of the Java operators and provides examples of their use. It covers operator precedence and shows how it is used in expression evaluation. It also covers casting and conversion and those situations where automatic type conversion comes into play. Read through this chapter and fill in any gaps that you may have. The review questions and exam questions will let you know how well you know this material and will give you an idea of how well you will do in operator-specific exam questions.

JAVA OPERATORS

Java's operators originate in C and C++. If you are a C or C++ programmer, I have good news and bad news. The good news is that many of Java's operators have the same behavior as they do in C and C++. The bad news is that some do not, and the ones that don't can trip you up on the exam. I don't assume that you have a background in C or C++, but I hope that you are far enough in your Java programming that most of the operators in Table 3.1 are familiar to you. Take the time now to go through the table and check off the ones you are familiar with. Then highlight the ones that you need to study. Pay careful attention to these operators when you work your way through this chapter.

TABLE 3.1

OPERATOR SUMMARY

Category	Operator	Example	Result
Arithmetic	+ (Unary)	+3	The int value 3.
	+ (Binary)	2 + 4	The value of x is 6.
	- (Unary)	-x	The sign of x is changed.
	- (Binary)	4 - 2	The value of x is 2.
	++ (Prefix)	x = 3	The value of x is 4 and
		y = ++x	the value of y is 4.
	++ (Postfix)	x = 3	The value of x is 4 and
		y = x++;	the value of y is 3.
	- - (Prefix)	x = 3	The value of x is 2 and
		y = --x	the value of y is 2.
	-- (Postfix)	x = 3	The value of x is 2 and
		y = x--	the value of y is 3.
	*	4 * 3	12
	/	11 / 4	2
	%	11 % 4	3
String	+	"ab" + "cd"	"abcd"
Bitwise	~	~3	-4
	&	3 & 4	0
	¦	3 ¦ 4	7
	^	5 ¦ 4	4
Shift	<<	3 << 2	12
	>>	-6 >> 2	-2
	>>>	-6 >>> 2	1073741822
Comparison	<	5 < 7	true
	<=	5 <= 7	true
	>	5 > 7	false
	>=	5 >= 7	false
	==	5 == 7	false
	!=	5 != 7	true
	instanceof	"abc" instanceof String	true

continues

TABLE 3.1	*continued*

OPERATOR SUMMARY

Logical	&	true & false	false
	¦	true ¦ false	true
	^	true ^ false	true
	!	!true	false
	&&	true && false	false
	¦¦	true ¦¦ false	true
Assignment	=	x = 5;	The value of x is 5.
	+=	x = 1; x += 5;	The value of x is 6.
	-=	x = 1; x - = 5;	The value of x is -4.
	*=	x = 1; x *= 5;	The value of x is 5.
	/=	int x = 1; x /= 5;	The value of x is 0.
	%=	x = 1; x %= 5;	The value of x is 1.
	&=	x = 1; x &= 5;	The value of x is 1.
	¦=	x = 1; x ¦= 5;	The value of x is 5.
	^=	x = 1; x ^= 5;	The value of x is 4.
	<<=	x = 1; x <<= 5;	The value of x is 32.
	>>=	x = 1; x >>= 5;	The value of x is 0.
	>>>=	x = 1; x >>>= 5;	The value of x is 0.
Cast	(*type*)	double d = 4.2;= byte b = (byte) d;	The value of b is 4.
Ternary	? :	x = 1; x = (x > 0) ? 5 : 10	The value of x is 5.

Unary Arithmetic Operators

The arithmetic operators consist of both unary and binary operators. *Unary* operators perform operations on a single operand. *Binary* operations perform operations on two operands. For example, in the expression, -x, the - operator is used as a unary operator. In the expression, x-y, the - operator is used as a binary operator.

The unary operators are used to increment, decrement, or change the sign of a value. The + unary operator has no effect on the sign of a value. The - unary operator changes the sign of a value. Both the + and - operators have subtle effects on byte, char, and short values. When the + or - operators are applied to a value of these types the value is first converted to an int value. The result of the operation is an int value. This process, referred to as *numeric promotion*, is discussed further for binary arithmetic operations, in the later section, "Numeric Promotion."

The ++ and -- operators are used to increment and decrement a value. For example, if x is 1 then ++x results in the value of 2 being assigned to x. If x is 6 then --x results in the value 5 of 5 being assigned to x. The ++ operators may appear before the value (prefix) or after the value (postfix). Examples are:

++x (prefix)

x++ (postfix)

--x (prefix)

x-- (postfix)

If x is 4 in the above expressions, then the first two expressions result in 5 being assigned to x, and the last two expressions result in 4 being assigned to x. Because the prefix and postfix forms of the increment and decrement operators both result in the same value being assigned to x, you may wonder what the difference is between the prefix and postfix forms. There is one significant difference between the prefix and postfix forms, and there's a fair chance that you'll encounter it on the test. The difference involves the use of prefix and postfix expressions in assignments. When a prefix expression is used in an expression, the value that is returned is the value that is calculated *after* the prefix operator is applied. When a postfix expression is used in an expression, the value that is returned is the value of the expression *before* the postfix operator is applied. The following examples illustrate these rules:

```
x = 10;
y = ++x;   // The value assigned to y is 11

x = 10;
y = x++;   // The value assigned to y is 10

x = 10;
y = --x;   // The value assigned to y is 9

x = 10;
y = x--;   // The value assigned to y is 10
```

You can see the difference in the results returned by the prefix and postfix operators in the preceding examples. If you want to make sure that the calculation is performed before returning a value, always use the prefix operator.

Binary Arithmetic Operators

Now that you've looked at the unary arithmetic operators, we'll cover the binary arithmetic operators + (addition), - (subtraction), * (multiplication), / (division), and % (modulo).

The binary arithmetic operators are fairly straightforward—they perform simple calculations on a pair of numeric values. However, there are a few special cases that need to be considered:

◆ When an operation is performed on operands of different types

◆ When the result of an integer division must be rounded

◆ Division by zero

◆ Modulo operations

◆ Operations that result in the throwing of runtime exceptions

◆ Operations that result in overflow or underflow

We'll cover each of the above special cases in the following sections, showing how they apply to each operator.

Numeric Promotion

When binary operations are applied to numeric arguments (integer and floating-point), *numeric promotion* is performed before the operation takes place. The numeric promotion consists of converting the values of the operands to a common type. The rules for this conversion are straightforward.

◆ If one of the operands is a `double`, then the other is converted to a `double`.

◆ Otherwise, if one of the operands is a `float`, then the other is converted to a `float`.

◆ Otherwise, if one of the operands is a `long`, then the other is converted to a `long`.

◆ Otherwise, both operands are converted to `int` values.

Make sure that you remember these rules. You won't be tested on the rules themselves, but you'll need to know them to work through related questions. One thing that you probably will see on the test is + operations involving a numeric value and a `String` value. These questions test your knowledge of the difference between the arithmetic + operator and the `String` + operator. The `String` + operator results in the concatenation of two `String` objects. For example, `"abc"` + `"def"` results in `"abcdef"`. But what about, `10` + `"0"` or `"2.4"` + `2.5`?

The rule that you should remember is that when one of the operands in a + operation is a `String`, then the other operand is converted to a `String`. Therefore, `10` + `"0"` results in the `String` `"100"` and `"2.4"` + `2.5` results in the `String` object `"2.42.5"`. The other operand is converted to a `String` object in one of two ways, depending on whether the operand is an object or a value of a primitive type. If the other operand is an object, then its `toString()` method is invoked to convert it to a `String` object. If the other operand is a value of a primitive type, then an object of the type's wrapper class is created (see Chapter 9, "The `java.lang` Package") and the object's `toString()` method is invoked to convert it to a `String` object.

Integer Division and Division by Zero

Java, like many other languages, supports division (/) operations on integer (`long`, `int`, `short`, `char`, and `byte`) values. In order to return the result of operations like `4/3` as an integer value, it rounds toward zero. This is the same as truncating the fractional part of the result. The following list provides some examples of integer division.

- ◆ `10 / 3` results in `3`
- ◆ `-10 / 3` results in `-3`
- ◆ `10 / -3` results in `-3`
- ◆ `11 / 3` results in `3`
- ◆ `-11 / 3` results in `-3`
- ◆ `11 / -3` results in `-3`

In mathematics, division by zero is undefined. In Java, division by zero results in different values, depending on whether the operation is performed on an integer value, a positive floating-point value, or a negative floating-point value.

Division of an integer by zero results in the throwing of an `ArithmeticException`. Division of a positive floating-point value by zero results in `POSITIVE_INFINITY`. Division of a negative floating point value by zero results in `NEGATIVE_INFINITY`. Note that when the sign of zero is negative, such as `-0`, the sign of the result is reversed. This only applies to floating point operations.

Modulo Operations

For many, the modulo operator `%`, also referred to as the remainder operator, is not as familiar as the other binary mathematical operators. First of all, it has nothing to do with percentages. It is the remainder that results when the first operand is divided by the second. That is, `x % y` is `x - ((int) (x/y)*y)`. Java, unlike C and C++, allows floating-point operands to be used with the `%` operator. The results of using the `%` operator with floating-point operands are calculated in a similar manner. The following list provides some examples of the `%` operator in action.

- ◆ `11 % 3` results in `2`.
- ◆ `11 % -3` results in `2`.
- ◆ `-11 % 3` results in `-2`.
- ◆ `-11 % -3` results in `-2`.
- ◆ `11.5 % 3.2` results in `1.8999999999999995`. (that is, approximately `1.9`)

◆ 11.5 % -3.2 results in 1.8999999999999995.

◆ -11.5 % 3.2 results in -1.8999999999999995.

◆ -11.5 % -3.2 results in -1.8999999999999995.

Note that if x is positive and y is not zero, x % y is positive. If x is negative and y is not zero, then x % y is negative. If x is an integer value and y is zero, then x % y results in the throwing of an ArithmeticException. If x is a floating-point value and y is zero, then x % y results in NaN (but no exception is thrown).

Runtime Exceptions

The only runtime exception that occurs during arithmetic operations is the ArithmeticException. This exception is never thrown in floating-point operations and only occurs in integer operations when dividing by 0 or taking the remainder of a number by 0. Although you won't be tested on this fact directly, remember it to help you to weed out bad answers in related questions.

Overflow and Underflow

A numeric overflow occurs when the result of a calculation is larger than the largest value that can be represented by a type. A numeric underflow occurs when the result of a calculation is smaller than the smallest value that can be represented by a type. Because arithmetic operations are performed using numeric values of limited size, some operations result in overflow and underflow. You can determine if an operation results in an overflow or underflow by calculating its result and determining whether the result is too large or small to be represented using the number of bytes available to the type. In cases of integer (but not floating point) overflow and underflow, the lower order bytes of the result that are capable of fitting into the type are returned as the result of the operation. Figure 3.1 shows how this occurs:

For example, consider the following program (see Listing 3.1):

FIGURE 3.1
How Java handles overflows and underflows.

Overflows and underflows occur when a calculated value becomes larger than or smaller than the number of bytes allowed by its type.

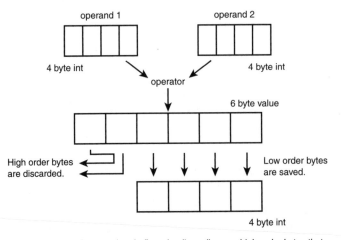

Java handles overflows and underflows by discarding any high-order bytes that won't fit into the number of bytes allowed by its type.

LISTING 3.1

OVERFLOW.JAVA—AN EXAMPLE OF THE RESULT OF AN OVERFLOW OPERATION

```java
class Overflow {
 public static void main(String args[]) {
  int n = 2000000000;
  System.out.println(n * n);
 }
}
```

The result displayed by this program is -1651507200, which is hardly the square of 2 billion. To determine how this result is calculated, look at the arithmetic that takes place.

◆ 2,000,000,000 is represented as 01110111 00110101 10010100 00000000 in binary form.

◆ 2,000,000,000 * 2,000,000,000 results in 4,000,000,000,000,000,000, which is 00110111 10000010 11011010 11001110 10011101 10010000 00000000 00000000 in binary form.

◆ This overflows the 32-bit `int` type. Therefore, we only save the last 4 bytes (`10011101 10010000 00000000 00000000`) as the result.

◆ The value of the last 4 bytes is the binary representation of the `int` value `-1651507200`.

The good news is that you won't see any questions that will ask you to calculate whether an operation results in an overflow or underflow. However, there may be some answers to multiple choice questions that say that an operation results in an overflow or underflow. By being familiar with how overflows and underflows occur, you will be able to tell which answers are obviously true and which are used as distractors.

BITWISE OPERATORS

The bitwise operators, ~ (inversion), & (and), ¦ (or), and ^ (exclusive-or) perform operations on integer values. The ~ operator is a unary operator, and the others are binary operators. Figure 3.2 summarizes how each operator performs its calculation.

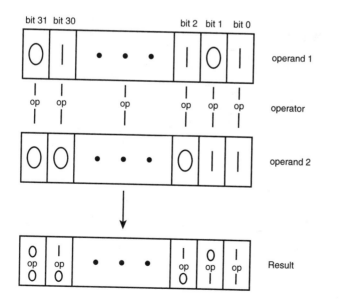

FIGURE 3.2
How the bitwise operators work.

The ~ operator inverts the bits which make up the integer value. That is, 0 bits become 1 bits and 1 bits become 0 bits. For example, ~3 yields the value -4. It is calculated as follows:

◆ 3 is represented as the binary int value 00000000 0000000000000000 00000011.

◆ Inverting each of the bits yields 11111111 1111111111111111 11111100, which is the bit pattern for -4 as an int value.

The &, ¦, and ^ operators calculate their results in a bit-by-bit fashion. That is, the *n*th bit of the result is calculated using only the *n*th bit of each operand. These bit-level operations are performed as follows:

◆ The & operator returns a 1 bit if the corresponding bits of its operands are both 1. It returns a 0 otherwise.

◆ The ¦ operator returns a 0 bit if the corresponding bits of its operands are both 0. It returns a 1 otherwise.

◆ The ^ operator returns a 0 bit if the corresponding bits of its operand are both 0 or both 1. It returns a 1 otherwise.

Table 3.2 summarizes the operation of these operators.

> **Numeric Promotion** Numeric promotion is used with both unary and binary bitwise operators. This means that byte, char, and short values are converted to int values before a bitwise operator is applied. If a binary bitwise operator has one long operand, the other operand is converted to a long value. The type of the result of a bitwise operation is the type to which the operands have been promoted.

TABLE 3.2

BINARY BITWISE OPERATORS

Operand 1	Operator	Operand 2	Result
0	&	0	0
0	&	1	0
1	&	0	0
1	&	1	1
0	¦	0	0
0	¦	1	1
1	¦	0	1
1	¦	1	1
0	^	0	0
0	^	1	1
1	^	0	1
1	^	1	0

Let's consider the expressions 63 & 252, 63 ¦ 252, and 63 ^ 252. To calculate the value of these expressions, we first represent the int values 63 and 252 as bit patterns:

```
00000000 00000000 00000000 00111111 = 63
00000000 00000000 00000000 11111100 = 252
```

Because & returns a 1 bit if, and only if, the corresponding bit from each operand is 1, we calculate 63 & 252 to be 60 as follows:

```
00000000 00000000 00000000 00111111 = 63
00000000 00000000 00000000 11111100 = 252
00000000 00000000 00000000 00111100 = 60
```

Because ¦ returns a 0 bit if and only if the corresponding bit from each operand is 0, we calculate 63 ¦ 252 to be 255 as follows:

```
00000000 00000000 00000000 00111111 = 63
00000000 00000000 00000000 11111100 = 252
00000000 00000000 00000000 11111111 = 255
```

Because ^ returns a 0 bit if, and only if, the corresponding bit from each operand match, we calculate 63 ¦ 252 to be 195 as follows:

```
00000000 00000000 00000000 00111111 = 63
00000000 00000000 00000000 11111100 = 252
00000000 00000000 00000000 11000011 = 195
```

The results of bitwise operations are easy to calculate after you've tried a few examples. The questions at the end of this chapter will help you study them. You may see an exam question that requires you to know how the bitwise operators work.

> **NOTE**
>
> **Java's Platform Independence**
> Because Java is implemented using a platform-independent virtual machine, bitwise operations always yield the same result, even when run on machines that use radically different CPUs.

SHIFT OPERATORS

The shift operators << (left shift), >> (right shift), and >>> (unsigned right shift) also work on the bit level. All of these operators are binary operators. If you took the JDK 1.1 Programmer Certification exam, you probably remember a few shift-related questions. Shift-related questions are not emphasized as much on the JDK 1.2 exam. However, you may still encounter a question that involves shifting. With a little bit of practice, you'll find that these operators are easy to use.

Numeric promotion is used with the shift operators. The left operand is promoted to an int if it is a byte, char, or short value. Then the right operand is promoted in the same manner. Note that when the left operand is an int, only the last 5 bits of the right operand are used to perform the shift. That's because an int is a 32-bit value and can only be shifted 0 through 31 times. When the left operand is a long value, only the last 6 bits of the right operand are used to perform the shift. Because long values are 64-bit values, they only can be shifted 0 through 63 times.

The << operator causes the bits of the left operand to be shifted to the left, based on the value of the right operand. The new bits that are used to fill in the shifted right bits have the value 0. Figure 3.3 illustrates the process of shifting left. Note that the leftmost bits shifted out of the operand are discarded.

The >> operator causes the bits of the left operand to be shifted to the right, based on the value of the right operand. The bits that fill in the shifted left bits have the value of the leftmost bit (before the shift operation). The >> operator is said to be a signed shift because it preserves the sign (positive or negative) of the operand. Figure 3.4 illustrates how the signed right shift is performed. The right-most bits that are shifted out of the operand are discarded.

The >>> operator is identical to the >> operator, except that the bits that fill in the shifted left bits have the value of 0. The >>> operator is said to be an unsigned shift because it does not preserve the sign of the operand. Figure 3.5 illustrates how the unsigned right shift is performed. The rightmost bits that are shifted out of the operand are discarded.

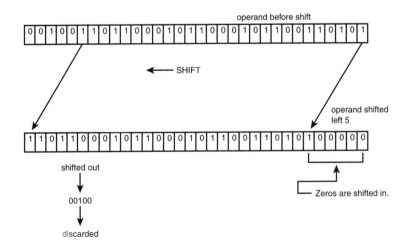

FIGURE 3.3
The << (left shift) operator.

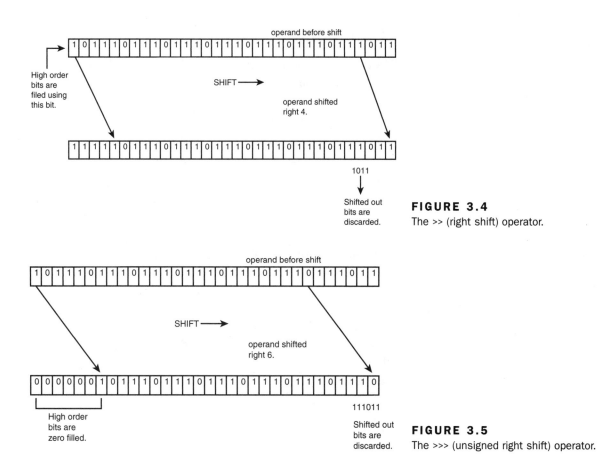

FIGURE 3.4
The >> (right shift) operator.

FIGURE 3.5
The >>> (unsigned right shift) operator.

Comparison Operators

The comparison operators are used to compare primitive values or object references. They are organized into three subgroups: the relational operators, the equality operators, and the instanceof operator. The relational operators are only defined for numeric values and the instanceof operator is only defined for object references.

The Relational Operators

The four relational operators are < (less than), <= (less than or equals), > (greater than), and >= (greater than or equals). These operators follow their mathematical definitions and produce a boolean value as their result. However, you should note that any relational expression with the NaN value evaluates to false.

The Equality Operators

The equality operators consist of == (is equal) and != (is not equal). These operators may be used with the eight primitive types, as well as object references. They return a boolean value in each case. When they are used with primitive values, the following rules apply:

◆ Numeric values cannot be compared to boolean values. Such a comparison results in a compilation error.

◆ Numeric promotion takes place before numeric values are compared. This enables any numeric value to be compared with any other numeric value.

Let's examine what happens in the following program (see Listing 3.2) as the result of the above rules.

LISTING 3.2

EQUALNUMBERS.JAVA—USING THE EQUALITY OPERATORS

```
class EqualValues {
 public static void main(String args[]) {
 byte b = 3;
  int i = 5;
  float f = 5.0f;
  double d = 3.0;
  System.out.println((b == d) == (i == f));
 }
}
```

The computation of interest takes place as an argument to the println() method. The expression (b==d) is evaluated. This results in the promotion of the byte value 3 to a double value. The == expression returns a value of true. The expression (i == f) is then evaluated. The int value of 5 is promoted to a float value and the == expression returns a value of true. This results in an expression true == true as the argument to the println() method. A value of true is printed as the result. (Note that the true value is converted to a String object by the println() method.)

When object references are compared, the == and != operators check to see if the objects being compared are the same object instance, and not whether the objects have the same values. For example, suppose objects A and B are both object of the same class and have exactly the same field values. If these objects are distinct (that is they are located in different areas of memory), then A == B evaluates to false, and A != B evaluates to true. Figure 3.6 summarizes the process used in evaluating expressions that use the equality operators.

Because String objects of identical values may be created during a program's execution, you must be careful not to compare the *values* of these objects using the == operator. For example, the following program (see Listing 3.3) displays a value of false when comparing two String objects with the same values.

LISTING 3.3

EQUALSTRINGS1.JAVA—AN EXAMPLE THAT USES THE == OPERATOR TO COMPARE String OBJECTS

```
class EqualStrings1 {
 public static void main(String args[]) {
  String s = "ab";
  String s1 = s + "cd";
  String s2 = "abcd";
  System.out.println(s1);
  System.out.println(s2);
  System.out.println(s1 == s2);
 }
}
```

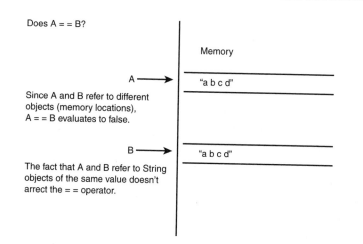

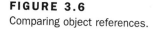

FIGURE 3.6
Comparing object references.

The equals() method is defined by the Object class as a means to tell whether two objects have the same value. It is overridden by subclasses of Object, such as String, to provide class-specific value comparisons. Let's use the equals() method to compare the values of the two String objects from Listing 3.3. The following program (Listing 3.4) displays a value of true when comparing the two String objects, referenced by s1 and s2.

LISTING 3.4

EQUALSTRINGS2.JAVA—AN EXAMPLE THAT USES THE Equals() METHOD TO COMPARE String OBJECTS

```
class EqualStrings2 {
 public static void main(String args[]) {
  String s = "ab";
  String s1 = s + "cd";
  String s2 = "abcd";
  System.out.println(s1);
  System.out.println(s2);
  System.out.println(s1.equals(s2));
 }
}
```

The instanceof Operator

The instanceof operator is a binary operator that determines whether an object reference (the left operand) is an instance of the class, interface, or array type specified by the right operand. The instanceof operator cannot be used with primitive types (this results in a compilation error).

The instanceof operator returns a boolean value of true if the left operand references a non-null object of class C (or array of type T), so that at least one of the following conditions holds.

- ◆ The right operand is a class name C' and C is a subclass of C'.

- ◆ The right operand is an interface name I, and C implements I.

- ◆ The right operand is an array of type T', the left operand is an array of type T, and T is a subclass or subinterface of T' or equal to T'.

The instanceof operator returns false if none of the above conditions are met or if the left operand is null.

The following program (see Listing 3.5) illustrates the use of the instanceof operator.

LISTING 3.5

INSTANCE.JAVA—USING THE instanceof OPERATOR TO DETERMINE AN OBJECT'S RUNTIME TYPE

```java
import java.util.*;

class Instance {
 public static void main(String args[]) {
  String s = "abcd";
  Vector v = new Vector();
  v.add(s);
  Object o = v.elementAt(0);
  System.out.println(s instanceof String);
  System.out.println(s instanceof Object);
  System.out.println(o instanceof String);
  System.out.println(o instanceof Object);
  System.out.println(o instanceof Vector);
 }
}
```

When you run the program, it produces the following results:

```
true
true
true
true
false
```

The first two output lines reflect the fact that s is a String and therefore an Object (because String is a subclass of Object). The third output line displays a value of true even though o is declared to be of type Object. How is this so? That's because the object assigned to o is the String object that was added to Vector v. The fourth and fifth output lines result from the fact that a String object is an Object object but not a Vector object.

LOGICAL OPERATORS

Java supports two groups of logical operators, the boolean operators ! (not), & (and), ¦ (or), and ^ (exclusive-or), and the logical short-circuit operators && (short-circuit and) and ¦¦ (short-circuit or). All of these operators are restricted to boolean operands.

The ! operator performs logical negation. Its operation is simply described:

◆ !x results in false if x is true.

◆ !x results in true if x is false.

The &, ¦, and ^ operators operate in the same manner that the bit-wise operators do when applied to each bit. This operation is described in Table 3.3.

TABLE 3.3

THE boolean OPERATORS &, ¦, AND ^

Operand 1	Operator	Operand 2	Result
false	&	false	false
false	&	true	false
true	&	false	false
true	&	true	true
false	¦	false	false
false	¦	true	true
true	¦	false	true
true	¦	true	true
false	^	false	false
false	^	true	true
true	^	false	true
true	^	true	false

The logical short-circuit operators, && and ¦¦, produce the same logical result as & and ¦, but differ in the way they are evaluated. Given an expression x & y, evaluation proceeds in the following order:

1. Evaluate x.

2. Evaluate y.

3. Apply Table 3.3 to determine the result of x & y.

However, the expression x && y is evaluated in the following manner:

1. Evaluate x.

2. If x is false, return `false`.

3. Otherwise, if x is true evaluate y.

4. Return the value of y.

The && operator is called a short-circuit operator because it skips the evaluation of the second operand, if the first operand is evaluated as false.

The ¦¦ operator also operates in a short-circuit fashion. The expression x ¦¦ y is evaluated as follows:

1. Evaluate x.

2. If x is true return `true`.

3. Otherwise, if x is false evaluate y.

4. Return the value of y.

If the first operand of ¦¦ is true then the evaluation of the second operand is skipped.

The following program (see Listing 3.6) illustrates the results of using the &, ¦, &&, and ¦¦ operators.

LISTING 3.6

LOGICAL.JAVA—USING THE boolean AND Logical SHORT-CIRCUIT OPERATORS

```
class Logical {
 static boolean sideEffect(boolean b) {
  System.out.print("Side effect! ");
  return b;
 }
 public static void main(String args[]) {
  boolean t = true;
  boolean f = false;
  System.out.println(false & sideEffect(true));
  System.out.println(false && sideEffect(true));
  System.out.println(true | sideEffect(true));
  System.out.println(true || sideEffect(true));
 }
}
```

When you run the program, it produces the following results:

```
Side effect! false
false
Side effect! true
true
```

ASSIGNMENT OPERATORS

Java provides a full suite of assignment operators, including the basic = assignment operator and the C *op=* style operators where *op* is a binary arithmetic operator. These operators are as follows:

◆ x = y The variable x is assigned the value of y.

◆ x += y The variable x is assigned the value of x + y.

◆ x -= y The variable x is assigned the value of x - y.

◆ x *= y The variable x is assigned the value of x * y.

◆ x /= y The variable x is assigned the value of x / y.

◆ x %= y The variable x is assigned the value of x % y.

◆ x &= y The variable x is assigned the value of x & y.

◆ x |= y The variable x is assigned the value of x | y.

◆ x ^= y The variable x is assigned the value of x ^ y.

◆ x <<= y The variable x is assigned the value of x <<= y.

◆ x >>= y The variable x is assigned the value of x >>= y.

◆ x >>>= y The variable x is assigned the value of x >>>= y.

With the exception of the = simple assignment operator and the += operator, all of the other above operators are used with primitive types. Note that the &, ¦, and ^ operators can be used with both Boolean and numeric arguments. The += operator may also be used with String objects.

The assignment operators of the form *op*= cast their result to the type of the left operand. For example, if b is of type byte, b += 3, assigns (byte) (b + 3) to b. This is important because the value of b is promoted to an int value before the addition takes place. The following program (Listing 3.7) compiles without a compilation error:

LISTING 3.7

Cast1.java—Casting and the += Operator

```
class Cast1 {
 public static void main(String args[]) {
  byte b = 0;
  b += 3;
  System.out.println(b);
 }
}
```

Unlike the *op*= operators, the = operator does not perform an implicit cast. The following program (Listing 3.8) results in a compilation error because casting is required to assign an int value to a byte value.

LISTING 3.8

Cast2.java—Casting and the = Operator

```
class Cast2 {
 public static void main(String args[]) {
  byte b = 0;
  b = b + 3;
  System.out.println(b);
 }
}
```

When the simple assignment operator is used with object references, a few rules apply:

◆ If the type of the left operand is a class C, then the type of the right operand must be a subclass of C or the null value.

◆ If the type of the left operand is an interface I, the type of the right operand must be a subinterface of I, or a class that implements I, or the null value.

The following section shows how casting can be used to change the type associated with the right operand before an assignment is made.

There are two more points to cover about the assignment operator:

◆ The value (and type) returned by an assignment is the value (and type) assigned to the left operand.

◆ The simple assignment operator is *right associative*. This means that a = b = c is evaluated as a = (b = c). All other operators are *left associative*. For example, a + b + c is evaluated as (a + b) + c.

The following program (see Listing 3.9) illustrates the above two rules. The statement i = j = k = l is evaluated as follows:

1. The value of l (4) is assigned to k.

2. The value of k = l (4) is assgined to j.

3. The value of j = k = l (4) is assigned to i.

LISTING 3.9

ASSIGN.JAVA—ASSOCIATIVITY AND THE = OPERATOR

```java
class Assign {
 public static void main(String args[]) {
  int i = 1;
  int j = 2;
  int k = 3;
  int l = 4;
  i = j = k = l;
  System.out.println(i);
  System.out.println(j);
  System.out.println(k);
  System.out.println(l);
 }
}
```

THE CAST OPERATOR

The cast operator (*type*) is used to convert numeric values from one numeric type to another or to change an object reference to a compatible type.

WIDENING AND NARROWING CONVERSIONS

A *widening conversion* is a conversion from a smaller numeric type to a larger numeric type. An example of a widening conversion is when a byte value is promoted to an int value. A *narrowing conversion* is a conversion from a larger numeric type to a smaller numeric type. A conversion from a long value to a short value would be an example of a narrowing conversion. Narrowing conversions require the use of the cast operator.

Casting can be used to enable numeric conversions that would normally be disallowed by the compiler. For example, the following program (see Listing 3.10) assigns the value 123 to the b variable. Without the (byte) cast operator, the compiler would generate an error message.

LISTING 3.10

CAST3.JAVA—CASTING NUMERIC VALUES

```
class Cast3 {
 public static void main(String args[]) {
  double d = 123.456;
  byte b;
  b = (byte) d;
  System.out.println(b);
 }
}
```

When casting is used with object references, the following rules apply:

1. A reference to any object can be cast into a reference to an object of class Object.

2. A reference to an object can be cast into a reference to an object of class C', if the actual class of the object is a subclass of C'.

3. A reference to an object can be cast into a reference to an object of interface I, if the actual class of the object implements I, if the object is of interface type I' and I' is a subinterface of I, or if the object is an array type and I is the `Cloneable` interface.

4. A reference to an object can be cast a reference to an object of an array type (with element reference type T), if the object is of an array type (with element reference type T') such that T' can be cast into T.

Let's examine each of the above rules.

The first rule is pretty simple. Any object reference can be cast to an `Object` object using the `(Object)` cast operator.

Figure 3.7 summarizes the second rule. When an object is created, it is an object of some specific class (referred to as the *actual* class in the rule). The object may be subsequently referenced by a superclass reference or an interface reference. For example, a `String` object may be created and then referenced as an `Object` object. Casting can be used to change the object's reference back to its original class (for example, `String`).

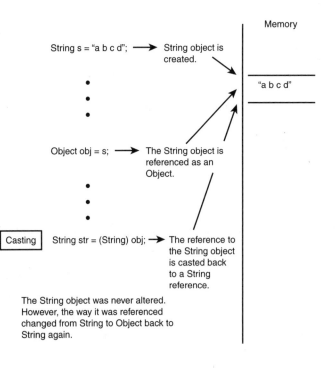

FIGURE 3.7
Casting between classes.

The third rule covers casting to interfaces. If the actual class of an object implements the interface, the object can be cast to that interface. For example, a `Vector` object can be cast to a `List` object, and a `List` object can be cast to a `Collection` object. Because the array type implements the `Cloneable` interface, any array can be cast into a `Cloneable` object.

Casting to array types is more complicated. In order to cast to an object reference to an array type reference, the object must be an array of a component type that is compatible with the component type of the array type reference. Figure 3.8 summarizes casting to array types.

As an example of object type casting, consider the following program (Listing 3.11). Without the `(String)` cast operator, the result returned by `v.elementAt(0)` is an object of the `Object` class. The compiler recognizes this inconsistency and generates an error message. When the `(String)` cast operator is used, the compiler recognizes that you are casting the reference to an `Object` object into a `String` object and proceeds with the compilation.

An object is an array of class T¹ objects

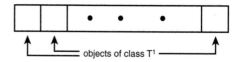

objects of class T¹

The object may be cast into an array of class T objects if and only if T¹ references may be cast into T references.

FIGURE 3.8
Casting to array types.

LISTING 3.11

CAST4.JAVA—CASTING OBJECT REFERENCES

```java
import java.util.*;

class Cast4 {
 public static void main(String args[]) {
  String s1 = "abc";
  String s2 = "def";
  Vector v = new Vector();
  v.add(s1);
  s2 = (String) v.elementAt(0);
  System.out.println(s2);
 }
}
```

THE TERNARY OPERATOR

The ternary operator ? :, also referred to as the conditional operator, has three operands and takes the following form:

operand1 ? operand2 : operand3

The first operand must be of boolean type. The first operand is evaluated and if true, the value of the second operand is returned. In this case, evaluation of the third operand does not take place. If the value of the first operand is false, evaluation of the second operand is skipped, and the value of the third operand is returned. The Java compiler requires that the second and third operands be promotable (numeric values) or castable (object references) to a common type.

For example, the program shown in Listing 3.12 produces the output 0xx3xx6xx9.

LISTING 3.12

TERNARY.JAVA—USING THE TERNARY OPERATOR

```java
class Ternary {
 public static void main(String args[]) {
  for(int i=0;i<10;++i)
   System.out.print((i%3==0)? ("" + i) : "x");
 }
}
```

OPERATOR PRECEDENCE AND ORDER OF EVALUATION

The order in which expressions are evaluated determines the values they produce. In Java, the operands of an expression are evaluated in a left-to-right fashion before any operations are performed. The only exceptions to this are operations involving the logical short-circuit operators && and ¦¦ and the ternary operator. After evaluating the operands of an expression, the operators are applied according to operator precedence and associativity. All binary operators are left associative except the = assignment operator. Parentheses are used to alter the effects of precedence and associativity.

Figure 3.9 shows Java's operator precedence hierarchy. Operators at the top of the hierarchy take precedence over lower level operators in the evaluation of an expression. Operators at the same level are evaluated in the order they appear in an expression, according to their associativity.

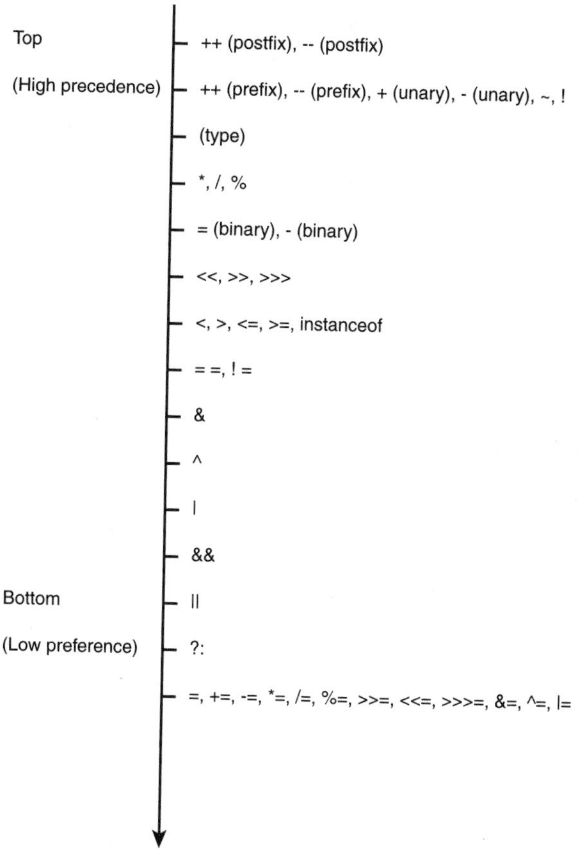

```
Top                    ++ (postfix), -- (postfix)

(High precedence)      ++ (prefix), -- (prefix), + (unary), - (unary), ~, !

                       (type)

                       *, /, %

                       = (binary), - (binary)

                       <<, >>, >>>

                       <, >, <=, >=, instanceof

                       = =, ! =

                       &

                       ^

                       |

                       &&

Bottom                 ||

(Low preference)       ?:

                       =, +=, -=, *=, /=, %=, >>=, <<=, >>>=, &=, ^=, |=
```

FIGURE 3.9
Java's operator precedence hierarchy.

Use Figure 3.9 to evaluate a complex expression. Consider the program shown in Listing 3.13. It displays the value abc9.

LISTING 3.13

PRECEDENCE.JAVA—USING THE OPERATOR PRECEDENCE TO EVALUATE COMPLEX EXPRESSIONS

```java
class Precedence {
 public static void main(String args[]) {
  String s = "abc";
  int x = 10;
  boolean b = false;
  s = s += x = x++ + 1 - 2 * 3 +
   ((Object) s instanceof String ? 4 << 5 / 6 & ++x:
   7 ^ 8 % --x) ¦ 9;
  System.out.println(s);
 }
}
```

The highest precedence operator is the postfix ++ operator. This increments the value of x to 11 but returns the value of 10. Our expression reduces to

```
s = s += x = 10 + 1 - 2 * 3 +    ((Object) s instanceof
String ? 4 << 5 / 6 & ++x:
    7 ^ 8 % --x) ¦ 9;
```

Now the highest precedence operators is *. Applying this operator, reduce the expression to

```
s = s += x = 10 + 1 - 6 +
    ((Object) s instanceof String ? 4 << 5 / 6
    & ++x: 7 ^ 8 % --x) ¦ 9;
```

The highest precedence operators becomes the + and - operators. Applying these operators enables us to reduce the expression to

```
s = s += x = 5 + ((Object) s instanceof String ? 4 << 5 / 6
& ++x:
    7 ^ 8 % --x) ¦ 9;
```

We must now evaluate the expression

```
(Object) s instanceof String ? 4 << 5 / 6 & ++x: 7 ^ 8 % --x
```

and then plug it back in to the overall expression. Within this expression the (Object) cast operator has the highest precedence. This causes s to be cast to an object of the Object class. (However, s remains fundamentally a String object.) We'll simplify the expression to

```
s instanceof String ? 4 << 5 / 6 & ++x: 7 ^ 8 % --x
```

The ternary operator evaluates the operand to the left of the ? before selecting which operand 4 << 5 / 6 & ++x or 7 ^ 8 % --x to evaluate next. The expression s instanceof String evaluates to true, and the overall expression simplifies to

```
4 << 5 / 6 & ++x
```

The ++ operator is evaluated next. Because the value of x is now 11, it is incremented to 12 and the expression simplifies to

```
4 << 5 / 6 & 12
```

The / is then evaluated, followed by << and then &. The expression is evaluated as follows:

```
4 << 0 & 12
4 & 12
4
```

Plugging this result back into the expression, you now have

```
s = s += x = 5 + 4 ¦ 9;
```

Because + has a higher precedence than ¦ the expression evaluates to

```
s = s += x = 9 ¦ 9;
```

and then to

```
s = s += x = 9;
```

The value 9 is then assigned to x leaving

```
s = s += 9;
```

The value of s becomes "abc9", and the expression simplifies to

```
s = "abc9";
```

The above example is much more complex than any you'll see in the exam. If you can work your way through this example, you should be able to tackle any exam question.

CHAPTER SUMMARY

This chapter reviewed all of the Java operators and provided examples of their use. It covered operator precedence and showed how it is used in expression evaluation. It also covered important points related to casting and numeric promotion. You should now be prepared to test your knowledge of these subjects. The following review questions and exam questions will let you know how well you understand this material and will give you an idea of how you'll do on operator-specific exam questions. They'll also indicate which material you need to study further.

KEY TERMS

- Operator
- Operand
- Expression
- Unary operator
- Binary operator
- Prefix operator
- Postfix operator
- Ternary operator
- Numeric promotion
- Casting
- Overflow
- Underflow
- Precedence
- Associativity
- Order of evaluation

APPLY YOUR KNOWLEDGE

Review Questions

1. What is the % operator?

2. What is the difference between the prefix and postfix forms of the ++ operator?

3. What are the legal operands of the instanceof operator?

4. What is the difference between the Boolean & operator and the && operator?

5. What is the difference between the >> and >>> operators?

6. How is it possible for two String objects with identical values not to be equal under the == operator?

7. Is &&= a valid Java operator?

8. Is the ternary operator written x : y ? z or x ? y : z?

9. Can a double value be cast to a byte?

10. Can a Byte object be cast to a double value?

11. Which arithmetic operations can result in the throwing of an ArithmeticException?

12. How is rounding performed under integer division?

13. What happens when you add a double value to a String?

14. How does Java handle integer overflows and underflows?

15. What factors determine the order of evaluation of an expression?

16. What is numeric promotion?

17. What is casting?

18. When can an object reference be cast to an interface reference?

19. What are order of precedence and associativity, and how are they used?

20. Which Java operator is right associative?

Exam Questions

1. What is the value of 111 % 13?

   A. 3

   B. 5

   C. 7

   D. 9

2. What is the value of 9 + 8 % 7 + 6?

   A. 17

   B. 16

   C. 13

   D. 4

3. What is the value of y after execution of the following statements?

   ```
   int x = 5;
   int y = 4;
   y = x++;
   ```

   A. 4

   B. 5

   C. 6

   D. 7

APPLY YOUR KNOWLEDGE

4. What is the value returned by `"abcd"` `instanceof Object`?

    A. `"abcd"`

    B. `true`

    C. `false`

    D. `String`

5. What is the value of `8 ¦ 9 & 10 ^ 11`?

    A. `8`

    B. `9`

    C. `10`

    D. `11`

6. What is the output displayed by the following program?

```
class Question {
 public static void main(String[] args) {
  int n = 7;
  n <<= 3;
  n = n & n + 1 ¦ n + 2 ^ n + 3;
  n >>= 2;
  System.out.println(n);
 }
}
```

    A. `0`

    B. `-1`

    C. `14`

    D. `64`

7. What is the value of `-31 >>> 5 >> 5 >>> 5 >> 5 >>> 5 >> 5`?

    A. `NaN`

    B. `-1`

    C. `3`

    D. `1024`

8. What is the value displayed by the following program?

```
class Question {
 public static void main(String[] args) {
  int x = 0;
  boolean b1, b2, b3, b4;
  b1 = b2 = b3 = b4 = true;
  x = (b1 ¦ b2 & b3 ^ b4) ? x++ : --x;
  System.out.println(x);
 }
}
```

    A. `-1`

    B. `0`

    C. `1`

    D. `2`

9. What line of output is displayed by the following program?

```
class Question {
 static boolean sideEffect(boolean b) {
  System.out.print(" side effect ");
  return b;
 }
 public static void main(String[] args) {
  boolean b1 = true;
  boolean b2 = false;
  if(b2 & sideEffect(b1))
System.out.println(1);
  else if(b1 ¦ sideEffect(b2))
System.out.println(2);
 }
}
```

    A. `1`

    B. `2`

    C. side effect 1

    D. side effect 2

    E. side effect side effect 1

    F. side effect side effect 2

APPLY YOUR KNOWLEDGE

10. What is the output displayed by the following program?

```
class Question {
 public static void main(String[] args) {
  String s1 = "ab";
  String s2 = "abcd";
  String s3 = "cd";
  String s4 = s1 + s3;
  s1 = s4;
  System.out.print("s1 "+((s1 == s2)? "==" :
"!=")+" s2");
 }
}
```

A. s1 == s2

B. s1 != s2

C. s1

D. s1 == "abcd"

11. Which statement (exactly one) is true about the following program?

```
class Question {
 public static void main(String[] args) {
  double d1 = 1.0;
  double d2 = 0.0;
  byte b = 1;
  d1 = d1 / d2;
  b = (byte) d1;
  System.out.print(b);
 }
}
```

A. It results in the throwing of an
   ArithmeticException.

B. It results in the throwing of a
   DivideByZeroException.

C. It displays the value 1.5.

D. It displays the value -1.

12. What is the result of the expression 5.4 + "3.2"?

A. The double value 8.6.

B. The String "8.6".

C. The long value 8.

D. The String "5.43.2".

13. What is the result of the following program?

```
class Question {
 public static void main(String[] args) {
  int i = 7;
  int j = 8;
  int n = (i ¦ j)  % (i & j);
  System.out.print(n);
 }
}
```

A. 0

B. 15

C. An ArithmeticException is thrown.

D. -15

14. Suppose that classes X and Y are subclasses of Z and Z implements the W interface. Which of the following are true?

A. A reference to an object of class X can be cast to a reference to an object of class Y.

B. A reference to an object of class Y can be cast to a reference to an object of class X.

C. A reference to an object of class X can be cast to a reference to an object of class Z.

D. A reference to an object of class Y can be cast to a reference to an object of class Z.

E. A reference to an object of class X can be cast to a reference to an object of interface W.

F. A reference to an object of class Y can be cast to a reference to an object of interface W.

G. A reference to an object of class Z can be cast to a reference to an object of interface W.

APPLY YOUR KNOWLEDGE

15. Which of the following are true?

    A. A reference to an array can be cast to a reference to an `Object`.

    B. A reference to an array can be cast to a reference to a `Cloneable`.

    C. A reference to an array can be cast to a reference to a `String`.

    D. None of the above.

Answers to Review Questions

1. It is referred to as the modulo or remainder operator. It returns the remainder of dividing the first operand by the second operand.

2. The prefix form performs the increment operation and returns the value of the increment operation. The postfix form returns the current value all of the expression and then performs the increment operation on that value.

3. The left operand is an object reference or `null` value and the right operand is a class, interface, or array type.

4. If an expression involving the Boolean `&` operator is evaluated, both operands are evaluated. Then the `&` operator is applied to the operand. When an expression involving the `&&` operator is evaluated, the first operand is evaluated. If the first operand returns a value of `true` then the second operand is evaluated. The `&&` operator is then applied to the first and second operands. If the first operand evaluates to `false`, the evaluation of the second operand is skipped.

5. The `>>` operator carries the sign bit when shifting right. The `>>>` zero-fills bits that have been shifted out.

6. The `==` operator compares two objects to determine if they are the same object in memory. It is possible for two `String` objects to have the same value, but be located in different areas of memory.

7. No, it is not.

8. It is written `x ? y : z`.

9. Yes, a `double` value can be cast to a `byte`.

10 No, an object cannot be cast to a primitive value.

11. Integer `/` and `%` can result in the throwing of an `ArithmeticException`.

12. The fractional part of the result is truncated. This is known as rounding toward zero.

13. The result is a `String` object.

14. It uses those low order bytes of the result that can fit into the size of the type allowed by the operation.

15. The order of the evaluation of an expression is determined by the use of parentheses, the operator precedence, and the operator associativity.

16. Numeric promotion is the conversion of a smaller numeric type to a larger numeric type, so that integer and floating-point operations may take place. In numerical promotion, `byte`, `char`, and `short` values are converted to `int` values. The `int` values are also converted to `long` values, if necessary. The `long` and `float` values are converted to `double` values, as required.

APPLY YOUR KNOWLEDGE

17. There are two types of casting, casting between primitive numeric types and casting between object references. Casting between numeric types is used to convert larger values, such as `double` values, to smaller values, such as `byte` values. Casting between object references is used to refer to an object by a compatible class, interface, or array type reference.

18. An object reference can be cast to an interface reference when the object implements the referenced interface.

19. Order of precedence determines the order in which operators are evaluated in expressions. Associativity determines whether an expression is evaluated left-to-right or right-to-left.

20 The = operator is right associative.

Answers to Exam Questions

1. C   `111 = 8 * 13 + 7`.

2. B   Order of precedence requires that the expression be evaluated as `(9 + (8 % 7) + 6)`.

3. B   The postfix operator returns the value of `x` before incrementing `x`.

4. B   The `String` `"abcd"` is an instance of `Object` so the value of `true` is returned.

5. D   Order of precedence requires the expression to be evaluated as `(8 ¦ ((9 & 10) ^ 11))`.

6. C   The variable `n` takes on the values `7`, `56`, `57`, and then `14`.

7. C   Use the process of elimination to answer this question. The expression returns a valid integer result, so answer A is eliminated. Because the first operation is an unsigned right shift, the final value of the expression must be non-negative. This rules out answer B. Because the original 32-bit value is shifted right 30 times, it would be impossible to produce a number as large as 1024. This rules out answer D. The only answer left is answer C.

8. B   From the ternary expression, the value of `x` must either be `0` or `-1`. Because `(b1 ¦ b2 & b3 ^ b4)` evaluates as `(b1 ¦ (b2 & (b3 ^ b4)))`, the answer is `0`.

9. F   Because we are not using the logical short-circuit operators, the `sideEffect()` method is invoked in both cases, resulting in `" side effect side effect 2"` being displayed.

10. B   Because `s1` and `s2` refer to different objects, `s1 != s2` is true.

11. D   Floating-point operations do not throw exceptions. This eliminates answers A and B. It would be impossible for a `byte` value to be displayed as `1.5`. The only answer left is D.

12. D   The floating point value is converted to a `String` and is then appended to `"3.2"`.

13. C   An `ArithmeticException` is thrown as the result of taking the remainder of a number by `0`.

14. C through G   References to `X` and `Y` objects can be cast to `Z` and `W` objects. References to `Z` objects can be cast to `W` objects. However, references to `X` and `Y` objects may not be cast to each other.

15. A and B   A and B hold for all array types. An array may never be cast to a `String`.

APPLY YOUR KNOWLEDGE

Suggested Readings and Resources

Gosling, James, Joy, Bill, and Steele, Guy, *The Java Language Specification.* Addison Wesley, 1996.

This chapter helps you to prepare for the exam by covering the following objectives:

Know how to write code that declares, constructs, and initializes arrays of any base type using any of the permitted forms both for declaration and for initialization.

Know how to declare `instance` variables, `static` variables, and `automatic` (method local) variables, making appropriate use of all permitted modifiers (such as `public`, `final`, `static`, `abstract`, and so forth). State the significance of each of these modifiers both singly and in combination and state the effect of package relationships on declared items qualified by these modifiers.

Know how to identify correctly constructed method declarations and variable declarations.

Know how to determine the effect upon objects and primitive values of passing variables into methods and performing assignments or other modifying operations in that method.

CHAPTER 4

Declarations and Access Control

OUTLINE

STUDY STRATEGIES

As you read through this chapter, you should concentrate on the following key items:

▶ How variables are declared and initialized

▶ How arrays are declared and initialized

▶ How methods are declared and used

▶ How arguments are passed to methods

▶ How methods may affect the original values and objects that are passed to them

▶ How access modifiers restrict access to classes, interfaces, variables, methods, and constructors

▶ How non-access modifers are used

CHAPTER INTRODUCTION

Declarations are basic to writing any program in Java. You must know how to declare classes, interfaces, variables, methods, and constructors to be a Java programmer. Although you are probably familiar with most basic declarations, there may be a few things that you haven't encountered or you have forgotten. This chapter will fill in any gaps in your knowledge. It covers variable and method declarations and the use of modifiers in these declarations. Class, constructor, and interface declarations are reviewed in Chapter 6, "Overloading, Overriding, Runtime Type, and Object Orientation."

DECLARING AND USING VARIABLES

Variable declarations are used to identify the type associated with a variable. They may also be used to initialize a variable to a particular value of that type. Variables may be declared as a primitive type or an object type. When a variable is declared as a primitive type, the variable's declaration identifies the type of primitive values that may be stored by the variable. When a variable is declared as an object type, the variable declaration identifies the type of object that may be referenced by the variable.

Java supports two different kinds of variables: field variables and local variables. Field variables are variables that are declared as members of a class. They are also referred to as member variables or as fields. Field variables store the information content of an object. Local variables are variables that are declared local to a method. They are temporary placeholders for storing values and references to objects that are used to perform a method's processing. Local variables are also referred to as automatic variables. We'll cover field variables first, followed by local variables.

Field Variables

Field variables are declared using the following syntax:

```
modifiers Type declarator;
```

Valid modifiers are the access modifiers—`public`, `protected`, and `private`—and the special modifiers—`final`, `static`, `transient`, and `volatile`. These modifiers are covered individually in later sections of this chapter.

The variable's type may be a primitive type (`boolean`, `byte`, `char`, `short`, `int`, `long`, `float`, or `double`), an object type (for example, `String` or `Vector`), or an array type. Array types are covered in the next section, "Working with Arrays."

The declarator may be a simple identifier (for example, `myVariable`), a simple identifier followed by an expression (for example, `myVariable = 3`), or an array identifier optionally followed by an expression or array initializer.

Working with Arrays

Arrays are Java objects. However, array declarations are very flexible (and sometimes confusing), so I'll cover them separately.

Array declarations might have the same modifiers as normal variable declarations. Array declarations differ from other variable declarations in that they must specify the array's dimensions. Technically, Java arrays are all one-dimensional arrays. Two-dimensional arrays are arrays of arrays. However, to simplify this discussion, I'll still refer to an array's dimensions as if Java supported multidimensional arrays.

The dimensions of an array may be specified to the right of its type or to the right of its identifier. Zero or more spaces may surround the brackets that are used to identify an array's dimensions. For example, all of the following array declarations are equivalent:

◆ `String[]s;`

◆ `String []s;`

◆ `String [] s;`

◆ `String [  ] s;`

◆ `String[] s;`

◆ `String[  ] s;`

◆ `String s[];`

◆ `String s [];`

◆ `String s [ ];`

Multidimensional arrays (arrays of arrays) may be specified with bracket sets appearing on either or both sides of the array name:

```
String[] s[];
String [][]s;
String s [] [ ];
```

Note that the actual size of each array dimension is not specified.

An array is created in one of two ways. The simplest way is to use an array initializer to create the array and initialize its elements:

```
String[] s = {"abc","def","ghi"};
```

Multidimensional arrays may be initialized by nesting array initializers:

```
int[][] i = {{1,2,3}, {4,5,6}, {7,8,9}};
```

Java keeps track of the number of elements specified in each dimension and creates and initializes an array of the correct size. However, listing array elements is only practical for very small arrays. To create larger arrays, you must use the new operator, followed by the array's base type and one or more sets of brackets. You specify the length of an array dimension by putting an integer within a bracket set. For example, the following creates an array of 100 String objects:

```
String[] s = new String[100];
```

You can supply the lengths of multiple array dimensions using this notation. For example, the following creates a 20 by 30 array of String objects:

```
String[][] s = new String[20][30];
```

The above notation is also equivalent to the following:

```
String[][] s = new String[20][];
for(int i=0; i<20; ++i)
 s[i] = new String[30];
```

When an array is created, its elements are automatically initialized to default values as described in Chapter 2, "Language Fundamentals."

Working with Objects

Objects are created using the new operator and the constructor of the object's class. For example, if an object is of class C, you use a constructor of the following form:

```
new C(argumentList)
```

The argument list must correspond to the actual parameters that are declared for the constructor being used.

When an object is created, it is typically (but not always) assigned to a variable of that type:

```
C myC = new C(argumentList);
```

The fields and methods of the object can then be referenced using the variable. For example, if C has a field f1 and a method m1, f1 may be accessed as myC.f1 and m1 may be invoked as myC.m1(argumentList).

In some cases, you may not want to store the newly created object before accessing it. For example, you could use new C().m1() to invoke the m1() method of a newly created C object.

The keywords this and super are used to refer to the current object instance. When this is used within a constructor, this refers to the object being created. When it is used within a non-static method, this refers to the object whose method is being executed. this should not be referenced in a static method because static methods are associated with the class as a whole rather than specific instances of a class.

The super keyword refers to the superclass of the current object instance. It is used to reference methods and field variables of the object's superclass that may have been hidden or overridden by those of the object's class. The ThisSuper program (Listing 4.1) illustrates the use of this and super.

The ThisSuper class extends SuperClass. Both ThisSuper and SuperClass define the s field variable and display() method. The ThisSuper s variable hides the SuperClass s variable and the ThisSuper display() method overrides the SuperClass display method. The ThisSuper constructor uses this and super as follows:

```
display(this.s);
display(super.s);
this.display(s);
super.display(s);
```

These statements produce the following output:

```
this: this
this: super
this: this
super: this
```

The first three statements use the display() method of ThisSuper to display the s field variable. The first and third statements refer to the current (ThisSuper) object instance. The second statement uses super to refer to the s variable of SuperClass. The last statement uses super to refer to the display() method and s variable of ThisSuper.

LISTING 4.1

THE ThisSuper PROGRAM

```
class ThisSuper extends SuperClass {
 String s = "this";
 public static void main(String[] args) {
  new ThisSuper();
 }
 ThisSuper() {
  display(this.s);
  display(super.s);
  this.display(s);
  super.display(s);
 }
 void display(String s) {
  System.out.println("this: "+s);
 }
}
class SuperClass {
 String s = "super";
 void display(String s) {
  System.out.println("super: "+s);
 }
}
```

Local Variables

Local variables are declared and initialized in the same manner as field variables. However, local variables may only specify the final modifier, which is used to identify those local variables that may be accessed from local inner classes. Chapter 6 covers the use of local inner classes and the final modifier.

The final Modifier The final modifier is used to indicate that the value of a variable cannot be changed once it is assigned a value.

The other major difference between local variables and field variables is their scope. A local variable may only be accessed from within the method that it is declared. It comes into existence when the method is executed and ceases to exist when the method's execution is completed.

The non-static field variables of an object come into existence when the object is created and continue to exist until the object is garbage collected. Static field variables come into existence when the class in which they are declared is loaded. Static field variables exist until their associated class is unloaded.

DECLARING AND USING METHODS

Methods are declared using the following syntax:

```
modifiers returnValue methodName(parameterList)
➡throwsClause {
  // Method body
}
```

A method may have any access modifier (public, protected, private, or package access) or the special modifiers (abstract, final, native, static, or synchronized). The use of these modifiers is covered later in this chapter.

The return type of a method may be any of the following:

◆ void—The method does not return a value.

◆ A primitive type—The primitive types boolean, byte, char, short, int, long, float, and double may be used as a method return type. The method must return a value that is promotable (refer to Chapter 3, "Operators and Assignments") to the specified return type.

◆ Object type—A method can return a reference to an object of any class or interface.

◆ Array type—Even though arrays are Java objects, I'll list them separately just to make sure they are not overlooked. A method may return a reference to any Java array. The return type is specified as the array type. For example, suppose the test() method returns an array of arrays of String objects. You could write its return type as String[][].

A method's parameter list is a comma-separated list of parameter declarations. Each parameter declaration identifies the parameter's type and a name by which the parameter can be referenced. A parameter may be referenced anywhere within the method. A parameter may also be declared as `final` so that it may be accessed from within a local inner class. The use of `final` with method parameters is covered in Chapter 6.

The `throws` clause of a method identifies all of the checked exception types that may be thrown (and not caught) during the execution of a method. This includes methods that are thrown by other methods invoked by the method. If a method throws (and does not catch) an exception of a particular type, the `throws` clause must identify a type which is a superclass of the exception type (and a subclass of `java.lang.Throwable`). The `throws` clause consists of a comma-separated list of checked exception types. Exception throwing is covered in more detail in Chapter 5, "Flow Control and Exception Handling."

Methods are used by invoking them with respect to an object reference. Methods are invoked using the following syntax:

```
variable.methodName(argumentList)
```

The keywords `this` and `super` may be used instead of a variable name.

`Static` methods (covered later in this chapter) are methods which apply to the class as a whole rather than an instance of a class. `Static` methods may be invoked using the same notation as non-static methods. However, since `static` methods are not associated with an instance of a class, it is more appropriate to invoke them using the class name rather than a variable name. The `StaticMethod` program shown in Listing 4.2 illustrates this point. It invokes the static `display()` method of `StaticClass` using the method invocation `StaticClass.display("sample output")`.

> **NOTE**
>
> **Method Signature** A method's signature consists of the method name and the sequence of types used to declare the method's parameters. It is illegal for a class to declare two methods with the same signature.

LISTING 4.2

THE StaticMethod PROGRAM

```
class StaticMethod {
 public static void main(String[] args) {
  StaticClass.display("sample output");
```

continues

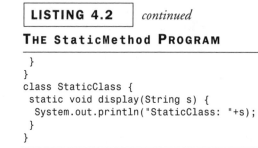

LISTING 4.2 | *continued*

THE StaticMethod PROGRAM

```
  }
}
class StaticClass {
 static void display(String s) {
  System.out.println("StaticClass: "+s);
 }
}
```

Passing Arguments

An argument that is passed to a method may be a primitive value or an object reference. When a primitive value is passed to a method, a copy of the value is made, and the copy is made available to the method. The original value is not modified as the result of any changes to the argument that occurs within the body of the method. The PassedValue program of Listing 4.3 illustrates this point. It displays a value of 100 as its output. The value of i is not modified by the modifyMethod() method.

LISTING 4.3

THE PassedValue PROGRAM

```
class PassedValue {
 public static void main(String args[]) {
  int i = 100;
  modifyMethod(i);
  System.out.println(i);
 }
 static void modifyMethod(int i) {
  i = i * 2;
 }
}
```

When an object is passed as an argument to a method, a copy of the object reference (but not the object itself) is made, and the copied object reference is passed to the method. Changes to the object reference that occur during the method's execution do not affect the original object reference. However, changes to the object itself that occur during the method's execution are made to the original object.

The PassedReference program of Listing 4.4 illustrates this distinction. The modifyReference() method has no effect on the Vector v declared that is in main() since it changes the object's reference. However, modifyReferencedObject() does have an effect on the Vector v that is declared in main() because it modifies the contents of the vector.

LISTING 4.4

THE PassedReference PROGRAM

```
import java.util.*;

class PassedReference {
 public static void main(String args[]) {
  Vector v = new Vector();
  v.add(new String("a"));
  v.add(new String("b"));
  v.add(new String("c"));
  System.out.println(v);
  modifyReference(v);
  System.out.println(v);
  modifyReferencedObject(v);
  System.out.println(v);
 }
 static void modifyReference(Vector v) {
  v = new Vector();
  v.add(new String("1"));
  v.add(new String("2"));
  v.add(new String("3"));
 }
 static void modifyReferencedObject(Vector v) {
  v.removeAllElements();
  v.add(new String("1"));
  v.add(new String("2"));
  v.add(new String("3"));
 }
}
```

DECLARING INITIALIZERS

Java classes may contain statements that support the initialization of program variables. Initialization is typically performed when a field variable is declared. Variable initializers are executed when a new instance of a class is created. Other initializers, referred to as static initializers, are used to initialize static variables. Static initializers are covered later in this chapter in the "Static" section.

ACCESS MODIFIERS

Access modifiers are an important part of any declaration that can be accessed outside the class or package in which it is made. Access modifiers enable you to determine whether a declaration is limited to a particular class, a class and its subclasses, a package, or if it is freely accessible. Although access modifiers are not iron-clad security controls, they can be used to limit access to your classes, interfaces, variables, methods, and constructors.

Java provides three access modifiers (`public`, `protected`, and `private`) and a fourth default access (package access). These modifiers are used as follows:

- `public`—Enables a class or interface to be accessed outside of its package. It also enables a variable, method, or constructor to be accessed anywhere its class may be accessed.

- `protected`—Enables a variable, method, or constructor to be accessed by classes or interfaces of the same package or by subclasses of the class in which it is declared.

- `private`—Prevents a variable, method, or constructor from being accessed outside of the class in which it is declared.

- Package access—Package access occurs when `public`, `protected`, or `private` are not specified. Package access applies to classes, interfaces, variables, methods, and constructors. It allows the declared item to be accessed by any class or interface of the same package.

Table 4.1 identifies the language elements that may be declared using the above access modifiers and the restrictions that are placed on these language elements as the result of these modifiers.

TABLE 4.1

ACCESS MODIFIERS

Modifier	Applies to	Description
public	Classes	A class may be accessed outside of its package.
	Interfaces	An interface may be accessed outside of its package.
	Field Variables	A variable may be accessed anywhere that its class may be accessed.

Modifier	Applies to	Description
	Methods	A method may be accessed anywhere that its class may be accessed.
	Constructors	A constructor may be accessed anywhere that its class may be accessed.
	Inner classes	An inner class may be accessed anywhere that its class may be accessed.
protected	Field variables	A variable may be accessed by classes or interfaces of the same package or by subclasses of the class in which it is declared.
	Methods	A method may be accessed by classes or interfaces of the same package or by subclasses of the class in which it is declared.
	Constructors	A constructor may only be accessed by classes or interfaces of the same package or by subclasses of the class in which it is declared.
	Inner classes	An inner class may only be accessed by classes or interfaces of the same package or by subclasses of the class in which it is declared.
private	Field variables	A variable may only be accessed within the class in which it is declared.
	Methods	A method may only be accessed within the class in which it is declared.
	Constructors	A constructor may only be accessed within the class in which it is declared.
	Inner classes	An inner class may only be accessed within the class in which it is declared.
(no access modifier package access)	Classes	A class may only be accessed within the package in which it is declared.
	Interfaces	An interface may only be accessed within the package in which it is declared.
	Field variables	A variable may only be accessed within the package in which it is declared.
	Methods	A method may only be accessed within the package in which it is declared.
	Constructors	A constructor may only be accessed within the package in which it is declared.
	Inner classes	An inner class may only be accessed within the package in which it is declared.

Java's access modifiers support an important programming feature known as *encapsulation*. Encapsulation allows access to a class to be restricted to a well-defined interface. Fully encapsulated classes declare all of their field variables as private and provide access to the properties they represent via special accessor methods. Encapsulation is covered in Chapter 6.

NOTE

Friendly Access

Package access is also referred to as *friendly* access by old C++ programmers.

NOTE

Access Modifiers and Inner Classes
Access modifiers are also used with
inner classes. Inner classes are covered in Chapter 6.

NOTE

Ordering Modifiers The order in
which modifiers appear in a declaration is not important. For example,
static final means the same thing
as final static.

NOTE

abstract and **final** Neither abstract
classes nor abstract methods may
be declared as final.

NOTE

abstract Subclasses If a class
extends an abstract class then it
must implement all methods declared
as abstract, if any, or be declared as
abstract, too.

OTHER MODIFIERS

Java supports several other modifiers besides the access modifiers.
These modifiers are covered in the following subsections.

abstract

The abstract modifier is used to identify abstract classes and methods. An abstract class defers its implementation to its subclasses and
may not be instantiated.

Abstract classes may declare abstract methods. An abstract
method is a method whose implementation is deferred. The body of
an abstract method is replaced by a semicolon. The AbstractClass
shown in Listing 4.5 is an abstract class that declares several
abstract methods.

LISTING 4.5

THE AbstractClass CLASS

```
abstract class AbstractClass {
 abstract void method1();
 abstract String method2(Object obj) throws
➥java.io.IOException;
 abstract int method3(long l);
 abstract boolean method4();
}
```

---

final

The final modifier is used to indicate that a declared item may not
be changed. When it is used with a class, it prevents the class from
being extended (subclassed). When it is used with a field variable, it
indicates that the variable may not be modified after it has been
assigned a value. Final variables are used to create constants.

Local variables and method parameters may also be declared as final
to enable them to be accessed by local inner classes. The use of final
with local variables is covered in Chapter 6.

When the final modifier is used with a method, it indicates that the method may not be overridden. Chapter 6 covers method overriding.

native

The native modifier is used to identify a native method declaration. native methods are methods that are written in code other than Java. The Java Native Interface (JNI) allows Java programs to access native methods that are made available as shared dynamic link libraries. native methods are declared using the following syntax:

```
modifiers native returnType methodName(parameterList)
➡throwsClause ;
```

Note that the method body is replaced by a semicolon in the same manner as an abstract method. However, native methods may not be declared as abstract.

static

The static modifier is used to indicate that a variable, method, or initializer applies to a class as a whole instead of specific instances of the class. static variables are shared by all instances of a class. Suppose that v is a static variable of class C, and c1 and c2 are variables that reference instances of C. Then v may be accessed as c1.v, c2.v, and C.v. Because static variables are shared by all instances of a class, c1.v, c2.v, and C.v all refer to the same value or object.

static methods are used to access the static variables of a class. They may also be used to invoke other static methods. However, static methods may not be used to access non-static variables or methods without specifying the class instance that the variable or method is associated with. Because static methods are not associated with an object instance, they may not refer to the current instance via the this identifier. The main() method of every Java application program is static. It is invoked before an instance of the application class is created.

N O T E

Non-static Methods and static Variables   Non-static methods may access both static and non-static variables.

Static initializers are used to perform processing when a class is first loaded. As such, static initializers are executed only once. Static initializers are identified by the static keyword followed by code that is surrounded in curly brackets.

The StaticApp program shown in Listing 4.6 illustrates the use of static variables, methods, and initializers. The static initializer is executed upon loading of the StaticApp class. This occurs before main() is executed. The s field variable is static and the t field variable is non-static. The display(s) statement invokes the static display() method with the static variable s. The app.display(app.t) statement invokes display() with the non-static t variable. The instance of StaticApp to which t applies (as in, app.t) must be supplied or else a compilation error results.

LISTING 4.6

THE StaticApp PROGRAM

```
class StaticApp {
 static String s = "This code is executed second.";
 String t  = "This code is executed last.";
 static {  // Static initializer
  display("This code is executed first.");
 }
 public static void main(String[] args) {
  display(s);
  StaticApp app = new StaticApp();
  app.display(app.t);
 }
 static void display(String s) {
  System.out.println(s);
 }
}
```

synchronized

The synchronized modifier is used to control access to objects that are shared among multiple threads. It is covered in Chapter 8, "Threads."

transient

The `transient` modifier is used with variables. It indicates that a variable may not be serialized. It is typically used to reduce the possibility that an object containing sensitive data might be written to a stream. A `transient` variable may not be declared as `final` or `static`.

volatile

The `volatile` modifier is used with variables. It is used to indicate that a variable may be modified asynchronously in a multiprocessor environment. This modifier is rarely used and not covered on the certification exam. However, it is good programming practice to use it with variables that may be accessed by several threads without synchronization.

CHAPTER SUMMARY

KEY TERMS

- Declaration
- Field variable
- Local variable
- Array
- this
- super
- Method
- void
- public
- protected
- private
- package access
- static
- final
- abstract class
- abstract method
- native method
- transient variable

This chapter covers variable and method declarations and the use of modifiers in these declarations. You learned the difference between field and local variables, how to declare and initialize arrays, and how methods are declared and used. You also learned how arguments are passed to methods, how access modifiers are used to restrict access to declared items, and how other modifiers are used. The following review and exam questions will test your knowledge of these topics and will help you to determine whether you need to study them further in preparation for the certification exam.

APPLY YOUR KNOWLEDGE

Review Questions

1. What is the difference between a field variable and a local variable?

2. What is the difference between `static` and non-static variables?

3. How are `this` and `super` used?

4. What is a `void` return type?

5. If a class is declared without any access modifiers, where may the class be accessed?

6. If a variable is declared as `private`, where may the variable be accessed?

7. If a method is declared as `protected`, where may the method be accessed?

8. What is an `abstract` method?

9. What is a `native` method?

10. What is a `transient` variable?

Exam Questions

1. What is the output of the following program?

```
class Question extends SuperClass {
  String s = "this";
  public static void main(String[] args) {
   new Question();
  }
  Question() {
   super.display(s);
  }
  void display(String s) {
   System.out.println("this: "+s);
  }
}
class SuperClass {
  String s = "super";
```

```
  void display(String s) {
   System.out.println("super: "+s);
  }
}
```

A. this: this

B. super: this

C. this: super

D. super: super

2. Which of the following declare an array of `String` objects?

A. String[] s;

B. String []s;

C. String [s];

D. String s[];

3. What is the value of `a[3]` as the result of the following array declaration?

```
int[] a = {1,2,3,4,5};
```

A. 1

B. 2

C. 3

D. 4

4. Which of the following are true about this method declaration?

```
void myMethod(String s) {
}
```

A. `myMethod()` is static.

B. `myMethod()` does not return a value.

C. `myMethod()` is abstract.

D. `myMethod()` may not be accessed outside of the package in which it is declared.

APPLY YOUR KNOWLEDGE

5. Which of the following are true about this variable declaration?

```
private static int i = 3;
```

   A. The value of i may not be changed after it is assigned a value.

   B. i may only be updated by a static method.

   C. The value of i is shared among all instances of the class in which it is declared.

   D. i may only be accessed within the class in which it is declared.

6. What is wrong with the following program?

```
class Question {
 String s = "abc";
 public static void main(String[] args) {
  System.out.println(s);
 }
}
```

   A. Nothing is wrong with the program.

   B. main() cannot be declared public because Question is not public.

   C. Because main() is static, it may not access non-static s without a reference to an instance of Question.

   D. The main() argument list is incorrect.

7. Which of the following are true?

   A. A top-level class may be declared as private.

   B. A method may be declared as transient.

   C. A constructor may be declared as volatile.

   D. A local variable may be declared as final.

8. What is the output of the following program?

```
class Question {
 static int i = 1;
 static {
  ++i;
 }
```

```
 public static void main(String[] args) {
  increment(i,5);
  display(i);
 }
 static void increment(int n, int m) {
  n += m;
 }
 static void display(int n) {
  System.out.print(n);
 }
 static {
  ++i;
 }
}
```

   A. 1

   B. 3

   C. 6

   D. 7

9. Which of the following are true?

   A. Local variables may be declared final.

   B. Methods may be declared final.

   C. Constructors may not be declared private.

   D. transient variables may not be serialized.

10. What is the output of the following program?

```
class Question {
 static int i = 1, j = 2;
 static {
  display(i);
 }
 public static void main(String[] args) {
  display(j);
 }
 static void display(int n) {
  System.out.print(n);
 }
}
```

   A. 1

   B. 2

   C. 12

   D. 21

APPLY YOUR KNOWLEDGE

Answers to Review Questions

1. A field variable is a variable that is declared as a member of a class. A local variable is a variable that is declared local to a method.

2. A static variable is associated with the class as a whole rather than with specific instances of a class. Non-static variables take on unique values with each object instance.

3. this is used to refer to the current object instance. super is used to refer to the variables and methods of the superclass of the current object instance.

4. A void return type indicates that a method does not return a value.

5. A class that is declared without any access modifiers is said to have package access. This means that the class can only be accessed by other classes and interfaces that are defined within the same package.

6. A private variable may only be accessed within the class in which it is declared.

7. A protected method may only be accessed by classes or interfaces of the same package or by subclasses of the class in which it is declared.

8. An abstract method is a method whose implementation is deferred to a subclass.

9. A native method is a method that is implemented in a language other than Java.

10. A transient variable is a variable that may not be serialized.

Answers to Exam Questions

1. B The display() method of SuperClass is invoked to display the s variable of Question.

2. A, B and D The identifier name may not be enclosed in brackets.

3. D Array indices begin with 0.

4. B and D myMethod() does not return a value and is declared with package access.

5. C and D Because i is static it is shared among all instances of its class. Because i is private it may only be accessed within the class in which it is declared.

6. C The non-static s variable may only be accessed with a reference to a Question object.

7. D A local variable may be declared as final. Only variables may be declared as volatile or final. Top-level classes may not be private.

8. B Both static initializers are executed before main() is executed. The increment() method has no effect on the value of i.

9. A, B, and D Constructors may be declared as final.

10. C The static initializer is executed followed by main().

Suggested Readings and Resources

Gosling, James; Joy, Bill; and Steele, Guy, *The Java Language Specification.* Addison Wesley, 1996.

This chapter helps you to prepare for the exam by covering the following objectives:

Know which statements are supported by Java and how each statement works.

▶ You must know what statements Java supports and how they work to be able to program in Java. The exam will contain questions that will require you to determine if a program or block of statements uses correct statement syntax.

Know how to analyze a sequence of statements, identify the flow of control, and determine the results of statement execution.

▶ Several exam questions require you to analyze a block of code and predict the output displayed by the code. You may also be required to identify specific points within the code that cause a particular action to occur.

Know how exceptions are handled and be able to trace through exception processing.

▶ Being able to handle exceptions is an important part of Java programming. You'll need to know how to throw and catch exceptions in order to correctly answer some exam questions. You'll also need to know how the finally clause of the try-catch statement works.

CHAPTER 5

Flow Control and Exception Handling

STUDY STRATEGIES

As you read through this chapter, concentrate on the following key items:

▶ What statements are supported by Java and how each statement works

▶ How to trace through statement execution

▶ How exceptions are thrown and caught

▶ How the `try-catch-finally` statement works

CHAPTER INTRODUCTION

This chapter covers Java statements. If you've written a few Java programs, then you're probably familiar with most of the statements covered in this chapter. Most of the material that is presented will seem pretty basic. However, pay attention just in case there is a detail or two that you're not familiar with. This chapter will fill in any gaps that you you might have. You'll see plenty of questions on the exam that will require you to analyze a small program or a block of Java code and determine the output that it will produce. The review questions and exam questions at the end of this chapter will test your understanding of Java statements and will give you an idea of the types of questions that you may see on the exam.

JAVA STATEMENTS

Java provides a wide range of programming statements that can be used to create structured object-oriented programs. These statements allow you to evaluate expressions, invoke methods, shape and control the flow of program execution, and throw and handle exceptions. Table 5.1 provides a summary of the programming statements that are provided by Java. You covered assignments in Chapter 3, "Operators and Assignments," and declarations in Chapter 4, "Declarations and Access Control." This chapter is limited to those statements that affect the flow of program execution.

TABLE 5.1

JAVA STATEMENTS

Statement	Description	Example
empty	A statement consisting of just ";" that performs no operation.	;
| block | A group of statements enclosed by { and }. The statement block is treated as a single statement when used with selection, iteration, and other statements. | ```
{
x += y;
if(x==100)
return y;
}
``` |

continues
```

TABLE 5.1	*continued*

JAVA STATEMENTS

Statement	*Description*	*Example*
declaration	Declares a variable as being of a particular type and optionally assigns a value to the variable.	`String s = "abcd";`
labeled	Statements may be labeled by preceding them with *identifier:*.	`loopA: for (;;) {}`
assignment	Evaluates an expression and assigns a value or object reference to a variable.	`c = (a*a + b*b)/2;`
invocation	Invokes a method of an object. `System.out.println("The end!");`	
return	Returns a value from a method invocation.	`return x*x + y*y;`
object creation	Creates a new object of a particular type	`new Application();`
if	Selects among two alternative courses of execution.	`if(x > y) ++y; else ++x;`
switch	Selects among several alternative courses of execution.	`switch (n) { case 1: case 2: case 3: default: }`
for	Iterates a variable over a range of values and repeatedly executes a statement or statement block.	`for(int i=0;i<100; ++i) {}`
while	Executes a statement or statement block while a condition is true.	`while } (!finished) {}`
do	Executes a statement or statement block until a condition is false.	`do { } while (!finished);`
break	Transfers control to a labeled statement or out of an enclosing statement.	`for (int i=0;i<100;++i) { if(x[i] == 0) break; }`
continue	Continues execution of a loop the next iteration.	`for (int i=0;i<100;++i) { if(i%10 == 0) continue;}`

Statement	*Description*	*Example*

`try-catch-finally`	Catches and processes exceptions that occur within the execution of a statement block.	`try {}`
		`catch`
		`(Exception e)`
		`{} finally {}`

`throw`	Throws an exception.	`throw new` `MyException();`

`synchronized`	Acquires a lock on an object and executes a statement block.	`synchronized`
		`(obj) {`
		`obj.setProperty`
		`(x);`
		`}`

Most, but not all, of the statements shown in Table 5.1, are covered in this chapter. The following list describes those that are not covered in this chapter:

◆ The `empty` statement is trivial and is not addressed further.

◆ The `block` statement is not a unique statement in and of itself. It consists of a semicolon-separated list (possible empty) of statements enclosed by { and }.

◆ Statement labels are covered in this chapter with the `break` statement.

◆ Assignments are covered in Chapter 3, "Operators and Assignments."

◆ Declarations, method invocations, the `return` statement, and object creation are covered in Chapter 4, "Declarations and Access Control."

◆ The `synchronized` statement is covered in Chapter 8, "Threads."

All the other statements shown in Table 5.1 are covered in the following sections.

SELECTION STATEMENTS

Java supports two statements, `if` and `switch`, that support the selection of alternative courses of execution. The `if` statement is used to select among two alternatives. The switch statement can be used to select among multiple courses of execution.

The if Statement

The Java if statement is similar to that of C and C++. Its syntax is as follows:

```
if (boolean expression) statement1;
```

or

```
if (boolean expression) statement1; else statement2;
```

In the first form, if the boolean expression evaluates to true, statement1 is executed. Otherwise, execution continues with the next statement following the if statement.

In the second form, if the boolean expression evalautes to true statement1 is executed. Otherwise, statement2 is executed.

In both forms of the if statement a statement block may be substituted for statement1 and statement2. if statements may be nested. This is accomplished when statement1 or statement2 are also if statements.

The switch Statement

The switch statement is also taken from C and C++. Its syntax follows:

```
switch(int expression) {
case n1:
 statements
case n2:
 statements
 .
 .
 .
case nm:
 statements
default:
 statements
}
```

The int expression must evaluate to a int value or a value that can be promoted to an int (that is byte, char, or short). The values following the case labels (n_1, n_2,...n_m) must be constant expressions that can be fully evaluated by the compiler. The default label is optional.

The switch statement is executed as follows:

1. The int is evaluated. If it matches any n_i of the n_1, n_2, ..., n_m then statement execution transfers to the statement following case n_i.

2. If the int expression does not match any of the n_1, n_2, ...n_m and a default label is supplied, then statement execution transfers to the statement following default.

3. If neither of the above two cases are satisfied, then statement execution continues with the next statement following the switch statement.

The cases of the switch statement are not mutually exclusive. For example, consider the program shown in Listing 5.1. It displays the following output:

```
3
4
5
6
7
default
```

In order to ensure that only one case of a switch statement is executed, you need to use the break statement. The break statement is covered in the next section.

LISTING 5.1

SWITCH1.JAVA—THE SWITCH STATEMENT

```
class Switch1 {
 public static void main(String[] args) {
  int n = 3;
  switch(n) {
   case 1:
    System.out.println(1);
   case 2:
    System.out.println(2);
   case 3:
    System.out.println(3);
   case 4:
    System.out.println(4);
```

continues

LISTING 5.1 | *continued*

SWITCH1.JAVA—THE SWITCH STATEMENT

```
      case 5:
       System.out.println(5);
      case 6:
       System.out.println(6);
      case 7:
       System.out.println(7);
      default:
       System.out.println("default");
    }
  }
}
```

NOTE

Labels Two or more statements may have the same label, provided that one statement is not enclosed by the other.

The break Statement

The break statement is used to transfer execution out of an enclosing statement. It may be used with or without a label. (A label consists of an identifier, followed by a colon.) When it is used without a label, it causes execution control to transfer out of the innermost switch, for, do, or while statement enclosing the break statement. When used with a label, the break statement transfers control out of any enclosing statement with a matching label.

Listing 5.2 shows how the break statement is used to ensure that only a single case of a switch statement is executed. This program displays the following single line of output:

    3

LISTING 5.2

SWITCH2.JAVA—USING THE BREAK STATEMENT WITHIN A SWITCH STATEMENT

```
class Switch2 {
 public static void main(String[] args) {
  int n = 3;
  switch(n) {
   case 1:
    System.out.println(1);
    break;
   case 2:
    System.out.println(2);
    break;
   case 3:
```

```
      System.out.println(3);
      break;
    case 4:
      System.out.println(4);
      break;
    case 5:
      System.out.println(5);
      break;
    case 6:
      System.out.println(6);
      break;
    case 7:
      System.out.println(7);
      break;
    default:
      System.out.println("default");
  }
 }
}
```

ITERATION STATEMENTS

Java provides three different types of iteration statements: for, while, and do. These statements, taken from C and C++, are used to repeat the execution of a statement or block of statements until a termination condition occurs.

The for Statement

The for statement repeatedly executes a statement or statement block and updates a variable (or group of variables) with each loop iteration. The syntax of the for statement is

```
for(initialization; boolean expression; iteration)
    statement block
```

A single statement may be used instead of the statement block. The execution of the for statement is executed as follows:

1. The initialization statement(s) are executed to initialize any variables that are used by the for loop.

2. The boolean expression is evaluated. If it is true then the statement block is executed. If it is false, then execution continues after the for statement.

3. After the statement block is executed, the iteration statement(s) are executed to increment any loop variables. Execution then continues with Step 2 above.

A typical example of a `for` statement is

```
for(int i=0;i<n;++i) {
  // Perform processing using i as an index.
}
```

The statement block is executed with values of i equal to 0 through n-1. Note that the scope of the variable i that is declared in the initialization statement is restricted to the `for` statement and enclosed statement block.

A little-known fact about the `for` statement (and one that you may be tested on) is that commas can be used to separate multiple statements in the initialization and iteration part of the statement. The only catch is, if you use a comma separator in the initialization block, you cannot declare variables within the initialization block. For example, the following `for` statement results in a compilation error:

```
for(int i=0,int j=0; i+j < 20; ++i, j += i) {
  System.out.println(i+j);
}
```

Listing 5.3 shows a version of the above statement that successfully compiles and produces the following output:

```
0
2
5
9
14
```

LISTING 5.3

FORTEST.JAVA—AN ADVANCED FOR STATEMENT

```
class ForTest {
 public static void main(String[] args) {
  int i,j;
  for(i=0, j=0; i+j < 20; ++i, j += i) {
   System.out.println(i+j);
  }
 }
}
```

The continue Statement

The continue statement is similar to the break statement in that it is used to alter the execution of for, do, and while statements. Like the break statement, it may be used with or without a label. When it is used without a label, it causes the statement block of the innermost for, do, or while statement to terminate and the loop's boolean expression to be reevaluated to determine whether the next loop repetition should take place. In the case of for statements, the iteration statement(s) are executed before the loop's boolean expression is reevaluated.

When used with a label, the continue statement transfers control to an enclosing for, do, or while statement with a matching label. If it is a for statement the iteration statements are executed, and the loop's boolean expression is reevaluated as a prelude to another loop iteration. If it is a do or while statement, the loop's boolean expression is reevaluated to determine whether the loop should be repeated.

Listing 5.4 shows how the continue statement is used with a set of nested for statements. The output that this program displays is as follows:

```
i = 1, j = 0
i = 1, j = 1
i = 1, j = 3
i = 2, j = 0
i = 2, j = 2
i = 3, j = 1
i = 4, j = 0
i = 6, j = 0
i = 6, j = 1
i = 6, j = 3
i = 7, j = 0
i = 7, j = 2
i = 8, j = 1
i = 9, j = 0
```

LISTING 5.4

CONTINUETEST.JAVA—USING A labeled continue STATEMENT

```
class ContinueTest {
 public static void main(String[] args) {
  outerloop: for(int i=0; i<10; ++i) {
   innerloop: for(int j=0; j<10; ++j) {
```

continues

<table>
<tr><td>**LISTING 5.4**</td><td>*continued*</td></tr>
</table>

CONTINUETEST.JAVA—USING A labeled continue STATEMENT

```
      if((i+j) % 5 == 0) continue outerloop;
      if((i+j) % 5 == 3) continue innerloop;
      System.out.println("i = "+i+", j = "+j);
    }
   }
  }
}
```

The while Statement

The while statement, like the for statement, repeatedly executes a statement or statement block. However, it is not explicitly designed to increment loop variables (although it can) and, as a consequence, has a much simpler syntax:

```
while (boolean expression)
  statement;
```

or

```
while (boolean expression) {
  statement(s)
}
```

The while statement's execution proceeds as follows:

1. The boolean expression is evaluated. If it evaluates to true, go to step 2. If it evaluates to false, control passes to the next statement after the while statement.

2. The enclosed statements are executed. Go to step 1.

An example of its use is shown in Listing 5.5. The while statement repeatedly executes until Math.random() produces a value greater than .5.

LISTING 5.5

WHILETEST.JAVA—USING THE while STATEMENT

```
class WhileTest {
 public static void main(String[] args) {
  boolean finished = false;
  while (!finished) {
```

```
      double d = Math.random();
      if(d > .5) finished = true;
      System.out.println(d);
    }
  }
}
```

The do Statement

The do statement is similar to the while statement. The only difference is that the loop condition is checked after the enclosed statement block is executed (rather than before it). The syntax of the do statement is

```
do statement while (loop expression);
```

or

```
do {
  statement(s)
} while (loop expression);
```

The do statement's execution proceeds as follows:

1. The enclosed statements are executed. Go to step 2.

2. The boolean expression is evaluated. If it evaluates to true, go to step 1. If it evaluates to false, control passes to the next statement after the do statement.

Listing 5.5 can be rewritten to use a do statement as follows (see Listing 5.6):

LISTING 5.6

DoTest.java—Using the do Statement

```
class DoTest {
 public static void main(String[] args) {
  boolean finished = false;
  do {
   double d = Math.random();
   if(d > .5) finished = true;
   System.out.println(d);
  } while (!finished);
 }
}
```

THROWING AND CATCHING EXCEPTIONS

Java provides superior support for runtime error and exception handling, enabling programs to check for anomalous conditions and respond to them with minimal impact on the normal flow of program execution. This allows error- and exception-handling code to be added easily to existing methods.

Exceptions are generated by the Java runtime system in response to errors that are detected as classes are loaded and their methods are executed. The runtime system is said to *throw* these *runtime exceptions*. Runtime exceptions are objects of the classes `java.lang.RuntimeException`, `java.lang.Error`, or of their subclasses. Runtime exceptions are also referred to as *unchecked* exceptions.

Exceptions may also be thrown directly by Java code using the `throw` statement. These exceptions are thrown when code detects a condition that could potentially lead to a program malfunction. The exceptions thrown by user programs are generally not objects of a subclass of `RuntimeException`. These non-runtime exceptions are referred to as *checked* exceptions or *program* exceptions.

Both program and runtime exceptions must be caught in order for them to be processed by exception-handling code. If a thrown exception is not caught, its thread of execution is terminated, and an error message is displayed on the Java console window.

The approach used by Java to catch and handle exceptions is to surround blocks of statements for which exception processing is performed by a `try` statement. The `try` statement contains a `catch` clause that identifies what processing is to be performed for different types of exceptions. When an exception occurs, the Java runtime system matches the exception to the appropriate `catch` clause. The `catch` clause then handles the exception in an appropriate manner. An optional `finally` clause is always executed whether or not an exception is thrown or caught. Figure 5.1 summarizes Java's approach to exception handling.

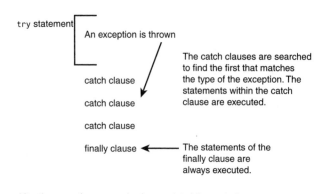

FIGURE 5.1
How Java's exception handling works.

The `throw` Statement

Exceptions are thrown using the `throw` statement. Its syntax is as follows:

```
throw Expression;
```

Expression must evaluate to an object that is an instance of a subclass of the `java.lang.Throwable` class. When an exception is thrown, execution does not continue after the `throw` statement. Instead, it continues with any code that catches the exception. If an exception is not caught, the current thread of execution is terminated, and an error is displayed on the console window. Specifically, the `uncaughtException()` method of the current `ThreadGroup` is invoked to display the error message.

For example, the following statement will throw an exception, using an object of class `ExampleException`:

```
throw new ExampleException();
```

The new operator is invoked with the `ExampleException()` constructor to allocate and initialize an object of class `ExampleException`. This object is then thrown by the `throw` statement.

A method's `throws` clause lists the types of exceptions that can be thrown during a method's execution. The `throws` clause appears immediately before a method's body in the method declaration. For example, the following method throws the `ExampleException`:

```
public void exampleMethod() throws ExampleException {
 throw new ExampleException();
}
```

NOTE

What to Throw? A `throw` statement can throw an object of any class that is a subclass of `java.lang.Throwable`; however, it is wise to stick with the standard convention of only throwing objects that are a subclass of class `Exception`.

N O T E

Runtime Exceptions and Errors
Because runtime exceptions or errors
can occur almost anywhere in a program's execution, the catch or declare
requirement does not apply to them.

When more than one exception can be thrown during the execution
of a method, the exceptions are separated by commas in the throws
clause. For example, the following method can throw either the
Test1Exception or the Test2Exception:

```
public void testMethod(int i) throws Test1Exception,
Test2Exception {
 if(i==1) throw new Test1Exception();
 if(i==2) throw new Test2Exception();
}
```

The types identified in the throws clause must be capable of being
legally assigned to the exceptions that may be thrown. In other
words, the class of the thrown exception must be castable to the class
of the exceptions identified in the throws clause.

If a program exception can be thrown during the execution of a
method, the method must either catch the exception or declare the
exception in its throws clause. This rule applies even if the exception
is thrown in other methods that are invoked during the method's
execution.

For example, suppose that method A of object X invokes method B of
object Y, which invokes method C of object Z. If method C throws an
exception, it must be caught by method C or declared in method C's
throws clause. If it is not caught by method C, it must be caught by
method B or declared in method B's throws clause. Similarly, if the
exception is not caught by method B, it must be caught by method A
or declared in method A's throws clause. The handling of exceptions
is a hierarchical process that mirrors the method invocation hierarchy (or call tree). Either an exception is caught by a method and
removed from the hierarchy, or it must be declared and propagated
back through the method invocation hierarchy. Figure 5.2 summarizes this process.

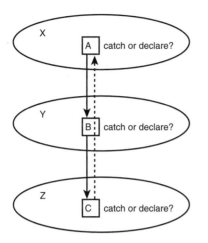

FIGURE 5.2
Declaring or catching exceptions.

The `try-catch-finally` Statement

Statements for which exception processing is to be performed are surrounded by a `try` statement with a valid `catch` or `finally` clause (or both). The syntax of the `try` statement is as follows:

```
try TryBlock CatchClauses FinallyClause;
```

At least one `catch` clause or `finally` clause must be defined. More than one `catch` clause may be used, but no more than one `finally` clause may be identified.

The `try` block is a sequence of Java statements that are preceded by an opening brace (`{`) and followed by a closing brace (`}`).

The `catch` clauses are a sequence of clauses of the form:

```
catch (Parameter) {
/*
* Exception handling statements
*/
}
```

The `Parameter` is a variable that is declared to be a subclass of `Throwable`. The statements within the `catch` clause are used to process the exceptions that they "catch," as I'll explain shortly.

The `finally` clause identifies a block of code that is to be executed at the conclusion of the `try` statement and after any `catch` clauses. Its syntax is as follows:

```
finally {
/*
```

```
 * Statements in finally clause
 */
}
```

The `finally` clause is always executed, no matter whether or not an exception is thrown.

The `try` statement executes a statement block. If an exception is thrown during the block's execution, it terminates execution of the statement block and checks the `catch` clauses to determine which, if any, of the `catch` clauses can catch the thrown exception. If none of the `catch` clauses can catch the exception, the exception is propagated to the next level `try` statement. This process is repeated until the exception is caught or no more `try` statements remain. Figure 5.3 summarizes the exception propagation process.

A `catch` clause can catch an exception if its argument may be legally assigned the object thrown in the `throw` statement. If the argument of a `catch` clause is a class, the `catch` clause can catch any object whose class is a subclass of this class.

The `try` statement tries each `catch` clause in order, and selects the first one that can catch the exception that was thrown. It then executes the statements in the `catch` clause. If a `finally` clause occurs in the `try` statement, the statements in the `finally` clause are executed after execution of the `catch` clause has been completed. Execution then continues with the statement following the `try` statement.

When an exception is caught in the `catch` clause of a `try` statement, that exception may be rethrown. When an exception is rethrown, it can then be caught and processed by the `catch` clause of a higher-level `try` statement. A higher-level `catch` clause can then perform any secondary clean-up processing.

FIGURE 5.3
Exception propagation.

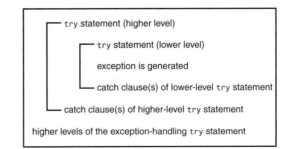

Listing 5.7 provides an example of exception handling. The ExceptionTest program reads a character entered by the user. It then throws and catches a VowelException, BlankException, or ExitException based on the user's input.

ExceptionTest provides two static methods, main() and processUserInput(). The main() method consists of a simple do statement that repeatedly tries to invoke processUserInput(). The try statement has three catch clauses and a finally clause. The three catch clauses notify the user of the type of exception they catch. The catch clause with an ExitException parameter causes the do statement and the program to terminate by setting finished to true. The finally clause just displays the fact that it has been executed.

The processUserInput() method prompts the user to enter a character. The actual reading of the character occurs within a try statement. IOException is caught by the try statement, eliminating the need to declare the exception in the processUserInput() throws clause. The IOException is handled by notifying the user that the exception occurred and continuing with program execution.

The processUserInput() method throws one of three exceptions based upon the character entered by the user. If the user enters a vowel, VowelException is thrown. If the user enters a line beginning with a non-printable character, BlankException is thrown. If the user enters x or X, ExitException is thrown.

When you run ExceptionTest, it produces the following prompt:

```
Enter a character:
```

Enter a blank line, and the following output is displayed:

```
A blank exception occurred.
This is the finally clause.
Enter a character:
```

The program notifies you that a blank exception has occurred and displays the fact that the finally clause of the main() try statement was executed. The processUserInput() method, upon encountering a space character returned by getChar(), throws the BlankException, which is caught by the main() method. The finally clause always executes no matter whether processUserInput() throws an exception or not.

Enter a at the program prompt, and the following output appears:

```
Enter a character: a
A vowel exception occurred.
This is the finally clause.
Enter a character:
```

Here the program notifies you that a vowel exception has occurred. The processing of the vowel exception is similar to the blank exception. See if you can trace the program flow of control involved in this processing.

Enter j, and the following is displayed:

```
Enter a character: j
This is the finally clause.
Enter a character:
```

No exceptions are thrown for the j character, but the `finally` clause is executed. The `finally` clause is always executed, no matter what happens during the execution of a `try` statement. Go ahead and type x to exit the `ExceptionTest` program. The program displays the following output:

```
Enter a character: x
An exit exception occurred.
This is the finally clause.
```

The program then returns you to the command prompt. The output acknowledges the fact that the exit exception was thrown by `processUserInput()` and caught by `main()`.

LISTING 5.7

EXCEPTIONTEST.JAVA—WORKING WITH EXCEPTIONS

```java
import java.io.*;

public class ExceptionTest {
 public static void main(String args[]) {
  boolean finished = false;
  do {
   try {
    processUserInput();
   }catch (VowelException x) {
    System.out.println("A vowel exception occurred.");
   }catch (BlankException x) {
    System.out.println("A blank exception occurred.");
   }catch (ExitException x) {
```

```
     System.out.println("An exit exception occurred.");
     finished = true;
    }finally {
     System.out.println("This is the finally clause.\n");
    }
   } while(!finished);
  }
  static void processUserInput() throws VowelException,
➡BlankException,
   ExitException {
  System.out.print("Enter a character: ");
  System.out.flush();
  char ch;
  try {
   BufferedReader kbd =
    new BufferedReader(new InputStreamReader(System.in));
   String line = kbd.readLine();
   if(line.length() == 0) ch = ' ';
   else ch=Character.toUpperCase(line.charAt(0));
  } catch (IOException x) {
   System.out.println("An IOException occurred.");
   return;
  }
  switch(ch) {
   case 'A':
   case 'E':
   case 'I':
   case 'O':
   case 'U':
    throw new VowelException();
   case ' ':
    throw new BlankException();
   case 'X':
    throw new ExitException();
  }
 }
}
class VowelException extends Exception {}
class BlankException extends Exception {}
class ExitException extends Exception {}
```

CHAPTER SUMMARY

KEY TERMS

- Programming statement
- Selection statement
- Iteration statement
- Exception
- Throwing an exception
- Exception handling

This chapter covered Java's flow of control and exception handling statements. You learned how to use the selection statements (`if` and `switch`), the iteration statements (`for`, `while`, and `do`), the control transfer statements (`break` and `continue`) and statements used in exception handling (`try-catch-finally` and `throw`). You've seen examples of these statements used in several small programs. You should now be prepared to test your knowledge of Java statements. The following review questions and exam questions will let you know how well you understand this material and will give you an idea of how you'll do in the certification exam questions. They'll also indicate which material you need to study further.

APPLY YOUR KNOWLEDGE

Review Questions

1. What is the purpose of a statement block?

2. For which statements does it make sense to use a label?

3. What is the difference between an `if` statement and a `switch` statement?

4. What restrictions are placed on the values of each case of a `switch` statement?

5. How are commas used in the initialization and iteration parts of a `for` statement?

6. What is the difference between a `while` statement and a `do` statement?

7. Can a `for` statement loop indefinitely?

8. What is the difference between a `break` statement and a `continue` statement?

9. What classes of exceptions can be caught by a `catch` clause?

10. What class of exceptions is generated by the Java run-time system?

11. What happens if an exception is not caught?

12. What is the purpose of the `finally` clause of a `try-catch-finally` statement?

13. What classes of exceptions can be thrown by a `throw` statement?

14. What is the relationship between a method's `throws` clause and the exceptions that can be thrown during the method's execution?

15. What is the catch or declare rule for method declarations?

16. What happens if a `try-catch-finally` statement does not have a `catch` clause to handle an exception that is thrown within the body of the `try` statement?

17. When is the `finally` clause of a `try-catch-finally` statement executed?

18. Can an exception be rethrown?

19. Can `try` statements be nested?

20. How does a `try` statement determine which `catch` clause should be used to handle an exception?

Exam Questions

1. What is wrong with the following `if` statement?

```
if(x++) {
  y = x * z;
  x /= 2;
else {
  y = y * y;
  ++z;
}
```

   A. The `if` condition should use a prefix operator instead of a postfix operator.

   B. The `if` condition must be a `boolean` expression, not a numeric expression.

   C. There is a missing } before the `else`.

   D. There is no `break` statement to allow control to transfer out of the `if` statement.

2. What is wrong with the following `switch` statement?

```
switch(i == 10) {
case '1':
  ++i;
  break;
```

APPLY YOUR KNOWLEDGE

```
case "2":
 --i;
case 3:
 i *= 5;
 break;
default
 i %= 3;
}
```

A. The switch expression must evaluate to an integer value.

B. The first case specifies a char value.

C. The second case specifies a String value.

D. There is a break statement missing in the second case.

E. An : should follow default.

3. What is wrong with the following for statement?

```
for(i=0; j=0, i<10; ++i, j += i) {
 k += i*i + j*j;
}
```

A. It should include more than one statement in the statement block.

B. There should be a comma between i=0 and j=0.

C. It uses more than one loop index.

D. There should be a semicolon between j=0 and i<10.

4. What is wrong with the following statement?

```
while (x >> 2) do {
 x *= y;
}
```

A. The loop expression is not a boolean expression.

B. The do should be removed.

C. The while should be capitalized.

D. There is nothing wrong with this statement.

5. What is wrong with the following statements:

```
for(int i=0; i<10; ++i) {
 if(x[i] > 100) break;
 if(x[i] < 0) continue;
 x[i+1] = x[i] + y[i];
}
```

A. It is illegal to have a break and continue statement within the same for statement.

B. The i variable cannot be declared in the initialization part of a for statement.

C. The prefix operator is not allowed in the iteration part of a for statement.

D. There's nothing wrong with the statements.

6. What Java statement is used to completely abort the execution of a loop?

A. The continue statement.

B. The goto statement.

C. The exit statement.

D. The break statement.

7. If you ran the following program, what lines would be included in its output?

```
class Question {
 public static void main(String[] args) {
  int i,j;
  for(i=0, j=0; i+j < 20; ++i, j += i) {
   System.out.println(i+j);
  }
 }
}
```

A. 5

B. 8

C. 13

D. The program cannot be compiled because the for statement's syntax is incorrect.

APPLY YOUR KNOWLEDGE

8. If you ran the following program, what lines would be included in its output?

```
class Question {
 public static void main(String[] args) {
  int i,j;
  for(i=0, j=0; i+j < 20; ++i, j += i--) {
   System.out.println(i+j);
  }
 }
}
```

A. 5

B. 8

C. 13

D. The program cannot be compiled because the for statement's syntax is incorrect.

9. If you ran the following program, which lines would be included in its output?

```
class Question {
 public static void main(String[] args) {
  int i = 1;
  int j = 2;
  outer: while (i < j) {
   ++i;
   inner: do {
    ++j;
    if(j % 3 == 0) continue outer;
    if(i % 3 == 0) break inner;
    if(i % 3 == 1) break outer;
    System.out.println(i*j);
   } while (j < i);
   System.out.println(i+j);
  }
 }
}
```

A. 5

B. 6

C. 7

D. The program does not display any output.

10. If you ran the following program, which lines would be included in its output?

```
class Question {
 public static void main(String[] args) {
  int i = 1;
  int j = 2;
  outer: while (i < j) {
   ++i;
   inner: do {
    ++j;
    if(i++ % 3 == 2) break inner;
    else if(j++ % 3 == 1) break outer;
    System.out.println(i*j);
   } while (j < i);
   System.out.println(i+j);
  }
 }
}
```

A. 5

B. 6

C. 7

D. The program does not display any output.

11. Which of the following must be true of the object thrown by a throw statement?

A. It must be assignable to the Throwable type.

B. It must be assignable to the Error type.

C. It must be assignable to the Exception type.

D. It must be assignable to the String type.

12. A catch clause may catch exceptions of which type?

A. The Throwable type.

B. The Error type.

C. The Exception type.

D. The String type.

13. Which of the following are true about the finally clause of a try-catch-finally statement?

A. It is only executed after a catch clause has executed.

APPLY YOUR KNOWLEDGE

B. It is only executed if a catch clause has not executed.

C. It is always executed unless its thread terminates.

D. It is only executed if an exception is thrown.

14. Which lines of output are displayed by the following program?

```java
class Question {
 public static void main(String[] args) {
  for(int i=0;i<10;++i) {
   try {
    if(i % 3 == 0) throw new Exception("E0");
    try {
     if(i % 3 == 1) throw new
     ➥Exception("E1");
     System.out.println(i);
    }catch (Exception inner) {
     i *= 2;
    }finally{
     ++i;
    }
   }catch (Exception outer) {
    i += 3;
   }finally{
    ++i;
   }
  }
 }
}
```

A. 4

B. 5

C. 6

D. 7

E. 8

F. 9

15. Which lines of output are displayed by the following program?

```java
class Question {
 public static void main(String[] args) {
```

```java
  for(int i=0;i<10;++i) {
   try {
    try {
     if(i % 3 == 0) throw new
     ➥Exception("E0");
     System.out.println(i);
    }catch (Exception inner) {
     i *= 2;
     if(i % 3 == 0) throw new
     ➥Exception("E1");
    }finally{
     ++i;
    }
   }catch (Exception outer) {
    i += 3;
   }finally{
    --i;
   }
  }
 }
}
```

A. 4

B. 5

C. 6

D. 7

E. 8

F. 9

Answers to Review Questions

1. A statement block is used to organize a sequence of statements as a single statement group.

2. The only statements for which it makes sense to use a label are those statements that can enclose a break or continue statement.

APPLY YOUR KNOWLEDGE

3. The `if` statement is used to select among two alternatives. It uses a `boolean` expression to decide which alternative should be executed. The `switch` statement is used to select among multiple alternatives. It uses an `int` expression to determine which alternative should be executed.

4. During compilation, the values of each case of a `switch` statement must evaluate to a value that can be promoted to an `int` value.

5. Commas are used to separate multiple statements within the initialization and iteration parts of a `for` statement.

6. A `while` statement checks at the beginning of a loop to see whether the next loop iteration should occur. A `do` statement checks at the end of a loop to see whether the next iteration of a loop should occur. The `do` statement will always execute the body of a loop at least once.

7. Yes, the `for` statement can loop indefinitely. For example, consider the statement `for(;;) ;`.

8. A `break` statement results in the termination of the statement to which it applies (`switch`, `for`, `do`, or `while`). A `continue` statement is used to end the current loop iteration and return control to the loop statement.

9. A `catch` clause can catch any exception that may be assigned to the `Throwable` type. This includes the `Error` and `Exception` types.

10. The Java runtime system generates `RuntimeException` and `Error` exceptions.

11. An uncaught exception results in the `uncaughtException()` method of the thread's `ThreadGroup` being invoked, which eventually results in the termination of the program in which it is thrown.

12. The `finally` clause is used to provide the capability to execute code no matter whether or not an exception is thrown or caught.

13. A `throw` statement may throw any expression that may be assigned to the `Throwable` type.

14. A method's `throws` clause must declare any checked exceptions that are not caught within the body of the method.

15. If a checked exception may be thrown within the body of a method, the method must either catch the exception or declare it in its `throws` clause.

16. The exception propagates up to the next higher level `try-catch` statement (if any) or results in the program's termination.

17. The `finally` clause of the `try-catch-finally` statement is always executed unless the thread of execution terminates or an exception occurs within the execution of the `finally` clause.

18. Yes, an exception can be rethrown.

19. `try` statements may be nested.

20. When an exception is thrown within the body of a `try` statement, the `catch` clauses of the `try` statement are examined in the order in which they appear. The first `catch` clause that is capable of handling the exception is executed. The remaining `catch` clauses are ignored.

APPLY YOUR KNOWLEDGE

Answers to Exam Questions

1. B and C   The if condition must be a boolean expression. A } is missing from in front of the else.

2. A, C, and E   The switch condition must be an integer expression. The case values must evaluate to integer values during compilation. A : should follow the default label.

3. B and D   Commas are used to separate statements within the initialization and iteration parts of a for statement. Semicolons are used to separate the initialization, loop condition, and iteration parts of the for statement.

4. A and B   The loop condition must be a boolean expression. There is no do in a while statement.

5. D   There's nothing wrong with the statements.

6. D   The break statement causes a loop's execution to be terminated.

7. A   The program displays the value 5. It does not display the values 8 or 13.

8. A, B, and C   The program displays the values 5, 8, and 13.

9. C   The program displays the value 7.

10. B   The program displays the value 6.

11. A   The object thrown by a throw statement must be assignable to the Throwable type. This includes the Error and Exception types.

12. A, B, and C   The exception caught by a catch clause must be assignable to the Throwable type. This includes the Error and Exception types.

13. C   The finally clause of a try-catch statement always executes unless its thread terminates.

14. B and E   The program only displays the values 5 and 8.

15. A and B   The program only displays the values 4 and 5.

Suggested Readings and Resources

Gosling, James; Joy, Bill; and Steele, Guy, *The Java Language Specification.* Addison Wesley, 1996.

This chapter helps you to prepare for the exam by covering the following objectives:

Know how to declare classes and inner classes, making appropriate use of all permitted modifiers (such as `public`, `final`, `static`, `abstract`, and so forth). State the significance of each of these modifiers both singly and in combination and state the effect of package relationships on declared items qualified by these modifiers.

For a given class, know how to determine if a default constructor will be created, and if so, state the prototype of that constructor.

State the legal return types for any method given the declarations of all related methods in this or parent classes.

Know how to identify correctly constructed class declarations (of all forms including inner classes), interface declarations, and implementations.

State the benefits of encapsulation in object-oriented design, and write code that implements tightly encapsulated classes and the relationships *is a* and *has a*.

Know how to write code to invoke overridden or overloaded methods and parental or overloaded constructors and describe the effect of invoking these methods.

Know how to write code to construct instances of any concrete class, including normal top-level classes, inner classes, static inner classes, and anonymous inner classes.

CHAPTER 6

Overloading, Overriding, Runtime Type, and Object Orientation

STUDY STRATEGIES

As you read through this chapter, you should concentrate on the following key items:

▶ How classes and interfaces are declared

▶ How inner and anonymous classes are declared and used

▶ How constructors are declared

▶ When a default constructor is created

▶ How one constructor may invoke another constructor of the same class or superclass

▶ How overriding and overloading differ

▶ What restrictions apply to an overriding method

▶ How classes are specified using *is a* and *has a*

▶ What a fully encapsulated class looks like

CHAPTER INTRODUCTION

Because Java is an object-oriented programming language, the certification exam requires you to be familiar with the basic concepts and techniques of object-oriented programming. In this chapter, you'll review object-oriented programming concepts, learn to create classes and interfaces, and learn how to use inner classes and adapter classes. You'll also learn how to declare and use constructors and overload and override methods.

OBJECT-ORIENTED PROGRAMMING AND JAVA

One of Java's many features is its extensive support of object-oriented programming. Java provides all of the basics of object-oriented programming: object reuse, class hierarchy, inheritance, encapsulation, polymorphism, and dynamic binding—in a programming context that is useful and efficient. The following subsections summarize these capabilities.

Object Composition and Reuse

The fact that one object can be composed of, or built from, other objects is the heart of object-oriented programming. This allows more complex objects to be constructed from basic building blocks. For example, suppose that you're developing a drawing program. Your drawing application would consist of objects such as windows, menus, a drawing canvas, a tool palette, a color palette, and so on. Some of these objects are available in class libraries and others are built from more primitive components. You develop your drawing application by gathering and building its component classes and assembling them into an integrated whole.

Object composition not only enables you to simplify the organization of your programs, it also lets you reuse the software you develop. For example, you could develop drawing classes as part of your drawing program and reuse those classes in a paint program and a desktop publishing program. You could also package your drawing classes and give or sell them to others so that they can use them as a foundation for building other custom classes. Object reuse provides you with the capability to build a core library of classes (such as the Java API) from which you can quickly and easily piece together your programs. Without object reuse, you are forced to start from scratch with every program that you develop.

Classification and Inheritance

Object reuse is not limited to object composition. It also exploits a powerful capability of object-oriented programming known as *inheritance*. Inheritance not only allows objects to be used as is, but also enables new objects to be created by extending and tailoring existing objects.

Classification is a way that we organize knowledge in general. We use classification whether or not we are doing object-oriented programming. When we encounter a new object in our daily experience, we try to fit that object in our existing classification scheme. If it fits an existing category, we know what kind of object it is. If it doesn't fit, we add a new category.

Figure 6.1 illustrates how we use classification to represent knowledge. When we classify objects in this hierarchical fashion, the classes at the top of the tree include all of the classes below them. If a class appears in the classification tree, it provides the properties of all object categories above it in the tree.

Figure 6.2 presents a classification tree for different types of vehicles. All categories in the tree below the category car, for example, share the common characteristics of having four wheels, being self-powered, and being designed for passenger transportation. The fact that a lower-level category shares the characteristics of the categories above it in the classification tree is known as inheritance. The lower-level categories are said to inherit the characteristics of the categories above them in the tree.

In Java, inheritance applies to the subclass relationship. When a class X extends another class Y, it inherits all of the (non-private) variables and methods of Y. This is very powerful feature for object reuse—not only can you reuse classes as they are defined, you can easily extend them and tailor their definitions by adding additional data and methods to their subclasses.

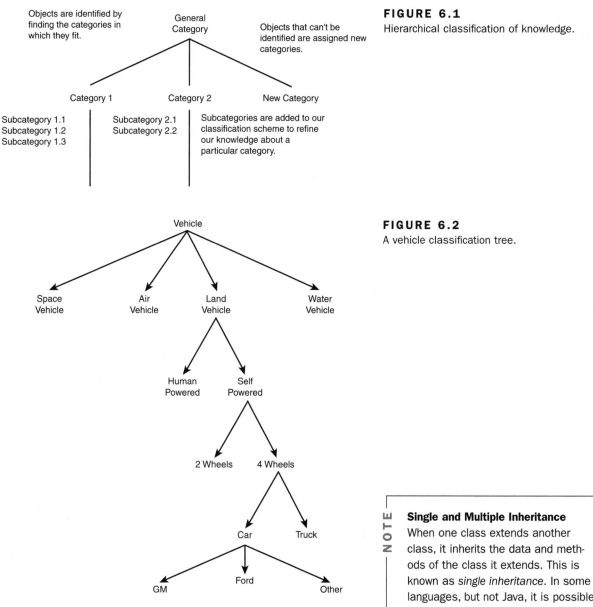

FIGURE 6.1
Hierarchical classification of knowledge.

FIGURE 6.2
A vehicle classification tree.

> **NOTE**
>
> **Single and Multiple Inheritance**
> When one class extends another class, it inherits the data and methods of the class it extends. This is known as *single inheritance*. In some languages, but not Java, it is possible for a class to extend multiple classes on different branches of the class hierarchy tree. This is known as *multiple inheritance*. Since Java classes may only have one parent, Java does not support multiple inheritance.

Encapsulation

One characteristic of object-oriented programming that is often touted is *encapsulation.* The term carries the connotation of an object being enclosed in some sort of container—that is exactly what it means. Encapsulation is the combining of data and the code that manipulates that data into a single component—that is, an object. Encapsulation also refers to the control of access to the details of an object's implementation. Object access is limited to a well-defined, controlled interface. This allows objects to be self-contained and protected from accidental misuse, both of which are important to reliable software design. When a class is fully encapsulated, it is possible to change the class's implementation without impacting other objects that use the class. A fully encapsulated class declares all of its variables as `private` and provides methods for getting and setting the properties represented by field variables.

Polymorphism

Polymorphism is the capability to assume different forms. In object-oriented programming, this refers to the capability of objects to have many methods of the same name, but with different types of arguments. The `print()` and `println()` method of the `PrintStream` class are an excellent example of polymorphism. These methods support printing of objects of different types.

The compiler and runtime system support polymorphism by matching each method invocation to the form of that method. The capability to figure out which method to use in complex situations is the essence of polymorphism.

Late Binding

Sometimes a program might need to interface with objects of many different classes. For example, consider a program that has the responsibility of receiving an object over a communication link. The program may not know what class an object belongs to until it receives it. The capability to defer until runtime the decision about what class an object belongs to is known as *late binding* or *dynamic binding*. Late binding is important in object-oriented programming because it allows programs to be developed in a more flexible manner. Without late binding, a program is required to know beforehand which classes of objects it will access at compile time. Late binding is key to supporting class inheritance because it allows an algorithm that is designed for a given class to work with any subclasses of that class. The runtime system identifies the actual class of an object and invokes any overriding methods of that class.

DECLARING CLASSES

Now that you've covered the concepts behind object-oriented programming, you will get down to its nuts and bolts. Most of what you do as a Java programmer involves declaring classes and interfaces and then fleshing them out with field variables and methods. Classes are declared using the following syntax:

```
modifiers class ClassName extendsClause  implementsClause {
// Class body
}
```

The modifiers, extends clause, and implements clause are optional. If they are supplied, they are used as follows:

> **NOTE**
>
> **Inner Classes** *Inner classes* are a special kind of classes that are declared within the context of other classes, interfaces, or statement blocks. This discussion applies to normal, top-level classes. You'll cover inner classes later in this chapter.

◆ Modifiers—A top-level class may be declared as public, final, or abstract. A public class may be accessed outside of its package. If a class is not declared as public, it may only be accessed by classes and interfaces that are part of the same package. A final class is a class that may not be extended. If a class attempts to extend a final class, a compilation error results. An abstract class is a class that declares one or more abstract methods. Because abstract methods must be overridden by a method with a method body (in order to be used), the declaration of an abstract class implies that it will be extended by a class or classes that will provide implementations of the abstract methods. A class may not be both final and abstract.

◆ extends clause—The extends clause consists of the keyword extends followed by the name of the class that is extended by the class being declared. The class identified in the extends clause is referred to as the *parent* or *direct superclass* of the class being declared. A class may have only one parent. If the extends clause is omitted, the class extends java.lang.Object as a default.

◆ implements clause—The implements clause identifies the interfaces that are implemented by a class. It consists of the keyword implements followed by a comma-separated list of interface names. In order for a class to implement an interface, it must provide a method with the same signature as each of the methods defined in the interface and inherited by the interface from the interfaces that it extends. An abstract class may provide abstract methods. Non-abstract classes must provide non-abstract methods. If a class is to implement an interface, the interface must be identified in the class's `implements` clause or in the `implements` clause of one of the class's superclasses. If an interface is not identified as an `implements` clause, the class does not implement that interface—even if the class supplies an implementation of all of the methods defined by the interface.

The class body declares *members* (field variables and methods), constructors, and initializers. Class members may also be inner classes or inner interfaces.

<table>
<tr><td>EXAM TIP</td><td>**Strict Subclasses**   All classes are considered to be subclasses of themselves. A *strict subclass* of a class X is any subclass of X except X.</td></tr>
</table>

Designing Classes Using *Is a* and *Has a*

You are likely to encounter several questions on the certification exam that test your ability to design a class using an English-language specification of the class's characteristics. This description will specify relationships using *is a* and *has a*. The *is a* specifies a subclass relationship and *has a* identifies a field variable. The following is an example of this type of class description:

A circle is a shape that has a center point and a radius.

The following code defines the class specified by the above description:

```
public class Circle extends Shape {
  Point center;
  double radius;
}
```

In general, whenever you see *is a,* think in terms of a class extending a superclass. Whenever you see *has a,* think in terms of a class having a field variable.

<table>
<tr><td>EXAM TIP</td><td>**"Is A" and "Has A"**   You should pay particular attention to the semantics of "is a" and "has a". A few test questions require you to design classes based on "is a" and "has a" descriptions.</td></tr>
</table>

CONSTRUCTORS

Objects are instances of classes that are created using constructors. Every class requires a constructor in order to create object instances. In fact, if a class does not declare a constructor, the compiler automatically creates a constructor for the class. However, in most cases, you won't rely on the compiler to create a constructor for you, and you'll declare your own constructors. The following is the syntax of a constructor declaration:

```
modifers ClassName(arguments) throwsClause {
  // Constructor body
}
```

The modifiers, arguments, and `throws` clause are optional. Valid modifiers are `public`, `protected`, `private`, or none. No modifier means that the constructor can only be accessed within the package where the class is declared. The `public`, `protected`, and `private` modifiers are used in the same manner as methods. The arguments and `throws` clause are also defined in the same way as methods. (Refer to Chapter 4, "Declarations and Access Control.")

One important way in which constructors differ from methods is that they are not inherited. Each class must define its own constructors. However, if no constructor is defined for a class, the compiler will supply a default constructor. The default constructor will not have any arguments and will simply invoke the constructor of the class's superclass to construct an object of the class.

> **EXAM TIP**
>
> **Private Constructors** Suppose that you want to create a class but you don't want it to be instantiated as an object. Just declare the class's constructors as `private`.

Using `this()` and `super()`

In some cases, you might want to define several constructors where each of the constructors takes some subset of the arguments used to create an object. One constructor takes all the arguments and supplies the code that constructs the object, and the other constructors take a partial list of arguments, supply default values, and invoke the main constructor. As an example, consider the example shown in Listing 6.1.

LISTING 6.1

Box's Constructors Use `this()` to Access One Another

```
public class Box {
 double x, y, width, height;
 public Box(double x, double y, double width, double height) {
  this.x = x;
```

continues

LISTING 6.1 *continued*

Box's Constructors Use this() to Access One Another

```
   this.y = y;
   this.width = width;
   this.height = height;
  }
  public Box(double x, double y) {
   this(x,y,10,10);
  }
  public Box() {
   this(1,1);
  }
 }
```

The first Box() constructor takes the arguments x, y, width, and height and assigns them to the appropriate field variables. The second Box() constructor takes just the box's coordinates as arguments and invokes the first constructor, passing 10 as the default value for the box's height and width. The third constructor has no arguments and invokes the second constructor with the default value of 1 for the box's x and y coordinates.

> **NOTE**
>
> **Using this()** If this() appears in a constructor, it must appear as the first statement in the constructor.

The this(x,y,10,10) and this(1,1) used in the second and third constructors is a special notation provided by Java to enable you to invoke a constructor of the same class from another constructor of that class. It is referred to as a constructor call statement. In order to use a constructor call statement, there must be a constructor whose argument list matches those supplied with this().

In other cases, instead of invoking the constructor of the same class as the object being constructed, you invoke the constructor of its superclass. To do this, you use the superclass constructor call statement, super(). To see how super() works consider the MyBox class declared by the following code (Listing 6.2).

LISTING 6.2

MyBox Uses super() to Access the Constructor of Box

```
import java.awt.Color;

public class MyBox extends Box {
 Color outerColor;
```

```
Color innerColor;
public MyBox(double x, double y, double width, double height,
    Color outer, Color inner) {
  super(x,y,width,height);
  outerColor = outer;
  innerColor = inner;
}
public MyBox(Color outer, Color inner) {
  super(10,10,100,100);
  outerColor = outer;
  innerColor = inner;
}
public MyBox() {
  super();
  outerColor = Color.black;
  innerColor = Color.white;
  }
}
```

The MyBox class extends Box with the capability to specify the box's outer (perimeter) and inner colors. The first constructor invokes super(x,y,width,height) to invoke the superclass (Box) constructor to initialize the box's location and dimensions. The second constructor also uses the superclass constructor and passes it the default values of 10 for the box's x and y coordinates and 100 for its width and height. The third constructor simply invokes super() to invoke the parameterless Box() constructor of its superclass.

If either this() or super() is used in a constructor, it must appear as the first statement of the constructor. This means that either this() or super() (but not both) may be used in a constructor. If neither this() nor super() is supplied, an implicit super() (with no arguments) is supplied by the compiler. This causes the superclass portion of an object to be created before that of the class itself. If a superclass does not have a parameterless constructor, an explicit constructor invocation must be used in the constructors of its subclasses. Also, if a class does not define an accessible constructor, it cannot be extended.

> **NOTE**
>
> **Using super()** If super() appears in a constructor, it must appear as the first statement in the constructor.

DECLARING INTERFACES

An interface defines a collection of methods that is implemented by a class. However, it may also be used to define constants, inner classes, and inner interfaces. The syntax of an interface declaration is as follows:

```
modifiers interface InterfaceName extendsClause {
  // Interface body
}
```

An interface may use the modifiers `public` and `abstract`. However, the use of `abstract` is redundant—all interfaces are `abstract` because they only declare `abstract` methods. An interface that is declared as `public` may be accessed outside its package.

The `extends` clause consists of the keyword `extends` followed by a comma-separated list of the interfaces that are extended. An extending interface inherits all the constants and methods of the interfaces that it extends.

An interface body may contain constant declarations, abstract method declarations, inner classes, and inner interfaces. Inner classes and interfaces are less common and covered later in this chapter. A constant definition declares and initializes a variable that is `public`, `static`, and `final` (a constant). If you omit these modifiers the compiler will supply them for you.

Abstract methods are covered in Chapter 4.

INNER AND ANONYMOUS CLASSES

Inner classes and inner interfaces were introduced in JDK 1.1. An inner class (also referred to as a nested class) is a class that is defined as a member of another class or local to a statement block. Inner interfaces are less common than inner classes. They are defined as members of another class or interface.

EXAM TIP

Inner and Anonymous Classes
Make sure that you understand how inner and anonymous classes are used. You'll see several exam questions that cover inner and anonymous classes.

Inner Classes

When an inner class is defined as a member of another class, it may have the access modifiers (`public`, `protected`, `private`, or package access). It may also be declared as `abstract`, `final`, or `static`. The access modifiers determine how the inner class may be accessed outside the class and outside the package in which it is declared. These modifiers are used in the same manner as with variables and methods.

Abstract or final inner classes are rarely used. However, the distinction between static and non-static inner classes is important.

The following is an example of a simple inner class declaration:

```
class Outer {
 class Inner {
  // Inner class body
 }
}
```

The Outer class is a normal top-level class. The Inner class is a simple class that is declared as an inner class of Outer.

Non-Static Inner Classes

Non-static inner classes may be used to create objects which are instances of the class. Every instance of a non-static inner class is associated with an instance of the outer class in which it is declared. In fact, an instance of an inner class cannot be created without first creating an instance of its outer class. The following program illustrates this point:

```
class Outer {
 public static void main(String[] args) {
  Inner inner = new Inner();
 }
 class Inner {
  Inner() {
  }
 }
}
```

If you attempt to compile the above program you'll get the following error message (assuming you're using the same version of the javac compiler):

```
Outer.java:4: No enclosing instance of class Outer is in
➥scope; an explicit one
must be provided when creating inner class Outer. Inner, as
➥in "outer. new Inner
()" or "outer. super()".
  Inner inner = new Inner();
                    ^
1 error
```

To fix the above problem, you can create an instance of Outer and pass it as the enclosing object instance for a new Inner object:

```
class Outer {
 public static void main(String[] args) {
  Outer outer = new Outer();
```

```
    Inner inner = outer.new Inner();
  }
  class Inner {
   Inner() {
   }
  }
}
```

The notation `outer.new Inner()` indicates that the `Outer` object referenced by `outer` is the enclosing object instance that is associated with the new instance of `Inner`.

You can also create an instance of `Inner` when `this` refers to the instance of the enclosing object. The following provides an example of this approach:

```
class Outer {
  public static void main(String[] args) {
   new Outer();
  }
  Outer() {
   new Inner();
  }
  class Inner {
   Inner() {
   }
  }
}
```

Because the `Inner()` constructor is invoked from within the `Outer()` constructor, `this` refers to the instance of the `Outer` object being created.

You can also construct the `Outer` and `Inner` objects within the same statement. The following example shows you how:

```
class Outer {
  public static void main(String[] args) {
   new Outer().new Inner();
  }
  class Inner {
  }
}
```

The statement `new Outer().new Inner()` creates the `Outer` object and the `Inner` object in a compact form.

Variables and methods that are declared in an outer class are accessible from within the inner class. However, `static` inner classes may only access `static` variables and methods in the outer class.

NOTE

Multiple Levels of Inner Classes
Multiple levels of inner classes are possible. However, this is seldom practical.

In some cases, it is important to distinguish between an instance of an inner class and an instance of an outer class. The this keyword refers to the current object instance. When it is used within the scope of an inner class, it refers to the inner class. When used within the scope of an outer class, it refers to the outer class. However, in some cases, it is desirable to refer to the instance of the outer class from within the inner class. The following example shows how this is done.

```
class Outer {
  String s = "Outer";
  public static void main(String[] args) {
   new Outer().new Inner();
  }
  class Inner {
   String s = "Inner";
   Inner() {
    System.out.println(this.s);
    System.out.println(Outer.this.s);
   }
  }
}
```

The program displays the line Inner followed by the line Outer. In the Inner() constructor, this.s, yields the value of the s variable corresponding to the Inner class and Outer.this.s refers to the s variable of the Outer class. To refer to the instance of an outer class prepend the outer class name and a period to this.

Static Inner Classes

Static inner classes differ from non-static inner classes in that (because they are static) they are not instantiated as separate object instances. In addition, static classes are not associated with an object instance of their surrounding class (although they may access static variables and methods of the surrounding class).

Static inner classes have a static enclosing scope and are treated as top-level classes. They are even referred to as top-level classes in some Java documentation. This leads to a contradiction in terms—that is, a top-level inner class.

The following is a simple example of a static inner class:

```
class Outer {
  public static void main(String[] args) {
   new Inner();
  }
  static class Inner {
```

```
    Inner() {
     System.out.println("some static");
    }
   }
  }
```

Note that because `Inner` is `static`, no instance of `Outer` is required before an instance of `Inner` can be created.

Local Inner Classes

Inner classes may also be declared local to a block of code. These inner classes are referred to as *local inner classes*. Since local inner classes are not class members they are not tied to an instance of an outer class. In addition, they may not be declared as `private`, `public`, `protected`, or `static`.

Because local inner classes are defined local to a code block (like a local variable), they may only access the local variables or method parameters of the code block in which they are defined. An additional restriction is placed on local inner classes in that they may only access variables or parameters that are declared as `final` and have been assigned a value. The following program illustrates the use of local inner classes.

```
class MyClass {
 public static void main(String[] args) {
  final String s = "some local results";
  class Local {
   Local() {
    System.out.println(s);
   }
  }
  new Local();
 }
}
```

The `Local` inner class is defined within the context of the `main()` method. Note that s must be declared `final` in order to be accessed from `Local`.

Anonymous Classes

It is sometimes convenient to declare and use a class on the spot. A good example of this is writing a class to implement an event listener interface or to extend an event adapter class.

Anonymous classes fill the need to define and use a class within a single statement. Anonymous classes (as their name implies) are classes without a name. They are declared using the name of the class that they extend or the interface that they implement. The following describes both forms of their syntax:

Extending a class

```
new SuperClassName(arguments) {
 // Class body
}
```

Implementing an interface

```
new InterfaceName() {
 // Implement interface methods
}
```

In the first form, the superclass of the class being declared is identified. No modifiers or `extends` clause are allowed. The arguments (optional) that are supplied are passed to the superclass constructor when the object is created. The superclass must have a constructor with a signature that accepts the arguments, or a compiler error will be generated. Anonymous classes do not have constructors.

In the second form, the anonymous class is declared in terms of the interface that it implements. The interface name is specified as the type of object being created. No `implements` clause is required or possible. When an anonymous class is defined in this fashion, it is declared as a subclass of `Object`. A valid declaration requires that the anonymous class implement all the methods of the interface. No arguments may be supplied when an anonymous class is created as an interface.

The following program (Listing 6.3) illustrates the use of both forms of anonymous inner classes.

LISTING 6.3

ANONYMOUS CLASSES ARE HANDY FOR DEFINING AND USING EVENT HANDLERS

```
import java.awt.*;
import java.awt.event.*;

class Anonymous extends Frame {
 public static void main(String[] args) {
```

continues

LISTING 6.3 | *continued*

ANONYMOUS CLASSES ARE HANDY FOR DEFINING AND USING EVENT HANDLERS

```
 new Anonymous();
}
Anonymous() {
 setTitle("Anonymous");
 setLayout(new FlowLayout());
 final Button button = new Button("Click here!");
 button.addActionListener(new ActionListener() {
  public void actionPerformed(ActionEvent e) {
   String label = button.getLabel();
   if(label.equals("Click here!"))
    button.setLabel("Try again");
   else
    button.setLabel("Click here!");
  }
 });
 add(button);
 addWindowListener(new WindowAdapter() {
  public void windowClosing(WindowEvent e) {
   System.exit(0);
  }
 });
 pack();
 setSize(200,200);
 show();
 }
}
```

The Anonymous program uses an anonymous inner class in two places. First, it creates an instance of the ActionListener interface, which it passes as an argument to the addActionListener() method of a Button object:

```
button.addActionListener(new ActionListener() {
 public void actionPerformed(ActionEvent e) {
  String label = button.getLabel();
  if(label.equals("Click here!"))
   button.setLabel("Try again");
  else
   button.setLabel("Click here!");
 }
});
```

The actionPerformed() method of the ActionListener interface is implemented to handle the clicking of the Button. You'll learn more about events in Chapter 13, "The java.awt Package: Event Handling."

The Anonymous program also uses an anonymous class to create an object that is passed as an argument to the addWindowListener() method. It extends the WindowAdapter class to handle the closing of the application window.

```
addWindowListener(new WindowAdapter() {
  public void windowClosing(WindowEvent e) {
    System.exit(0);
  }
});
```

FIGURE 6.3
The opening window of the Anonymous program.

The Anonymous program displays the window shown in Figure 6.3. When you click the button, it changes its label as shown in Figure 6.4.

FIGURE 6.4
The button's label changes when you click it.

OVERLOADING METHODS

Earlier in the chapter, polymorphism was mentioned as an important feature of object-oriented programming languages. Although polymorphism is not unique to object-oriented programming, it tends to provide the greatest benefit in an object-oriented setting. Method overloading is the primary way in which polymorphism is implemented in Java. Method overloading consists of using the same method name with different arguments and return types within the same class. The only restriction placed on overloading is that two methods may not have the same name and the same argument list. In other words, at least one argument must be different. Argument lists differ if they are a different sequence of types. The argument names do not matter.

A great example of overloading are the print() and println() methods of the java.io.PrintStream class. These methods are overloaded to support each of the primitive types as well as objects.

OVERRIDING METHODS

In addition to overloading, Java also supports overriding. Overriding is similar to overloading in that it deals with the use of functions of the same name. However, overriding is different in that it applies to the use of methods with the same name, arguments, and return type between a class and its superclasses. Where overloading allows more

> **NOTE**
>
> **Operator Overloading** Some languages, such as C++, support operator overloading. Operator overloading allows the same operator to be used with different types of operands. Java does not allow new operators to be defined. However, it does overload the + operator, which can be used for both arithmetic and String operations.

> **NOTE**
>
> **Constraints on Overloading** Overloaded methods may have different return types. However, it is illegal to define two methods with the same arguments and a different return type. Remember, overloaded methods have the same name but different arguments.

methods of the same name to be defined, overriding allows a sub-class to redefine the methods it inherits from its superclasses and therefore specialize the behavior of the superclass.

When a class extends its superclass, it inherits all of the non-private methods of its superclass. In some cases, you may want to redefine some of the methods that are inherited. If the subclass creates a method with the same name as an inherited method, but with different arguments, that is overloading. However, if the subclass declares a method with the same name and same arguments, that's overriding. The following rules apply to overriding:

◆ The overriding (subclass) and overridden (superclass) methods must have the same return type.

◆ The accessibility of the overriding method must not be more restrictive than the overridden method.

◆ The throws clause of the overriding method must only specify exceptions that are in the throws clause of the overridden method.

Let's look at each of the restrictions. The first one follows from the golden rule that a class may not have two methods with the same name, same arguments, and a different return type. If a class were allowed to declare a method with the same name, same arguments, and a different return type than a superclass method, the method would conflict with the one inherited from the superclass.

The second restriction is a little more complicated. Its purpose is to ensure that an extending class does not make the extended class's methods less accessible. However, what is more or less accessible is sometimes difficult to ascertain. The following rules apply:

◆ If the overridden method is public, the overriding method must also be public.

◆ If the overridden method is protected, the overriding method must be public or protected.

◆ If the overridden method is package access (that is, having no modifiers), the overriding method must be public, package access, or protected.

◆ If the superclass method is private, it is not inherited by its subclasses, and overriding is not an issue.

The third restriction requires that any exception thrown by the overriding method be throwable by the overridden method. This means that the exception must be a subclass of some exception that is thrown by the overridden method.

CHAPTER SUMMARY

In this chapter, you reviewed the object-oriented programming used by Java. You learned how to declare top-level classes and interfaces, and how to use inner classes and adapter classes. You also learned how to declare and use constructors, and overload and override methods. The following review questions will test your knowledge of these topics and help to prepare you for the certification exam.

KEY TERMS

- Object reuse
- Classification
- Single inheritance
- Multiple inheritance
- Encapsulation
- Polymorphism
- Late binding
- Parent class
- Superclass
- Direct superclass
- Subclass
- Strict subclass
- Class member
- Abstract class
- Inner class
- Local inner class
- Anonymous class
- Overloading
- Overriding

APPLY YOUR KNOWLEDGE

Review Questions

1. What is the difference between multiple inheritance and single inheritance? Which does Java support?

2. What modifiers may be used with a top-level class?

3. Can an abstract class be final?

4. What is the difference between a public and a non-public class?

5. What must a class do to implement an interface?

6. Is a class a subclass of itself?

7. Does a class inherit the constructors of its superclass?

8. When does the compiler supply a default constructor for a class?

9. How are this() and super() used with constructors?

10. What modifiers may be used with an interface declaration?

11. What modifiers may be used with an inner class that is a member of an outer class?

12. What is the difference between a static and a non-static inner class?

13. What modifiers can be used with a local inner class?

14. Can an anonymous class be declared as implementing an interface and extending a class?

15. What restrictions are placed on method overloading?

16. What restrictions are placed on method overriding?

Exam Questions

1. What is the output of the following program?

```java
class S1 {
 public static void main(String[] args) {
  new S2();
 }
 S1() {
  System.out.print("S1");
 }
}
class S2 extends S1 {
 S2() {
  System.out.print("S2");
 }
}
```

A. S1

B. S2

C. S1S2

D. S2S1

2. Which of the following are characteristic of a fully encapsulated class?

A. All variables are private.

B. All methods are private.

C. Methods are provided to access the class's properties.

D. The class's design may be changed with minimal impact on its implementation.

3. What is an example of polymorphism?

A. Inner classes

B. Anonymous classes

C. Method overloading

D. Method overriding

APPLY YOUR KNOWLEDGE

4. Which of the following modifiers may not be used with a top-level class?

   A. `public`

   B. `private`

   C. `abstract`

   D. `final`

5. Which of the following are true about constructors?

   A. A class inherits its constructors from its parent.

   B. The compiler supplies a default constructor if no constructors are provided for a class.

   C. All constructors have a `void` return type.

   D. A constructor may throw an exception.

6. What is the output of the following program?

```
class Outer {
 String s = "Outer";
 public static void main(String[] args) {
  new Outer().new Inner();
 }
 Outer() {
  System.out.print(s);
 }
 class Inner {
  String s = "Inner";
  Inner() {
   System.out.print(s);
  }
 }
}
```

   A. Outer

   B. Inner

   C. OuterInner

   D. InnerOuter

7. Which of the following are true about method overriding?

   A. The overriding and overridden methods must have the same name, argument list, and return type.

   B. The overriding method must not limit access more than the overridden method.

   C. The overriding method must not throw any exceptions that may not be thrown by the overridden method.

   D. The overriding method may not be `private`.

8. Which of the following are true about local inner classes?

   A. They are not associated with an instance of an outer (enclosing) class.

   B. They may access `final` initialized variables and parameters that are in the scope of the statement block in which the class is declared.

   C. They may be declared `public`, `protected`, or `private`.

   D. They may not implement an interface.

9. Given non-static classes `Outer` and `Inner` where `Inner` is declared as an inner class of `Outer`, how is an instance of `Outer` accessed from within the scope of `Inner`?

   A. `this`

   B. `this.Outer`

   C. `Outer.this`

   D. `this.this`

APPLY YOUR KNOWLEDGE

10. What is the output of the following program?

```
class Question {
 String s = "Outer";
 public static void main(String[] args) {
  S2 s2 = new S2();
  s2.display();
 }
}
class S1 {
 String s = "S1";
 void display() {
  System.out.println(s);
 }
}
class S2 extends S1 {
 String s = "S2";
}
```

A. S1

B. S2

C. null

D. S1S2

Answers to Review Questions

1. Multiple inheritance occurs when a class extends multiple direct superclasses. Single inheritance occurs when a class extends a single direct superclass. Since Java classes may have only one parent, Java does not support multiple inheritance. However, Java does support single inheritance.

2. A top-level class may be public, abstract, or final.

3. An abstract class may not be declared as final.

4. A public class may be accessed outside of its package. A non-public class may not be accessed outside of its package.

5. It must provide all of the methods in the interface and identify the interface in its implements clause.

6. A class is a subclass of itself.

7. A class does not inherit constructors from any of its superclasses.

8. The compiler supplies a default constructor for a class if no other constructors are provided.

9. this() is used to invoke a constructor of the same class. super() is used to invoke a superclass constructor.

10. An interface may be declared as public or abstract.

11. A (non-local) inner class may be declared as public, protected, private, static, final, or abstract.

12. A non-static inner class may have object instances that are associated with instances of the class's outer class. A static inner class does not have any object instances.

13. A local inner class may be final or abstract.

14. An anonymous class may implement an interface or extend a superclass, but may not be declared to do both.

15. Two methods may not have the same name and argument list but different return types.

16. Overridden methods must have the same name, argument list, and return type. The overriding method may not limit the access of the method it overrides. The overriding method may not throw any exceptions that may not be thrown by the overridden method.

APPLY YOUR KNOWLEDGE	

Answers to Exam Questions

1. C   The superclass (S1) constructor is invoked before the subclass (S2) constructor.

2. A and C   A fully encapsulated class declares its variables as private and provides methods to access the properties represented by these variables.

3. C   Method overloading is an example of polymorphism.

4. B   A top-level class may not be declared as private.

5. B and D   The compiler supplies a default constructor if no constructors are provided for a class. Constructors may throw exceptions. These exceptions must be declared in the constructors' throws clause.

6. C   An instance of Outer is created, followed by an instance of Inner.

7. All are true.

8. A and B   Local inner classes may not be declared public, protected, or private. They may implement interfaces.

9. C   An instance of Outer is accessed as Outer.this.

10. A   The display() method displays the s variable of the S1 class.

Suggested Readings and Resources

Gosling, James; Joy, Bill; and Steele, Guy, *The Java Language Specification*. Addison Wesley, 1996.

This chapter helps you to prepare for the exam by covering the following objectives:

Know what garbage collection is and how it is performed.

▶ You must know what garbage collection is and how it is performed to be able to think through exam questions related to this topic.

Know when an object is subject to garbage collection. State the behavior that is guaranteed by the garbage collection system and write code that explicitly makes objects eligible for collection.

▶ Several exam questions require you to know when an object is no longer being referenced and can be garbage collected. You'll be required to examine examples of program code and identify specific points within the code where an object becomes subject to garbage collection.

Know under which conditions finalization takes place.

▶ Finalization allows objects to perform cleanup operations before they are discarded. Knowledge of how finalization takes place is required to evaluate the behavior of code segments that appear in some exam questions.

CHAPTER 7

Garbage Collection

STUDY STRATEGIES

As you read through this chapter, you should
concentrate on the following key items:

▶ How the garbage collector works

▶ When is an object subject to garbage collection

▶ How is an object garbage collected

▶ What finalization is used for

▶ How finalization works

CHAPTER INTRODUCTION

This chapter addresses a very specific topic—garbage collection—and is very short. However, the concepts described in this chapter are important. You're very likely to see questions that require a solid understanding of garbage collection. This chapter provides you with the background you need to understand the Java garbage-collection mechanism. The review questions and exam questions at the end of this chapter will test your understanding and will give you an idea of the types of questions that you may see on the exam. The concepts presented in this chapter are easy to pick up. With a little study, you should be able to correctly answer all garbage-collection-related questions on the certification exam.

WHAT IS GARBAGE COLLECTION?

During the course of a Java program's (or applet's) execution, the program may create and use many different objects. Each object takes up some amount of valuable memory space and possibly other resources, such as windows or communication buffers. While the memory and other resources taken up by each individual object may be neglible, when viewed collectively, the resource drain may be significant. A program may become unable to perform its processing because it needs memory and operating system resources which are no longer available.

Garbage collection helps to solve this resource drain. It consists of the following activities:

◆ Monitoring the objects used by a program and determining when they are no longer needed.

◆ Informing selected objects that they are no longer in use and that they should release any nonmemory resources.

◆ Destroying objects that are no longer in use and reclaiming their resources.

Figure 7.1 summarizes the garbage-collection process. The following section describes how garbage collection is supported by Java.

NOTE

Applets and Garbage Collection
Although this chapter's discussion is oriented toward Java programs, it applies equally as well to Java applets. Just think of applets as special types of Java programs.

FIGURE 7.1

The garbage-collection process.

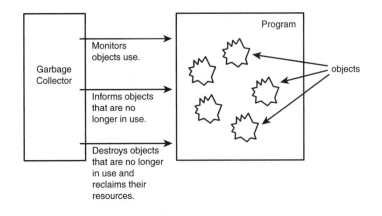

HOW DOES THE GARBAGE COLLECTOR WORK?

The Java garbage collector helps to recycle memory and other resources when they are no longer needed. It consists of a separate thread of execution that executes in the background and keeps track of all the objects that are used in a Java program. When an object is no longer needed, it becomes subject to garbage collection.

At this point, you are probably wondering what it means for an object to be no longer needed and how the garbage collector determines which objects are needed and which are not. An object is no longer needed by a program if it is no longer in use and cannot be brought back into use. The garbage collector determines that an object cannot be used if it is no longer *reachable* by the program. A reachable object is an object that can be accessed directly or indirectly through the variables that are currently available to the program.

The garbage collector keeps track of the objects that are created and used during a program's execution. It identifies all objects that can be accessed by the program and those that cannot. An object becomes *unreachable* and subject to garbage collection when it is no longer accessible to the program. I'll give you a concrete example of how this occurs and then come back to the general discussion.

Listing 7.1 shows the code for the GarbageDemo program. This program is designed to quickly use up all of your memory resources by creating increasingly longer arrays of increasingly longer String objects. The program takes an integer command-line argument which you can use to specify the amount of resources it uses. I set the default to 15, which allows the program to execute to completion when I run it under Windows 98 on a notebook with 96 megabytes of RAM. If your computer has less RAM, you may need to run the program with a value less than 15. Start at 14 and work backwards until your program is able to execute without running out of memory.

When I run the program on my computer, it displays the following output:

```
1 is being collected.
2 is being collected.
3 is being collected.
4 is being collected.
5 is being collected.
6 is being collected.
7 is being collected.
8 is being collected.
9 is being collected.
10 is being collected.
11 is being collected.
12 is being collected.
```

This output is displayed by the finalize() method of each Garbage object, indicating that the garbage collector has determined that the object has become unreachable. (The finalize() method is invoked on an object by the garbage collector so that the object may perform cleanup before it is reclaimed by the garbage collector.)

The above output indicates that 12 Garbage objects were being finalized by the garbage collector. These objects had become unreachable because they no longer were referenced by the g field variable of the GarbageDemo class. To understand how this happened, let's look at the run() method:

```
void run() {
  for(int i=1;i<max;++i) {
   g = new Garbage(i);
  }
 }
```

With each iteration of the for statement, a new Garbage object is created and assigned to the g variable. When a new object is assigned to the g variable, the previous object that was referenced by the g variable is no longer accessible by g or any other variable or object. Hence, that object becomes subject to garbage collection.

LISTING 7.1

GARBAGEDEMO.JAVA—AN EXAMPLE OF GARBAGE COLLECTION IN ACTION

```java
public class GarbageDemo {
 Garbage g;
 int max;
 public static void main(String[] args) {
  int n = 15;
  if(args.length > 0) n = (new Integer(args[0])).intValue();
  GarbageDemo app = new GarbageDemo(n);
  app.run();
 }
 public GarbageDemo(int n) {
  max = n;
 }
 void run() {
  for(int i=1;i<max;++i) {
   g = new Garbage(i);
  }
 }
}
class Garbage {
 String[] trash;
 int value;
 public Garbage(int n) {
  value = n;
  trash = new String[n];
  trash[0] = "This String uses up memory resources. ";
  for(int i=1;i<n;++i)
   trash[i] = trash[i-1] + trash[i-1];
 }
 protected void finalize() {
  System.out.println(value+" is being collected.");
 }
}
```

Having seen an example of garbage collection in action, let's take a look at how it works. Figure 7.2 summarizes the operation of the garbage collector. The garbage collector keeps track of all variables that are accessible to the program. These variables reference objects, which in turn may reference other objects, and so on. These are the set of reachable objects. An object becomes unreachable when it is no longer referenced by the program variables or reachable objects. When this happens it is subject to garbage collection.

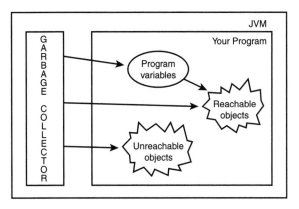

FIGURE 7.2
How the garbage collector works.

If an object is not reachable from a program variable or a reachable program
object then it is unreachable and subject to garbage collection.

WHEN IS AN OBJECT SUBJECT TO GARBAGE COLLECTION?

When an object becomes subject to garbage collection, it is not necessarily garbage collected immediately. It may, in fact, never be garbage collected. The program may terminate before the garbage collector gets around to reclaiming the object. Being subject to garbage collection simply means that an object is eligible to be reclaimed.

In the previous section, I displayed the results of running GarbageDemo on my computer. Note that only 12 objects had their finalize() method invoked by the garbage collector. What happened to Garbage(13) and Garbage(14)? Garbage(13) was subject to garbage collection, but the garbage collector never got around to invoking its finalize() method. Garbage(14) remained reachable until the program's termination.

The important point to remember about garbage collection is that an object becomes subject to garbage collection when it is no longer accessible. If and when the object is collected is subject to the garbage collector. Because the garbage collector runs asynchronously to your program (as a separate thread), there is no telling when it will execute, which unreachable objects it will reclaim, and when it will reclaim those objects.

Where in a program's execution does an object become subject to garbage collection? This occurs when the object becomes unreachable. If you are asked a multiple-choice, garbage-collection–related question that has an answer choice specifically stating when an object is actually collected, reject that answer. Garbage collection is non-determinable. There is no way of telling if and when an object will be collected.

How Is Finalization Performed?

The example of Listing 7.1 makes use of the finalize() method of the Garbage objects to indicate for which objects the garbage collector has initiated the garbage-collection process. An object's finalize() method is invoked by the garbage collector when it determines that the object has become unreachable.

The finalize() method is defined in the Object class. However, the Object implementation of finalize() performs no action. Classes override finalize() to perform cleanup prior to garbage collection. For example, a networking object may close down a TCP connection prior to garbage collection.

If an object becomes unreachable, there is no guarantee that the object's finalize() method will be invoked. However, if an object does have a finalize() method, this method will be invoked before the object is garbage collected. Figure 7.3 illustrates this fine point.

> **N O T E**
>
> **Finalization**   An object may invoke the finalize() method of its super-class to perform any required finalization.

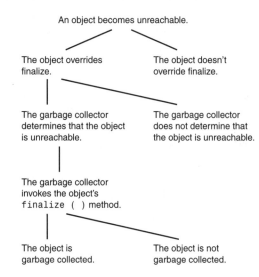

FIGURE 7.3

Reachability, finalization, and garbage collection.

When an object's finalize() method is invoked, the object may perform an action that will make the object reachable again. For example, the object may invoke a method that results in its being included in a Vector of reachable objects.

After the finalize() method has completed its processing and returned to the garbage collector, the garbage collector performs no reclamation processing until the garbage collector has again identified the object as being unreachable and subject to collection. At this point, the object is discarded, and its memory resources are reclaimed. Note that the finalize() method is never invoked more than once for a given object.

CHAPTER SUMMARY

This chapter described the operation of the garbage collector and covered the circumstances in which an object is subject to garbage collection. It explained the difference between being subject to garbage collection and having garbage collection actually performed. This chapter also covered finalization and explained how finalization fits into the garbage-collection process. You should now be prepared to test your knowledge of these subjects. The following review questions and exam questions will let you know how well you understand this material and will give you an idea of how you'll do in garbage-collection–specific exam questions. They'll also indicate which material you need to study further.

KEY TERMS

- Garbage collection
- Reachable
- Unreachable
- Finalization

APPLY YOUR KNOWLEDGE

Review Questions

1. What is the purpose of garbage collection?

2. When is an object subject to garbage collection?

3. How many times may an object's `finalize()` method be invoked?

4. Can an unreachable object become reachable again?

5. Under what conditions is an object's `finalize()` method invoked by the garbage collector?

6. What is the purpose of finalization?

7. Does garbage collection guarantee that a program will not run out of memory?

8. If an object is garbage collected, can it become reachable again?

9. Can an object be garbage collected while it is still reachable?

10. Can an object's `finalize()` method be invoked while it is reachable?

Exam Questions

1. At which line in the following code is the `Vector` object created in line 4 first subject to garbage collection?

```
1. import java.util.*;
2. public class Question {
3.   public static void main(String[] args) {
4.     Vector v1 = new Vector(); a
5.     Vector v2 = new Vector();
6.     v1.add("This");
7.     v1.add(v2);
8.     String s = (String) v1.elementAt(0);
9.     v1 = v2;
10.    v2 = v1;
11.    v1.add(s);
12. }
13.}
```

A. Line 5

B. Line 6

C. Line 8

D. Line 9

2. At which line in the following code is the `Vector` object, created in line 4, first subject to garbage collection?

```
1. import java.util.*;
2. public class Question {
3.   public static void main(String[] args) {
4.     Vector v1 = new Vector();
5.     Vector v2 = new Vector();
6.     v1 = null;
7.     Vector v3 = v1;
8.     v1 = v2;
9.     v1.add("This");
10.    v1.add(v2);
11.    String s = (String) v1.elementAt(0);
12.    v1 = v2;
13.    v2 = v1;
14.    v1.add(s);
15. }
16.}
```

A. Line 6

B. Line 7

C. Line 8

D. Line 12

3. How can you force an object to be garbage collected?

A. Invoke its `finalize()` method.

B. Remove all references to the object.

C. Use all memory that is available to the program.

D. You cannot force an object to be garbage collected.

APPLY YOUR KNOWLEDGE

4. If an object with a `finalize()` method has been garbage collected, which of the following are true about that object?

   A. The object became unreachable.

   B. The object's `finalize()` method was invoked by the garbage collector.

   C. The memory used by the object is subject to reuse.

   D. The object did not implement any interfaces.

5. Which of the following are true about an unreachable object?

   A. It will be garbage collected.

   B. Its `finalize()` method will be invoked.

   C. It can become reachable again.

   D. It has a `null` value.

6. Which of the following are true about the Java garbage collector as implemented by the Java 2 Platform?

   A. It guarantees that Java programs will never run out of memory.

   B. It executes as a low-priority, background thread.

   C. It keeps track of which objects are reachable and unreachable.

   D. It can be directed to garbage collect specific objects.

7. Which of the following are true about an object's `finalize()` method?

   A. It can be invoked multiple times by the garbage collector.

   B. If it is invoked, the object will be garbage collected.

   C. If the object has been garbage collected, its `finalize()` method has been invoked.

   D. It must perform cleanup operations.

Answers to Review Questions

1. The purpose of garbage collection is to identify and discard objects that are no longer needed by a program so that their resources may be reclaimed and reused.

2. An object is subject to garbage collection when it becomes unreachable to the program in which it is used.

3. An object's `finalize()` method may only be invoked once.

4. An unreachable object may become reachable again. This can happen when the object's `finalize()` method is invoked and the object performs an operation which causes it to become accessible to reachable objects.

5. The garbage collector invokes an object's `finalize()` method when it detects that the object has become unreachable.

6. The purpose of finalization is to give an unreachable object the opportunity to perform any cleanup processing before the object is garbage collected.

7. Garbage collection does not guarantee that a program will not run out of memory. It is possible for programs to use up memory resources faster than they are garbage collected. It is also possible for programs to create objects that are not subject to garbage collection. Try running the `GarbageDemo` program of Listing 7.1 with a command-line argument of 100.

APPLY YOUR KNOWLEDGE

8. Once an object is garbage collected, it ceases to exist. It can no longer become reachable again.

9. A reachable object cannot be garbage collected. Only unreachable objects may be garbage collected.

10. An object's `finalize()` method cannot be invoked by the garbage collector while the object is still reachable. However, an object's `finalize()` method may be invoked by other objects.

Answers to Exam Questions

1. D The object created in line 4 is assigned to the v1 variable up to line 9. At this point, a new object is assigned to the v1 variable, and the object created in line 4 is no longer accessible to the program.

2. A In line 6, the `null` value is assigned to the v1 variable. This causes the object created in line 4 to become unreachable.

3. D The garbage collector operates in a non-determined manner. It cannot be forced to garbage collect a specific object.

4. A, B, and C Only unreachable objects are garbage collected. If an object has a `finalize()` method, the garbage collector will invoke the object's `finalize()` method before garbage collecting the object. After an object has become garbage collected, its memory is subject to reuse.

5. C There's no guarantee that an unreachable object will be garbage collected or that its `finalize()` method will be invoked. However, an unreachable object can become reachable again. This can happen if the object makes itself accessible to other reachable objects when its `finalize()` method is invoked. There is no restriction that requires an unreachable object to have a `null` value.

6. B and C The garbage collector cannot prevent a program from running out of memory. It does, however, execute as a low-priority background thread and keep track of which objects are reachable and unreachable. It cannot be directed to garbage collect an object.

7. C An object's `finalize()` method may only be invoked once by the garbage collector. If an object's `finalize()` method is invoked, there is no guarantee that it will be garbage collected. However, if the object has been garbage collected, then its `finalize()` method must have been invoked. The purpose of the `finalize()` method is to perform cleanup operations prior to garbage collection. However, it is not required to do so.

Suggested Readings and Resources

Pawlan, Monica, *Reference Objects and Garbage Collection.* `http://developer.javasoft.com/developer/technicalArticles/monicap/RefObj/refobj.html`.

This chapter helps you to prepare for the exam by covering the following objectives:

Know what multithreading is and how it is implemented in Java.

▶ Java is a multithreaded language. You must know what multithreading is in order to develop programs and applets that take advantage of Java's multithreading capabilities. You also need to know this in order to answer exam questions related to this topic.

Know how threads are created and executed. Write code to define instantiate and start new threads using both `java.lang.Thread` and `java.lang.Runnable`.

▶ Several exam questions require you to know the different ways threads are created, how they are executed, and the methods they implement. You may be required to examine examples of program code and identify specific points within the code where threads are created and executed.

Know when and how thread scheduling takes place.

▶ Scheduling enables threads to share the processing resources of one or more CPUs. Knowledge of when and how threads are scheduled is required to evaluate the behavior of code segments that appear in some exam questions.

Recognize conditions that might prevent a thread from executing.

▶ Executing threads may perform actions that result in them entering a wait state. Other events may also cause a thread to wait. Some threads may be prevented from reentering a running state. Exam questions will test your knowledge of these topics.

CHAPTER 8

Threads

OBJECTIVES

Know how threads are synchronized. Write code using synchronized wait(), notify(), **and** notifyAll() **to protect against concurrent access problems and to communicate between threads. Define the interaction between threads and between threads and object locks when executing** synchronized wait(), notify(), **or** notifyAll().

▶ Synchronization allows threads to share information in a controlled manner. Without synchronization, multithreading would be dangerous at best. Several exam questions require you to know how synchronization is accomplished through object locks.

OUTLINE

As you read through this chapter, you should concentrate on the following key items:

▶ How multithreading works

▶ How threads are created

▶ How threads are executed

▶ How threads are scheduled

▶ What methods are used to control thread states

▶ How synchronization works

Chapter Introduction

This chapter covers the very important topic of Java threads. It describes how multithreading works and how Java supports multithreading, and explains thread-related topics, such as scheduling and synchronization. The concepts and techniques described in this chapter are important—you'll see questions that will test your understanding of threads on the certification exam. This chapter will provide you with the background you need to understand how threads work. The review questions and exam questions at the end of this chapter will test your understanding and will give you an idea of the types of questions that you may see on the exam. The concepts presented in this chapter can be complicated, especially if you are new to multithreading. However, by studying the material and questions presented in this chapter, you should be able to prepare for the thread-related questions that you'll see on the certification exam.

How Multithreading Works

Multithreaded programs support more than one concurrent thread of execution—that is, they are able to simultaneously execute multiple sequences of instructions. Each instruction sequence has its own unique flow of control that is independent of all others. These independently executed instruction sequences are known as *threads*.

If your computer has only a single CPU, you might be wondering how it can execute more than one thread at the same time. In single-processor systems, only a single thread of execution occurs at a given instant. The CPU quickly switches back and forth between several threads to create the illusion that the threads are executing at the same time. Single-processor systems support logical concurrency, not physical concurrency. Logical concurrency is the characteristic exhibited when multiple threads execute with separate, independent flows of control. On multiprocessor systems, several threads do, in fact, execute at the same time, and physical concurrency is achieved. The important feature of multithreaded programs is that they support logical concurrency, not that physical concurrency is actually achieved.

Many programming languages support multiprogramming. Multiprogramming is the logically concurrent execution of multiple programs. For example, a program can request that the operating system execute programs A, B, and C by having it spawn a separate process for each program. These programs can run in a parallel manner, depending upon the multiprogramming features supported by the underlying operating system. Multithreading differs from multiprogramming in that multithreading provides concurrency within the context of a single process, but multiprogramming also provides concurrency between processes. Threads are not complete processes in and of themselves. They are a separate flow of control that occurs within a process. Figure 8.1 illustrates the difference between multithreading and multiprogramming.

> **NOTE** **Processes** A process is the operating system object that is created when a program is executed.

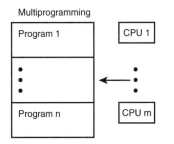

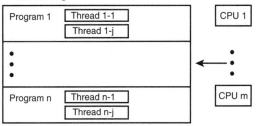

FIGURE 8.1

Multithreading versus multiprogramming.

The advantage of multithreading is that concurrency can be used within a process to implement multiple instances of simultaneous services. Multithreading also requires less processing overhead than multiprogramming because concurrent threads are able to share common resources more effectively. An example of a multithreaded application is a multithreaded Web server, which is able to efficiently handle multiple browser requests—one request per each processing thread.

CREATING THREADS

Java, unlike many other programming languages, provides native support for multithreading. This support is centered around the `java.lang.Thread` class, the `java.lang.Runnable` interface, and methods of the `java.lang.Object` class. Support is also provided through `synchronized` methods and statements.

The `Thread` class provides the capability to create objects of class `Thread`, each with their own separate flow of control. The `Thread` class encapsulates the data and methods associated with separate threads of execution and enables multithreading to be integrated within Java's object-oriented framework. The minimal multithreading support required of the `Thread` class (or other classes that support multithreading) is specified by the `java.lang.Runnable` interface. This interface defines an important method—the `run()` method—which provides the entry point for a separate thread of execution. The `Object` class supports multithreading through the `wait()`, `notify()`, and `notifyAll()` methods. These methods allow threads to suspend their execution to wait for processing resources and to be informed when to resume execution as the resources become available. Other classes of the `java.lang` package, such as `ThreadGroup`, also support multithreading.

Java provides two approaches to creating threads. In the first approach, you create a subclass of class `Thread` and override the `run()` method to provide an entry point into the thread's execution. When you create an instance of your `Thread` subclass, you invoke its `start()` method to cause the thread to execute as an independent sequence of instructions. The `start()` method is inherited from the `Thread` class. It initializes the `Thread` object, using your operating system's multithreading capabilities, and invokes the `run()` method. Listing 8.1 provides an example of creating threads in this manner. When I run the program on my computer, it displays the following output:

```
thread2: Java
thread1: Java
thread2: is
thread1: is
thread2: hot,
thread1: hot,
thread1: aromatic,
thread2: aromatic,
thread2: and
```

NOTE

Java API Documentation This chapter makes heavy use of the Java API methods defined for class `Thread`, `Throwable`, and `Object`. If you haven't obtained and installed a copy of the Java API documentation, now is a good time to do so. The API documentation is available at JavaSoft's Web site, `http://www.javasoft.com`.

```
thread1: and
thread2: invigorating.
Thread 2 is dead.
thread1: invigorating.
Thread 1 is dead.
```

The above output shows how two threads execute in sequence, displaying information to the console window. The program creates two threads of execution, thread1 and thread2, from the MyThread class. It then starts both threads and executes a do statement that waits for the threads to die. The threads display the Java is hot, aromatic, and invigorating. message word by word, while waiting a short, random amount of time between each word. Because both threads share the console window, the program's output identifies which threads wrote to the console at various times during the program's execution.

LISTING 8.1

THREAD1.JAVA—SUBCLASSING THE THREAD CLASS

```
class Thread1 extends Thread {
 static String message[] =
{"Java","is","hot,","aromatic,","and",
  "invigorating."};
 public static void main(String args[]) {
  Thread1 thread1 = new Thread1("thread1: ");
  Thread1 thread2 = new Thread1("thread2: ");
  thread1.start();
  thread2.start();
  boolean thread1IsAlive = true;
  boolean thread2IsAlive = true;
  do {
   if(thread1IsAlive && !thread1.isAlive()){
    thread1IsAlive = false;
    System.out.println("Thread 1 is dead.");
   }
   if(thread2IsAlive && !thread2.isAlive()){
    thread2IsAlive = false;
    System.out.println("Thread 2 is dead.");
   }
  }while(thread1IsAlive ¦¦ thread2IsAlive);
 }
 public Thread1(String id) {
  super(id);
 }
 public void run() {
  String name = getName();
```

continues

LISTING 8.1   *continued*

THREAD1.JAVA—SUBCLASSING THE THREAD CLASS

```
    for(int i=0;i<message.length;++i) {
      randomWait();
      System.out.println(name+message[i]);
    }
  }
  void randomWait(){
    try {
      sleep((long)(3000*Math.random()));
    }catch (InterruptedException x){
      System.out.println("Interrupted!");
    }
  }
}
```

The approach to creating threads shown in Listing 8.1 is very simple and straightforward. However, it has the drawback of requiring your `Thread` objects to be under the `Thread` class in the class hierarchy. In some cases, such as applets, this requirement can be somewhat limiting.

Java's other approach to creating threads does not limit the location of your `Thread` objects within the class hierarchy. In this approach, your class implements the `java.lang.Runnable` interface. The `Runnable` interface consists of a single method, the `run()` method, which must be overridden by your class. The `run()` method provides an entry point into your thread's execution. In order to run an object of your class as an independent thread, you pass it as an argument to a constructor of class `Thread`. Listing 8.2 shows how this is done.

LISTING 8.2

THREAD2.JAVA—IMPLEMENTING RUNNABLE

```
class Thread2 {
  public static void main(String args[]) {
    Thread thread1 = new Thread(new MyClass("thread1: "));
    Thread thread2 = new Thread(new MyClass("thread2: "));
    thread1.start();
    thread2.start();
```

```
 boolean thread1IsAlive = true;
 boolean thread2IsAlive = true;
 do {
  if(thread1IsAlive && !thread1.isAlive()){
   thread1IsAlive = false;
   System.out.println("Thread 1 is dead.");
  }
  if(thread2IsAlive && !thread2.isAlive()){
   thread2IsAlive = false;
   System.out.println("Thread 2 is dead.");
  }
 }while(thread1IsAlive || thread2IsAlive);
 }
}
class MyClass implements Runnable {
 static String message[] =
 ➡{"Java","is","hot,","aromatic,","and",
  "invigorating."};
 String name;
 public MyClass(String id) {
  name = id;
 }
 public void run() {
  for(int i=0;i<message.length;++i) {
   randomWait();
   System.out.println(name+message[i]);
  }
 }
 void randomWait(){
  try {
   Thread.currentThread().sleep((long)(3000*Math.random()));
  }catch (InterruptedException x){
   System.out.println("Interrupted!");
  }
 }
}
```

The Thread2 program is very similar to Thread1. It even displays the same ouput when I run it on my computer. Thread2 differs from Thread1 only in the way that the threads are created.

Because these two examples are so similar, you might be wondering why you would pick one approach to creating a class over another. The advantage of using the Runnable interface is that your class does not need to extend the Thread class. This is a very helpful feature when you create multithreaded applets. The only disadvantage to this approach is that you have to do a little more work to create and execute your threads.

THREAD STATES

In the discussion of Listings 8.1 and 8.2, I referred to threads as being *dead* when their processing had completed. I wasn't trying to be morose. This is the standard Java term for referring to that state of a thread's execution. After a thread reaches the dead state, it can't be restarted. The thread still exists as an object (that is as a Thread or Runnable object), it just doesn't execute as a separate thread of execution.

Threads have several other well-defined states in addition to the dead state. These states are

- ◆ Ready—When a thread is first created, it doesn't begin executing immediately. You must first invoke its start() method, and then the thread scheduler must allocate it CPU time. A thread may also enter the ready state if, after previously executing, it stopped for a while and then became ready to resume its execution.

- ◆ Running—Threads are born to run. A thread is in the running state when it is actually executing. It may leave this state for a number of reasons, which we'll cover in this section and next section.

- ◆ Waiting—A running thread may perform a number of actions that will cause it to wait. A common example is when the thread performs some type of input or output operation. In Listings 8.1 and 8.2, threads are waiting because they invoked their sleep() methods.

In general, a thread is either ready, running, waiting, or dead. Figure 8.2 shows the interaction between these states.

A thread begins as a ready thread and then enters the running state when it is scheduled by the thread scheduler. The thread may be preempted by other threads and returned to the ready state, or it may wait on a resource, object lock, or simply go to sleep. When this happens, the thread enters the waiting state. To run again, the thread must enter the ready state. Eventually, the thread will cease its execution and enter the dead state.

FIGURE 8.2

Interaction between thread states.

SCHEDULING

After examining the thread state diagram shown in Figure 8.2, you may wonder exactly what causes a thread to move from one state to another. In this section, we'll look at how threads move between the ready and running state. In later sections, we'll look at movement in and out of the waiting state.

A thread moves back and forth between the ready and running state because multithreading requires multiple threads to share execution time with each other, based on the availability of the system's CPU (or CPUs). The approach used to determine which threads should execute at a given time is referred to as scheduling. Scheduling is performed by the Java runtime system. It schedules threads based on their priority. Higher priority threads are run before lower priority threads. Threads of equal priority have an equal chance of running. While the above rules guide thread scheduling, the actual details of thread scheduling are platform-dependent.

Most operating systems support one of two common approaches to thread scheduling:

◆ Preemptive scheduling—The highest priority thread continues to execute unless it dies, waits, or is preempted by a higher priority thread coming into existence. The latter can occur as the result of a thread lowering its priority or creating a higher priority thread.

◆ Time slicing—A thread executes for a specific slice of time and then enters the ready state. At this point, the thread scheduler determines whether it should return the thread to the ready state or schedule a different thread.

Both approaches have their advantages and disadvantages. Preemptive scheduling is more predictable. However, its disadvantage is that a higher priority thread could execute forever, preventing lower priority threads from executing. The time slicing approach is less predictable but better able to handle selfish threads. Windows and Macintosh implementations of Java follow a time slicing approach. Solaris and other Unix implementations follow a preemptive scheduling approach.

NOTE

Thread Priority   A thread's *priority* is an integer value between `MIN_PRIORITY` and `MAX_PRIORITY`. These constants are defined in the `Thread` class. A thread's priority is set when it is created. It is set to the same priority as the thread that created it. The default priority of a thread is `NORM_PRIORITY`. The priority of a thread can be changed using the `setPriority()` method.

NOTE

Yielding   The simplest way for a running thread to enter the ready state is for it to invoke its `yield()` method. The `yield()` method is a `static` method of the `Thread` class. When a thread invokes its `yield()` method, it simply returns to the ready state. It then returns to the running state at the discretion of the thread scheduler.

SLEEPING AND WAKING

As shown in Listings 8.1 and 8.2, a thread can enter the waiting state by invoking its sleep() method. The sleep() method, like the yield() method, is a static method of the Thread class. It takes a millisecond time value and an optional nanosecond time value as arguments. When a thread invokes its sleep() method, it enters the waiting state. It returns to the ready state after the specified time has expired.

It is possible for another thread to awaken a sleeping thread by invoking the sleeping thread's interrupt() method. The sleeping thread then enters the ready state. When it reenters the running state, execution continues with the thread's InterruptedException handler.

STOPPING, SUSPENDING, AND RESUMING

Prior to JDK 1.2, it was possible for one thread to stop or suspend the execution of another thread (or itself). The stop(), suspend(), and resume() methods have been identified as problematic and are deprecated in JDK 1.2.

BLOCKING ON I/O

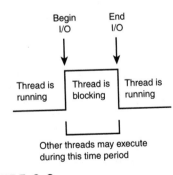

FIGURE 8.3
Blocking on I/O.

A thread may also enter the waiting state as the result of performing an input/output operation. I/O operations, such as disk writes or socket reads, are slow when compared to the execution speed of a CPU. While one thread waits for an I/O operation to complete, it is possible for other threads to perform quite a bit of processing. This is illustrated in Figure 8.3. When a thread performs an I/O operation, it enters the waiting state. It remains in the waiting state until the I/O operation is completed. The thread is said to be blocked on I/O or blocking on I/O. When the I/O operation is completed, the thread transitions to the ready state.

SYNCHRONIZATION

There are many situations in which multiple threads must share access to common objects. For example, Listings 8.1 and 8.2 illustrate the effects of multithreading by having multiple executing threads write to the Java console, a common shared object. These examples do not require any coordination or synchronization in the way the threads access the console window: Whichever thread is currently executing is able to write to the console window.

There are times when you might want to coordinate access to shared resources. For example, in a database system, you might not want one thread to be updating a database record while another thread is trying to read it. Java enables you to coordinate the actions of multiple threads using synchronized methods and synchronized statements. I'll cover synchronized methods first, and then synchronized statements.

Synchronized methods are used to coordinate access to objects that are shared among multiple threads. These methods are declared with the synchronized keyword. Only one synchronized method can be invoked for an object at a given point in time. This keeps synchronized methods in multiple threads from conflicting with each other.

All classes and objects are associated with a unique lock. The lock is used to control the way in which synchronized methods are allowed to access the class or object. When a synchronized method is invoked for a given object, it tries to *acquire* the lock for that object. If it succeeds, no other synchronized method may be invoked for that object until the lock is released. A lock is automatically released when the method completes its execution and returns. A lock may also be released when a synchronized method executes certain methods, such as wait(). We'll cover the wait() method in a later section.

The following example shows how synchronized methods and object locks are used to coordinate access to a common object by multiple threads. This example adapts the Thread1 program for use with synchronized methods, as shown in Listing 8.3.

> **NOTE**
>
> **Class Locks** Although we speak of a lock on a class, technically a class lock is a lock that is acquired on the class's Class object.

> **NOTE**
>
> **Locks and States** When a thread is waiting for a lock on an object, the thread leaves the running state and enters the waiting state. When the thread acquires the lock on the object, it moves from the waiting state to the ready state.

LISTING 8.3

USING Synchronized METHODS

```
class Thread3 extends Thread {
 static String message[] =
 ➥{"Java","is","hot,","aromatic,","and",
 "invigorating."};
 public static void main(String args[]) {
 Thread3 thread1 = new Thread3("thread1: ");
 Thread3 thread2 = new Thread3("thread2: ");
 thread1.start();
 thread2.start();
 boolean thread1IsAlive = true;
 boolean thread2IsAlive = true;
 do {
  if(thread1IsAlive && !thread1.isAlive()){
   thread1IsAlive = false;
   System.out.println("Thread 1 is dead.");
  }
  if(thread2IsAlive && !thread2.isAlive()){
   thread2IsAlive = false;
   System.out.println("Thread 2 is dead.");
  }
 }while(thread1IsAlive ¦¦ thread2IsAlive);
 }
 public Thread3(String id) {
 super(id);
 }
 public void run() {
 SynchronizedOutput.displayList(getName(),message);
 }
 void randomWait(){
  try {
  sleep((long)(3000*Math.random()));
  }catch (InterruptedException x){
  System.out.println("Interrupted!");
  }
 }
}
class SynchronizedOutput {
 public static synchronized void
  displayList(String name,String list[]) {
 for(int i=0;i<list.length;++i) {
  Thread3 t = (Thread3) Thread.currentThread();
  t.randomWait();
  System.out.println(name+list[i]);
 }
 }
}
```

Here are the results of an example run on my system:

```
thread1: Java
thread1: is
thread1: hot,
thread1: aromatic,
thread1: and
thread1: invigorating.
Thread 1 is dead.
thread2: Java
thread2: is
thread2: hot,
thread2: aromatic,
thread2: and
thread2: invigorating.
Thread 2 is dead.
```

Now edit Thread3.java and delete the synchronized keyword in the declaration of the displayList() method of class SynchronizedOutput. It should look like this when you are finished:

```
class SynchronizedOutput {
  public static void displayList(String name,String
  ➥list[]) {
```

Save Thread3.java, recompile it, and rerun it with the change in place. You may now get output similar to this:

```
thread2: Java
thread1: Java
thread1: is
thread2: is
thread2: hot,
thread1: hot,
thread2: aromatic,
thread1: aromatic,
thread2: and
thread2: invigorating.
Thread 2 is dead.
thread1: and
thread1: invigorating.
Thread 1 is dead.
```

The difference in the program's output should give you a feel for the effects of synchronization upon multithreaded program execution.

What difference does the fact that displayList() is synchronized have on the program's execution? When displayList() is not synchronized, it may be invoked by one thread (for example thread1), display some output, and wait while thread2 executes. When

N O T E

Static Synchronized Methods
Methods that are declared as both static and synchronized must acquire the lock on their **class** (their class's Class object) before they are allowed to execute. That's because static methods operate on their class as a whole rather than on instances of their class.

thread2 executes, it too invokes displayList() to display some output. Two separate invocations of displayList(), one for thread1 and the other for thread2, execute concurrently. This explains the mixed output display.

When the synchronized keyword is used, thread1 invokes displayList() and acquires a lock for the SynchronizedOutput class (because displayList() is a static method). After this, displayList() proceeds with the output display for thread1. Because thread1 acquired a lock for the SynchronizedOutput class, thread2 must wait until the lock is released before it is able to invoke displayList() to display its output. This explains why one task's output is completed before the other's.

The synchronized Statement

The synchronized statement is similar to a synchronized method in that it is used to acquire a lock on an object before performing an action. The synchronized statement differs from a synchronized method in that it can be used with the lock of any object—the synchronized method can only be used with its object's (or class's) lock. It also differs in that it applies to a statement block, rather than an entire method. The syntax of the synchronized statement is as follows:

```
synchronized (object) {
  statement(s)
}
```

The statements enclosed by the braces are only executed when the current thread acquires the lock for the object or class enclosed by parentheses. Listing 8.4 shows how the synchronized statement may be used in this chapter's extended example.

LISTING 8.4

USING THE Synchronized STATEMENT

```
class Thread4 extends Thread {
 static String message[] =
➥{"Java","is","hot,","aromatic,","and",
  "invigorating."};
 public static void main(String args[]) {
  Thread4 thread1 = new Thread4("thread1: ");
  Thread4 thread2 = new Thread4("thread2: ");
```

```
   thread1.start();
   thread2.start();
   boolean thread1IsAlive = true;
   boolean thread2IsAlive = true;
   do {
    if(thread1IsAlive && !thread1.isAlive()){
     thread1IsAlive = false;
     System.out.println("Thread 1 is dead.");
    }
    if(thread2IsAlive && !thread2.isAlive()){
     thread2IsAlive = false;
     System.out.println("Thread 2 is dead.");
    }
   }while(thread1IsAlive || thread2IsAlive);
  }
  public Thread4(String id) {
   super(id);
  }
  public void run() {
   synchronized(System.out) {
    for(int i=0;i<message.length;++i) {
     randomWait();
     System.out.println(getName()+message[i]);
    }
   }
  }
  void randomWait(){
   try {
    sleep((long)(3000*Math.random()));
   }catch (InterruptedException x){
    System.out.println("Interrupted!");
   }
  }
}
```

WAITING AND NOTIFYING

The wait(), notify(), and notifyAll() methods of the Object class
are used to provide an efficient way for threads to wait for resources.
They also provide additional synchronization support. These methods are used to implement a synchronization scheme where threads
that have acquired an object's (or class's) lock, wait until they are
notified that access to the object is permitted. The wait(), notify()
and notifyAll() methods provide you with finer control over shared
resources. They enable you to place threads in a waiting pool until
resources become available to satisfy the threads' requests. A separate
resource monitor or controller process can be used to notify waiting
threads that they are able to execute.

When a thread has acquired an object's lock, either through a syn-chronized method or a synchronized statement, the thread invokes the object's wait() method. This causes the thread to lose the object's lock and enter the waiting state. It is possible for several threads to be waiting as the result of invoking an object's wait() method. These threads are referred to as the waiting pool.

A thread typically invokes an object's wait() method by invoking a synchronized method of the object. The call to wait() is embedded in the synchronized method. For example, a service-providing object would provide a method of the following form:

```
public synchronized returnType requestService(parameters) {
 while(resourceNotAvailable) {
  wait();
 }
 // Perform service
}
```

When another thread acquires the object's lock and invokes the object's notify() method, one of the waiting threads is returned to the ready state. (The notifyAll() method is used to return all of the threads in the waiting pool to the ready state.) When a waiting thread reenters the running state, it reacquires the lock on the object and can then continue its processing.

Listing 8.5 shows how the wait() and notify() methods are used to control access to a shared resource. A Resource object is shared among a Controller object and several User objects. The Resource object provides access to the console display. The User objects execute as separate threads and use the Resource object to display their output. The Controller object also executes as a separate thread and controls access to the Resource object, making it available for output every 10 seconds.

The displayOutput() method of the Resource object displays a mes-sage on the console when okToSend is true. If a User thread invokes displayOutput() when okToSend is false, it enters the waiting pool. The allowOutput() method of Resource is periodically invoked by the Controller to allow a User thread to exit the waiting pool and display output via the Resource object.

Note that the wait() method, like the sleep() method of the Thread class, throws the InterruptedException. This exception is thrown when a thread's interrupt() method is invoked while it is in the waiting state.

LISTING 8.5

USING wait() AND notify() TO CONTROL ACCESS TO A SHARED RESOURCE

```java
class Thread5 {
 public static void main(String args[]) {
  Resource resource = new Resource();
  Thread controller = new Thread(new Controller(resource));
  Thread[] user = new Thread[3];
  for(int i=0;i<user.length;++i)
   user[i] = new Thread(new User(i,resource));
  controller.start();
  for(int i=0;i<user.length;++i)
   user[i].start();
  boolean alive;
  out: do {
   alive = false;
   for(int i=0;i<user.length;++i)
    alive |= user[i].isAlive();
   Thread.currentThread().yield();
  } while(alive);
  controller.interrupt();
 }
}
class Resource {
 boolean okToSend = false;
 public synchronized void displayOutput(int id,String[]
➥message) {
  try{
   while(!okToSend) {
    wait();
   }
   okToSend = false;
   for(int i=0;i<message.length;++i) {
    Thread.currentThread().sleep((long)1000);
     System.out.println(id+": "+message[i]);
   }
  }catch(InterruptedException ex){
  }
 }
 public synchronized void allowOutput() {
  okToSend = true;
  notify();
 }
}
class Controller implements Runnable {
 Resource resource;
 public Controller(Resource resource) {
  this.resource = resource;
 }
 public void run() {
  try{
   while(true) {
```

continues

N O T E **Class Synchronization**   A thread may synchronize on a class as well as an object of a class.

| **LISTING 8.5** | *continued* |

USING wait() AND notify() TO CONTROL ACCESS TO A SHARED RESOURCE

```
        Thread.currentThread().sleep((long)10000);
        resource.allowOutput();
      }
    }catch(InterruptedException ex){
    }
  }
}
class User implements Runnable {
  static String message[] =
➥{"Java","is","hot,","aromatic,","and",
  "invigorating."};
  int id;
  Resource resource;
  public User(int id,Resource resource) {
    this.id = id;
    this.resource = resource;
  }
  public void run() {
    resource.displayOutput(id,message);
  }
}
```

CHAPTER SUMMARY

KEY TERMS

- Multithreading
- Thread state
- Scheduling
- Shared resource
- Synchronization
- Object lock

This chapter described how multithreading works, and how multithreading is supported by Java. It also covered the thread-related topics of scheduling and synchronization. It explained how thread prority is used to determine which thread is executed. It also explained how object locks are used to control access to shared resources. You should now be prepared to test your knowledge of these topics. The following review questions and exam questions will let you know how well you understand this material and will give you an idea of how you'll do in thread-related exam questions. They'll also indicate which material you need to study further.

APPLY YOUR KNOWLEDGE

Review Questions

1. How does multithreading take place on a computer with a single CPU?

2. What are the two basic ways in which classes that can be run as threads may be defined?

3. What method must be implemented by all threads?

4. What method is invoked to cause an object to begin executing as a separate thread?

5. What invokes a thread's run() method?

6. What are the high-level thread states?

7. When a thread is created and started, what is its initial state?

8. What state is a thread in when it is executing?

9. When a thread blocks on I/O, what state does it enter?

10. What state does a thread enter when it terminates its processing?

11. How can a dead thread be restarted?

12. What are three ways in which a thread can enter the waiting state?

13. What is a task's priority and how is it used in scheduling?

14. What is the difference between preemptive scheduling and time slicing?

15. What is the difference between yielding and sleeping?

16. What happens when you invoke a thread's interrupt method while it is sleeping or waiting?

17. What's new with the stop(), suspend() and resume() methods in JDK 1.2?

18. Why do threads block on I/O?

19. What is synchronization and why is it important?

20. What is an object's lock and which object's have locks?

21. Can a lock be acquired on a class?

22. What are synchronized methods and synchronized statements?

23. What happens when a thread cannot acquire a lock on an object?

24. What is the purpose of the wait(), notify(), and notifyAll() methods?

Exam Questions

1. Which of the following are true?

   A. Multithreading is unique to Java.

   B. Multithreading requires more than one CPU.

   C. Multithreading requires that a computer have a single CPU.

   D. Multithreading is supported by Java.

2. How can a class that is run as a thread be defined?

   A. By subclassing the Thread class.

   B. By implementing the Throwable interface.

   C. By implementing the Multithread interface.

   D. By implementing the Runnable interface.

APPLY YOUR KNOWLEDGE

3. The `Runnable` interface declares which methods?

   A. `start()`

   B. `run()`

   C. `stop()`

   D. `yield()`

4. Given an object t that implements `Runnable`, which method of the `Thread` class should you invoke to cause t to be executed as a separate thread?

   A. `start()`

   B. `init()`

   C. `run()`

   D. `main()`

5. Which of the following are thread states?

   A. ready

   B. running

   C. open

   D. waiting

   E. dead

   F. unwound

6. Which of the following thread state transitions are valid?

   A. From ready to running.

   B. From running to ready.

   C. From running to waiting.

   D. From waiting to running.

   E. From waiting to ready.

   F. From ready to waiting.

7. When a thread blocks on I/O, which of the following are true?

   A. The thread enters the ready state.

   B. The thread enters the dead state.

   C. No other thread may perform I/O.

   D. The thread enters the waiting state.

8. Which of the following are true about a dead thread?

   A. The thread's object is discarded.

   B. The thread must wait until all other threads execute before it is restarted.

   C. The thread cannot be restarted.

   D. The thread is `synchronized`.

9. Which of the following are true?

   A. Java only supports preemptive scheduling.

   B. Java only supports time slicing.

   C. The JVM has been implemented on operating systems that use time slicing.

   D. The JVM has been implemented on operating systems that use preemptive scheduling.

10. Which of the following are true?

   A. The `sleep()` method puts a thread in the ready state.

   B. The `yield()` method puts a thread in the waiting state.

   C. The `suspend()` method is the preferred method for stopping a thread's execution.

   D. A thread's `interrupt()` method results in the throwing of the `InterruptedException`.

APPLY YOUR KNOWLEDGE

11. Which of the following are true?

    A. Only threads have locks.

    B. Classes have locks.

    C. Primitive types have locks.

    D. Only Runnable objects have locks.

12. Which of the following are true?

    A. The Thread class inherits the wait() and notify() methods.

    B. The Object class declares the wait() and notify() methods.

    C. Only the Synchronized class supports the wait() and notify() methods.

    D. The wait() and notify() methods have been deprecated in JDK 1.2.

13. Which of the following lines of output are displayed by the following program?

```
class Question {
 public static void main(String args[]) {
  MyThread t = new MyThread();
  t.displayOutput("t has been created.");
  t.start();
 }
}
class MyThread extends Thread {
 public void displayOutput(String s) {
  System.out.println(s);
 }
 public void run() {
  displayOutput("t is running.");
 }
}
```

    A. t has been created.

    B. t is running.

C. The program will display different output depending on whether the underlying operating system supports preemptive scheduling or time slicing.

D. None of the above. The program does not compile.

14. Which of the following are true about the following program?

```
class Question {
 public static void main(String args[]) {
  MyThread t1 = new MyThread("t1");
  MyThread t2 = new MyThread("t2");
  t1.start();
  t2.start();
 }
}
class MyThread extends Thread {
 public void displayOutput(String s) {
  System.out.println(s);
 }
 public void run() {
  for(int i=0;i<10;++i) {
   try {
    sleep((long)(3000*Math.random()));
   }catch(Exception ex) {
   }
   displayOutput(getName());
  }
 }
 public MyThread(String s) {
  super(s);
 }
}
```

A. The program always displays t1 10 times, followed by t2 10 times.

B. The program always displays t1 followed by t2.

C. The program displays no output.

D. The output sequence will vary from computer to computer.

APPLY YOUR KNOWLEDGE

15. Which of the following are true about the following program?

```java
class Question {
 public static void main(String args[]) {
  MyThread t1 = new MyThread("t1");
  MyThread t2 = new MyThread("t2");
  t1.start();
  t2.start();
 }
}
class MyThread extends Thread {
 public static Resource resource = new
 ➥Resource();
 public void run() {
  for(int i=0;i<10;++i) {
   resource.displayOutput(getName());
  }
 }
 public MyThread(String s) {
  super(s);
 }
}
class Resource {
 public Thread controller;
 boolean okToSend = false;
 public synchronized void
 ➥displayOutput(String s) {
  try{
   while(!okToSend) {
    wait();
   }
   okToSend = false;
   System.out.println(s);
  }catch(InterruptedException ex){
  }
 }
 public synchronized void allowOutput() {
  okToSend = true;
  notifyAll();
 }
 public Resource() {
  Thread controller = new Thread(new
  ➥Controller(this));
  controller.start();
 }
}
class Controller implements Runnable {
 Resource resource;
 public Controller(Resource resource) {
  this.resource = resource;
 }
```

```java
 public void run() {
  try{
   for(int i=0;i<100;++i) {
    Thread.currentThread().sleep(2000);
    resource.allowOutput();
   }
  }catch(InterruptedException ex){
  }
 }
}
```

A. The program always displays t1 10 times, followed by t2 10 times.

B. The program always displays t1 followed by t2.

C. The program displays no output.

D. The output sequence will vary from computer to computer.

Answers to Review Questions

1. The operating system's task scheduler allocates execution time to multiple tasks. By quickly switching between executing tasks, it creates the impression that tasks execute sequentially.

2. A thread class may be declared as a subclass of Thread, or it may implement the Runnable interface.

3. All tasks must implement the run() method, whether they are a subclass of Thread or implement the Runnable interface.

4. The start() method of the Thread class is invoked to cause an object to begin executing as a separate thread.

5. After a thread is started, via its start() method or that of the Thread class, the JVM invokes the thread's run() method when the thread is initially executed.

APPLY YOUR KNOWLEDGE

6. The high-level thread states are ready, running, waiting, and dead.

7. A thread is in the ready state after it has been created and started.

8. An executing thread is in the running state.

9. A thread enters the waiting state when it blocks on I/O.

10. When a thread terminates its processing, it enters the dead state.

11. A dead thread cannot be restarted.

12. A thread can enter the waiting state by invoking its `sleep()` method, by blocking on I/O, by unsuccessfully attempting to acquire an object's lock, or by invoking an object's `wait()` method. It can also enter the waiting state by invoking its (deprecated) `suspend()` method.

13. A task's priority is an integer value that identifies the relative order in which it should be executed with respect to other tasks. The scheduler attempts to schedule higher priority tasks before lower priority tasks.

14. Under preemptive scheduling, the highest priority task executes until it enters the waiting or dead states or a higher priority task comes into existence. Under time slicing, a task executes for a predefined slice of time and then reenters the pool of ready tasks. The scheduler then determines which task should execute next, based on priority and other factors.

15. When a task invokes its `yield()` method, it returns to the ready state. When a task invokes its `sleep()` method, it returns to the waiting state.

16. When a task's `interrupt()` method is executed, the task enters the ready state. The next time the task enters the running state, an `InterruptedException` is thrown.

17. The `stop()`, `suspend()` and `resume()` methods have been deprecated in JDK 1.2.

18. Threads block on I/O (that is enters the waiting state) so that other threads may execute while the I/O operation is performed.

19. With respect to multithreading, synchronization is the capability to control the access of multiple threads to shared resources. Without synchronization, it is possible for one thread to modify a shared object while another thread is in the process of using or updating that object's value. This often leads to significant errors.

20. An object's lock is a mechanism that is used by multiple threads to obtain synchronized access to the object. A thread may execute a synchronized method of an object only after it has acquired the object's lock. All objects and classes have locks. A class's lock is acquired on the class's `Class` object.

21. Yes, a lock can be acquired on a class. This lock is acquired on the class's `Class` object.

22. Synchronized methods are methods that are used to control access to an object. A thread only executes a `synchronized` method after it has acquired the lock for the method's object or class. Synchronized statements are similar to `synchronized` methods. A `synchronized` statement can only be executed after a thread has acquired the lock for the object or class referenced in the `synchronized` statement.

APPLY YOUR KNOWLEDGE

23. If a thread attempts to execute a `synchronized` method or `synchronized` statement and is unable to acquire an object's lock, it enters the waiting state until the lock becomes available.

24. The `wait()`, `notify()`, and `notifyAll()` methods are used to provide an efficient way for threads to wait for a shared resource. When a thread executes an object's `wait()` method, it enters the waiting state. It only enters the ready state after another thread invokes the object's `notify()` or `notifyAll()` methods.

Answers to Exam Questions

1. D   Multithreading is not unique to Java and can be implemented on systems with one or more CPUs.

2. A and D   Subclassing `Thread` and implementing `Runnable` are the two approached to creating a thread class.

3. B   The `run()` method is the only method declared by `Runnable`.

4. A   The `start()` method is used to execute an object as a separate thread.

5. A, B, D, and E   Thread states are ready, running, waiting, and dead.

6. A, B, C, E   Threads do not transition from waiting to running or ready to waiting.

7. D   Threads enter the waiting state when they block on I/O.

8. C   Dead threads may not be restarted.

9. C and D   Solaris supports preemptive scheduling, and Windows supports time slicing.

10. D   The `interrupt()` method results in the throwing of the `InterruptedException` when an interrupted thread enters the running state.

11. B   Classes have locks, but primitive types do not.

12. A and B   A follows from B.

13. A and B   Both A and B are displayed.

14. D   The output may vary because it is not `synchronized`.

15. D   The output is only `synchronized` one line at a time.

Suggested Readings and Resources

Gosling, James; Joy, Bill; and Steele, Guy, *The Java Language Specification*. Addison Wesley, 1996.

This chapter helps you to prepare for the exam by covering the following objectives:

Know the important classes and interfaces provided by the `java.lang` package.

▶ The `java.lang` package is the main Java API package. It provides the fundamental classes and interfaces, such as `Object`, `Class` and `System`, upon which the rest of the Java API is built. You need to know how these classes and interfaces are used in order to answer several exam questions.

Know what the wrapped classes are and how they are used.

▶ Several exam questions require you to be familiar with the `java.lang` classes that are used to represent primitive values as objects. You need to know how to create object wrappers for primitive types, what methods the wrapped classes support, and how to convert from wrapped objects back to primitive values.

Know the differences between the `String` and `StringBuffer` classes. Describe the significance of the immutability of String objects.

▶ Several exam questions require knowledge of the `String` and `StringBuffer` classes. To correctly answer these exam questions, you need to know the relationships between these classes and the types of methods that they support.

Know how the methods of the `Math` class are used to perform mathematical calculations. Write code using the following methods of the `java.lang.Math` class: `abs()`, `ceil()`, `floor()`, `max()`, `min()`, `random()`, `round()`, `sin()`, `cos()`, `tan()`, and `sqrt()`.

▶ Knowledge of the methods of the `Math` class were required for the JDK 1.1 exam. Although these methods are not emphasized as much on the JDK 1.2 exam, you'll still need to know them in order to answer a few exam questions.

CHAPTER 9

The `java.lang` Package

Know how other `java.lang` classes and interfaces are used.

▶ Although the certification exam focuses on classes described for the previous objectives, knowledge of other classes and interfaces is important to be able to program in Java. Familiarity with these other classes and interfaces may help you answer some exam questions.

As you read through this chapter, you should concentrate on the following key items:

▶ What classes and interfaces are provided by `java.lang`

▶ How the `Object`, `Class`, and `System` classes are used

▶ How the wrapped classes are used

▶ The differences between the `String` and `StringBuffer` classes

▶ How the methods of the `Math` class are used

CHAPTER INTRODUCTION

This chapter covers the classes and interfaces of the java.lang package. This chapter is important because there are several exam questions that require knowledge of this package. This chapter, like the exam, focuses on the few important classes of java.lang: Object, Class, System, String, StringBuffer, Math, and the wrapped classes. It also briefly covers the other classes and interfaces of java.lang. If you read through this chapter and master the review questions, then you should be able to significantly improve your score on the certification exam.

The java.lang package provides 30 classes and 3 interfaces (not counting the Error and Exception classes (and their subclasses)) that are fundamental to Java programming. These classes and interfaces are described in the following sections.

THE Object, Class, AND Package CLASSES

Object and Class are two of the most important classes in the Java API. The Object class is at the top of the Java class hierarchy. All classes are subclasses of Object and, therefore, inherit its methods. The Class class is used to provide information about each class loaded by the Java Virtual Machine. The Package class is new to JDK 1.2. It is used to provide version information about a package.

Object

The Object class does not have any variables and has only one constructor. However, it provides 11 methods that are inherited by all Java classes and support general operations used by all objects. For example, the equals() and hashCode() methods are used to compare Java objects. *Hash tables* are like arrays, but are indexed by key values (referred to as *hash codes*) and dynamically grow in size. A hash table associates objects with hash codes, so that the objects can be efficiently stored and retrieved. They make use of hash functions that map objects to their hash codes. The hashCode() method creates a hash code for an object and is an example of a hash function. Hash codes can be used used to quickly determine whether two objects are different.

The `clone()` method creates an identical copy of an object. (Object references are copied but not the objects referenced by the references.) A cloned object must implement the `clonable` interface. This interface is defined within the `java.lang` package. It contains no methods and is used only to differentiate `clonable` classes from `nonclonable` classes.

The `getClass()` method identifies the class of an object by returning an object of `Class`. The `toString()` method creates a `String` representation of the value of an object. This method is handy for quickly displaying the contents of an object. When an object is displayed, using `print()` or `println()`, the `toString()` method of its class is automatically called to convert the object into a string before printing. Classes that override the `toString()` method can easily provide a custom display for their objects.

The `finalize()` method of an object is executed when an object is garbage-collected. The method performs no action, by default, and needs to be overridden by any class that requires specialized finalization processing.

The `Object` class provides three `wait()` and two `notify()` methods that support thread synchronization control. These methods are implemented by the `Object` class so that they can be made available to threads that are not created from subclasses of class `Thread`. The `wait()` methods cause a thread to wait until it is notified or until a specified amount of time has elapsed. The `notify()` methods are used to notify waiting threads that their wait is over.

Class

The `Class` class provides over 30 methods that support the runtime processing of an object's class and interface information. This class does not have a constructor. Objects of this class, referred to as *class descriptors*, are automatically created as classes are loaded by the Java virtual machine. Despite their name, class descriptors are used for interfaces as well as classes.

The getName() and toString() methods return the String containing the name of a class or interface. The toString() method differs in that it prepends the string class or interface, depending on whether the class descriptor is a class or an interface. The static forName() method loads the class specified by a String object and returns a class descriptor for that class.

The getSuperclass() method returns the class descriptor of the superclass of a class. The isInterface() method identifies whether a class descriptor applies to a class or an interface. The getInterfaces() method returns an array of Class objects that specify the interfaces of a class, if any.

The newInstance() method creates an object that is a new instance of the specified class. It can be used in lieu of a class's constructor, although it is generally safer and clearer to use a constructor rather than newInstance(). The newInstance() method is useful to create instances of classes not known at compile time.

The getClassLoader() method returns the class loader of a class, if one exists. Classes are not usually loaded by a class loader. However, if a class is loaded from outside the CLASSPATH, such as over a network, a class loader is used to convert the class byte stream into a class descriptor. The ClassLoader class is covered later in this chapter in the "ClassLoader, Security Manager, and Runtime Classes" section.

The Class class contains a number of other methods that begin with get and is. These methods are used to obtain detailed information about classes and interfaces. You don't have to remember all the methods of the Class class. For the purposes of the exam, remember that the Class class supports the runtime processing of an object's class and interface information and that the methods of Class provide detailed access to this information.

Package

Java software development is based upon the use and reuse of packages. Both Java 1.0 and Java 1.1 used packages. However, the Package class is new to JDK 1.2. It provides methods for obtaining package version information stored in the manifest of .jar files. The

Package class provides several methods that can be used to retrieve information about packages. The static getPackage() and getAllPackages() methods provide Package objects that are known to the current class loader. Other methods return name, title, version, security, and vendor information about the specification and implementation of packages. The isCompatibleWith() method is used to determine whether a package is comparable with a particular version.

THE ClassLoader, SecurityManager, AND Runtime CLASSES

The ClassLoader, SecurityManager, and Runtime classes provide a fine level of control over the operation of the Java runtime system. Most of the time, however, you will not want or need to exercise this control because Java is set up to perform optimally for a variety of applications. The ClassLoader class enables you to define custom loaders for classes that you load outside of your CLASSPATH—for example, over a network. The SecurityManager class enables you to define a variety of security policies that govern the accesses that classes may make to threads, executable programs, your network, and your file system. The Runtime class provides you with the capability to control and monitor the Java runtime system. It also allows you to execute external programs.

THE System CLASS

The System class is one of the most important and useful classes provided by java.lang. It provides a standard interface to common system resources and functions. It implements the standard input, output, and error streams, and supplies a set of methods that provide control over the Java runtime system. Some of these methods duplicate those provided by the Runtime class.

Standard Streams

The in, out, and err variables are, by default, assigned to the standard input, output, and error streams, which are used to support console I/O. The setIn(), setOut(), and setErr() methods can be used to reassign these variables to other streams.

Properties-Related Methods

The System class provides several properties-related methods. *Properties* are extensions of the Dictionary and Hashtable classes and are defined in the java.util package. Properties are a list of key–value pairs where the keys are String objects that specify a property's name and the values are String objects that specify the property's value. Properties are used for storing configuration information. A set of system properties is available through the System class that describes the general characteristics of the operating system and runtime system you are using. The getProperties() method gets all the system properties and stores them in an object of class Properties. The getProperty() method gets a single property, as specified by a key. The setProperties() method sets the system properties to the values of a Properties object. The setProperty() method sets the value of a particular property. The identityClone() method returns the hash code associated with an object.

Security Manager-Related Methods

The getSecurityManager() and setSecurityManager() methods provide access to the security manager that is currently in effect. The setSecurityManager() method can be used to implement a custom security policy. However, as of JDK 1.2, the best way to implement a custom policy is via an external security policy.

Runtime-Related Methods

Several of the methods defined for the Runtime class are made available through the System class. These methods include exit(), gc(), load(), loadLibrary(), runFinalizersOnExit(), and runFinalization().

Odds and Ends

The arraycopy() method is used to copy data from one array to another. This function provides the opportunity for system-specific, memory-copying operations to optimize memory-to-memory copies.

The currentTimeMillis() method returns the current time in milli-seconds since January 1, 1970. If you want more capable date and time methods, check out the Date class in java.util.

The getenv() method is used to obtain the value of an environment variable. However, this method is identified as obsolete in the Java API documentation and can no longer be used.

THE WRAPPED CLASSES

Variables that are declared using the primitive Java types are not objects and cannot be created and accessed using methods. Primitive types also cannot be subclassed. To get around the limitations of primitive types, the java.lang package defines class *wrappers* for these types. These class wrappers furnish methods that provide basic capabilities such as class conversion, value testing, hash codes, and equality checks. The constructors for the wrapped classes allow objects to be created and converted from primitive values and strings. Be sure to browse the API pages for each of these classes to familiarize yourself with the methods they provide.

The Boolean Class

The Boolean class is a wrapper for the boolean primitive type. It pro-vides the getBoolean(), toString(), valueOf(), and booleanValue() methods to support type and class conversion. The toString(), equals(), and hashCode() methods override those of class Object.

The Character Class

The Character class is a wrapper for the char primitive type. It pro-vides several methods that support case, type, and class testing and conversion.

The Byte, Short, Integer, and Long Classes

These classes wrap the byte, short, int, and long primitive types. They provide the MIN_VALUE and MAX_VALUE constants, as well as a number of type and class testing and conversion methods. The parseInt() and parseLong() methods are used to parse String objects and convert them to Byte, Short, Integer, and Long objects.

The Double and Float Classes

The Double and Float classes wrap the double and float primitive types. They provide the MIN_VALUE, MAX_VALUE, POSITIVE_INFINITY, and NEGATIVE_INFINITY constants, as well as the NaN (not-a-number) constant. NaN is used as a value that is not equal to any value, including itself. These classes provide a number of type and class testing and conversion methods, including methods that support conversion to and from integer bit representations.

The Number Class

The Number class is an abstract numeric class that is subclassed by Byte, Short, Integer, Long, Float, and Double. It provides several methods that support conversion of objects from one class to another.

All Wrapped Up

The program in Listing 9.1 shows some of the methods that can be used with the primitive types when they are wrapped as objects. Look up these methods in the API pages for each class and try to figure out how they work before moving on to their explanations.

LISTING 9.1

USING WRAPPER CLASSES

```
public class WrappedClassApp {
  public static void main(String args[]) {
   Boolean b1 = new Boolean("TRUE");
```

```
    Boolean b2 = new Boolean("FALSE");
    System.out.println(b1.toString()+" or "+b2.toString());
    for(int j=0;j<16;++j)
     System.out.print(Character.forDigit(j,16));
    System.out.println();
    Integer i = new Integer(Integer.parseInt("ef",16));
    Long l = new Long(Long.parseLong("abcd",16));
    long m=l.longValue()*i.longValue();
    System.out.println(Long.toString(m,8));
    System.out.println(Float.MIN_VALUE);
    System.out.println(Double.MAX_VALUE);
   }
}
```

The program examines some of the more useful methods provided
by the wrapped classes. It creates two objects of class Boolean from
string arguments passed to their constructors. It assigns these objects
to b1 and b2 and then converts them back to String objects when it
displays them. They are displayed in lowercase, as boolean values are
traditionally represented.

The program then executes a for loop that prints out the character
corresponding to each of the hexadecimal digits. The static
forDigit() method of the Character class is used to generate the
character values of digits in a number system of a different radix.

The static parseInt() and parseLong() methods are used to parse
strings according to different radices. In the example, they are used
to convert strings representing hexadecimal numbers into Integer
and Long values. These values are then multiplied together and converted to a string that represents the resulting value in base 8. This
is accomplished using an overloaded version of the toString()
method.

The sample program concludes by displaying the minimum float
value and the maximum double value, using the predefined class
constants of the Float and Double classes.

The program's output is as follows:

```
true or false
0123456789abcdef
50062143
1.4E-45
1.7976931348623157E308
```

THE Math CLASS

The Math class provides an extensive set of mathematical methods in the form of a static class library. It also defines the mathematical constants E and PI. The supported methods include arithmetic, trigonometric, exponential, logarithmic, random number, and conversion routines. You should browse the API page of this class to get a feel for the methods it provides. The example in Listing 9.2 only touches on a few of these methods.

LISTING 9.2

USING THE METHODS OF THE Math CLASS

```
public class MathApp {
 public static void main(String args[]) {
  System.out.println(Math.E);
  System.out.println(Math.PI);
  System.out.println(Math.abs(-1234));
  System.out.println(Math.cos(Math.PI/4));
  System.out.println(Math.sin(Math.PI/2));
  System.out.println(Math.tan(Math.PI/4));
  System.out.println(Math.log(1));
  System.out.println(Math.exp(Math.PI));
  for(int i=0;i<3;++i)
   System.out.print(Math.random()+" ");
  System.out.println();
  }
}
```

This program prints the constants e and π, $|-1234|$, $\cos(\pi/4)$, $\sin(\pi/2)$, $\tan(\pi/4)$, $\ln(1)$, e^{π}, and then three random double numbers between 0.0 and 1.1. Its output is as follows:

```
2.718281828459045
3.141592653589793
1234
0.7071067811865476
1.0
0.9999999999999999
0.0
23.14069263277926
0.5214844573332809 0.7036104523989761 0.15555052349418896
```

The random numbers you generate may differ from those shown here.

THE Comparable INTERFACE

The Comparable interface is a new interface that was added with JDK 1.2. This interface defines the compareTo() method. Objects of classes that implement the Comparable interface can be compared to each other and sorted.

THE String AND StringBuffer CLASSES

The String and StringBuffer classes are used to support operations on strings of characters. The String class supports constant (unchanging or immutable) strings, whereas the StringBuffer class supports growable, modifiable strings. String objects are more compact than StringBuffer objects, but StringBuffer objects are more flexible.

String Literals

String literals are strings that are specified using double quotes. "This is a string" and "xyz" are examples of string literals. String literals are different than the literal values used with primitive types. When the javac compiler encounters a String literal, it converts it to a String constructor. For example, this

```
String str = "text";
```

is equivalent to this

```
String str = new String("text");
```

Because the compiler automatically supplies String constructors, you can use String literals everywhere that you can use objects of the String class.

The + Operator and StringBuffer

If String objects are constant, how can they be concatenated with the + operator and be assigned to existing String objects? In the following example, the code will result in the string "ab" being assigned to the s object:

```
String s = "";
s = s + "a" + "b";
```

How can this be possible if strings are constant? The answer lies in the fact that the Java compiler uses StringBuffer objects to accomplish the string manipulations. This code would be rendered as something similar to the following by the Java compiler:

```
String s = "";
s = new
➥StringBuffer("").append("a").append("b").toString();
```

A new object of class StringBuffer is created with the "" argument. The StringBuffer append() method is used to append the strings "a" and "b" to the new object, and then the object is converted to an object of class String via the toString() method. The toString() method creates a new object of class String before it is assigned to the s variable. In this way, the s variable always refers to a constant (although new) String object.

String **Constructors**

The String class provides several constructors for the creation and initialization of String objects. These constructors enable strings to be created from other strings, string literals, arrays of characters, arrays of bytes, and StringBuffer objects. Browse through the API page for the String class to become familiar with these constructors.

String **Access Methods**

The String class provides a very powerful set of methods for working with String objects. These methods enable you to access individual characters and substrings; test and compare strings; copy, concatenate, and replace parts of strings; convert and create strings; and perform other useful string operations.

The most important String methods are the length() method, which returns an integer value identifying the length of a string; the charAt() method, which allows the individual characters of a string to be accessed; the substring() method, which allows substrings of a string to be accessed; and the valueOf() method, which enables primitive data types to be converted into strings.

In addition to these methods, the Object class provides a toString() method for converting other objects to String objects. This method is often overridden by subclasses to provide a more appropriate object-to-string conversion.

Character and Substring Methods

Several String methods enable you to access individual characters and substrings of a string. These include charAt(), getBytes(), getChars(), indexOf(), lastIndexOf(), and substring(). Whenever you need to perform string manipulations, be sure to check the API documentation to make sure that you don't overlook an easy-to-use, predefined String method.

String Comparison and Test Methods

Several String methods allow you to compare strings, substrings, byte arrays, and other objects with a given string. Some of these methods are compareTo(), endsWith(), equals(), equalsIgnoreCase(), regionMatches(), and startsWith().

Copy, Concatenation, and Replace Methods

The following methods are useful for copying, concatenating, and manipulating strings: concat(), copyValueOf(), replace(), and trim().

String Conversion and Generation

A number of string methods support String conversion. These are intern(), toCharArray(), toLowerCase(), toString(), toUpperCase(), and valueOf(). You'll explore the use of some of these methods in the following section.

Stringing Along

The program in Listing 9.3 provides a glimpse at the operation of some of the methods identified in the previous subsections. Because strings are frequently used in application programs, learning to use the available methods is essential to being able to use the String class most effectively.

LISTING 9.3

WORKING WITH STRINGS

```
public class StringApp {
 public static void main(String args[]) {
  String s = "  Java 2 Certification ";
  System.out.println(s);
  System.out.println(s.toUpperCase());
  System.out.println(s.toLowerCase());
  System.out.println("["+s+"]");
  s=s.trim();
  System.out.println("["+s+"]");
  s=s.replace('J','X');
  s=s.replace('C','Y');
  s=s.replace('2','Z');
  System.out.println(s);
  int i1 = s.indexOf('X');
  int i2 = s.indexOf('Y');
  int i3 = s.indexOf('Z');
  char ch[] = s.toCharArray();
  ch[i1]='J';
  ch[i2]='C';
  ch[i3]='2';
  s = new String(ch);
  System.out.println(s);
 }
}
```

This program performs several manipulations of a string s, which is initially set to " Java 2 Certification ". It prints the original string and then prints uppercase and lowercase versions of it, illustrating the use of the toUpperCase() and toLowerCase() methods. It prints the string enclosed between two braces to show that it contains leading and trailing spaces. It then trims away these spaces using the trim() method and reprints the string to show that these spaces were removed.

The program uses the replace() method to replace 'J', 'C', and '2' with 'X', 'Y', and 'Z', and prints out the string to show the changes. The replace() method is case sensitive. It uses the indexOf() method to get the indices of 'X', 'Y', and 'Z' within s. It uses the toCharArray() to convert the string to a char array. It then uses the indices to put 'J', 'C', and '2' back in their proper locations within the character array. The String() constructor is used to construct a new string from the character array. The new string is assigned to s and is printed.

The program's output is as follows:

```
Java 2 Certification
  JAVA 2 CERTIFICATION
  java 2 certification
[   Java 2 Certification ]
[Java 2 Certification]
Xava Z Yertification
Java 2 Certification
```

The StringBuffer Class

The StringBuffer class is the force behind the scenes for most complex string manipulations. The compiler automatically declares and manipulates objects of this class to implement common string operations.

The StringBuffer class provides three constructors: an empty constructor, a constructor with a specified initial buffer length, and a constructor that creates a StringBuffer object from a String object. In general, you will find yourself constructing StringBuffer objects from String objects, and the last constructor will be the one you use most often.

The StringBuffer class provides several versions of the append() method to convert and append other objects and primitive data types to StringBuffer objects. It provides a similar set of insert() methods for inserting objects and primitive data types into StringBuffer objects. It also provides methods to access the character-buffering capacity of StringBuffer and methods for accessing the characters contained in a string. It is well worth a visit to the StringBuffer API pages to take a look at the methods that it has to offer.

Strung Out

The program in Listing 9.4 shows how StringBuffer objects can be manipulated using the append(), insert(), and setCharAt() methods.

LISTING 9.4

USING THE StringBuffer OBJECT

```java
public class StringBufferApp {
 public static void main(String args[]) {
  StringBuffer sb = new StringBuffer(" is ");
  sb.append("Hot");
  sb.append('!');
  sb.insert(0,"Java");
  sb.append('\n');
  sb.append("This is ");
  sb.append(true);
  sb.setCharAt(21,'T');
  sb.append('\n');
  sb.append("Java is #");
  sb.append(1);
  String s = sb.toString();
  System.out.println(s);
  }
}
```

The program creates a StringBuffer object using the string " is ". It appends the string "Hot" using the append() method and the character '!' using an overloaded version of the same method. The insert() method is used to insert the string "Java" at the beginning of the string buffer.

Three appends are used to tack on a newline character (\n), the string "This is ", and the boolean value true. The append() method is overloaded to support the appending of the primitive data types as well as arbitrary Java objects.

The setCharAt() method is used to replace the letter 't' at index 21 with the letter 'T'. The charAt() and setCharAt() methods allow StringBuffer objects to be treated as arrays of characters.

Finally, another newline character is appended to sb, followed by the string "Java is #" and the int value 1. The StringBuffer object is then converted to a string and displayed to the console window.

The output of the program is as follows:

```
Java is Hot!
This is True
Java is #1
```

THREADS AND PROCESSES

This section describes the classes and interfaces of java.lang that support multithreading. Chapter 8, "Threads," covers the important ones in more detail. It also covers the Process class, which is used to manipulate processes that are executed using the System.exec() methods.

Runnable

The Runnable interface provides a common approach to identifying the code to be executed as part of an active thread. It consists of a single method, run(), which is executed when a thread is activated. The Runnable interface is implemented by the Thread class and by other classes that support threaded execution.

Thread

The Thread class is used to construct and access individual threads of execution that are executed as part of a multithreaded program. It defines the priority constants that are used to control task scheduling: MIN_PRIORITY, MAX_PRIORITY, and NORM_PRIORITY. It provides seven constructors for creating instances of class Thread. The four constructors with the Runnable parameters are used to construct threads for classes that do not subclass the Thread class. The other constructors are used for the construction of Thread objects from Thread subclasses.

Thread supports many methods for accessing Thread objects. These methods provide the capabilities to work with a thread's group; obtain detailed information about a thread's activities; set and test a thread's properties; and cause a thread to wait, be interrupted, or be destroyed.

ThreadGroup

The ThreadGroup class is used to encapsulate a group of threads as a single object so that it can be accessed as a single unit. A number of access methods is provided for manipulating ThreadGroup objects. These methods keep track of the threads and thread groups contained in a thread group and perform global operations on all threads in the group. The global operations are group versions of the operations that are provided by the Thread class.

ThreadLocal

The ThreadLocal class is used to implement variables that are local to a thread. The get(), set(), and initialize() methods are used to set and retrieve the values of these variables.

Process

The Process class is used to encapsulate processes that are executed with the System.exec() methods. An instance of class Process is returned by the Runtime class exec() method when it executes a process that is external to the Java runtime system. This Process object can be destroyed using the destroy() method and waited on using the waitFor() method. The exitValue() method returns the system exit value of the process. The getInputStream(), getOutputStream(), and getErrorStream() methods are used to access the standard input, output, and error streams of the process.

THE Compiler CLASS

The Compiler class consists of static methods that are used to compile Java classes in the rare event that you want to compile classes directly from a program or applet. These methods enable you to build your own customized Java development environment.

EXCEPTIONS AND ERRORS

The java.lang package establishes the Java exception hierarchy and declares numerous exceptions and errors. Errors are used to indicate the occurrence of abnormal and fatal events that should not be handled within application programs.

The Throwable Class

The Throwable class is at the top of the Java error-and-exception hierarchy. It is extended by the Error and Exception classes and provides methods that are common to both classes. These methods consist of stack tracing methods, the getMessage() method, and the toString() method, which is an override of the method inherited from the Object class. The getMessage() method is used to retrieve any messages that are supplied in the creation of Throwable objects.

The fillInStackTrace() and printStackTrace() methods supply and print information that is used to trace the propagation of exceptions and errors throughout a program's execution.

The Error Class

The Error class is used to provide a common superclass to define abnormal and fatal events that should not occur. It provides two constructors and no other methods. Four major classes of errors extend the Error class: AWTError, LinkageError, ThreadDeath, and VirtualMachineError.

The AWTError class identifies fatal errors that occur in the Abstract Window Toolkit packages. It is a single identifier for all AWT errors and is not subclassed.

The LinkageError class is used to define errors that occur as the result of incompatibilities between dependent classes. These incompatibilities result when class Y depends on class X, which is changed before class Y can be recompiled. The LinkageError class is extensively subclassed to identify specific manifestations of this type of error.

The ThreadDeath error class is used to indicate that a thread has been stopped. Instances of this class can be caught and then rethrown to ensure that a thread is gracefully terminated, although this is not recommended. The ThreadDeath class is not subclassed.

The VirtualMachineError class is used to identify fatal errors occurring in the operation of the Java Virtual Machine. It has four subclasses: InternalError, OutOfMemoryError, StackOverflowError, and UnknownError.

The Exception Class

The Exception class provides a common superclass for the exceptions that can be defined for Java programs and applets.

THE Void CLASS

The Void class is used to reference the Class object representing the void type. It is provided for completeness and is used for reflection. It has no constructors or methods.

CHAPTER SUMMARY

KEY TERMS

- Wrapped class
- String
- StringBuffer
- Random number
- Object
- Class
- Class loaded
- Security manager

This chapter covered the classes and interfaces of the java.lang package. It focused on the wrapped classes, String and StringBuffer, and the Math class. It presented several examples of how these classes are used. It also covered the Object, Class, System, and other important classes and interfaces of java.lang. You should now be prepared to test your knowledge of these topics. The following review questions and exam questions will let you know how well you understand this material and will give you an idea of how you'll do in related exam questions. They'll also indicate which material you need to study further.

APPLY YOUR KNOWLEDGE

Review Questions

1. What are the `Object` and `Class` classes used for?

2. What are wrapped classes?

3. What is the difference between the `String` and `StringBuffer` classes?

4. Why are the methods of the `Math` class static?

5. Which class is extended by all other classes?

6. Which class should you use to obtain design information about an object?

7. What is the purpose of the `Runtime` class?

8. What is the purpose of the `System` class?

9. Which `Math` method is used to calculate the absolute value of a number?

10. What are `E` and `PI`?

Exam Questions

1. Which of the following are true?

   A. The `Class` class is the superclass of the `Object` class.

   B. The `Object` class is `final`.

   C. The `Class` class can be used to load other classes.

   D. The `ClassLoader` class can be used to load other classes.

2. Which of the following classes is used to perform basic console I/O?

   A. `System`

   B. `SecurityManager`

   C. `Math`

   D. `Runtime`

3. Which of the following is not a wrapper class?

   A. `String`

   B. `Integer`

   C. `Boolean`

   D. `Character`

4. What's wrong with the following code?

```
public class Question {
 public static void main(String args[]) {
  Boolean b = new Boolean("TRUE");
  if(b) {
   for(Integer i=0;i<10;++i) {
    System.out.println(i);
   }
  }
 }
}
```

   A. There is nothing wrong with the code. It compiles and runs fine.

   B. The `if` condition should be a `boolean` instead of a `Boolean`.

   C. The index of the `for` statement should be an `int` instead of an `Integer`.

   D. It is illegal to construct a `Boolean` value.

APPLY YOUR KNOWLEDGE

5. Which of the following methods cause the `String` object referenced by s to be changed?

   A. `s.concat()`

   B. `s.toUpperCase()`

   C. `s.replace()`

   D. `s.valueOf()`

6. What is the output of the following program?

```
public class Question {
 public static void main(String args[]) {
  String s1 = "abc";
  String s2 = "def";
  String s3 = s1.concat(s2.toUpperCase());
  System.out.println(s1+s2+s3);
 }
}
```

   A. `abcdefabcdef`

   B. `abcabcDEFDEF`

   C. `abcdefabcDEF`

   D. None of the above

7. Which of the following methods are methods of the `Math` class?

   A. `absolute()`

   B. `log()`

   C. `cosine()`

   D. `sine()`

8. Which of the following methods are methods of the `String` class?

   A. `delete()`

   B. `append()`

   C. `reverse()`

   D. `replace()`

9. Which of the following are true about the `Error` and `Exception` classes?

   A. Both classes extend `Throwable`.

   B. The `Error` class is final and the `Exception` class is not.

   C. The `Exception` class is final and the `Error` class is not.

   D. Both classes implement `Throwable`.

10. Which of the following are true?

   A. The `Void` class extends the `Class` class.

   B. The `Float` class extends the `Double` class.

   C. The `System` class extends the `Runtime` class.

   D. The `Integer` class extends the `Number` class.

Answers to Review Questions

1. The `Object` class is the highest-level class in the Java class hierarchy. The `Class` class is used to represent the classes and interfaces that are loaded by a Java program.

2. Wrapped classes are classes that allow primitive types to be accessed as objects.

3. `String` objects are constants. `StringBuffer` objects are not.

4. So they can be invoked as if they are a mathematical code library.

5. The `Object` class is extended by all other classes.

6. The `Class` class is used to obtain information about an object's design.

APPLY YOUR KNOWLEDGE

7. The purpose of the Runtime class is to provide access to the Java runtime system.

8. The purpose of the System class is to provide access to system resources.

9. The abs() method is used to calculate absolute values.

10. E is the base of the natural logarithm and PI is mathematical value *pi*.

Answers to Exam Questions

1. C and D   The Object class is the highest-level class in the Java 2 API and therefore cannot be a subclass of Class or final.

2. A   System.in, System.err, and System.out support console I/O.

3. A   There is no primitive string type to wrap.

4. B and C

5. A and B   The toUpperCase() and concat() methods change their associated String object.

6. D   String objects are immutable and cannot be changed.

7. B   The absolute() value method, cosine(), and sine() methods are abbreviated abs(), cos(), and since().

8. D   A, B, and C look like String methods, but they are not.

9. A   Throwable is the superclass of both Error and Exception.

10. D

Suggested Readings and Resources

The JDK 1.2 java.lang package API description.

This chapter helps you to prepare for the exam by covering the following objectives:

Know the important classes and interfaces provided by the `java.util` package.

▶ The `java.util` package is a core Java package. This package has been expanded in JDK 1.2 to cover include several new classes and interfaces. Some of these classes and interfaces will be on the certification exam. You need to become familiar with these classes and interfaces in order to answer related exam questions.

Know what the Collections API is and how it is used. Make appropriate selection of collection classes/interfaces to suit specified behavior requirements.

▶ Several exam questions require you to be familiar with classes and interfaces that are part of the new Collections API. You will be required to know how these classes are used and the subclass relationships between these classes.

Know how the date-related classes of the `java.util` package are used.

▶ Several exam questions require knowledge of data-related classes, such as `Calendar` and `GregorianCalendar`. You need to know the relationships between these classes and the types of methods that they support to correctly answer some exam questions.

Know how other `java.util` classes and interfaces are used.

Although the certification exam focuses on Collections API classes of `java.util`, knowledge of other classes and interfaces is important to being a good Java programmer. Familiarity with these other classes and interfaces may help you answer some exam questions.

CHAPTER 10

The `java.util` Package

STUDY STRATEGIES

As you read through this chapter, you should
concentrate on the following key items:

▶ The classes and interfaces are provided by
  `java.util`

▶ How the Collections API is used

▶ The class and inteface hierarchy supported by
  the Collections API

▶ How the date-related classes of `java.util` are
  used

CHAPTER INTRODUCTION

This chapter covers the classes and interfaces of `java.util` package. Although you won't see a lot of questions about this package, every question counts, and you should familiarize yourself with this material. This chapter, like the exam, focuses on the new Collections API. It also covers date-related classes and other prominent classes of `java.util`. If you read through this chapter and master the review questions, you should have no problem with the `java.util` questions on the certification exam.

THE CLASSES AND INTERFACES OF THE `java.util` PACKAGE

The `java.util` package provides 34 classes and 13 interfaces that support the new Collections API, date/calendar operations, internationalization, change observation, parsing, random number generation, and basic event processing. These classes and interfaces are organized as summarized in Figure 10.1 and described in the following sections.

THE COLLECTIONS API

The most notable change to the `java.util` package in JDK 1.2 is the introduction of the classes and interfaces of the Collections API. These classes and interfaces provide an implementation-independent framework for manipulating collections of objects. You'll first review the pre-JDK 1.2 collections classes and interfaces, and then you'll cover the new classes and interfaces introduced with JDK 1.2.

FIGURE 10.1

The classes and interfaces of `java.util`.

Collections
  Pre-JDK 1.2
    BitSet
    Dictionary
    Enumeration
    Hashtable
    Properties
    Stack
    Vector
  New to JDK 1.2
    AbstractCollection
    AbstractLIst
    AbstractMap
    AbstractSequentialList
    AbstractSet
    ArrayList
    Arrays
    Collection
    Collections
    Comparator
    HashMap
    HashSet
    Iterator
    LInkedList
    List
    ListIterator
    Map
    MapEntry
    Set
    SortedMap
    SortedSet
    TreeMap
    TreeSet
    WeakHashMap

Date/Calendar
  Calendar
  Date
  GregorianCalendar
  SimpleTimeZone
  TimeZone

Internationalization
  ListResourceBundle
  Locale
  PropertyResourceBundle
  ResourceBundle

Change Observation
  Observer
  Observable

Parsing
  StringTokenizer

Random Number Generation
  Random

Basic Event Support
  EventListener
  EventObject

Other
  PropertyPermission

Pre-JDK 1.2 Collections Classes and Interfaces

JDK 1.1 provided the `Enumeration` interface and the following six classes for working with collections of objects:

- ◆ `Vector`—An expandable array of objects

- ◆ `Stack`—A last-in, first-out stack of objects

- ◆ `BitSet`—A growable bit vector

- ◆ `Dictionary`—A list of key-value pairs

- ◆ `Hastable`—A dictionary that implements a hash table

- ◆ `Properties`—A hash table that provides the capability to associate a list of properties with their values

The `Enumeration` interface and the preceding six classes are very valuable in working with different types of object collections. Their success inspired the JDK 1.2 Collections API. The following subsections cover the `Enumeration` interface and the six classes in the preceding list.

The `Enumeration` Interface

The `Enumeration` interface provides two methods for stepping through an ordered set of objects or values: `hasMoreElements()` and `nextElement()`. The `hasMoreElements()` method enables you to determine whether more elements are contained in an `Enumeration` object. The `nextElement()` method returns the `nextElement()` contained by an object.

`Enumeration`-implementing objects are said to be consumed by their use. This means that the `Enumeration` objects cannot be restarted to reaccess through the elements they contain. Their elements may be accessed only once.

The `Vector` Class

The `Vector` class provides the capability to implement a growable array. The array grows larger as more elements are added to it. The array may also be reduced in size after some of its elements have been deleted. This is accomplished using the `trimToSize()` method.

`Vector` operates by creating an initial storage capacity and then adding capacity to this as needed. It grows by an increment defined by the `capacityIncrement` variable. The initial storage capacity and `capacityIncrement` can be specified in `Vector`'s constructor. A second constructor is used when you want to specify only the initial storage capacity. A third, default constructor specifies neither the initial capacity nor the `capacityIncrement`. This constructor lets Java figure out the best parameters to use for `Vector` objects. Finally, a fourth constructor was added with JDK 1.2 to create a `Vector` out of a `Collection` object.

The access methods provided by the `Vector` class support array-like operations and operations related to the number of objects contained in a `Vector`. The array-like operations enable elements to be added, deleted, and inserted into vectors. They also allow tests to be performed on the contents of vectors and specific elements to be

N O T E

Enumeration and Iterator The `Enumeration` interface has been replaced by the `Iterator` interface in the JDK 1.2 Collections API. You can still use `Enumeration`, but it is being phased out.

NOTE

Vector Update   The Vector class has been retrofitted in JDK 1.2 to extend the AbstractList class and implement the List interface.

retrieved. The size-related operations enable the byte size and number of elements of the vector to be determined. It also enables the vector size to be increased to a certain capacity or trimmed to the minimum capacity needed. (A vector's capacity is the number of elements it can hold. Its size is the number of elements it does hold.) Consult the Vector API page for a complete description of these methods.

The Stack Class

The Stack class provides the capability to create and use storage objects called *stacks* within your Java programs. You store information by pushing it onto a stack and remove and retrieve information by popping it off the stack. Stacks implement a last-in-first-out storage capability. The last object pushed onto a stack is the first object that can be retrieved from the stack. The Stack class extends the Vector class.

The Stack class provides a single default constructor, Stack(), that is used to create an empty stack.

Objects are placed on the stack using the push() method and retrieved from the stack using the pop() method. The search() method enables you to search through a stack to see if a particular object is contained on the stack. The peek() method returns the top element of the stack without popping it off. The empty() method is used to determine whether a stack is empty. The pop() and peek() methods both throw the EmptyStackException if the stack is empty. Use of the empty() method can help to avoid the generation of this exception.

The BitSet Class

The BitSet class is used to represent and manipulate a set of bits. Each individual bit is represented by a boolean value, and can be indexed much like an array or Vector. A bit set is a growable set, the capacity of which is increased as needed. The bits of a bit set are sometimes referred to as *flags*.

Two BitSet constructors are provided. One enables the initial capacity of a BitSet object to be specified. The other is a default constructor that initializes a BitSet to a default size.

The BitSet access methods provide and, or, and exclusive or logical operations on bit sets, enable specific bits to be set and cleared, and override general methods declared for the Object class.

The Dictionary Class

The Dictionary, Hashtable, and Properties classes are three generations of classes that implement the capability to provide key-based data storage and retrieval. The Dictionary class is the abstract superclass of Hashtable, which is, in turn, the superclass of Properties.

Dictionary provides the abstract functions used to store and retrieve objects by key-value associations. The class allows any object to be used as a key or value. This provides great flexibility in the design of key-based storage and retrieval classes. Hashtable and Properties are two examples of these classes.

The Dictionary class can be understood using its namesake. A hard-copy dictionary maps words to their definitions. The words can be considered the keys of the dictionary, and the definitions are the values of the keys. Java dictionaries operate in the same fashion. One object is used as the key to access another object. This abstraction will become clearer as you investigate the Hashtable and Properties classes.

The Dictionary class defines several methods that are inherited by its subclasses. The elements() method is used to return an Enumeration object containing the values of the key-value pairs stored within the dictionary. The keys() method returns an enumeration of the dictionary keys. The get() method is used to retrieve an object from the dictionary based on its key. The put() method puts a Value object in the dictionary and indexes it using a Key object. The isEmpty() method determines whether a dictionary contains any elements, and the size() method identifies the dictionary's size in terms of the number of elements it contains. The remove() method deletes a key-value pair from the dictionary, based on the object's key.

> **NOTE** **Dictionary is Obsolete** The Dictionary class has been rendered obsolete by the Map interface, as of JDK 1.2. However, its Hashtable and Properties subclasses are still in use.

The Hashtable Class

The Hashtable class implements a hash table data structure. A *hash table* indexes and stores objects in a dictionary using hash codes as the objects' keys. *Hash codes* are integer values that identify objects. They are computed in such a manner that different objects are very likely to have different hash values and, therefore, different dictionary keys.

The `Object` class implements the `hashCode()` method. This method enables you to calculate the hash code of an arbitrary Java object. All Java classes and objects inherit this method from `Object`. The `hashCode()` method is used to compute the hash code key for storing objects within a hash table. `Object` also implements the `equals()` method. This method is used to determine whether two objects with the same hash code are, in fact, equal.

The Java `Hashtable` class is very similar to the `Dictionary` class from which it is derived. Objects are added to a hash table as key-value pairs. The object used as the key is hashed, using its `hashCode()` method, and the hash code is used as the actual key for the `value` object. When an object is to be retrieved from a hash table, using a key, the key's hash code is computed and used to find the object.

The `Hashtable` class provides three constructors. The first constructor allows a hash table to be created with a specific initial capacity and load factor. The *load factor* is a `float` value between `0.0` and `1.0` that identifies the percentage of hash table usage that causes the hash table to be rehashed into a larger table. For example, suppose a hash table is created with a capacity of 100 entries and a 0.70 load factor. When the hash table is 70 percent full, a new, larger hash table will be created, and the current hash table entries will have their hash values recalculated for the larger table.

The second `Hashtable` constructor just specifies the table's initial capacity and ignores the load factor. The default hash table constructor does not specify either hash table parameter.

The methods defined for the `Hashtable` class allow key-value pairs to be added to and removed from a hash table. These methods are also used to search the hash table for a particular key or object value, to create an enumeration of the table's keys and values, to determine the size of the hash table, and to recalculate the hash table as needed. Many of these methods are inherited or overridden from the `Dictionary` class.

The Properties Class

The `Properties` class is a subclass of `Hashtable` that can be read from or written to a stream. It also provides the capability to specify a set of default values to be used if a specified key is not found in the table. The default values themselves are specified as an object of class `Properties`. This allows an object of class `Properties` to have a default `Properties` object, which in turn has its own default properties, and so on.

`Properties` supports two constructors: a default constructor with no parameters and a constructor that accepts the default properties to be associated with the `Properties` object being constructed.

The `Properties` class declares several new access methods. The `getProperty()` method enables a property to be retrieved using a `String` object as a key. A second overloaded `getProperty()` method allows a value string to be used as the default, in case the key is not contained in the `Properties` object.

The `load()` and `save()` methods are used to load a `Properties` object from an input stream and save it to an output stream. The `save()` method enables an optional header comment to be saved at the beginning of the saved object's position in the output stream.

The `propertyNames()` method provides an enumeration of all the property keys, and the `list()` method provides a convenient way to print a `Properties` object on a `PrintStream` object.

JDK 1.2 Collections Classes and Interfaces

The Collections API of JDK 1.2 added 10 new interfaces and 14 new classes to those that you studied in the previous section. These additional classes and interfaces provide a powerful API for working with different types of object collections.

The new Collections interfaces introduced with JDK 1.2 are as follows:

◆ `Collection`—Defines methods that implement the concept of an unordered group of objects, referred to as *elements*. The `Collection` interface corresponds to a mathematical *bag*, which is a collection that allows duplicate objects. It defines a full spectrum of methods for adding, removing, and retrieving objects from the collection, as well as methods that operate on the collection itself.

◆ List—Extends the Collection interface to implement an ordered collection of objects. Because lists are ordered, List's objects can be indexed. The ListIterator interface provides methods for iterating through the elements of a list.

◆ Set—Extends the Collection interface to implement a finite mathematical set. Sets differ from lists in that they do not allow duplicate elements.

◆ SortedSet—A Set whose elements are sorted in ascending order.

◆ Comparator—Provides a generic way to compare the elements of a collection.

◆ Iterator—Provides methods for iterating through the elements of a collection. In JDK 1.2, the Iterator interface replaces the Enumeration interface.

◆ ListIterator—Extends the Iterator interface to support bidirectional iteration of lists.

◆ Map—Replaces the Dictionary class as a means to associate keys with values. The Map interface provides similar methods for performing operations on the map and its elements.

◆ SortedMap—A Map whose elements are sorted in ascending order.

◆ Map.Entry—An inner interface of the Map interface that defines methods for working with a single key-value pair.

Figure 10.2 shows the hierarchical relationships between the classes and interfaces of the Collections API.

```
          Collections API Hierarchy

     Interfaces                    Classes

Enumeration                   java.lang.Object
Collection                        AbstractCollection
     List                              AbstractList
     Set                                   AbstractSequentialList
          Sorted Set                          LinkedList
Comparator                                ArraytList
Iterator                                  Vector
     List Iterator                             Stack
Map                               AbstractSet
     SortedMap                        HashSet
Map.Entry                            TreeSet
                              AbstractMap
                                HashMap
                                TreeMap
                                WeakHashMap
                              Arrays
                              BitSet
                              Collections
                              Dictionary
                                  HashTable
                                      Properties
```

FIGURE 10.2

The Collections API class and interface hierarchy.

The new collections classes introduced with JDK 1.2 are as follows:

◆ `AbstractCollection`— The `AbstractCollection` class provides a basic implementation of the `Collection` interface. It is extended by other classes that tailor `AbstactCollection` to more specific implementations.

◆ `AbstractList`—The `AbstractList` class extends the `AbstractCollection` class to provide a basic implementation of the `List` interface.

◆ `AbstractSequentialList`—The `AbstractSequentialList` class extends the `AbstractList` class to provide a list that is tailored to sequential access, as opposed to random access.

◆ LinkedList—The LinkedList class extends the AbstractSequentialList class to provide an implementation of a doubly linked list. A linked list is a list in which each element references the next element in the list. A doubly linked list is a list in which each element references both the previous and next elements in the list.

◆ ArrayList—The ArrayList class extends AbstractList to implement a resizable array.

◆ AbstractSet—The AbstractSet class extends the AbstractCollection class to provide a basic implementation of the Set interface.

◆ HashSet—The HashSet class extends AbstractSet to implement a set of key-value pairs. It does not allow the use of the null element.

◆ TreeSet—The TreeSet class extends AbstractSet to implement the Set interface using a TreeMap.

◆ AbstractMap—The AbstractMap class provides a basic implementation of the Map interface.

◆ HashMap—The HashMap class extends AbstractMap to implement a hash table that supports the Map interface.

◆ WeakHashMap—The WeakHashMap class extends AbstractMap to provide a hashtable-based Map implementation with weak keys. An entry in a WeakHashMap is automatically removed when its key is garbage collected.

◆ TreeMap—The TreeMap class extends AbstractMap to implement a sorted binary tree that supports the Map interface.

◆ Arrays—The Arrays class provides static methods for searching and sorting arrays and converting them to lists.

◆ Collections—The Collections class provides static methods for searching, sorting, and performing other operations on objects that implement the Collection interface.

The right half of Figure 10.2 shows the Collections API class hierarchy. The following subsections show how to work with the new

Collections classes and interfaces. Four examples are provided that show you how to work with lists, sets, maps, and the conversion capabilities of the Arrays class.

Working with Lists

Lists are collections whose objects are ordered. Because lists are ordered, their elements can be indexed. Lists allow duplicate elements. Most lists allow the null value to be an element.

The ListApp program of Listing 10.1 shows how to create and use lists. This program creates a LinkedList object that is referenced by the list variable. The add() method if used to add the strings "is", "is", "a", and "a" to the LinkedList object. The add() method is then used to add the null value to the list. The addLast() method is used to add "test" as the last element of the list. The addFirst() method is used to add "This" as the first element of the list. The displayList() method is then invoked to display the elements of the list.

The displayList() method displays the following results:

```
The size of the list is: 7
This
is

is
a
a
null
test
```

The displayList() method uses the size() method to determine the number of elements in the list. It invokes the listIterator() method to return an object that implements the ListIterator interface. The argument to the listIterator() method is the index of the first element of the list to return in the ListIterator object. In this case, I used 0 so that the whole list would be returned.

The hasNext() method of the ListIterator interface is used to iterate through the list, and the next() method is used to retrieve the next element of the list. Note that the list can contain the null value, and special provisions are made for printing this value.

LISTING 10.1

THE ListApp PROGRAM

```
import java.util.*;

public class ListApp {
 public static void main(String args[]){
    LinkedList list = new LinkedList();
    list.add("is");
    list.add("is");
    list.add("a");
    list.add("a");
    list.add(null);
    list.addLast("test");
    list.addFirst("This");
    displayList(list);
 }
 static void displayList(LinkedList list) {
  System.out.println("The size of the list is: "+list.size());
  ListIterator i = list.listIterator(0);
  while(i.hasNext()){
   Object o = i.next();
   if(o == null) System.out.println("null");
   else System.out.println(o.toString());
  }
 }
}
```

Working with Sets

Sets differ from lists in that they are unordered and cannot contain duplicates of the same element. The SetApp program, shown in Listing 10.2, illustrates the use of sets. It performs the same type of processing as ListApp, but it does so using sets instead of lists.

LISTING 10.2

THE SetApp PROGRAM

```
import java.util.*;

public class SetApp {
 public static void main(String args[]){
    HashSet set = new HashSet();
    set.add("This");
    set.add("is");
```

```
    set.add("is");
    set.add("a");
    set.add("a");
    set.add(null);
    set.add("test");
    displaySet(set);
 }
 static void displaySet(HashSet set) {
  System.out.println("The size of the set is: "+set.size());
  Iterator i = set.iterator();
  while(i.hasNext()){
   Object o = i.next();
   if(o == null) System.out.println("null");
   else System.out.println(o.toString());
  }
 }
}
```

SetApp begins by creating an HashSet object and assigning it to the
set variable. It then adds the same elements to the set as ListApp did
to its list. Note that because sets are not ordered, there are no
addFirst() and addLast() methods. The displaySet() method is
invoked to display the set. It displays the following results:

```
The size of the set is: 5
This
is
a
null
test
```

Note that the set did not allow duplicate elements, but did allow the
null value as an element. The displaySet() method uses the size()
method to determine the number of elements in the set. It uses the
iterator() method to create an Iterator object. The Iterator
object is used to step through and display the elements of the set.

Working with Maps
Maps differ from lists and sets in that they are ordered collections of
key-value pairs. Maps are a generalization of the Dictionary,
Hashtable, and Properties classes that you studied earlier in this
chapter. The MapApp program of Listing 10.3 uses an object of the
TreeMap class to create a sorted list of key-value pairs. The TreeMap
class implements a sorted binary tree.

LISTING 10.3

THE MapApp PROGRAM

```
import java.util.*;

public class MapApp {
 public static void main(String args[]){
    TreeMap map = new TreeMap();
    map.put("one","1");
    map.put("two","2");
    map.put("three","3");
    map.put("four","4");
    map.put("five","5");
    map.put("six","6");
    displayMap(map);
 }
 static void displayMap(TreeMap map) {
  System.out.println("The size of the map is: "+map.size());
  Collection c = map.entrySet);
  Iterator i = c.iterator();
  while(i.hasNext()){
   Object o = i.next();
   if(o == null) System.out.println("null");
   else System.out.println(o.toString());
  }
 }
}
```

The MapApp program begins by creating a TreeMap object and assigning it to the map variable. It then adds six key-value pairs to the map. These key-value pairs associate the names of the numbers from 1 through 6 with their values. The displayMap() method is then invoked to display the program's results:

```
The size of the map is: 6
five=5
four=4
one=1
six=6
three=3
two=2
```

The displayMap() method uses the size() method to determine the number of elements (key-value pairs) in the map. It invokes the entrySet) method to create a Collection object containing the values of the map. The iterator() method of the Collection object is used to obtain an Iterator object for the collection. The Iterator object is used to step through and display the elements of the collection. You should note that the TreeMap object uses the key to sort its key-value pairs.

Sorting and Converting

The Arrays and Collections classes provide a number of static methods for searching, sorting, and converting arrays and Collection objects. The ConvertApp program of Listing 10.4 provides an example of these capabilities. This program creates an array of names, sorts the array, converts it to a list, and then displays the values of the list.

LISTING 10.4

THE ConvertApp PROGRAM

```java
import java.util.*;

public class ConvertApp {
 public static void main(String args[]){
  String strings[] = {"Jason","Emily","Lisa","Jamie","Pierre",
   "Stanley","Gloria","Ben","Ken","Lela"};
  Arrays.sort(strings);
  List list = Arrays.toList(strings);
  displayList(list);
 }
 static void displayList(List list) {
  System.out.println("The size of the list is: "+list.size());
  ListIterator i = list.listIterator(0);
  while(i.hasNext()){
   Object o = i.next();
   if(o == null) System.out.println("null");
   else System.out.println(o.toString());
  }
 }
}
```

ConvertApp begins by creating an array of first names. It then uses the static sort() method of the Arrays class to sort the array. The toList() method of Arrays is invoked to convert the array to a List object. The displayList() method is then invoked to display the list. Its output follows:

```
The size of the list is: 10
Ben
Emily
Gloria
Jamie
Jason
Ken
Lela
Lisa
Pierre
Stanley
```

The displayList() method uses the method of the List interface to determine the size of the list and step through the elements of the list.

DATE AND CALENDAR-RELATED CLASSES

Another major set of classes supported by the java.util package are classes for working with dates and calendars. The original JDK 1.0 provided the Date class to encapsulate date and time as an object. In JDK 1.1, many of the functions of the Date class were deprecated in favor of more international handling of date and time. The Calendar, GregorianCalendar, SimpleTimeZone, and TimeZone classes were added to provide more comprehensive and international support of date and time. The DateFormat class of the java.text package was also added to support international date formatting.

> **NOTE**
>
> **Deprecation** A *deprecated* API element is one that has been replaced by an improved alternative. In most cases, the deprecated element may still be used. However, compiler warnings are generated to inform you that an improved alternative exists.

Date

The Date class encapsulates date and time information and enables date objects to be accessed in a system-independent manner.

Four of the six Date JDK 1.0 constructors have been deprecated. Only the default constructor that creates a Date object with the current system date and time, and a constructor that creates a Date object from a long value, are not deprecated in JDK 1.2.

The access methods defined by the Date class support comparisons between dates and provide access to specific date information, including the time zone offset. However, many of the JDK 1.0 methods have been deprecated in favor of methods provided by the Calendar and TimeZone classes.

Calendar

The Calendar class provides support for date conversions that were previously implemented by the Date class. The support provided by Calendar is more comprehensive and international. The Calendar class is an abstract class that can be extended to provide conversions for specific calendar systems. The GregorianCalendar subclass supports the predominant calendar system used by many countries.

The Calendar class provides two constructors: a default parameterless constructor that constructs a calendar with the default TimeZone and Locale objects and a constructor that allows the TimeZone and Locale objects to be specified. It supplies many constants for accessing days of the week, months of the year, hours, minutes, seconds, milliseconds, and other values.

The Calendar class provides a number of methods for performing data comparisons, arithmetic, and conversions. The getInstance() method returns a locale-specific calendar that is a GregorianCalendar object, by default.

GregorianCalendar

The GregorianCalendar class is a subclass of the Calendar class that supports calendar operations for most of the world. It supports the eras B.C. and A.D. by defining them as class constants. It provides seven constructors that enable GregorianCalendar objects to be created using a combination of different date, time, time zone, and locale values. Its methods override those provided by the Calendar class.

TimeZone

The TimeZone class is used to encapsulate the notion of a time zone. It allows you to work in the local time zone, as well as time zones that are selected by a time zone ID. The TimeZone class keeps track of daylight savings time.

The TimeZone class provides a single, parameterless constructor that creates a TimeZone object corresponding to the local time zone. The TimeZone class does not define any field variables.

The access methods of TimeZone allow you to get a list of available time zone IDs, retrieve the local time zone (from the operating system), get the local time zone offset (and adjust it for daylight savings time), and create TimeZone objects for other time zone IDs.

SimpleTimeZone

The SimpleTimeZone class extends TimeZone to provide support for GregorianCalendar objects. It creates SimpleTimeZone objects using the time zone IDs and offsets defined in the TimeZone class. It provides methods for changing the way daylight savings time is calculated.

DateApp

The DateApp program illustrates the use of the date-related classes covered in the previous sections. It shows how Date, GregorianCalendar, and TimeZone objects are created and how to use their methods to access date/time information. The DateApp program is presented in Listing 10.5.

LISTING 10.5

USING DATES AND CALENDARS

```
import java.util.*;

public class DateApp {
 public static void main(String args[]){
  Date today = new Date();
  GregorianCalendar cal = new GregorianCalendar();
  cal.setTime(today);
  System.out.println("Today: ");
  displayDateInfo(cal);
  cal.clear();
  cal.set(2000,0,1);
  System.out.println("\nNew Years Day 2000: ");
  displayDateInfo(cal);
 }
 static void displayDateInfo(GregorianCalendar cal){
  String days[] =
  ➥{"","Sun","Mon","Tue","Wed","Thu","Fri","Sat"};
  String months[] =
  ➥{"January","February","March","April","May",
   "June","July","August","September","October","November",
   "December"};
  String am_pm[] = {"AM","PM"};
  System.out.println("Year: "+cal.get(Calendar.YEAR));
  System.out.println("Month:
  ➥"+months[cal.get(Calendar.MONTH)]);
  System.out.println("Date: "+cal.get(Calendar.DATE));
  System.out.println("Day:
  ➥"+days[cal.get(Calendar.DAY_OF_WEEK)]);
  System.out.println("Hour: "+(cal.get(Calendar.HOUR)+12)%13);
```

```
    System.out.println("Minute: "+cal.get(Calendar.MINUTE));
    System.out.println("Second: "+cal.get(Calendar.SECOND));
    System.out.println(am_pm[cal.get(Calendar.AM_PM)]);
    TimeZone tz=cal.getTimeZone();
    System.out.println("Time Zone: "+tz.getID());
 }
}
```

The program creates a Date object and a GregorianCalendar object using the default Date() and GregorianCalendar() constructors. The Date object is assigned to the today variable, and the GregorianCalendar object is assigned to the cal variable. The cal variable is updated with the current date by invoking its setTime() method with the Date object stored in today. The displayDateInfo() method is then invoked to display date and time information about the cal variable.

The clear() method of the Calendar class is invoked to reset the date of the GregorianCalendar object stored in cal. The set() method is used to set its date to New Year's 2000. There are several versions of the set() method, each of which takes a different set of parameters. The version used in DateApp takes the year, month, and date as parameters. Note that the month value ranges from 0 to 12, where the year and date values begin at 1. The displayDateInfo() method is invoked again to display information about the new calendar date.

The displayDateInfo() method creates the days, months, and am_pm arrays to define string values corresponding to the days of the week, months of the year, and a.m./p.m. It then prints a line corresponding to date and time values. These values are retrieved using the get() method of the Calendar class and the Calendar constants corresponding to date/time values. The getTimeZone() method of Calendar is invoked to retrieve the local TimeZone object. The getID() method of the TimeZone class is used to retrieve the local time zone ID string.

INTERNATIONALIZATION CLASSES

The java.util package provides a number of classes that support internationalization. These classes are not emphasized on the certification exam and are covered in this section somewhat briefly.

The `Locale` Class

The `Locale` class supports internationalization by describing geographic, political, or cultural regions. Locale objects are used to tailor program output to the conventions of that region. They are created using the `Locale()` constructors, which take `language` and `country` arguments and an optional `variant` argument. The `variant` argument is used to specify software-specific characteristics, such as operating system or browser. The `Locale` class defines constants for the most popular languages and countries. The access methods of `Locale` support the setting and retrieving of language, country, and variant-related values.

The `ResourceBundle` Class

The `ResourceBundle` class also supports internationalization. `ResourceBundle` subclasses are used to store locale-specific resources that can be loaded by a program to tailor the program's appearance to the particular locale in which it is being run. Resource bundles provide the capability to isolate a program's locale-specific resources in a standard and modular manner.

The `ResourceBundle` class provides a single parameterless constructor. The `parent` field variable is used to identify the `ResourceBundle` class that is the parent of a particular class. This parent can be set using the `setParent()` method. The parent is used to find resources that are not available in a particular resource bundle.

The `ResouceBundle` methods are used to retrieve the resources that are specific to a particular locale.

The `ListResourceBundle` Class

The `ListResourceBundle` class extends the `ResourceBundle` class to simplify access to locale-specific resources. It organizes resources in terms of an array of object pairs, where the first object is a `String` key and the second object is the key's value. The `getContents()` method returns the key-value array.

The PropertyResourceBundle Class

The PropertyResourceBundle class extends the ResourceBundle class to organize locale-specific resources using a property file. An InputStream object is supplied to the PropertyResourceBundle() constructor to enable reading of the property file.

OTHER java.util CLASSES AND INTERFACES

The java.util package contains a number of other classes and interfaces that provide capabilities for many of your programs. These remaining classes and interfaces are covered in the following subsections.

The Random Class

The Random class provides a template for the creation of random number generators. It differs from the random() method of the java.lang.Math class in that it allows any number of random number generators to be created as separate objects. The Math.random() method provides a static function for the generation of random double values. This static method is shared by all program code.

Objects of the Random class generate random numbers using a linear congruential formula. Two constructors are provided for creating Random objects. The default constructor initializes the seed of the random number generator using the current system time. The other constructor allows the seed to be set to an initial long value.

The Random class provides eight access methods, seven of which are used to generate random values. The next(), nextInt(), nextLong(), nextFloat(), and nextDouble() methods generate values for the numeric data types. The values generated by nextFloat() and nextDouble() are between 0.0 and 1.0. The nextGaussian() method generates a Gaussian distribution of double values with mean 0.0 and standard deviation 1.0. The nextBytes() method generates a random byte array.

The setSeed() method is used to reset the seed of the random number generator.

The StringTokenizer Class

The StringTokenizer class is used to create a parser for String objects. It parses strings according to a set of delimiter characters. It implements the Enumeration interface in order to provide access to the tokens contained within a string.

StringTokenizer provides three constructors. All three have the input string as a parameter. The first constructor includes two other parameters: a set of delimiters to be used in the string parsing and a boolean value used to specify whether the delimiter characters should be returned as tokens. The second constructor accepts the delimiter string, but not the return token's toggle. The last constructor uses the default delimiter set consisting of the space, tab, newline, and carriage-return characters.

The access methods provided by StringTokenizer include the Enumeration methods, hasMoreElements() and nextElement(), hasMoreTokens() and nextToken(), and countTokens(). The countTokens() method returns the number of tokens in the string being parsed.

Observer and Observable

The Observer interface and Observable class are used to implement an abstract system by which observable objects can be observed by objects that implement the Observer interface. Observable objects are objects that subclass the Observable class. These objects maintain a list of observers. When an observable object is updated, it invokes the update() method of its observers to notify them that it has changed state.

The update() method is the only method that is specified in the Observer interface. The method takes the Observable object and a second notification message Object as its parameters.

The Observable class is an abstract class that must be subclassed by Observable objects. It provides several methods for adding, deleting, and notifying observers and for manipulating change status. These methods are described in the class's API page.

The EventObject Class and the EventListener Interface

The EventObject class is the top-level class of the Java event hierarchy. *Events* represent actions that occur during the course of program execution. Most events are generated as the result of user actions, such as mouse clicks and keyboard actions. The java.awt.event package declares event classes that are subclasses of EventObject. The EventObject class contains a single constructor that identifies the object that is the source of the event. This object is accessible through the source field variable. The EventObject class also provides the getSource() method for accessing the event source.

Event handlers handle events by responding to the the events' occurrence and providing feedback to the user. Java 1.1 provided the capability to deliver events to specific objects—a capability that was lacking in Java 1.0.

JDK 1.1 event handling makes use of special classes, called *adapter classes*, whose objects listen for the occurrence of events on behalf of objects of other classes. These classes implement event listener interfaces that specify methods for identifying and responding to the occurrence of related events. The EventListener interface is the top-level interface that all listener interfaces must implement. It is an empty interface and does not declare any methods.

The PropertyPermission Class

The PropertyPermission class is used to create permissions to access specific system properties. You should not use this class yourself. Instead, specify property permissions in your local security policy.

CHAPTER SUMMARY

KEY TERMS

- Collection
- List
- Map
- Vector
- Set
- Stack
- Hashtable
- Dictionary
- Iterator
- Gregorian Calendar
- Time Zone
- Locale
- Internationalization
- Resource Bundle

This chapter covered the classes and interfaces of the `java.util` package. It focused on the new Collections API and presented several examples of how these classes are used. It also covered date-related and other prominent classes and interfaces of `java.util`. You should now be prepared to test your knowledge of these topics. The following review questions and exam questions will let you know how well you understand this material and will give you an idea of how you'll do in related exam questions. They'll also indicate which material you need to study further.

APPLY YOUR KNOWLEDGE

Review Questions

1. What is the Collections API?

2. What is the Vector class?

3. What is the Stack class?

4. What is the Dictionary class?

5. What is the Collection interface?

6. What is the List interface?

7. What is the Map interface?

8. What is the Set interface?

9. What is an Iterator interface?

10. What is the GregorianCalendar class?

11. What is the SimpleTimeZone class?

12. What is the Locale class?

13. What is the ResourceBundle class?

14. How are Observer and Observable used?

15. Which java.util classes and interfaces support event handling?

Exam Questions

1. What changes are needed to make the following program compile?

```
import java.util.*;
class Question {
 public static void main(String args[]) {
   String s1 = "abc";
   String s2 = "def";
   Vector v = new Vector();
   v.add(s1);
   v.add(s2);
```

```
   String s3 = v.elementAt(0) +
➥v.elementAt(1);
   System.out.println(s3);
 }
}
```

A. Declare Question as public.

B. Cast v.elementAt(0) to a String.

C. Cast v.elementAt(1) to an Object.

D. Import java.lang.

2. What output does the following program display?

```
import java.util.*;
class Question {
 public static void main(String args[]) {
   String s1 = "abc";
   String s2 = "def";
   Stack stack = new Stack();
   stack.push(s1);
   stack.push(s2);
   try {
     String s3 = (String) stack.pop() +
➥(String) stack.pop();
     System.out.println(s3);
   }catch(EmptyStackException ex){
   }
 }
}
```

A. abcdef

B. defabc

C. abcabc

D. defdef

3. Which of the following extend the Collection interface?

A. Dictionary

B. List

C. Map

D. Set

APPLY YOUR KNOWLEDGE

4. Which JDK 1.1 interface is the `Iterator` interface intended to replace?

   A. `Runnable`

   B. `Throwable`

   C. `Enumeration`

   D. `List`

5. Which of the following may have duplicate elements?

   A. `Collection`

   B. `List`

   C. `Map`

   D. `Set`

6. Can a `null` value be added to a `List`?

   A. Yes.

   B. Yes, but only if the `List` is linked.

   C. Yes, provided that the `List` is non-empty.

   D. No.

7. What is the output of the following program?

```
import java.util.*;
class Question {
 public static void main(String args[]) {
  HashSet set = new HashSet();
  String s1 = "abc";
  String s2 = "def";
  String s3 = "";
  set.add(s1);
  set.add(s2);
  set.add(s1);
  set.add(s2);
  Iterator i = set.iterator();
  while(i.hasNext()){
   s3 += (String) i.next();
  }
  System.out.println(s3);
 }
}
```

   A. `abcdefabcdef`

   B. `defabcdefabc`

   C. `fedcbafedcba`

   D. `defabc`

8. What is the output of the following program?

```
import java.util.*;
class Question {
 public static void main(String args[]) {
  TreeMap map = new TreeMap();
  map.put("one","1");
  map.put("two","2");
  map.put("three","3");
  displayMap(map);
 }
 static void displayMap(TreeMap map) {
  Collection c = map.entrySet();
  Iterator i = c.iterator();
  while(i.hasNext()){
   Object o = i.next();
   System.out.print(o.toString());
  }
 }
}
```

   A. `onetwothree`

   B. `123`

   C. `one=1three=3two=`

   D. `onethreetwo`

9. Which of the following `java.util` classes support internationalization?

   A. `Locale`

   B. `ResourceBundle`

   C. `Country`

   D. `Language`

APPLY YOUR KNOWLEDGE

10. Which of the following are true about Observer and Observable?

    A. Observer is an interface and Observable is a class?

    B. When an Observable object is updated it invokes the update() method of its observers.

    C. Observable objects must be GUI components.

    D. They are in the Collections API.

Answers to Review Questions

1. The Collections API is a set of classes and interfaces that support operations on collections of objects.

2. The Vector class provides the capability to implement a growable array of objects.

3. The Stack class implements a last-in first-out stack.

4. The Dictionary class provides the capability to store key-value pairs.

5. The Collection interface provides support for the implementation of a mathematical bag—an unordered collection of objects that may contain duplicates.

6. The List interface provides support for ordered collections of objects.

7. The Map interface replaces the JDK 1.1 Dictionary class and is used associate keys with values.

8. The Set interface provides methods for accessing the elements of a finite mathematical set. Sets do not allow duplicate elements.

9. The Iterator interface is used to step through the elements of a Collection.

10. The GregorianCalendar provides support for traditional Western calendars.

11. The SimpleTimeZone class provides support for a Gregorian calendar.

12. The Locale class is used to tailor program output to the conventions of a particular geographic, political, or cultural region.

13. The ResourceBundle class is used to store locale-specific resources that can be loaded by a program to tailor the program's appearance to the particular locale in which it is being run.

14. Objects that subclass the Observable class maintain a list of observers. When an Observable object is updated it invokes the update() method of each of its observers to notify the observers that it has changed state. The Observer interface is implemented by objects that observe Observable objects.

15. The EventObject class and the EventListener interface support event processing.

Answers to Exam Questions

1. B   The elementAt() method of Vector returns an Object reference.

2. B   Stacks are last-in first out.

3. B and D   Dictionary is a class. Map does not extend Collection.

4. C   It is intended to replace the Enumeration interface.

APPLY YOUR KNOWLEDGE

5. A and B   Neither a `Map` nor a `Set` may have duplicate elements.

6. A   Yes, a `null` value may be added to any `List`.

7. D   Sets may not have duplicate elements.

8. C   A `TreeMap` sorts its elements by their keys.

9. A and B   `Country` and `Language` are not `java.util` classes.

10. A and B   `Observer` and `Observable` are not part of the Collections API. They do not have any relationship to GUI components.

Suggested Readings and Resources

The JDK 1.2 `java.util` package API description.

This chapter helps you to prepare for the exam by covering the following objectives:

Know what the AWT is and how it is used.

▶ A general knowledge of what the AWT is and how it is used is required for the certification exam.

Know what components and containers are supported by the AWT and how they are used.

▶ Although you don't need to know all the details about the AWT's components and containers, the exam assumes that you know the basics about how each component and container is used. You will be required to know the components by name and have a basic familiarity with their constructors, properties, and methods.

Know how to use components and containers to build GUI-based applications and applets.

▶ To build a basic GUI application or applet, you need to assemble the AWT's component and container pieces into a final program. You need to have some hands-on experience using the AWT components and containers to correctly answer these exam questions.

> **NOTE**
>
> **Layouts and Event Handlers** This chapter uses layouts and event handlers to build simple GUI applications and applets. However, these topics are covered in more detail in subsequent chapters.

CHAPTER 11

The java.awt Package: Components and Facilities

STUDY STRATEGIES

As you read through this chapter, you should concentrate on the following key items:

▶ How the AWT is used to build graphical user interfaces

▶ What components and containers are supported by the AWT

▶ How each component and container is used

▶ How components and containers are assembled into applets and applications

CHAPTER INTRODUCTION

This chapter covers the GUI components and containers of `java.awt`. You'll work with labels, buttons, text fields, check boxes, choices, lists, and scrollbars. You'll also learn how to use components and containers. Familiarity with these AWT classes and interfaces is essential to developing a Java-based GUI, and you can expect to see several exam questions that require knowledge of them. By studying the component and container descriptions in this chapter and working the programming examples, you should be able to do well on related exam questions. Subsequent chapters will expand on the material introduced in this chapters.

COMPONENTS AND CONTAINERS

The AWT supports the development of graphical user interfaces through the use of components and containers. *Components* refer to visible user interface elements, such as labels, buttons, text fields, and scrollbars. *Containers* are components that contain and organize other components. Examples of containers are windows, dialog boxes, and applets. In general, components extend the `Component` class and containers extend the `Container` class. Since containers are also components, the `Container` class is a subclass of the `Component` class. Some components extend the `MenuComponent` class, which is not a subclass of `Component`, but a separate component class hierarchy that is devoted to menu-related components. Figure 11.1 provides an overview of how the AWT's components and containers are organized into a class hierarchy.

We'll start with the `Container` class and describe the non-container components that it supports. Then we'll cover the `Component` class and describe its subclasses. Finally, we'll wrap up with `MenuComponent` and the menu-related classes of java.awt.

AWT COMPONENTS

The `Component` class is the superclass of the set of AWT classes that implement graphical user interface controls. These components

```
Object
    Component
        Box.Filler
        Button
        Canvas
        Checkbox
        Choice
        Container

            . . .
            Panel
                        Applet
                ScrollPane
            Window
                    Frame
                    Dialog
                            FileDialog

        Label
        List
        Scrollbar
        TextComponent
            TextField
            TextArea

    MenuComponent
        MenuBar
        MenuItem
                Menu
                    PopupMenu
            CheckboxMenuItem
```

FIGURE 11.1
The AWT component and container class hierarchy.

include windows, dialog boxes, buttons, labels, text fields, and other common GUI components. The Component class provides a common set of methods that are used by all these subclasses, including methods for working with event handlers, images, fonts, and colors. More than 100 methods are implemented by this class. It is a good idea to browse the API pages of the Component class to get a feel for the kinds of methods that are available because they are inherited by all the subclasses of Component. While the certification exam will not test you on all these methods, there are a few that you should be familiar with:

◆ getBounds() and setBounds()—Gets and sets the size and position of a component. These parameters are usually determined by a layout manager, as described in Chapter 12, "The java.awt Package: Layout."

◆ getBackground(), setBackground(), getForeground(), and setForeground()—Gets and sets the component's background and foreground colors. By default, these colors are inherited from the component's parent container.

◆ getEnabled() and setEnabled()—Causes a component to be enabled or disabled. A disabled component is displayed in a way that indicates that it is nonoperational (usually grayed-out).

◆ getFont() and setFont()—Gets and sets the font used with the component. By default, the font is inherited from the component's container.

◆ getParent()—Returns the component's container (if any).

◆ getSize(), setSize(), getPreferredSize(), and setPreferredSize()—Gets and sets the actual and preferred (minimum required) size of a component. The size set by these methods may be (and usually is) overridden by layout managers.

◆ setVisible()—Causes a component to be displayed or hidden.

The above methods are important in that they are typically used when working with any Component and Container subclasses.

The subclasses of Component define the major components of the AWT. They are summarized here and covered in the following subsections:

◆ Button—A push button

◆ Canvas—A canvas used for drawing and painting

◆ Checkbox—A check box or radio button

◆ Choice—A pulldown list of choices.

◆ Container—Superclass of containers, such as windows, dialog boxes, and applets.

◆ Label—A text label

◆ List—A list from which one or more selections may be made

◆ Scrollbar—A scrollbar

◆ TextComponent—Superclass of single- and multiple-line text fields

The Box.Filler class also extends Component. However, it is not part of the java.awt package and does nothing other than to take up space when components of a container are laid out.

Labels

The most basic GUI component is the *label*, which is simply text that is displayed at a particular location of a GUI container. The Label class of the java.awt package provides the capability to work with labels. This class provides three Label() constructors: a default parameterless constructor for creating blank Label objects, a constructor that takes a String object that specifies the label's text, and a constructor that takes a String object (the label's text) and an alignment constant. The alignment constant may be LEFT, CENTER, or RIGHT.

The alignment constants determine the justification of text within the label. The Label class provides methods for working with the label's text and alignment, and for performing other operations. The setText() and getText() methods are used to access the label's text.

FIGURE 11.2
The window displayed by ButtonApp.

Buttons

Buttons are another fundamental GUI component. Unlike labels, which are used solely to provide information to the user, buttons enable users to interact with applets and applications.

The Button class of java.awt provides the capability to create labeled buttons. The Button class has two constructors: a default parameterless constructor that creates unlabeled buttons and a constructor that takes a String object (the button's label) as a parameter. The Button class provides methods for getting and setting the button's label—getLabel() and setLabel()—and for handling button-related events.

The ButtonApp (Listing 11.1) program illustrates the use of the Button and Label classes. Figure 11.2 shows the default window that it displays. Click on any of the buttons and the text label is updated with the button's label.

LISTING 11.1

THE ButtonApp PROGRAM

```
import java.awt.*;
import java.awt.event.*;

public class ButtonApp extends Frame {
 Label label = new Label("Default Label");
 Button button1 = new Button("One");
 Button button2 = new Button("Two");
 Button button3 = new Button("Three");
 Panel panel1 = new Panel();
 Panel panel2 = new Panel();
 public static void main(String[] args) {
  ButtonApp app = new ButtonApp();
 }
 public ButtonApp() {
  super("ButtonApp");
  panel1.add(label);
  button1.addActionListener(new ButtonHandler());
  button2.addActionListener(new ButtonHandler());
  button3.addActionListener(new ButtonHandler());
  panel2.add(button1);
  panel2.add(button2);
  panel2.add(button3);
  add("North",panel1);
  add("Center",panel2);
  addWindowListener(new WindowEventHandler());
  pack();
  show();
 }
 class ButtonHandler implements ActionListener {
```

```
 public void actionPerformed(ActionEvent e){
  String s = e.getActionCommand();
  label.setText(s);
 }
}
class WindowEventHandler extends WindowAdapter{
 public void windowClosing(WindowEvent e) {
  System.exit(0);
 }
 }
}
```

Text Components

The TextComponent class is the superclass of all text-based classes. It provides a common set of methods used by its TextField and TextArea subclasses. It does not provide any constructors and cannot be instantiated. It provides methods for getting and setting the text that is displayed in a text object—getText() and setText()—setting the text object to an editable or read-only state—setEditable()—handling text-editing events, and selecting text that is contained within an object.

TextField

The TextField class implements a one-line text entry field. It provides four constructors that are used to specify the width of the text field in character columns and the default text to be displayed within the field. It provides several methods for accessing the field's size and for specifying whether the characters typed by the user should be displayed. The setEchoCharacter() method is used to specify a character that is to be displayed in lieu of text typed by the user. This method is used to implement password-like fields, fields that display a string of asterisks instead of the characters that the user is typing.

TextArea

The TextArea class implements scrollable text entry objects that span multiple lines and columns. It provides five constructors that enable you to specify the number of rows and columns and the default text display. It provides several methods that return the dimensions of the text area and then insert, append, and replace the text that is

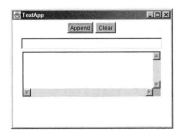

FIGURE 11.3
The TextApp default window.

contained in that text area. It also provides the capability to set the text to read-only or edit mode.

The TextApp program (Listing 11.2) illustrates the use of the TextField and TextArea classes. See the program running in Figure 11.3. Enter text into the text field and click the Append button. The text is appended to the text area. Click the Clear button and the text area is cleared.

LISTING 11.2

THE TextApp PROGRAM

```
import java.awt.*;
import java.awt.event.*;

public class TextApp extends Frame {
 TextField textField = new TextField(40);
 TextArea textArea = new TextArea(5,40);
 Button append = new Button("Append");
 Button clear = new Button("Clear");
 public static void main(String[] args) {
  TextApp app = new TextApp();
 }
 public TextApp() {
  super("TextApp");
  Panel panel1 = new Panel();
  Panel panel2 = new Panel();
  append.addActionListener(new ButtonHandler());
  clear.addActionListener(new ButtonHandler());
  panel1.add(append);
  panel1.add(clear);
  panel2.add(textField);
  panel2.add(textArea);
  add("North",panel1);
  add("Center",panel2);
  addWindowListener(new WindowEventHandler());
  pack();
  setSize(350,250);
  show();
 }
 class ButtonHandler implements ActionListener {
  public void actionPerformed(ActionEvent ev){
   String s=ev.getActionCommand();
   if(s.equals("Append")) {
    String text = textArea.getText();
    if(!text.equals("")) text += "\n"+textField.getText();
    else text = textField.getText();
    textArea.setText(text);
   }else if(s.equals("Clear")) textArea.setText("");
  }
```

```
   }
  class WindowEventHandler extends WindowAdapter{
   public void windowClosing(WindowEvent e) {
    System.exit(0);
   }
  }
}
```

Check Boxes

The Checkbox class is used to implement labeled check box and radio button GUI controls. If a Checkbox object is not associated with a CheckboxGroup object, it is implemented as a traditional check box. If a Checkbox object is associated with a CheckboxGroup object, it is implemented as a radio button.

The Checkbox class provides five constructors that enable you to specify the check box label, initial state, and CheckboxGroup object. The Checkbox class provides methods for getting and setting the label—getLabel() and setLabel()—and state of the check box—getState() and setState()—and its CheckboxGroup object, if any. The state of the check box is boolean. The Checkbox class also provides methods for identifying event handling code.

The CheckboxGroup class is used with the Checkbox class to implement radio buttons. All Checkbox objects that are associated with a CheckboxGroup object are treated as a single set of radio buttons. Only one button in the group may be set to On at a given point in time. The setState() method of a Checkbox object can be used to set the state of a radio button to "on." It also resets the state of all other radio buttons in the CheckboxGroup to the "off" state. The CheckboxGroup provides a single, parameterless constructor. It also provides methods for getting and setting the Checkbox object.

The CheckboxApp program (Listing 11.3) shows how Checkbox objects can be used as both check boxes and radio buttons. Figure 11.4 shows the default window displayed by CheckboxApp. Click any of the radio buttons or check boxes, and the text area displays the results of your click.

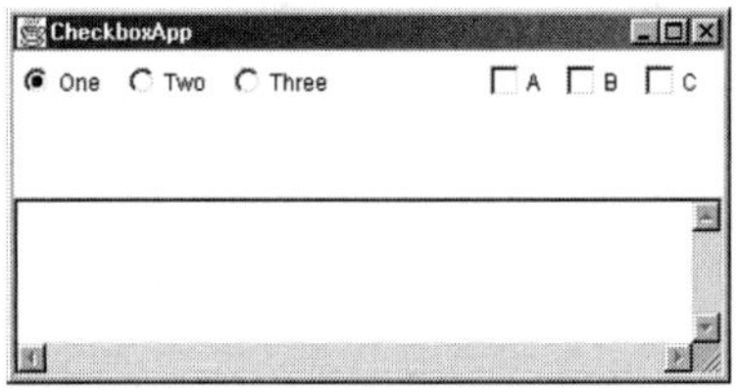

FIGURE 11.4

The window displayed by CheckboxApp

LISTING 11.3

THE CheckboxApp PROGRAM

```java
import java.awt.*;
import java.awt.event.*;

public class CheckboxApp extends Frame {
 TextArea textArea = new TextArea(5,10);
 public static void main(String[] args) {
  CheckboxApp app = new CheckboxApp();
 }
 public CheckboxApp() {
  super("CheckboxApp");
  Panel panel1 = new Panel();
  Panel panel2 = new Panel();
  Checkbox one = new Checkbox("One");
  Checkbox two = new Checkbox("Two");
  Checkbox three = new Checkbox("Three");
  CheckboxGroup group = new CheckboxGroup();
  one.setCheckboxGroup(group);
  two.setCheckboxGroup(group);
  three.setCheckboxGroup(group);
  one.setState(true);
  Checkbox a = new Checkbox("A");
  Checkbox b = new Checkbox("B");
  Checkbox c = new Checkbox("C");
  CheckboxHandler ch = new CheckboxHandler();
  one.addItemListener(ch);
  two.addItemListener(ch);
  three.addItemListener(ch);
  a.addItemListener(ch);
  b.addItemListener(ch);
  c.addItemListener(ch);
  panel1.add(one);
  panel1.add(two);
  panel1.add(three);
  panel2.add(a);
  panel2.add(b);
  panel2.add(c);
  add(panel1,"West");
  add(panel2,"East");
  add(textArea,"South");
  addWindowListener(new WindowEventHandler());
  pack();
  setSize(400,200);
  show();
 }
 class CheckboxHandler implements ItemListener {
  public void itemStateChanged(ItemEvent e){
   String status;
   Checkbox checkbox = (Checkbox) e.getItemSelectable();
   if(checkbox.getState()) status = "You checked: ";
   else status = "You unchecked: ";
   status += checkbox.getLabel();
   textArea.setText(status);
```

```
  }
 }
 class WindowEventHandler extends WindowAdapter{
  public void windowClosing(WindowEvent e) {
   System.exit(0);
  }
 }
}
```

Choices and Lists

The Choice class is used to implement pull-down lists that can be placed in the main area of a window. These lists are known as *option menus*. These are pop-up menus that enable the user to select a single menu value. The Choice class provides a single, parameterless constructor. It also provides access methods that are used to add items to the list, count the number of items contained in the list, select a list item, handle events, and determine which list item is selected.

The List class implements single- and multiple-selection list GUI controls. The lists provided by the List class are more sophisticated than those provided by the Choice class. The List class lets you specify the size of the scrollable window in which the list items are displayed and select multiple items from the list. The List class has the following three constructors:

- ◆ List()

- ◆ List(int rows)

- ◆ List(int rows, boolean multipleMode)

The first one takes no parameters and constructs a generic List object. The second one allows you to select the number of rows in the visible window. The third one enables you to specify the number of rows and also whether or not multiple selections are allowed.

The List class provides several access methods that are used to add, delete, and replace list items, count the number of items in the list, determine which items are selected, handle events, and select items within the list. I recommend that you browse the API description of the List class to get an idea of the methods that it supports.

FIGURE 11.5
The ChooserApp window.

The ChooserApp program (Listing 11.4) shows how Choice and List objects are used in a GUI. Figure 11.5 shows the ChooserApp program running. Use the Choice object on the left of the screen to select a meal. Use the menu item List object on the right of the screen to select one or more items to order for that meal. The results of your order are displayed in the TextField object.

LISTING 11.4

THE ChooserApp PROGRAM

```java
import java.awt.*;
import java.awt.event.*;

public class ChooserApp extends Frame {
 MyChoice mealChoice;
 MyList currentList;
 MyList mealList[];
 String meals[] = {"Breakfast","Lunch","Dinner"};
 String mealChoices[][] = {
  {"pancakes","eggs","bacon","ham","sausage","cereal",
   "toast","coffee","juice"},
  {"pizza","hamburger","hot dog","burrito","salad","fries",
   "chips","soda","milk"},
  {"spaghetti","carne asada","barbequed
chicken","soup","salad",
   "bread","wine","beer","soda","milk"}
 };
 TextField text;
 public static void main(String[] args) {
  ChooserApp app = new ChooserApp();
 }
 public ChooserApp() {
  super("ChooserApp");
  setupChoice();
  setupLists();
  text = new TextField(40);
  add("North",new Label("Place your order:"));
  add("South",text);
  add("West",mealChoice);
  currentList = mealList[0];
  add("East",currentList);
  addWindowListener(new WindowEventHandler());
  pack();
  setSize(300,200);
  show();
 }
 void setupChoice(){
  mealChoice = new MyChoice(meals);
  mealChoice.addItemListener(new ChoiceHandler());
 }
 void setupLists(){
```

```
    mealList = new MyList[meals.length];
    ListHandler lh = new ListHandler();
    for(int i=0;i<meals.length;++i){
     mealList[i] = new MyList(5,true,mealChoices[i]);
     mealList[i].addItemListener(lh);
    }
   }
   class ChoiceHandler implements ItemListener {
    public void itemStateChanged(ItemEvent e){
     for(int i=0;i<meals.length;++i)
      if(meals[i].equals(mealChoice.getSelectedItem())){
       remove(currentList);
       currentList = mealList[i];
       add("East",currentList);
       text.setText(meals[i]);
      }
     validate();
    }
   }
   class ListHandler implements ItemListener {
    public void itemStateChanged(ItemEvent e){
     String order = mealChoice.getSelectedItem()+": ";
     String items[] = currentList.getSelectedItems();
     for(int i=0;i<items.length;++i) order += items[i]+" ";
     text.setText(order);
    }
   }
   class WindowEventHandler extends WindowAdapter{
    public void windowClosing(WindowEvent e) {
     System.exit(0);
    }
   }
  }
  class MyList extends List {
   public MyList(int rows,boolean multiple,String labels[]) {
    super(rows,multiple);
    int length = labels.length;
    for(int i=0;i<length;++i) {
     try {
      add(labels[i]);
     }catch (NullPointerException ex) {
      add("");
     }
    }
   }
  }
  class MyChoice extends Choice {
   public MyChoice(String labels[]) {
    super();
    int length = labels.length;
    for(int i=0;i<length;++i) {
     try {
```

continues

| LISTING 11.4 | *continued* |

THE ChooserApp PROGRAM

```
   add(labels[i]);
  }catch (NullPointerException ex) {
   add("");
  }
 }
}}
```

Scrollbars

The Scrollbar class is used to implement vertical and horizontal scrollbars. It provides three constructors that enable you to specify the orientation of the scrollbar and the parameters that control the scrollbar's operation. It provides several methods that allow the scrollbar's parameters and current value to be read and set.

When you use scrollbars in your Java programs, you will probably use them to scroll through a Graphics object that is associated with a Canvas object or the main application window. (These objects are covered in the following chapter.) You create and place scrollbars in your window in the same manner as any other window component. Their position and size within the window are determined by the layout associated with the window.

Scrollbars are created using the Scrollbar()constructor. Three forms of this constructor are provided. The default constructor takes no parameters and is not particularly useful, unless you want to create a Scrollbar object and then specify its orientation and use later in your program. The second constructor allows the orientation of a Scrollbar object to be specified. The third Scrollbar() constructor uses the five parameters that are needed to create a working scrollbar: orientation, value, visible, minimum, and maximum.

The orientation of a scrollbar is specified by the VERTICAL and HORI-ZONTAL constants defined by the Scrollbar class. The minimum and maximum parameters specify the range of the scrollbar. These values should map to the object being scrolled. For example, if you are scrolling a 1,000-line text object, appropriate minimum and maximum values for a vertical scrollbar would be 0 and 999. Horizontal values can be determined using the maximum width of the text to be scrolled (in pixels).

The value parameter identifies the starting value associated with the scrollbar. The value parameter is usually set to the minimum value of the scrollbar. However, suppose you wanted to initiate the display of an object with its center displayed on the screen. You would then set the scrollbar's value parameter to the average of its minimum and maximum values.

The visible parameter is used to specify the size of the viewable area of the object being scrolled. For example, if you are scrolling a 1,000-line text object and the viewable area of the window is 25 lines long, you would set the visible variable to 25. The visible parameter also determines the actual maximum value of the scrollbar. In this example, the maximum value would be 1000 - 25 = 975.

The Scrollbar class provides several methods for getting and setting the parameters of a Scrollbar object. The getOrientation(), getValue(), getVisibleAmount(), getMinimum(), and getMaximum() methods retrieve the parameter values discussed so far. The getValue() method is used to determine the position to which the user has scrolled.

The setUnitIncrement() and setBlockIncrement() methods are used to specify the size of a scrollable unit and page relative to the minimum and maximum values associated with a scrollbar. For example, when scrolling text, you can set the unit increment of a vertical scrollbar to one so that only one line of text is vertically scrolled. You can set the page increment to 10 to allow 10 lines of text to be scrolled when the user clicks between the tab and arrows of a scrollbar. The getUnitIncrement() and getBlockIncrement() methods provide access to the current unit- and page-increment values. The block increment is equal or slightly less than the visible amount.

The setValue() method enables you to directly set the current position of a scrollbar. The setValues() method allows you to specify a scrollbar's value, visible, minimum, and maximum parameters.

The ScrollerApp program (Listing 11.5) shows how scrollbars are used. Figure 11.6 shows the ScrollerApp program running. Move the vertical or horizontal scrollbar and the text label is updated to display the scrollbar's new position.

FIGURE 11.6
The ScrollerApp window.

LISTING 11.5

THE ScrollerApp PROGRAM

```java
import java.awt.*;
import java.awt.event.*;

public class ScrollerApp extends Frame {
 Label label = new Label("Scrollbar Position");
 MyScrollbar hscroll = new MyScrollbar(Scrollbar.HORIZONTAL,
  50,1,0,100,label);
 MyScrollbar vscroll = new MyScrollbar(Scrollbar.VERTICAL,
  500,10,0,1000,label);
 public static void main(String[] args) {
  ScrollerApp app = new ScrollerApp();
 }
 public ScrollerApp() {
  super("ScrollerApp");
  add("Center",label);
  add("West",vscroll);
  add("North",hscroll);
  addWindowListener(new WindowEventHandler());
  pack();
  setSize(200,200);
  show();
 }
 class WindowEventHandler extends WindowAdapter{
  public void windowClosing(WindowEvent e) {
   System.exit(0);
  }
 }
}
class MyScrollbar extends Scrollbar {
 Label position;
 String direction = "     Horizontal";
 public MyScrollbar(int orientation,int value,int visible,int
➡min,int max,
  Label label) {
  super(orientation,value,visible,min,max);
  position=label;
  if(orientation==Scrollbar.VERTICAL) direction = "
➡Vertical";
  addAdjustmentListener(new MyScrollbar.HandleScrolling());
 }
 class HandleScrolling implements AdjustmentListener {
  public void adjustmentValueChanged(AdjustmentEvent e){
   position.setText(direction+" Position:  "+e.getValue());
  }
 }
}
```

Canvas

The Canvas class provides an area of the screen that is used for drawing and painting. You generally extend the Canvas class and override its paint() method to accomplish custom drawing and painting. Each Canvas object is associated with a Graphics object that is used to perform the actual drawing and painting. Chapter 14, "The java.awt.Package: Painting," covers the Canvas class in more detail.

AWT CONTAINERS

Although Component contains many GUI-related subclasses, its Container subclass is used to define components that can contain other components. It provides methods for adding, retrieving, displaying, counting, and removing the components that it contains. The Container class also provides methods for working with layouts, which are used to control the layout of components within a container. Methods that you should become familiar with are:

◆ add()—Used to add a component to the container (usually under the control of a layout class).

◆ getComponent() and getComponentAt()—Obtains a reference to a component in the container.

◆ getInsets()—Returns information about a container's border.

◆ remove() and removeAll()—Removes components from the container.

◆ getLayout() and setLayout()—Gets and sets the way in which the components of the container are organized.

◆ validate() and validateTree()—Causes the container to be laid out and redisplayed.

The Container class has three major AWT subclasses: Window, Panel, and ScrollPane. Window provides a common superclass for application main windows (Frame objects) and Dialog windows. The Panel class is a generic container that can be displayed within an applet or window. It is subclassed by the java.applet.Applet class as the base class for all Java applets. The ScrollPane class is a scrollable container that can have vertical and horizontal scrollbars.

NOTE

Swing Containers The `Container` class also has several Swing subclasses. However, because Swing is not part of the certification exam (and a large topic of its own) I do not cover the Swing subclasses.

Window

The `Window` class provides an encapsulation of a generic `Window` object. It is subclassed by `Frame` and `Dialog` to provide the capabilities needed to support application main windows and dialog box support.

The `Window` class provides two constructors that create `Window` objects with a `Frame` or a `Window` as the parent. The parent must be specified because only objects of the `Frame` class or its subclasses contain the functionality needed to implement a main application window.

The `Window` class provides important methods that are used by its `Frame` and `Dialog` subclasses. The `pack()` method is used to size the components of a window according to their preferred size and arrange them according to the window layout style. The `pack()` method should be invoked before a window is displayed. The `setSize()` method sets the vertical and horizontal dimensions of the window. The `show()` method is used to display a window. Windows are hidden (invisible) by default, and are only displayed as a result of invoking their `show()` method. The `toFront()` and `toBack()` methods are used to position windows relative to their frame window and all other windows of the same program. The `dispose()` method releases the resources associated with a window and deletes the `Window` object. The `getWarningString()` method is used to retrieve the warning message associated with untrusted windows. Warning messages are associated with windows that are created by applets.

A `Window` object does not have a border or a menubar when it is created. In this state, it may be used to implement a pop-up window.

Frame

The `Frame` class is used to provide the main window of an application. It is a subclass of `Window` that supports the capabilities to specify a window icon, cursor, menu bar, and title. Because it implements the `MenuContainer` interface, it is capable of working with `MenuBar` objects.

The `Frame` class defines several constants that can specify different types of cursors to be used within the frame. As of JDK 1.1, a separate `Cursor` class is available for working with cursors.

Frame provides two constructors: a default parameterless constructor that creates an untitled frame window and a constructor that accepts a String argument to be used as the frame window's title. The second constructor is typically used.

Frame extends the set of access methods that it inherits from Window by adding methods to get and set the window title, icon image, and menu bar. It also provides methods for removing the menu bar and specifying whether the window is resizable.

Dialog

The Dialog class is a subclass of the Window class that is used to implement dialog box windows. A dialog box is usually a smaller temporary window that contains a number of GUI controls for interacting with the user. Common examples of dialog boxes are the file open or save dialog boxes that are used to select files and directories. The Dialog class enables you to construct modal and non-modal dialog boxes. *Modal* dialog boxes must be closed before control returns to the window that launched them. *Non-modal* dialog boxes that do not need to be closed before other program windows can be accessed.

The Dialog constructors enable you to specify the Frame or Dialog object containing the dialog box., as well as the modal flag and the dialog box's title.

The Dialog class provides only a handful of access methods. These methods get and set the dialog box's title, determine whether it is modal, and get and set its resizable properties.

FileDialog

The FileDialog class is used to construct dialog boxes that support the selection of files for input and output operations. It is a subclass of the Dialog class and provides three constructors. These constructors take as arguments the Frame window that contains the dialog box, the title to be used at the top of the dialog box, and a mode parameter that can be set to the LOAD or SAVE constants defined by FileDialog.

FileDialog provides methods that are used to access the directory and filename of the user-selected file and to specify an object that implements the FileNameFilter interface. The FileNameFilter

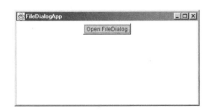

FIGURE 11.7

The FileDialogApp window.

interface is defined in the java.io package. It defines the accept() method, which is used to determine the filenames that should be included in a file list.

Listing 11.6 shows the FileDialogApp program. It displays the window shown in Figure 11.7. Click on the Open FileDialog button and a file dialog box is displayed. Select a filename and click Open. The directory and name of the file that you selected are displayed.

LISTING 11.6

THE FileDialogApp PROGRAM

```java
import java.awt.*;
import java.awt.event.*;

public class FileDialogApp extends Frame {
 Label label1 = new Label("");
 Label label2 = new Label("");
 public static void main(String[] args) {
  FileDialogApp app = new FileDialogApp();
 }
 public FileDialogApp() {
  super("FileDialogApp");
  Panel panel = new Panel();
  Panel panel1 = new Panel();
  Panel panel2 = new Panel();
  Panel panel3 = new Panel();
  panel.setLayout(new GridLayout(3,1));
  Button button = new Button("Open FileDialog");
  panel1.add(button);
  panel2.add(label1);
  panel3.add(label2);
  panel.add(panel1);
  panel.add(panel2);
  panel.add(panel3);
  add("Center",panel);
  button.addActionListener(new ButtonHandler());
  addWindowListener(new WindowEventHandler());
  pack();
  setSize(400,200);
  show();
 }
 class ButtonHandler implements ActionListener {
  public void actionPerformed(ActionEvent e){
   FileDialog fd = new FileDialog(FileDialogApp.this);
   fd.show();
   label1.setText(fd.getDirectory());
   label2.setText(fd.getFile());
   validate();
  }
 }
 class WindowEventHandler extends WindowAdapter{
```

```
  public void windowClosing(WindowEvent e) {
   System.exit(0);
  }
 }
}
```

Panel

The Panel class is a subclass of Container that provides a rectangular area for organizing components. Panel objects typically organize a set of components into a group that can then be ordered and laid out as if it were a single component.

Applet

The Applet class is a subclass of Panel that that is designed to be embedded in a Web page. Applet objects are automatically constructed by the user agent (usually a browser) when it displays the page, and contains several methods to interact with this environment. It contains a single default parameterless constructor, which is generally not used. Applets are constructed by the runtime environment when they are loaded and do not have to be explicitly constructed.

The Applet class contains methods that can display images, play audio files, respond to events, and obtain information about an applet's execution environment. This environment is referred to as the applet's *context*.

Even though applets are an important part of Java programming, you probably won't see any applet-related questions on the certification exam. However, you'll see several examples of their use in the following chapter on layouts.

ScrollPane

The ScrollPane class simplifies the development of scrollable applications. The ScrollPane class is like a combination of a panel and vertical and horizontal scrollbars. The great thing about it is that it performs all the scrollbar event handling and screen redrawing internally. The fact that the ScrollPane class handles events is significant.

By handling events internally, it enables scrolling-related operations to run significantly faster.

The ScrollPane class extends the Container class and, therefore, can contain other components. It is designed to automate scrolling for a single, contained component, such as a Canvas object. It provides two constructors—a single parameterless constructor and a constructor that takes an int argument. The parameterless constructor creates a ScrollPane object that displays scrollbars only when they are needed. The other constructor takes one of the three constants: SCROLLBARS_ALWAYS, SCROLLBARS_AS_NEEDED, and SCROLLBARS_NEVER. These constants determine if and when scrollbars are displayed by the ScrollPane object.

The initial size of the ScrollPane object is 100×100 pixels. The setSize() method can be used to resize it. The ScrollPane class provides methods for accessing and updating its internal scrollbars, but in most cases this is both unnecessary and ill-advised. Other methods are provided to get and set the current scrollbar positions.

Menus

Java provides a rich set of menu-related classes for creating and interacting with pull-down menus. The MenuComponent class is the superclass of all menu-related classes. Since it extends the Object class instead of Component, it defines a separate AWT component class hierarchy. It provides several methods, the most useful of which are the following:

◆ getFont() and setFont()—Gets and sets the font associated with the menu component.

◆ getName() and setName()—Gets and sets the name of the menu component.

◆ getParent()—Returns the parent container of the menu component.

The MenuComponent class has two direct superclasses, MenuBar and MenuItem, which provide most of the methods for creating and using menus.

MenuBar

The MenuBar class defines the menu bar that is displayed at the top of an application window by a Frame object. A Frame object can have one and only one MenuBar object, which is set using the setMenuBar() method of the Frame class. A MenuBar object is assigned a set of Menu objects, each of which is displayed as a separate pull-down menu. Common examples are the File, Edit, and Help pull-down menus found in many window applications. Menu objects are added to a MenuBar object using the add() method of the MenuBar class. The MenuBar class lets a special menu be designated as a Help menu. It is set using the setHelpMenu() method. The getMenu() and getHelpMenu() methods are used to retrieve the Menu objects that have been added to a MenuBar.

MenuItem

The MenuItem class extends the MenuComponent class and defines the individual items that may be added to a Menu object. Some of its important methods are:

◆ getLabel() and setLabel()   Gets and sets the menu item's label.

◆ getShortcut() and setShortcut()   Gets and sets the MenuShortcut object associated with the menu item. A MenuShortcut object defines keystrokes that can be entered to select a menu item.

◆ isEnabled() and setEnabled()   Allows the enabled status of the menu item to be checked and set.

Since MenuItem is the superclass of the Menu class, it enables Menu objects to be used as MenuItem objects. This enables cascading, multi-level menus to be constructed. MenuItem is also the superclass of the CheckboxMenuItem class and provides the capability to implement menu items that can be checked or unchecked.

FIGURE 11.8
The MenuApp window.

Menu

The Menu class is a subclass of MenuItem that implements a pull-down menu. For example, an application's File menu would be implemented as a Menu object that is added to a MenuBar. A Menu object contains one or more MenuItem objects, which can be a normal user-selectable MenuItem object, a CheckboxMenuItem object, or another Menu object. Java supports *tear-off menus*, which are menus that can be removed from a menu bar. A tear-off menu is constructed in the same manner as a regular menu—you only need to set the Boolean tear-off value in the Menu() constructor. Tear-off menus are not implemented within Windows 95 or NT, but they are implemented in Solaris and other UNIX derivatives.

The Menu class provides several methods for working with MenuItem objects, including the add(), insert(), remove(), and removeAll() methods. The getItem() and getItemCount() methods are used to access the MenuItem objects that have been added to a menu. The insertSeparator() method inserts a separator line between menu items.

CheckboxMenuItem

The CheckboxMenuItem class extends the MenuItem class and supports menu items that can be checked on or off. The getState() and setState() methods are used to access the checked state of the menu item.

The MenuApp program shown in Listing 11.7 shows how the MenuBar, Menu, MenuItem, and CheckboxMenuItem classes are used. It displays the window shown in Figure 11.8. This window has a menu bar with File, Edit, and Help pulldown menus. When you select a menu item, the result of your selection is displayed in the middle of the window.

LISTING 11.7

THE MENUAPP PROGRAM

```
import java.awt.*;
import java.awt.event.*;

public class MenuApp extends Frame {
  MenuBar mb = new MenuBar();
```

```
Label label = new Label("");
public static void main(String[] args) {
 MenuApp app = new MenuApp();
}
public MenuApp() {
 super("MenuApp");
 Panel panel = new Panel();
 panel.add(label);
 add("Center",panel);
 addWindowListener(new WindowEventHandler());
 setupMenuBar();
 setMenuBar(mb);
 pack();
 setSize(400,400);
 show();
}
void setupMenuBar() {
 Menu fileMenu =  new Menu("File");
 Menu editMenu =  new Menu("Edit");
 Menu helpMenu = new Menu("Help");
 MenuItem newFileMenu = new MenuItem("New");
 MenuItem exitFileMenu = new MenuItem("Exit");
 fileMenu.add(newFileMenu);
 fileMenu.addSeparator();
 fileMenu.add(exitFileMenu);
 MenuItem cutEditMenu = new MenuItem("Cut");
 MenuItem copyEditMenu = new MenuItem("Copy");
 MenuItem pasteEditMenu = new MenuItem("Paste");
 Menu statusMenu = new Menu("Status");
 CheckboxMenuItem textMode = new CheckboxMenuItem("Text
 ➥Mode",true);
 CheckboxMenuItem wordWrap = new CheckboxMenuItem("Word
 ➥Wrap",true);
 statusMenu.add(textMode);
 statusMenu.add(wordWrap);
 editMenu.add(cutEditMenu);
 editMenu.add(copyEditMenu);
 editMenu.add(pasteEditMenu);
 editMenu.addSeparator();
 editMenu.add(statusMenu);
 MenuItem aboutHelp = new MenuItem("About");
 helpMenu.add(aboutHelp);
 mb.add(fileMenu);
 mb.add(editMenu);
 mb.setHelpMenu(helpMenu);
 MenuHandler mh = new MenuHandler();
 newFileMenu.addActionListener(mh);
 exitFileMenu.addActionListener(mh);
 cutEditMenu.addActionListener(mh);
 copyEditMenu.addActionListener(mh);
 pasteEditMenu.addActionListener(mh);
 textMode.addItemListener(mh);
 wordWrap.addItemListener(mh);
 aboutHelp.addActionListener(mh);
```

continues

LISTING 11.7 | *continued*

THE MenuApp PROGRAM

```
  }
  class MenuHandler implements ActionListener, ItemListener {
    public void actionPerformed(ActionEvent e){
      String s = e.getActionCommand();
      label.setText(s);
      validate();
      if(s.equals("Exit")) System.exit(0);
    }
    public void itemStateChanged(ItemEvent e){
      CheckboxMenuItem item = (CheckboxMenuItem)
e.getItemSelectable();
      String status;
      if(item.getState()) status = "You checked: ";
      else status = "You unchecked: ";
      status += item.getLabel();
      label.setText(status);
      validate();
    }
  }
  class WindowEventHandler extends WindowAdapter{
    public void windowClosing(WindowEvent e) {
      System.exit(0);
    }
  }
}
```

Pop-up Menus

In addition to the traditional menus that are pulled down from a menu bar, Java provides support for *pop-up menus*, which are menus that appear when you perform a mouse action that triggers them.

Pop-up menus are supported via the PopupMenu class, which is a subclass of the Menu class. This class provides two constructors—a default parameterless constructor and a constructor that takes a String parameter. The String parameter is used as the pop-up menu's title. In Windows, the title is not displayed.

The show() method of the PopupMenu class causes a pop-up menu to be displayed. Its arguments are the Component object in which the menu is to be popped up and the x, y coordinate where the menu is to be placed (relative to the component).

CHAPTER SUMMARY

CHAPTER SUMMARY

This chapter covered the classes and interfaces of java.awt that are used to implement GUI components and containers. You were introduced to each of the major AWT components and learned how they are organized into containers. You also built several small Java applications and applets that illustrated the use of component and containers. You should now be prepared to test your knowledge of these topics. The following review questions and exam questions will let you know how well you understand this material and will give you an idea of how you'll do in related exam questions. They'll also indicate which material you need to study further.

KEY TERMS

- Abstract Windowing Toolkit
- Component
- Container
- Button
- Label
- Text Field
- Text Area
- Checkbox
- Radio Button
- Selection List
- Window
- Frame
- Dialog
- Panel
- Applet

APPLY YOUR KNOWLEDGE

Review Questions

1. Which class is the immediate superclass of the `Container` class?

2. Which method of the `Component` class is used to set the position and size of a component?

3. Name three subclasses of the `Component` class.

4. What methods are used to get and set the text label displayed by a `Button` object?

5. Name two subclasses of the `TextComponent` class.

6. Which `TextComponent` method is used to set a `TextComponent` to the read-only state?

7. How can the `Checkbox` class be used to create a radio button?

8. Name four `Container` classes.

9. Which class is the immediate superclass of the `MenuComponent` class.

10. What `Checkbox` method allows you to tell if a `Checkbox` is checked?

11. What is the difference between a `Choice` and a `List`?

12. Which `Container` method is used to cause a container to be laid out and redisplayed?

13. What is the difference between a `Window` and a `Frame`?

14. What is the immediate superclass of the `Dialog` class?

15. What is the immediate superclass of the `Applet` class?

16. What is the difference between a `Scrollbar` and a `ScrollPane`?

17. Which containers may have a `MenuBar`?

18. What is the immediate superclass of `Menu`?

19. What is the difference between a `MenuItem` and a `CheckboxMenuItem`?

20. Which `Component` subclass is used for drawing and painting?

Exam Questions

1. Which of the following are true?

    A. `Component` extends `Container`.

    B. `MenuItem` extends `Component`.

    C. `Container` extends `Component`.

    D. `MenuComponent` extends `Component`.

2. Which of the following are direct or indirect subclasses of `Component`?

    A. `Button`

    B. `Label`

    C. `CheckboxMenuItem`

    D. `Toolbar`

    E. `Frame`

3. Which of the following are direct or indirect subclasses of `Container`?

    A. `Frame`

    B. `TextArea`

    C. `MenuBar`

    D. `FileDialog`

    E. `Applet`

APPLY YOUR KNOWLEDGE

4. Which `Component` method is used to access a component's immediate `Container`?

    A. `getVisible()`

    B. `getImmediate()`

    C. `getParent()`

    D. `getContainer()`

5. Which method is used to set the text of a `Label` object?

    A. `setText()`

    B. `setLabel()`

    C. `setTextLabel()`

    D. `setLabelText()`

6. Which of the following are true?

    A. `TextComponent` extends `TextArea`.

    B. `TextArea` extend `TextField`.

    C. `TextField` extends `TextComponent`.

    D. `TextComponent` extends `TextField`.

    E. `TextArea` extends `TextComponent`.

7. Which of the following are true?

    A. The `Checkbox` class extends the `RadioButton` class.

    B. The `CheckboxGroup` class is used to define radio buttons.

    C. The `RadioGroup` class is used to define radio buttons.

    D. A `Checkbox` is a `RadioButton` that has been associated with a `CheckboxGroup`.

    E. A `Checkbox` is a `RadioButton` that has been associated with a `RadioGroup`.

8. Which constructor creates a `TextArea` with 10 rows and 20 columns?

    A. `new TextArea(10,20)`

    B. `new TextArea(20,10)`

    C. `new TextArea(new Rows(10), new Colums(20))`

    D. `new TextArea(200)`

9. Which of the following creates a `List` with 5 visible items and multiple selection enabled?

    A. `new List(5, true)`

    B. `new List(true, 5)`

    C. `new List(5, false)`

    D. `new List(false, 5)`

10. Which are true about the `Container` class?

    A. The `validate()` method is used to cause a `Container` to be laid out and redisplayed.

    B. The `add()` method is used to add a `Component` to a `Container`.

    C. The `getBorder()` method returns information about a container's insets.

    D. The `getComponent()` method is used to access a `Component` that is contained in a `Container`.

11. Which of the following are true?

    A. `Window` extends `Frame`.

    B. `Applet` extends `Window`.

    C. `Panel` extends `Container`.

    D. `ScrollPane` extends `Panel`.

APPLY YOUR KNOWLEDGE

12. Which of the following are true?

    A. A `Dialog` can have a `MenuBar`.

    B. `MenuItem` extends `Menu`.

    C. A `MenuItem` can be added to a `Menu`.

    D. A `Menu` can be added to a `Menu`.

13. Suppose a `Panel` is added to a `Frame` and a `Button` is added to the `Panel`. If the `Frame`'s font is set to 12-point TimesRoman, the `Panel`'s font is set to 10-point TimesRoman, and the `Button`'s font is not set, what font will be used to display the `Button`'s label?

    A. 12-point TimesRoman

    B. 11-point TimesRoman

    C. 10-point TimesRoman

    D. 9-point TimesRoman

14. A `Frame`'s background color is set to `Color.Yellow`, and a `Button`'s background color is set to `Color.Blue`. Suppose the `Button` is added to a `Panel`, which is added to the `Frame`. What background color will be used with the `Panel`?

    A. `Color.Yellow`

    B. `Color.Blue`

    C. `Color.Green`

    D. `Color.White`

15. Which methods will cause a `Frame` to be displayed?

    A. `show()`

    B. `setVisible()`

    C. `display()`

    D. `displayFrame()`

Answers to Review Questions

1. `Component`

2. `setBounds()`

3. `Box.Filler, Button, Canvas, Checkbox, Choice, Container, Label, List, Scrollbar, or TextComponent`

4. `getLabel()` and `setLabel()`

5. `TextField` and `TextArea`

6. `setEditable()`

7. By associating `Checkbox` objects with a `CheckboxGroup`.

8. `Window, Frame, Dialog, FileDialog, Panel, Applet, or ScrollPane`

9. `Object`

10. `getState()`

11. A `Choice` is displayed in a compact form that requires you to pull it down to see the list of available choices. Only one item may be selected from a `Choice`. A `List` may be displayed in such a way that several `List` items are visible. A `List` supports the selection of one or more `List` items.

12. `validate()`

13. The `Frame` class extends `Window` to define a main application window that can have a menu bar.

14. `Window`

15. `Panel`

16. A `Scrollbar` is a `Component`, but not a `Container`. A `ScrollPane` is a `Container`. A `ScrollPane` handles its own events and performs its own scrolling.

APPLY YOUR KNOWLEDGE

17. `Frame`

18. `MenuItem`

19. The `CheckboxMenuItem` class extends the `MenuItem` class to support a menu item that may be checked or unchecked.

20. `Canvas`

Answers to Exam Questions

1. C The `Container` class is a subclass of `Component`. `MenuItem` extends `MenuComponent` which extends `Object`.

2. A, B, and E `CheckboxMenuItem` is not in the `Component` class hierarchy. `Toolbar` is not an AWT class.

3. A, D, and E `TextArea` and `MenuBar` are not subclasses of `Container`.

4. C The `getParent()` method is used to access a component's container.

5. A The `setText()` method sets the text of a `Label`.

6. C and E `TextComponent` is extended by `TextField` and `TextArea`.

7. B The `CheckboxGroup` class is used to define radio buttons.

8. A Usage is `TextArea(rows,columns)`.

9. A Usage is `List(rows, multipleMode)`.

10. A, B, and D The `getBorder()` method is not defined for the `Container` class.

11. C `Panel` extends `Container`. The others are false.

12. C and D A `MenuItem` (and therefore a `Menu`) can be added to a `Menu`.

13. C Since the `Button`'s parent is the `Panel`, the `Button` inherits the `Panel`'s font.

14. A The `Panel` inherits the `Frame`'s background color.

15. A and B Either `show()` or `setVisible()` may be used.

Suggested Readings and Resources

The JDK 1.2 `java.awt` package API description.

This chapter helps you to prepare for the exam by covering the following objectives:

Know what layout managers are and how they are used.

▶ A general knowledge of what layout managers are and how they are used to organize components in containers is required for some exam questions. You should also learn the advantages of layout managers developing platform-independent GUIs.

Know what layout managers are supported by the AWT.

▶ The AWT supports five basic layout managers. You will be required to know what these layout managers are and be able to identify examples of their use.

Know how to write code using component container and layout manager classes of the `java.awt` package to present a GUI with specified appearance and resize the behavior and distinguish the responsibilities of layout managers from those of containers.

▶ This is the key objective of this chapter. Several exam questions require you to know the basics of how layout managers are used. You need to have some practical experience using the AWT layout managers to correctly answer these exam questions.

Know how to position components without a layout manager.

▶ Although you probably won't get tested on this, knowledge of how to position components without a layout manager will help you to understand layout managers better and make you a better Java programmer.

C H A P T E R 12

The java.awt Package: Layout

OUTLINE

STUDY STRATEGIES

As you read through this chapter, you should concentrate on the following key items:

▶ What classes and interfaces support layouts.

▶ How layout managers simplify the process of organizing GUI components.

▶ How each layout manager is used.

▶ How layouts are displayed by Java.

CHAPTER INTRODUCTION

This chapter covers the classes and interfaces of java.awt that are used to organize the display of GUI components. Knowledge of these classes and interfaces is essential to developing a Java-based GUI. As a consequence, you will see quite a few questions about the material covered in this chapter. Fortunately, this material is not difficult. With some study and a little programming, you should be able to master this material. If you read through this chapter, compile and run the programs, and master the review questions, you should have no problem with layout managers on the certification exam.

WORKING WITH LAYOUT MANAGERS

The way that Java organizes GUI components within containers differs from traditional windowing systems like Windows, the MacOS, and the X Window system. These older systems require that programmers specify the absolute position and size of components within containers. This approach is OK if you are working with a single windowing system. But Java is platform-independent and is not confined to an particualr windowing system. Instead, Java's AWT provides the capability to organize components within containers using relative component sizes and positions.

Java's unique approach uses *layout managers*, which implement *layout policies*. Layout policies are rules for organizing components within a container. A layout manager is an object that carries out the policy for a particular set of components and containers. Layout managers provide a significant benefit because you can create a custom GUI without having to worry about the exact size and position of your GUI elements. It's true that modern visual programming tools simplify this aspect of GUI building; however, this is still a major consideration when building a platform-independent GUI. You don't have to worry about how a particular button will look when it is displayed by Netscape Navigator under Linux, Internet Explorer under Windows 98, or under a Macintosh windows program. Java's layout managers can make sure that your GUI will be laid out consistently across browsers and windowing systems.

NOTE **GUI Differences and Layouts**   Many GUI components differ slightly in size and appearance across browsers and windowing systems. Java's layout managers accomodates these differences when they display your GUI on different platforms.

NOTE **Absolute Positioning and Sizing**   The AWT will also let you use absolute positioning and sizing. This is accomplished through a null layout manager.

USING LAYOUTS

The method by which the components of a `Container` object are organized is determined by an object that implements the `LayoutManager` interface. The layout of a `Container` is specified using the `setLayout()` method of the `Container` class. It passes an object that implements the `LayoutManager` interface as a parameter.

The `LayoutManager` interface provides a set of methods that are implemented by classes that control the layout of a container. These methods include those that add or remove components from a layout, calculate the size of the container, and lay out the components of the container. The `LayoutManager2` interface extends the `LayoutManager` interface to deal with constraint-based layouts.

The `BorderLayout` Class

The `BorderLayout` class is used to lay out the GUI components contained in a `Container` object. It lays out components along the North, South, East, and West borders of the container and in the center of the container. The center component gets any space left over from the North, South, East, and West border components. It is the default layout for `Window`, `Frame`, and `Dialog` objects and provides the capability to specify the horizontal and vertical gap between the laid-out components and the container.

The `CardLayout` Class

The `CardLayout` class is used to lay out the components of a `Container` object in the form of a deck of cards in which only one card is visible at a time. The class provides methods that are used to specify the first, last, next, and previous components in the container.

The `FlowLayout` Class

The `FlowLayout` class is used to lay out the components of a `Container` object in a left-to-right, top-to-bottom fashion. It is the default layout used with `Panel` and `Applet` objects. It specifies the alignment of the components it lays out by the LEFT, CENTER, and RIGHT constants.

The GridLayout Class

The GridLayout class lays out the components of a Container object in a grid in which all components are the same size. The GridLayout constructor is used to specify the number of rows and columns of the grid.

The GridBagLayout Class

The GridBagLayout class lays out the components of a Container object in a grid-like fashion. Some components may occupy more than one row or column. The GridBagConstraints class identifies the positioning and resizing parameters of a component contained within an object that is laid out using a GridBagLayout. The Insets class is used to specify the margins associated with an object that is laid out using a GridBagLayout object. An Insets object is a representation of the borders of a container. It specifies the space that a container must leave at each of its edges.

> **NOTE**
>
> **Layout Managers and Preferred Sizes**
> Layout managers always try to accommodate the *preferred* size of a component, which is the minimal component size needed to display the component normally. However, when making a tradeoff between layout policy and preferred size, layout policy always wins. The preferred size of a component is returned by its getPreferredSize() method.

The Layouts Applet

The Layouts applet, shown in Listing 12.1, provides an example of using containers and layouts. This applet is run using the HTML file provided in Listing 12.2. When you run the Layouts applet using appletviewer, it displays the opening window shown in Figure 12.1. You can click the Border, Flow, Card, Grid, and GridBag buttons in the top panel to change the layout displayed in the panel below it. Figures 12.2 through 12.5 show the other layouts that are displayed. When you select the Card layout, a bottom panel is displayed (see Figure 12.2) containing the First, Last, Next, and Previous buttons. These buttons move you through the card deck of buttons displayed in the middle panel. Play with the applet to familiarize yourself with its operation before going on to the next section, which describes how the Layouts applet works.

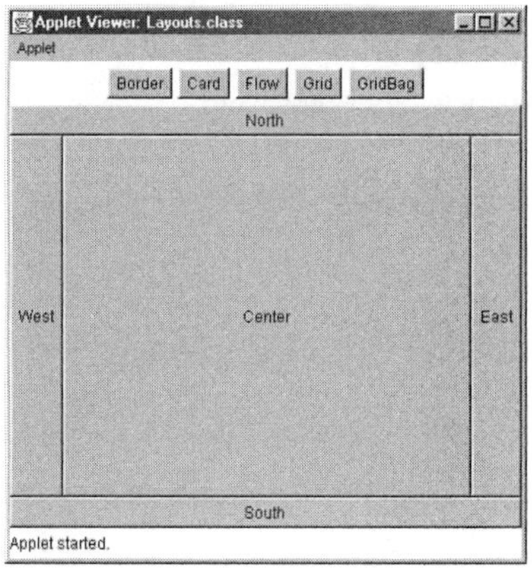

FIGURE 12.1
An example of a BorderLayout.

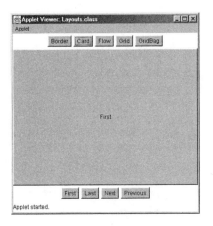

FIGURE 12.2
An example of a CardLayout.

FIGURE 12.3
An example of a FlowLayout.

LISTING 12.1

THE Layouts APPLET

```
import java.applet.*;
import java.awt.*;
import java.awt.event.*;

public class Layouts extends Applet {
 Panel[] panels;
 Panel currentPanel;
 static int border=0;
 static int card=1;
 static int flow=2;
 static int grid=3;
 static int gridBag=4;
 String[] layouts = {"Border","Card","Flow","Grid","GridBag"};
 String[] cards = {"First","Last","Next","Previous"};
 Button[] layoutButtons = new Button[layouts.length];
 Button[] navigateButtons = new Button[cards.length];
 Panel layoutButtonPanel = new Panel();
 Panel navigateButtonPanel = new Panel();
 public void init(){
  setLayout(new BorderLayout());
  setupButtons();
  add("North",layoutButtonPanel);
  setupDisplayPanels();
 }
 void setupButtons() {
  for(int i=0;i<layouts.length;++i) {
   layoutButtons[i] = new Button(layouts[i]);
   layoutButtons[i].addActionListener(new ButtonHandler());
   layoutButtonPanel.add(layoutButtons[i]);
  }
  for(int i=0;i<cards.length;++i) {
   navigateButtons[i] = new Button(cards[i]);
   navigateButtons[i].addActionListener(new ButtonHandler());
   navigateButtonPanel.add(navigateButtons[i]);
  }
 }
 void setupDisplayPanels() {
 panels = new Panel[5];
 for(int i=0;i<5;++i) panels[i]=new Panel();
 panels[border].setLayout(new BorderLayout());
 panels[card].setLayout(new CardLayout());
 panels[flow].setLayout(new FlowLayout());
 panels[grid].setLayout(new GridLayout(2,3));
 GridBagLayout gridBagLayout = new GridBagLayout();
 panels[gridBag].setLayout(gridBagLayout);
 panels[border].add("North",new Button("North"));
 panels[border].add("South",new Button("South"));
 panels[border].add("East",new Button("East"));
 panels[border].add("West",new Button("West"));
 panels[border].add("Center",new Button("Center"));
 String cardButtons[] =
➥{"First","Second","Third","Fourth","Last"};
```

```
String flowButtons[] = {"One","Two","Three","Four","Five"};
String gridButtons[] = {"(0,0)","(1,0)","(2,0)",
 "(0,1)","(1,1)","(2,1)"};
for(int i=0;i<cardButtons.length;++i)
 panels[card].add("next card",new Button(cardButtons[i]));
for(int i=0;i<flowButtons.length;++i)
 panels[flow].add(new Button(flowButtons[i]));
for(int i=0;i<gridButtons.length;++i)
 panels[grid].add(new Button(gridButtons[i]));
Button gridBagButtons[] = new Button[9];
for(int i=0;i<9;++i) gridBagButtons[i] = new
➥Button("Button"+i);
int gridx[] = {0,1,2,0,2,0,1,1,0};
int gridy[] = {0,0,0,1,1,2,2,3,4};
int gridwidth[] = {1,1,1,2,1,1,1,2,3};
int gridheight[] = {1,1,1,2,2,1,1,1,1};
GridBagConstraints gridBagConstraints[] = new
➥GridBagConstraints[9];
for(int i=0;i<9;++i) {
 gridBagConstraints[i] = new GridBagConstraints();
 gridBagConstraints[i].fill=GridBagConstraints.BOTH;
 gridBagConstraints[i].gridx=gridx[i];
 gridBagConstraints[i].gridy=gridy[i];
 gridBagConstraints[i].gridwidth=gridwidth[i];
 gridBagConstraints[i].gridheight=gridheight[i];
 gridBagLayout.setConstraints(gridBagButtons[i],
  gridBagConstraints[i]);
 panels[gridBag].add(gridBagButtons[i]);
 }
 add("Center",panels[border]);
 currentPanel=panels[border];
}
void switchPanels(Panel newPanel,boolean setNavigateButtons) {
 remove(currentPanel);
 currentPanel=newPanel;
 add("Center",currentPanel);
 remove(navigateButtonPanel);
 if(setNavigateButtons) add("South",navigateButtonPanel);
 validate();
}
class ButtonHandler implements ActionListener {
 public void actionPerformed(ActionEvent ev){
  String s=ev.getActionCommand();
  if(s.equals("Border")) switchPanels(panels[border],false);
  else if(s.equals("Card")) switchPanels(panels[card],true);
  else if(s.equals("Flow")) switchPanels(panels[flow],false);
  else if(s.equals("Grid")) switchPanels(panels[grid],false);
  else if(s.equals("GridBag"))
  ➥switchPanels(panels[gridBag],false);
  else if(s.equals("First")){
   CardLayout
   ➥currentLayout=(CardLayout)currentPanel.getLayout();
   currentLayout.first(currentPanel);
```

continues

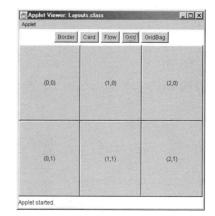

FIGURE 12.4

An example of a `GridLayout`.

FIGURE 12.5

An example of a `GridBagLayout`.

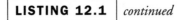

LISTING 12.1 | *continued*

THE Layouts APPLET

```
 }else if(s.equals("Last")){
  CardLayout
  ➥currentLayout=(CardLayout)currentPanel.getLayout();
  currentLayout.last(currentPanel);
 }else if(s.equals("Next")){
  CardLayout
  ➥currentLayout=(CardLayout)currentPanel.getLayout();
  currentLayout.next(currentPanel);
 }else if(s.equals("Previous")){
  CardLayout
  ➥currentLayout=(CardLayout)currentPanel.getLayout();
  currentLayout.previous(currentPanel);
  }
 }
 }
}
```

LISTING 12.2

AN HTML FILE FOR DISPLAYING THE Layouts APPLET

```
<HTML>
<HEAD>
<TITLE>Layouts</TITLE>
</HEAD>
<BODY>
<APPLET CODE="Layouts.class" WIDTH=400 HEIGHT=350>
</APPLET>
</BODY>
</HTML>
```

How the Layouts Applet Works

The Layouts applet begins by declaring a number of variables for use in the applet. These variables are used as follows:

◆ panels—An array of panels used to hold an example of each of the five layouts

◆ currentPanel—Identifies the current panel being displayed

◆ border—Constant used to identify a BorderLayout

◆ card—Constant used to identify a CardLayout

◆ flow—Constant used to identify a FlowLayout

◆ grid—Constant used to identify a GridLayout

◆ gridBag—Constant used to identify a GridBagLayout

◆ layouts—An array of labels for the layout buttons

◆ cards—An array of labels for the card navigation buttons

◆ layoutButtons—The buttons displayed in the top panel

◆ navigateButtons—The buttons displayed in the bottom panel when a CardLayout is selected

◆ layoutButtonPanel—The panel used to display the layout buttons

◆ navigateButtonPanel—The panel used to display the card navigation buttons

The init() method sets the applet's layout to a BorderLayout. Note that this layout does not change. Only the layout of the middle panel is changed by clicking the layout buttons. The init() method invokes the setupButtons() method to initialize the layout and navigation buttons. It adds the panel which displays the layout buttons at the top (North) of the applet's display. It then invokes the setupDisplayPanels() method to set up the panels that are used to display the various layouts.

The setupButtons() method initializes the elements of the layoutButtons and navigateButtons arrays, sets up their event handlers, and adds the buttons to the layoutButtonPanel and navigateButtonPanel.

The setupDisplayPanels() method creates each of the five layout panels, lays them out, and adds buttons to them. The buttons are used for display purposes and do not handle any events. The panels are indexed by the border, flow, card, grid, and gridBag constants. The gridx, gridy, gridwidth, and gridheight arrays set up the GridBagConstraints object for the GridBagLayout. These constraints determine the position and dimension of the objects being laid out. The panel with the BorderLayout is the first panel displayed and is added to the center of the applet's display area.

The switchPanels() method is used to remove the current layout panel being displayed and to add the new panel identified by the newPanel parameter. The setNavigateButtons parameter determines whether the card navigation buttons panel is displayed at the bottom of the applet's display area. The validate() method causes the applet to be laid out and its components to be redisplayed.

The ButtonHandler class provides the event handling for the layout and card navigation buttons. This event handling is performed by the actionPerformed() method. The layout buttons are handled by invoking the switchPanels() method to display a new layout panel. The navigation buttons are handled by invoking the first(),last(),next(), and previous() methods of the CardLayout class to display other buttons in the card deck.

LAYOUT MANAGERS, LAYOUT POLICIES, AND CONTAINERS

The Layouts applet provides a great way to study the interaction between layout managers, layout policies, and containers. Use appletviewer to display the Layouts applet and resize the appletviewer window to see how each of the layout managers respond to changes in the container's size. Several exam questions will require you to be familiar with how a container's layout is updated when the container is resized.

ABSOLUTE POSITIONING

In the preceding sections, you learned how to use the standard AWT layouts to organize the way GUI components are displayed within a container. But what if you want to organize your GUI using the traditional absolute positioning approach. In that case, use a null layout and position and size your components using absolute values. The setBounds() method of the Component class specifies both the position and dimensions of the component displayed. Because setBounds() is defined in the Component class, it can be used with all the Component subclasses.

> **NOTE**
>
> **The validate(), invalidate(), and doLayout() methods** The validate(), invalidate() and doLayout() methods can be used to cause a container to be laid out again. The validate() method is used by the AWT to cause a container to lay out its subcomponents after the components it contains have been added to or modified. The invalidate() method causes a component and all of its containers to be marked as needing to be laid out. The doLayout() method is used to tell a layout manager to layout a component.

The Positions Applet

The Positions applet, shown in Listing 12.3, illustrates the use of the null layout. The HTML file contained in Listing 12.4 is used to display this applet. The applet's display is shown in Figure 12.6. Note that this GUI organization is not easily supported by any of the standard layouts.

The Positions applet is short and simple, but it shows how the null layout can be used to produce custom layouts. Two labels and two buttons are declared and initialized. These buttons and labels identify the x, y coordinate at which they are located. The init() method sets the applet's layout to null, invokes the setBounds() method for each of the labels and buttons, and then adds the labels and buttons to the applet container. The setBounds() method used in this example takes the following four parameters:

◆ The horizontal position of the component.

◆ The vertical position of the component.

◆ The component's width.

◆ The component's height.

Other variations of the setBounds() method are also available, as described in the API description of the Component class.

NOTE
The Origin The upper-left corner of a container is position (0,0). The x coordinate increases as you move to the right. The y coordinate increases as you move down.

LISTING 12.3

THE POSITIONS APPLET

```
import java.applet.*;
import java.awt.*;
import java.awt.event.*;

public class Positions extends Applet {
 Label label1 = new Label("Label at (10,10)");
 Label label2 = new Label("Label at (100,100)");
 Button button1 = new Button("Button at (150,150)");
 Button button2 = new Button("Button at (200,200)");
 public void init() {
  setLayout(null);
  label1.setBounds(10,10,200,30);
  label2.setBounds(100,100,200,30);
  button1.setBounds(150,150,150,30);
  button2.setBounds(200,200,250,60);
```

continues

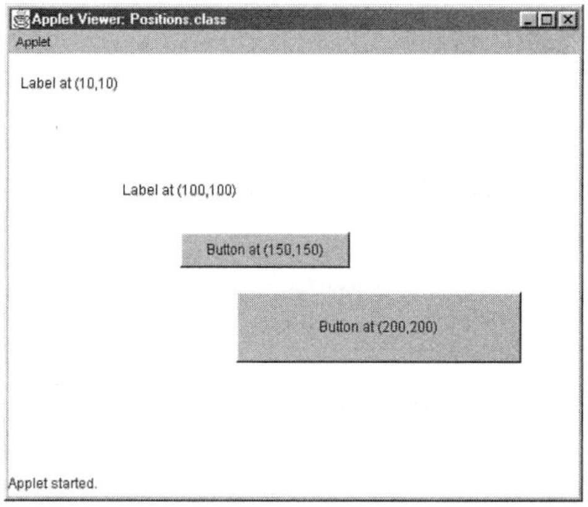

FIGURE 12.6

The Positions applet displays GUI components using a null layout.

LISTING 12.3 *continued*

THE Positions APPLET

```
  add(label1);
  add(label2);
  add(button1);
  add(button2);
  }
}
```

LISTING 12.4

AN HTML FILE DISPLAYING THE Positions APPLET

```
<HTML>
<HEAD>
<TITLE>Positions</TITLE>
</HEAD>
<BODY>
<APPLET CODE="Positions.class" WIDTH=500 HEIGHT=350>
</APPLET>
</BODY>
</HTML>
```

CHAPTER SUMMARY

KEY TERMS

- Layout
- Layout manager
- Border layout
- Card layout
- Flow layout
- Grid layout
- Gridbag layout
- Gridbag constraint
- Inset
- Absolute positioning

CHAPTER SUMMARY

This chapter covered the classes and interfaces of java.awt that are used to layout GUI components. You were introduced to each of the AWT layout managers and learned how they work through a programming example. You also learned how components are laid out in the absence of a layout manager. You should now be prepared to test your knowledge of these topics. The following review questions and exam questions will let you know how well you understand this material and will give you an idea of how you'll do in related exam questions. They'll also indicate which material you need to study further.

APPLY YOUR KNOWLEDGE

Review Questions

1. What is a layout manager?

2. What advantage do Java's layout managers provide over traditional windowing systems?

3. What are the problems faced by Java programmers who don't use layout managers?

4. What method is used to specify a container's layout?

5. How are the elements of a BorderLayout organized?

6. How are the elements of a CardLayout organized?

7. How are the elements of a FlowLayout organized?

8. How are the elements of a GridLayout organized?

9. How are the elements of a GridBagLayout organized?

10. Which containers use a BorderLayout as their default layout?

11. Which containers use a FlowLayout as their default layout?

12. What is the preferred size of a component?

Exam Questions

1. The following is an example of which layout?

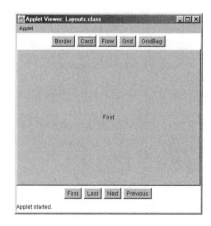

A. CardLayout

B. null Layout

C. BorderLayout

D. SetLayout

2. The follwwowing is an example of which layout?

A. CardLayout

B. null Layout

C. BorderLayout

D. SetLayout

APPLY YOUR KNOWLEDGE

3. The following is an example of which layout?

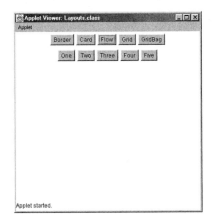

A. GridLayout

B. FlowLayout

C. GridLineLayout

D. LineLayout

4. The following is an example of which layout?

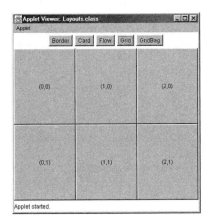

A. GridLayout

B. null Layout

C. GridBagLayout

D. GridBagConstraintLayout

5. The following is an example of which layout?

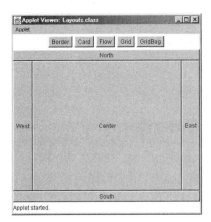

A. GridLayout

B. null Layout

C. GridBagLayout

D. GridBagConstraintLayout

6. The following is an example of which layout?

A. CardLayout

B. null Layout

C. BorderLayout

D. SetLayout

APPLY YOUR KNOWLEDGE

7. Given a component, comp, and a container, cont, that is organized according to a BorderLayout, which of the following should be used to add comp to the top of the container.

    A. addTop(cont,comp);

    B. comp.add("North",cont);

    C. cont.add("North",comp);

    D. cont.addTop(comp);

8. Given a component, comp, and a container, cont, that is organized according to a FlowLayout, which of the following should be used to add comp to the container.

    A. cont.add(comp);

    B. comp.add(cont);

    C. cont.addComponent(comp);

    D. cont.addAllComponents();

9. Which method is used to set the layout of a container?

    A. startLayout()

    B. initLayout()

    C. layoutContainer()

    D. setLayout()

10. Which method returns the preferred size of a component?

    A. getPreferredSize()

    B. getPreferred()

    C. getRequiredSize()

    D. getLayout()

11. Which method sets the size and position of a component?

    A. setBounds()

    B. setSizeAndPosition()

    C. setComponentSize()

    D. setComponent()

12. Which layout should you use to organize the components of a container in a tabular form?

    A. CardLayout

    B. BorderLayout

    C. FlowLayout

    D. GridLayout

Answers to Review Questions

1. A layout manager is an object that is used to organize components in a container.

2. Java uses layout managers to lay out components in a consistent manner across all windowing platforms. Since Java's layout managers aren't tied to absolute sizing and positioning, they are able to accommodate platform-specific differences among windowing systems.

3. Without layout managers, Java programmers are faced with determining how their GUI will be displayed across multiple windowing systems and finding a common sizing and positioning that will work within the constraints imposed by each windowing system.

4. The setLayout() method is used to specify a container's layout.

APPLY YOUR KNOWLEDGE

5. The elements of a BorderLayout are organized at the borders (North, South, East, and West) and the center of a container.

6. The elements of a CardLayout are stacked, one on top of the other, like a deck of cards.

7. The elements of a FlowLayout are organized in a top to bottom, left to right fashion.

8. The elements of a GridBad layout are of equal size and are laid out using the squares of a grid.

9. The elements of a GridBagLayout are organized according to a grid. However, the elements are of different sizes and may occupy more than one row or column of the grid. In addition, the rows and columns may have different sizes.

10. The Window, Frame, and Dialog classes use a BorderLayout as their default layout.

11. The Panel and Applet classes use the FlowLayout as their default layout.

12. The preferred size of a component is the minimum component size that will allow the component to display normally.

Answers to Exam Questions

1. C

2. A

3. B

4. A

5. C

6. B

7. C   The container's add method is invoked, passing it the orientation and component as arguments.

8. A   The container's add method is invoked, passing it the component as an argument.

9. D

10. A

11. A

12. D   The GridLayout is best if the table elements are of equal size. Otherwise, use a GridBagLayout.

Suggested Readings and Resources

The JDK 1.2 java.awt package API description.

This chapter helps you to prepare for the exam by covering the following objectives:

Know how AWT event handling takes place.

▶ Event handling enables GUI applications to respond to user actions. A general knowledge of how event handling is performed is required for the certification exam.

Know the difference between the JDK 1.0 event handling model and that of JDK 1.1 and later.

▶ JDK 1.0 supported an event-handling model based on event inheritance or "bubbling." This model was replaced with an event-delegation model in JDK 1.1. Knowledge of the differences between the old and new models is needed to correctly answer some exam questions.

Know which classes and interfaces support the event delegation model.

▶ Although you don't need to know all the details about the AWT's event handling classes and interfaces, the exam assumes that you have a general familiarity with how each is used. You will be required to recognizes the names of these classes and interfaces and have a basic familiarity with their constructors, properties, and methods.

Know how listeners and adapters are used in event handling.

▶ To build a basic GUI application or applet, you'll need to handle the events that result from user interaction with the GUI. You need to have some hands-on experience using listeners and event handlers to correctly answer these exam questions.

CHAPTER 13

The java.awt Package: Event Handling

Know how to override event dispatching methods.

▶ While the preferred way of handling AWT events is through the event-delegation facilities, it is also possible for a component to explicitly handle its own events by overriding its event-dispatching methods.

As you read through this chapter, you should concentrate on the following key items:

▶ How the AWT event-delegation model works

▶ Which classes and interfaces support event handling

▶ How listeners and adapters are used to implement the event-delegation model

▶ How to override a component's event-dispatching methods

CHAPTER INTRODUCTION

This chapter covers the event-handling classes and interfaces of `java.awt.event`, `java.awt`, and `java.util`. Familiarity with these classes and interfaces is essential to writing event handling code. A few exam questions will test your knowledge of the material covered in this chapter. By studying the descriptions of the event-handling classes and interfaces presented in this chapter, you'll refresh your knowledge of event handling and be ready for any related exam questions.

HANDLING EVENTS

The user communicates with window programs by performing actions such as clicking a mouse button or pressing a key on the keyboard. These actions result in the generation of events. The process of responding to an event is known as *event handling*. The invocation of an event handling method is the end result of an event's generation. Window programs are said to be *event-driven* because they operate by performing actions in response to events.

The JDK 1.02 supported an approach to event handling referred to as an *inheritance model*. In this approach, events are handled by subclassing window components and overriding their `action()`, `handleEvent()`, and other methods. These methods return `True` or `False` to indicate whether they have successfully handled an event. If a `True` value is returned, the event processing is complete. Otherwise, the event is sent to the object's container for further processing. In this model, a container *inherits* all the events that are not handled by its components. The component events are said to *bubble up* the containment hierarchy. One of the problems with this approach is that a significant number of processing resources are expended in bubbling up events that are never handled.

The JDK 1.02 approach to event handling was replaced by an *event-delegation model* in JDK 1.1. However, the old inheritance event model was still supported. The old model is now fully deprecated in Java 2.

The event-delegation model provides the capability to deliver events to programmer-selected classes—a capability that was lacking in JDK 1.02. The event-delegation approach is less complex and more efficient. It uses special interfaces, called *event listeners*, whose methods listen for the occurrence of events. In this model, a source object generates events that are listened for by a listener object. The source object is usually a window GUI component, such as a button. The listener object is a class that implements an event-listener interface appropriate for the source object. The source object provides methods that allow listener objects to register themselves to listen for its events. For example, an object that handles the clicking of a button implements the ActionListener interface. This object is registered with a particular button via the button's addActionListener() method.

The event-delegation model is a significant improvement over that of Java 1.02, which required GUI components to be subclassed in order to handle events. Although it is still possible to do this in the event-delegation model, it is no longer necessary. Events can be handled by classes that are separate from the component in which the event is generated.

THE JDK 1.02 Event Class

In the JDK 1.02 inheritance model, the Event class encapsulates all Windows event processing. The Event class defines the entire list of events handled by window programs using *class constants*. These constants are used to identify the events that are passed to event-handling methods. You can review the Java API description of the Event class to familiarize yourself with these constants.

The Event class provides three constructors for creating events, but you probably won't need to use these constructors because events are internally generated by the Java runtime system in response to user interface actions. The Event class also provides methods for determining whether the Ctrl, Shift, or Meta (Alt) keys are pressed during the generation of an event.

THE CLASSES AND INTERFACES OF THE EVENT DELEGATION MODEL

In the event-delegation model that was introduced with JDK 1.1 (and extended in Java 2), the java.util.EventObject class is the top-level class of the event-class hierarchy. This class provides a source field variable to identify the object that is the source of an event, a getSource() method to retrieve this object, and a toString() method to convert an event into a String representation. It provides a single constructor that takes the object that is the source of the event as an argument.

The java.awt.AWTEvent class extends the java.util.EventObject class to support AWT events. It provides several variables, constants, and methods that are used to identify events and determine whether they are consumed. The AWTEvent class is extended by the following classes of java.awt.event:

◆ ActionEvent—Generated by user interface actions, such as clicking on a button or selecting a menu item.

◆ AdjustmentEvent—Generated by scrolling actions.

◆ AncestorEvent—Generated when the ancestor of a component is added or removed from visibility or moved.

◆ ComponentEvent—Generated by changes to the position, focus, or sizing of a window component, or by a keyboard input or other mouse action.

◆ InputMethodEvent—Generated by changes to the text being entered via an input method.

◆ InternalFrameEvent—Generated as the result of changes to a Swing JInternalEvent object. (Knowledge of Swing is not required for the certification exam.)

◆ InvocationEvent—Generated by the invokeLater() and invokeAndWait() methods of the EventQueue object.

◆ ItemEvent—Generated by a component-state change, such as selecting an item from a list.

◆ TextEvent—Generated by text-related events, such as changing the value of a text field.

The ComponentEvent class is further extended by the following classes:

◆ FocusEvent—Generated by a change in the status of a component's input focus

◆ InputEvent—Subclassed by KeyEvent and MouseEvent to cover events generated by keyboard actions and low-level mouse events

◆ ContainerEvent—Generated by events associated with adding and removing components from a container

◆ PaintEvent—Generated by the painting/repainting of a window

◆ WindowEvent—Generated by events such as the opening, closing, and minimizing of a window

The AWTEvent class and its subclasses enable window-related events to be directed to specific objects that listen for those events. These objects implement EventListener interfaces. The java.util.EventListener interface is the top-level interface of the event-listener hierarchy. It is an interface in name only because it does not define any constants or methods. It is extended by the following interfaces of java.awt.event:

◆ ActionListener—Implemented by objects that handle ActionEvent events

◆ AWTEventListener—Implemented by objects that monitor AWTEvent events

◆ AdjustmentListener—Implemented by objects that handle AdjustmentEvent events

◆ ComponentListener—Implemented by objects that handle ComponentEvent events

◆ ContainerListener—Implemented by objects that handle ContainerEvent events

◆ FocusListener—Implemented by objects that handle FocusEvent events

◆ InputMethodListener—Implemented by objects that handle InputMethodEvent events

◆ `ItemListener`—Implemented by objects that handle `ItemEvent` events

◆ `KeyListener`—Implemented by objects that handle `KeyEvent` events

◆ `MouseListener`—Implemented by objects that handle clicking-related `MouseEvent` events

◆ `MouseMotionListener`—Implemented by objects that handle movement-related `MouseEvent` events

◆ `TextListener`—Implemented by objects that handle `TextEvent` events

◆ `WindowListener`—Implemented by objects that handle `WindowEvent` events

As a convenience, the `java.awt.event` package provides *event adapter* classes that implement the event listener interfaces. These classes may be subclassed to override specific event-handling methods of interest. The adapter classes of `java.awt.event` are as follows:

◆ `ComponentAdapter`—Implements the `ComponentListener` interface and handles `ComponentEvent` events

◆ `ContainerAdapter`—Implements the `ContainerListener` interface and handles `ContainerEvent` events

◆ `FocusAdapter`—Implements the `FocusListener` interface and handles `FocusEvent` events

◆ `KeyAdapter`—Implements the `KeyListener` interface and handles `KeyEvent` events

◆ `MouseAdapter`—Implements the `MouseListener` interface and handles clicking-related `MouseEvent` events

◆ `MouseMotionAdapter`—Implements the `MouseListener` interface and handles movement-related `MouseEvent` events

◆ `WindowAdapter`—Implements the `WindowListener` interface and handles `WindowEvent` events

These adapter classes are convenience classes because they provide stubs for the methods of the interfaces that you don't want to implement yourself.

In addition to the classes and interfaces covered so far in this section, the following two classes of java.awt also support the event-delegation model:

◆ java.awt.EventQueue—supports the queuing of events. It enables event listeners to monitor the queue and retrieve specific events for processing. The EventQueue is automatically created and managed by the runtime system to queue the events generated by GUI components.

◆ java.awt.AWTEventMulticaster—provides the capability to listen for multiple events and then forward the events to multiple-event listeners. It provides a thread-safe mechanism by which event listeners can be added and removed from its event-listening destination list.

An object may handle the events of more than one object. Conversely, an object may have one of its events handled by more than one event-handling object. In the latter case, the order of invocation of the event handlers cannot be predicted.

AN EVENT DELEGATION EXAMPLE

Now that you've covered the event-handling classes and interfaces, let's work through a programming example so that you can see how they are used in a window application. Listing 13.1 presents the Event Sampler program. This program shows how the events of common AWT components are handled.

When you run EventApp, it displays the window shown in Figure 13.1. It provides samples of the following GUI components:

◆ Text field   Typing Enter in the text field causes the contents of the text field to be converted to uppercase.

◆ Text area   The text area is used to display the results of handling the events of the other GUI components.

◆ Button   Clicking the button clears the contents of the text area.

◆ Canvas   Clicking in the canvas results in a little red square being displayed.

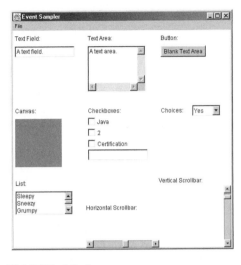

FIGURE 13.1

The Event Sampler default window.

◆ Check box   Checking the check boxes results in text being displayed in the associated text field.

◆ Choice   The selection of a choice is displayed in the text area.

◆ List   Selection of a list item is displayed in the text area. Double-clicking of a list item also updates the text area.

◆ Horizontal scrollbar   Any change to the horizontal scrollbar is displayed in the text area.

◆ Vertical scrollbar   Any change to the vertical scrollbar is displayed in the text area.

LISTING 13.1

THE EventApp PROGRAM

```
import java.awt.*;
import java.awt.event.*;

public class EventApp extends Frame {
 // Used to display the results of event handling.
 TextArea textArea;
 public static void main(String args[]){
  EventApp app = new EventApp();
 }
 public EventApp() {
  super("Event Sampler");
  setup();
  setSize(480,480);
  // Add event handler for closing the frame.
  addWindowListener(new WindowEventHandler());
  show();
 }
 void setup() {
  setupMenuBars();
  setupPanels();
 }
 void setupMenuBars() {
  MenuBar menuBar = new MenuBar();
  Menu fileMenu = new Menu("File");
  MenuItem fileExit = new MenuItem("Exit");
  MenuItemHandler mh = new MenuItemHandler();
  // Add an action listener for File -> Exit.
  fileExit.addActionListener(mh);
  fileMenu.add(fileExit);
  menuBar.add(fileMenu);
  setMenuBar(menuBar);
 }

 void setupPanels() {
  Panel mainPanel = new Panel();
```

```
// Divide the main panel into a 3-by-3 grid.
mainPanel.setLayout(new GridLayout(3,3));
// Create each of the subpanels.
Panel panels[][] = new Panel[3][3];
for(int i=0;i<3;++i){
 for(int j=0;j<3;++j){
  panels[j][i] = new Panel();
  panels[j][i].setLayout(new FlowLayout(FlowLayout.LEFT));
 }
}
// Set up the text field
panels[0][0].add(new Label("Text Field:"));
TextField textField = new TextField("A text field.",15);
// Handle the text field's action event
textField.addActionListener(new HandleTextField());
panels[0][0].add(textField);
// Set up the text area
panels[1][0].add(new Label("Text Area:"));
textArea = new TextArea("A text area.",5,15);
panels[1][0].add(textArea);
// Set up the button
panels[2][0].add(new Label("Button:"));
Button button = new Button("Blank Text Area");
// Handle the button's action event.
button.addActionListener(new HandleButton());
panels[2][0].add(button);
// Set up the canvas. It handles its own events.
panels[0][1].add(new Label("Canvas:"));
panels[0][1].add(new MyCanvas());
// Set up the checkbox panel. It also handles its own
➥events.
String checkboxStrings[] =
➥{"Checkboxes:","Java","2","Certification"};
panels[1][1].add(new MyCheckboxGroup(checkboxStrings));
// Set up the choice component.
panels[2][1].add(new Label("Choices:"));
String choiceStrings[] = {"Yes","No","Maybe"};
Choice choice = new Choice();
for(int i=0;i<choiceStrings.length;++i)
 choice.addItem(choiceStrings[i]);
// Handle the selection of a choice.
choice.addItemListener(new HandleChoice());
panels[2][1].add(choice);
// Set up the list.
panels[0][2].add(new Label("List:"));
String listStrings[] =
➥{"Sleepy","Sneezy","Grumpy","Dopey","Doc",
 "Happy","Bashful"};
List list = new List(3,false);
for(int i=0;i<listStrings.length;++i)
 list.add(listStrings[i]);
// Handle the selection and double-click events.
list.addItemListener(new HandleListSelect());
list.addActionListener(new HandleListDoubleClick());
```

continues

> **LISTING 13.1** | *continued*
>
> ### THE EventApp PROGRAM

```
  panels[0][2].add(list);
  // Set up the horizontal scrollbar.
  panels[1][2].setLayout(new BorderLayout());
  panels[1][2].add("Center",new Label("Horizontal
➥Scrollbar:"));
  Scrollbar hScroll = new
➥Scrollbar(Scrollbar.HORIZONTAL,50,10,0,100);
  // Handle the scrollbar's adjustment event.
  hScroll.addAdjustmentListener(new HandleScrolling());
  panels[1][2].add("South",hScroll);
  // Set up the vertical scrollbar.
  panels[2][2].setLayout(new BorderLayout());
  panels[2][2].add("North",new Label("Vertical Scrollbar:"));
  Scrollbar vScroll = new
➥Scrollbar(Scrollbar.VERTICAL,50,10,0,1000);
  // Handle the scrollbar's adjustment event.
  vScroll.addAdjustmentListener(new HandleScrolling());
  panels[2][2].add("East",vScroll);
  for(int i=0;i<3;++i)
   for(int j=0;j<3;++j)
    mainPanel.add(panels[j][i]);
  add("Center",mainPanel);
 }
class WindowEventHandler extends WindowAdapter {
 // Handle the window's closing
 public void windowClosing(WindowEvent e){
  System.exit(0);
 }
}
class MenuItemHandler implements ActionListener {
 // Handle menu selections
 public void actionPerformed(ActionEvent ev){
  String s=ev.getActionCommand();
  if(s.equals("Exit")) System.exit(0);
 }
}

class HandleTextField implements ActionListener {
 // Handle changes to the text field
 public void actionPerformed(ActionEvent ev){
  TextField textField = (TextField) ev.getSource();
  String text = textField.getText();
  textField.setText(text.toUpperCase());
 }
}
class HandleButton implements ActionListener {
 // Handle the clicking of a button
 public void actionPerformed(ActionEvent ev){
  textArea.setText("");
 }
}
class HandleChoice implements ItemListener {
```

```
  // Handle a choice selection
  public void itemStateChanged(ItemEvent e){
   Choice ch = (Choice) e.getItemSelectable();
   textArea.setText(ch.getSelectedItem());
  }
 }
 class HandleListSelect implements ItemListener {
  // Handle a list selection
  public void itemStateChanged(ItemEvent e){
   int change = e.getStateChange();
   List l = (List) e.getItemSelectable();
   if(change==ItemEvent.SELECTED){
    textArea.setText("Selected:\n"+l.getSelectedItem());
   }else if(change==ItemEvent.DESELECTED){
    textArea.setText("Selected:");
   }
  }
 }
 class HandleListDoubleClick implements ActionListener {
  // Handle the double-clicking of a list item
  public void actionPerformed(ActionEvent e){
   textArea.setText("Double-clicked:\n
   ➥"+e.getActionCommand());
  }
 }
 class HandleScrolling implements AdjustmentListener {
  // Handle scrolling
  public void adjustmentValueChanged(AdjustmentEvent e){
   textArea.setText("Position: "+e.getValue());
  }
 }
}
class MyCanvas extends Canvas {
 int x = -1;
 int y = -1;
 int boxSize = 10;
 public MyCanvas() {
  super();
  setSize(100,100);
  setVisible(true);
  addMouseListener(new MouseHandler());
  repaint();
 }
 public void paint(Graphics g) {
  setBackground(Color.gray);
  setForeground(Color.red);
  if(x>=0 && y>=0) g.fillRect(x,y,boxSize,boxSize);
 }
 class MouseHandler extends MouseAdapter {
  public void mouseClicked(MouseEvent ev){
   x = ev.getX();
   y = ev.getY();
   repaint();
  }
```

continues

LISTING 13.1 | *continued*

THE EventApp PROGRAM

```
  }
}
class MyCheckboxGroup extends Panel {
 String labelString;
 String checkboxLabels[];
 Checkbox checkboxes[];
 int numBoxes;
 TextField results;
 public MyCheckboxGroup(String strings[]) {
  super();
  labelString = strings[0];
  numBoxes = strings.length-1;
  checkboxLabels = new String[numBoxes];
  for(int i=0;i<numBoxes;++i)
   checkboxLabels[i] = strings[i+1];
  results = new TextField("",15);
  setupPanel();
  setVisible(true);
 }
 void setupPanel() {
  setLayout(new GridLayout(numBoxes+2,1));
  add(new Label(labelString));
  checkboxes = new Checkbox[numBoxes];
  MyCheckboxGroup.HandleCheck hrc =
   new MyCheckboxGroup.HandleCheck();
  for(int i=0;i<numBoxes;++i){
   checkboxes[i] = new Checkbox(checkboxLabels[i]);
   checkboxes[i].addItemListener(hrc);
   add(checkboxes[i]);
  }
  add(results);
 }
 class HandleCheck implements ItemListener {
  public void itemStateChanged(ItemEvent e){
   String newResults = "";
   for(int i=0;i<numBoxes;++i)
    if(checkboxes[i].getState())
     newResults = newResults + " " +checkboxes[i].getLabel();
   results.setText(newResults);
  }
 }
}
```

EventApp provides you with numerous examples of event handling. You should work your way through the program code and study the operation of the following event handlers:

◆ WindowEventHandler   Extends the WindowAdapter class and overrides its windowClosing() method to handle the closing of the application window.

◆ MenuItemHandler   Implements the ActionListener interface. Uses the getActionCommand() method of the ActionEvent class to get the label of the selected menu item.

◆ HandleTextField   Implements the ActionListener interface. Sets the text field to its contents converted to uppercase. The getSource() method of the java.util.EventObject class is used to obtain a reference to the text field.

◆ HandleButton   Implements the ActionListener interface. Sets the text area to a blank string.

◆ HandleChoice   Implements the ItemListener interface. Sets the text area to the selected item. This item is retrieved through the getSelectedItem() method of the ItemEvent class.

◆ HandleListSelect   Implements the ItemListener interface. Sets the text area to the selected item. This item is retrieved through the getSelectedItem() method of the ItemEvent class.

◆ HandleListDoubleClick   Implements the ActionListener interface. Sets the text area to the clicked item. This item is retrieved through the getActionCommand() method of the ActionEvent class.

◆ HandleScrolling   Implements the AdjustmentListener interface. Sets the text area to the scrollbar's current position.

◆ MouseHandler   Extends the MouseAdapter class. Sets the x and y variables to the location of the mouse click and invokes the repaint() method to cause the canvas to be redisplayed with the results of the mouse click.

◆ HandleCheck   Implements ItemListener by displaying the check boxes' labels in a text field. It uses the getState() method of the Checkbox class to determine which check box is checked.

Note that the EventApp, MyCanvas, and MyCheckboxGroup classes handle their events using inner classes. The other event handlers are inner classes of EventApp, but they handle the events of other GUI components.

OVERRIDING A COMPONENT'S EVENT DISPATCHER

A GUI component may handle its own events by simply implementing the associated event-handling interfaces. However, it is also possible to extend the component's class and override its event dispatching methods. AWT components have methods of the form processXEvent(), where X refers to the event generated by the component. These methods dispatch events to the appropriate event listeners. You can override these methods to control the way in which events are dispatched. For example, the Button class uses the processActionEvent() method to dispatch ActionEvents to event listeners. You can override processActionEvent() in a subclass of Button to control how event dispatching takes place.

In addition to overriding the component's event-dispatching method, you may also need to enable the event. This automatically takes place when an event listener is added to a component. However, if you do not add an event listener for the component, you'll have to invoke its enableEvents() method, passing the event identifier (defined in the AWTEvent class) as an argument. For example, to enable the ActionEvent in an object that is a subclass of Button, you invoke the following method for that object:

```
object.enableEvents(AWTEvent.ACTION_EVENT_MASK);
```

The API description of the AWTEvent class lists and describes the event mask constants that are used with enableEvents(). These constants are of the form *EVENTNAME*_EVENT_MASK.

Listing 13.2 (EventOverrideApp) provides an example of overriding the processActionEvent() method of the Button class. When the button is clicked, it displays a message in the text area as shown in Figure 13.2.

Note how the MyButton constructor uses the enableEvents() method to enable the action event and how the processActionEvent() method performs the event handling.

FIGURE 13.2

The EventOverrideApp program displays the results of the button click in the text area.

LISTING 13.2

THE EventOverrideApp PROGRAM

```java
import java.awt.*;
import java.awt.event.*;

public class EventOverrideApp extends Frame {
 public static void main(String args[]){
  EventOverrideApp app = new EventOverrideApp();
 }
 public EventOverrideApp() {
  super("Event Override");
  setup();
  setSize(300,300);
  // Add event handler for closing the frame.
  addWindowListener(new WindowEventHandler());
  show();
 }
 void setup() {
  setupMenuBars();
  setupPanels();
 }
 void setupMenuBars() {
  MenuBar menuBar = new MenuBar();
  Menu fileMenu = new Menu("File");
  MenuItem fileExit = new MenuItem("Exit");
  MenuItemHandler mh = new MenuItemHandler();
  // Add an action listener for File -> Exit.
  fileExit.addActionListener(mh);
  fileMenu.add(fileExit);
  menuBar.add(fileMenu);
  setMenuBar(menuBar);
 }
void setupPanels() {
  Panel panel = new Panel();
  TextArea textArea = new TextArea(15,20);
  MyButton button = new MyButton("Click here!",textArea);
  panel.add(button);
  panel.add(textArea);
  add(panel);
 }
 class WindowEventHandler extends WindowAdapter {
  public void windowClosing(WindowEvent e){
   System.exit(0);
  }
 }
 class MenuItemHandler implements ActionListener {
  public void actionPerformed(ActionEvent ev){
   String s=ev.getActionCommand();
   if(s.equals("Exit")) System.exit(0);
  }
 }
```

continues

| LISTING 13.2 | *continued* |

THE EventOverrideApp PROGRAM

```
}
class MyButton extends Button {
 TextArea textArea;
 public MyButton(String s, TextArea textArea) {
  super(s);
  this.textArea = textArea;
  enableEvents(AWTEvent.ACTION_EVENT_MASK);
 }
 public void processActionEvent(ActionEvent event) {
  String s = textArea.getText();
  s += "\nThe button was clicked.";
  textArea.setText(s);
  // super.processActionEvent(event);
  // Uncomment the above line to allow event listeners to
  // also handle this event.
 }
}
```

CHAPTER SUMMARY

KEY TERMS

- Event handling
- Event inheritance model
- Event bubbling
- Event delegation model
- Event listener
- Event adapter

This chapter covered the classes and interfaces that support AWT event handling. You were introduced to each of the major AWT events and learned how they are handled using event listeners and adapters. You also learned how to enable components to handle their own events by overriding their event-dispatching methods. You should now be prepared to test your knowledge of these topics. The following review and exam questions will let you know how well you understand this material and give you an idea of how you'll do on the certification exam. These questions will also indicate what material you need to study further.

APPLY YOUR KNOWLEDGE

Review Questions

1. What is the difference between the JDK 1.02 event model and the event-delegation model introduced with JDK 1.1?

2. What is the highest-level event class of the event-delegation model?

3. What interface is extended by AWT event listeners?

4. What class is the top of the AWT event hierarchy?

5. What event results from the clicking of a button?

6. What is the relationship between an event-listener interface and an event-adapter class?

7. In which package are most of the AWT events that support the event-delegation model defined?

8. How can a GUI component handle its own events?

9. What is the advantage of the event-delegation model over the earlier event-inheritance model?

10. What is the purpose of the enableEvents() method?

Exam Questions

1. Which of the following are true?

   A. The event-inheritance model has replaced the event-delegation model.

   B. The event-inheritance model is more efficient than the event-delegation model.

   C. The event-delegation model uses event listeners to define the methods of event-handling classes.

   D. The event-delegation model uses the handleEvent() method to support event handling.

2. Which of the following is the highest class in the event delegation class hierarchy?

   A. java.util.EventListener

   B. java.util.EventObject

   C. java.awt.AWTEvent

   D. java.awt.event.AWTEvent

3. Which of the following are true?

   A. Event listeners are interfaces that define the methods that event-handling classes must implement.

   B. An event adapter is a class that provides a default implementation of an event listener.

   C. The event listener and adapter classes are deprecated in Java 2.

   D. The WindowAdapter class is used to handle window-related events.

4. When two or more objects are added as listeners for the same event, which listener is first invoked to handle the event?

   A. The first object that was added as a listener.

   B. The last object that was added as a listener.

   C. There is no way to determine which listener will be invoked first.

   D. It is impossible to have more than one listener for a given event.

APPLY YOUR KNOWLEDGE

5. Which of the following components generate action events?

   A. Buttons

   B. Labels

   C. Check boxes

   D. Windows

6. Which of the following are true?

   A. A `TextField` object may generate an `ActionEvent`.

   B. A `TextArea` object may generate an `ActionEvent`.

   C. A `Button` object may generate an `ActionEvent`.

   D. A `MenuItem` object may generate an `ActionEvent`.

7. Which of the following are true?

   A. The `MouseListener` interface defines methods for handling mouse clicks.

   B. The `MouseMotionListener` interface defines methods for handling mouse clicks.

   C. The `MouseClickListener` interface defines methods for mouse clicks.

   D. The `ActionListener` interface defines methods for handling the clicking of a button.

8. Suppose that you want to have an object eh handle the `TextEvent` of a `TextArea` object t. How should you add eh as the event handler for t?

   A. `t.addTextListener(eh);`

   B. `eh.addTextListener(t);`

   C. `addTextListener(eh,t);`

   D. `addTextListener(t,eh);`

9. What is the preferred way to handle an object's events in Java 2?

   A. Override the object's `handleEvent()` method.

   B. Add one or more event listeners to handle the events.

   C. Have the object override its `processEvent()` methods.

   D. Have the object override its `dispatchEvent()` methods.

10. Which of the following are true?

   A. A component may handle its own events by adding itself as an event listener.

   B. A component may handle its own events by overriding its event-dispatching method.

   C. A component may not handle its own events.

   D. A component may handle its own events only if it implements the `handleEvent()` method.

Answers to Review Questions

1. The JDK 1.02 event model uses an event inheritance or bubbling approach. In this model, components are required to handle their own events. If they do not handle a particular event, the event is inherited by (or bubbled up to) the component's container. The container then either handles the event or it is bubbled up to its container and so on, until the highest-level container has been tried.

   In the event-delegation model, specific objects are designated as event handlers for GUI components. These objects implement event-listener

APPLY YOUR KNOWLEDGE

interfaces. The event-delegation model is more efficient than the event-inheritance model because it eliminates the processing required to support the bubbling of unhandled events.

2. The `java.util.EventObject` class is the highest-level class in the event-delegation class hierarchy.

3. All AWT event listeners extend the `java.util.EventListener` interface.

4. The `java.awt.AWTEvent` class is the highest-level class in the AWT event-class hierarchy.

5. The `ActionEvent` event is generated as the result of the clicking of a button.

6. An event-listener interface defines the methods that must be implemented by an event handler for a particular kind of event. An event adapter provides a default implementation of an event-listener interface.

7. Most of the AWT-related events of the event-delegation model are defined in the `java.awt.event` package. The `AWTEvent` class is defined in the `java.awt` package.

8. A component can handle its own events by implementing the required event-listener interface and adding itself as its own event listener.

9. The event-delegation model has two advantages over the event-inheritance model. First, it enables event handling to be handled by objects other than the ones that generate the events (or their containers). This allows a clean separation between a component's design and its use. The other advantage of the event-delegation model is that it performs much better in applications where many events are generated. This

performance improvement is due to the fact that the event-delegation model does not have to repeatedly process unhandled events, as is the case of the event-inheritance model.

10. The `enableEvents()` method is used to enable an event for a particular object. Normally, an event is enabled when a listener is added to an object for a particular event. The `enableEvents()` method is used by objects that handle events by overriding their event-dispatch methods.

Answers to Exam Questions

1. C   The event-delegation model uses event listeners to define the methods of event-handling classes. It does not make use of the `handleEvent()` method of the older, less-efficient event-inheritance model.

2. B   The `java.util.EventObject` class is at the top of the event-delegation class hierarchy.

3. A, B, and D   Answer C is false because event-listener and adapter classes are used by the event-delegation model, which is the preferred approach to Java 2 event handling.

4. C   When more than one event listener is added for an event, there is no way to determine which listener will be invoked first.

5. A   Buttons generate `ActionEvents`. `Labels`, `Checkboxes`, and `Windows` do not.

6. A, C, and D   `TextAreas` do not generate `ActionEvents`. But, `TextFields`, `Buttons`, and `MenuItems` do.

APPLY YOUR KNOWLEDGE

7. A and D   The MouseListener interface handles general mouse clicks. However, the ActionListener interface handles the clicking of Button objects.

8. A   You must invoke the TextArea object's addTextListener() method and pass it a reference to the event handler.

9. B   The event-delegation model uses event listeners to handle events.

10. A and B   A component may handle its own events by adding itself as an event handler or overriding its event-dispatching method.

Suggested Readings and Resources

The JDK 1.2 java.awt.event package API description.

This chapter helps you to prepare for the exam by covering the following objectives:

Know how the AWT supports painting, repainting, and clipping operations.

▶ A general knowledge of how the AWT supports painting, repainting, and clipping is required for the certification exam.

Know how the Canvas and Graphics classes are used to implement drawing and painting operations.

▶ The Canvas and Graphics classes are fundamental to painting. You need to know the relationship between these classes and the types of methods that are available for drawing shapes, text, and images.

Know how text is drawn using the Font, FontMetrics, and Graphics classes.

▶ The Font and FontMetrics classes are used to draw text on a Graphics object. A general understanding of how this occurs is useful for developing painting-based applets and applications.

Know how images are created and displayed.

▶ The certification exam requires a basic understanding of how images are created and displayed using a Graphics object.

CHAPTER 14

The java.awt Package: Painting

STUDY STRATEGIES

As you read through this chapter, you should concentrate on the following key items:

▶ How the Canvas and Graphics classes relate to each other

▶ How painting and repainting occurs

▶ What types of methods are provided by the Graphics class

▶ How geometric shapes are drawn using a Graphics object

▶ How the Font, FontMetrics, and Graphics classes are used to draw text

▶ How images are created and displayed

▶ How clipping works

CHAPTER INTRODUCTION

The `Canvas`, `Graphics`, and `Image` classes of the `java.awt` package are fundamental to AWT painting and drawing. You"ll learn how to use these classes to display bitmapped images and draw geometric shapes. You'll also learn how to use the `Font` class to control the way text is displayed. Understanding these classes is essential to developing GUI-based applets and applications. The certification exam may have a few questions that will call upon your knowledge of these classes. By studying the class descriptions of this chapter and working the programming examples, you should be able to do well on related exam questions.

THE Canvas AND Graphics CLASSES

The `Canvas` class of `java.awt` provides a general GUI component (it extends `Component`) for drawing images and text (or anything else) on the screen. It does not support any drawing methods of its own, but provides access to a `Graphics` object via its `paint()` method.

The `paint()` method is invoked upon the creation and update of a `Canvas` object. It enables the `Graphics` object associated with the `Canvas` object to be updated. The `paint()` method should not be directly invoked, but it can be indirectly accessed using the `repaint()` method. The AWT creates a background thread that automatically causes the `paint()` methods of `Canvas`, `Frame`, `Panel`, `Applet`, and other GUI components as required to update any areas that need repainting. You can implement custom drawing and painting operations in your applet or application by extending the `Canvas` class and overriding its `paint()` method.

NOTE

Graphics Context A `Graphics` object is sometimes referred to as a *graphics context*.

NOTE

Graphics Object A `Graphics` object is also available via the `paint()` methods of the `Applet`, `Frame`, `Panel`, and other classes that extend `Component`.

N O T E

The update() Method   The AWT invokes an object's update() method (inherited from Component) when the object's repaint() method is invoked. The update() method fills the component with its background color, set the component's foreground color, and then invokes the component's paint() method.

N O T E

The repaint() Method   When an object's repaint() method is invoked, the AWT schedules a repaint operation. Repainting typically occurs every .1 seconds. Multiple repaint() requests that occur within this interval are combined. This prevents repainting from consuming all the processing resources of an applet or application.

N O T E

Colors   Colors are available via the Color class. This class defines constants, such as Color.red, Color.white, and Color.blue, that can be used to identify colors by name. Colors can also be created using their red, blue, and green color values.

The Graphics class is where all the low-level drawing methods are implemented. These methods can be used directly to draw objects and text or can be combined to display more elaborate screen objects. The Graphics drawing methods enable you to draw and fill a number of geometrical shapes, including lines, arcs, ovals, rectangles, rounded rectangles, and polygons. A special draw3DRect() method is provided for drawing rectangles that are shaded to give them a three-dimensional appearance. The Graphics class also provides the capability to draw bitmapped images and text on the canvas. Some of the important Graphics drawing methods are as follows:

- draw3DRect() and fill3DRect()—Draws/fills a 3D rectangle
- drawArc() and fillArc()—Draws/fills an arc
- drawImage()—Draws an image on the screen
- drawLine()—Draws a line segment
- drawOval() and fillOval()—Draws/fills an oval
- drawPolygon() and fillPolygon()—Draws/fills a polygon
- drawPolyline() and fillPolyline()—Draws/fills a sequence of line segments
- drawRect() and fillRect()—Draws/fills a rectangle
- drawRoundRect() and fillRoundRect()—Draws/fills a rounded rectangle
- drawString()—Draws a String of text at a specified location
- getColor() and setColor()—Gets and sets the drawing (foreground) color
- getFont() and setFont()—Gets and sets the current font

We'll cover shape drawing, text drawing, and image drawing the following sections.

DRAWING SHAPES

Some programs, such as the Microsoft Windows Paint program, are used to construct images by *painting* on the screen. These paint programs create an image array of color pixels and update the array based on user paint commands. These commands may consist of pixel-level drawing operations or more general operations that draw geometrical objects such as circles, rectangles, and lines. Painting programs are characterized by the fact that the pixel array is the focus for the drawing that takes place.

Drawing programs, such as CorelDRAW, support drawing operations using a more object-oriented approach. When you draw a circle or line with a drawing program, you do not merely update the pixels of the canvas—you add an object to the list of objects that are displayed on the canvas. Because drawing programs operate at a higher object level, you can select, move, resize, group, and perform other operations on the objects that you've drawn.

The `Graphics` class is oriented toward providing the methods that are needed to support higher-level drawing programs rather than lower-level painting programs. However, it does support important painting operations, such as displaying bitmapped images, as you'll see in the `ImageApp` program later in this chapter.

When using the `Graphics` class to support graphical operations, you will generally maintain a list of the objects that you've drawn and use that list of objects to repaint the screen, as required.

The `DrawApp` Program

The `DrawApp` program shows how the higher-level drawing operations of the `Graphics` class are used to display and maintain a list of the objects that are drawn on a canvas. The source code of the `DrawApp` program is shown in Listing 14.1.

LISTING 14.1

THE SOURCE CODE FOR THE DrawApp PROGRAM

```
import java.awt.*;
import java.awt.event.*;
import java.util.*;

public class DrawApp extends Frame {
 // Create buttons
 Button lineButton = new Button("Line");
 Button ovalButton = new Button("Oval");
```

continues

LISTING 14.1 | *continued*

THE SOURCE CODE FOR THE DrawApp PROGRAM

```java
Button rectButton = new Button("Rectangle");
Button clearButton = new Button("Clear");
// Create Canvas object
MyCanvas canvas = new MyCanvas(TwoPointObject.LINE);
public static void main(String[] args) {
 DrawApp app = new DrawApp();
}
public DrawApp() {
 super("DrawApp");
 add("Center",canvas);
 setupButtons();
 addWindowListener(new WindowEventHandler());
 pack();
 setSize(400,400);
 show();
}

void setupButtons() {
 // Connect event handlers
 lineButton.addActionListener(new ButtonHandler());
 ovalButton.addActionListener(new ButtonHandler());
 rectButton.addActionListener(new ButtonHandler());
 clearButton.addActionListener(new ButtonHandler());
 Panel panel = new Panel();
 panel.add(lineButton);
 panel.add(ovalButton);
 panel.add(rectButton);
 panel.add(clearButton);
 add("North",panel);
}
class ButtonHandler implements ActionListener {
 public void actionPerformed(ActionEvent ev){
  // Handle button clicks
  String s=ev.getActionCommand();
  if(s.equals("Clear")) canvas.clear();
  else if(s.equals("Line"))
   canvas.setTool(TwoPointObject.LINE);
  else if(s.equals("Oval"))
   canvas.setTool(TwoPointObject.OVAL);
  else if(s.equals("Rectangle"))
   canvas.setTool(TwoPointObject.RECTANGLE);
 }
}
class WindowEventHandler extends WindowAdapter{
 public void windowClosing(WindowEvent e) {
  System.exit(0);
 }
}
}
class MyCanvas extends Canvas {
 // Define the default drawing tool
```

```
int tool = TwoPointObject.LINE;
Vector objects = new Vector();
TwoPointObject current;
boolean newObject = false;
public MyCanvas(int toolType) {
 super();
 tool = toolType;
 // Handle mouse clicking and movement
 addMouseListener(new MouseHandler());
 addMouseMotionListener(new MouseMotionHandler());
}
public void setTool(int toolType) {
 tool = toolType;
}
public void clear() {
 objects.removeAllElements();
 repaint();
}
public void paint(Graphics g) {
 // Draw/redraw canvas
 int numObjects = objects.size();
 for(int i=0;i<numObjects;++i) {
  TwoPointObject obj = (TwoPointObject) objects.elementAt(i);
  obj.draw(g);
 }
 if(newObject) current.draw(g);
}
class MouseHandler extends MouseAdapter {
 public void mousePressed(MouseEvent e){
  // Handle mouse down
  current = new TwoPointObject(tool,e.getX(),e.getY());
  newObject = true;
 }
 public void mouseReleased(MouseEvent e){
  // Handle mouse up
  if(newObject) {
   objects.addElement(current);
   newObject = false;
  }
 }
}
class MouseMotionHandler extends MouseMotionAdapter {
 public void mouseDragged(MouseEvent e){
  // Handle mouse movement
  int x = e.getX();
  int y = e.getY();
  if(newObject) {
   int oldX = current.endX;
   int oldY = current.endY;
   if(tool != TwoPointObject.LINE) {
    if(x > current.startX) current.endX = x;
    if(y > current.startY) current.endY = y;
    int width = Math.max(oldX,current.endX) -
    ➥current.startX + 1;
```

continues

LISTING 14.1 | *continued*

THE SOURCE CODE FOR THE DrawApp PROGRAM

```java
        int height = Math.max(oldY,current.endY) -
   ➥current.startY + 1;
        repaint(current.startX,current.startY,width,height);
      }else{
        current.endX = x;
        current.endY = y;
        int startX =
   ➥Math.min(Math.min(current.startX,current.endX),oldX);
        int startY =
   ➥Math.min(Math.min(current.startY,current.endY),oldY);
        int endX =
   ➥Math.max(Math.max(current.startX,current.endX),oldX);
        int endY =
   ➥Math.max(Math.max(current.startY,current.endY),oldY);
        repaint(startX,startY,endX-startX+1,endY-startY+1);
      }
    }
  }
}
}
class TwoPointObject {
// Encapsulates objects that can be described using two
➥points
public static int LINE = 0;
public static int OVAL = 1;
public static int RECTANGLE = 2;
public int type, startX, startY, endX, endY;
public TwoPointObject(int objectType,int x1,int y1,int x2,int
➥y2) {
  type = objectType;
  startX = x1;
  startY = y1;
  endX = x2;
  endY = y2;
}
public TwoPointObject(int objectType,int x,int y) {
  this(objectType,x,y,x,y);
}
public TwoPointObject() {
  this(LINE,0,0,0,0);
}
public void draw(Graphics g) {
  if(type == LINE) g.drawLine(startX,startY,endX,endY);
  else{
    int w = Math.abs(endX - startX);
    int l = Math.abs(endY - startY);
    if(type == OVAL) g.drawOval(startX,startY,w,l);
    else g.drawRect(startX,startY,w,l);
  }
}
}
```

When you run DrawApp, you will see the opening window shown in Figure 14.1.

The DrawApp program is initially configured for you to draw lines in its window area. You can draw a line by clicking the left mouse button and dragging the mouse. When you have finished drawing the line, release the left mouse button and the drawn line will be completed. The coordinate where you press the left mouse button is the beginning of the line, and the coordinate where you release the left mouse button is the end of the line. Go ahead and draw several lines, as shown in Figure 14.2.

The DrawApp program supports the drawing of lines, ovals, and rectangles. Click the Oval button to change the drawing tool to draw ovals. You draw an oval in the same way that you draw a line. When you click the left button of your mouse, you mark the upper-left corner of an invisible bounding box surrounding the oval. Drag the mouse to where you want the lower-right corner of the oval's bounding box and release the left mouse button. Try drawing a few ovals, as shown in Figure 14.3.

Now click the Rectangle button to begin drawing rectangles. You draw rectangles in the same way that you draw ovals. Go ahead and draw a rectangle, as shown in Figure 14.4.

You can experiment with the program before going on to find out how it works. If you want to clear the drawing screen, click the Clear button.

The DrawApp program is a little longer than the programs you've seen so far in this book. It consists of three major classes and three event-handling inner classes. The DrawApp class is the main class used to implement the program. The MyCanvas class is used to implement the program's main canvas component. The TwoPointObject class is used to implement the line, oval, and rectangle objects that are drawn on the screen. It is called TwoPointObject because it supports objects that can be characterized by a starting point (mouse down) and an ending point (mouse up).

DrawApp declares the canvas variable to refer to the MyCanvas object that implements the drawing. This object is constructed by passing the TwoPointObject.LINE constant as an argument. This tells the constructed object that the line tool should be initially used to support drawing. The height and width of the DrawApp window is set to 400 pixels.

FIGURE 14.1
The DrawApp opening window.

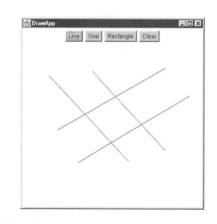

FIGURE 14.2
Drawing lines with DrawApp.

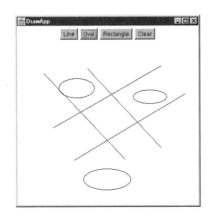

FIGURE 14.3
Drawing ovals with DrawApp.

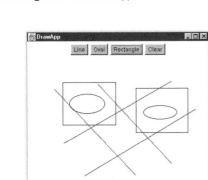

FIGURE 14.4
Drawing rectangles with DrawApp.

The actionPerformed() method of the ButtonHandler class handles the clicking of the buttons. The Clear button is handled by invoking the clear() method of the MyCanvas class to clear the canvas to a blank state. The Line, Oval, and Rectangle buttons are handled by invoking the setTool() method of the MyCanvas class to set the current drawing tool. It uses the LINE, OVAL, and RECTANGLE constants defined in the TwoPointObject class.

MyCanvas

The MyCanvas class extends the Canvas class to provide custom drawing capabilities. The tool variable is used to identify the current drawing tool that is in effect. The objects variable is declared as a Vector. It is used to store all the objects drawn by the user. The current variable is used to refer to the current TwoPointObject object being drawn by the user. The newObject flag is used to track whether the user has begun drawing a new object.

The MyCanvas constructor invokes the constructor of the Canvas class using the superclass constructor call statement, and then sets the tool variable to the toolType argument passed to the constructor.

The setTool() method changes the tool used to draw an object.

The clear() method invokes the removeAllElements() method of the Vector class to remove all drawing objects stored in the Vector referenced by the objects variable.

The paint() method is used to paint and repaint the screen. It uses the size() method of the Vector class to determine how many objects are stored in the objects vector and sets the numObjects variable to this value. It then iterates through each object stored in objects and draws each one on the canvas. The elementAt() method of the Vector class is used to retrieve an object from the objects vector. The object is cast into an object of class TwoPointObject and assigned to the obj variable. The draw() method of the TwoPointObject class is invoked to draw the object on the current Graphics context.

Notice that the paint() method does not have to know how to support limited area repainting. Only full canvas painting needs to be implemented by paint(). Support of limited area repainting is provided by the local AWT implementation.

The MouseHandler and MouseMotionHandler inner classes handle the events associated with pressing, releasing, and dragging the mouse. They do this by extending the MouseAdapter and MouseMotionAdapter classes of java.awt.event. The MouseHandler class handles the pressing and releasing of the mouse button via the mousePressed() and mouseReleased() methods. The MouseMotionHandler class handles the dragging of the mouse via the mouseDragged() method.

The mousePressed() method handles the event that is generated when the user clicks the left mouse button in the canvas. The method is called by the Java runtime system with the position of the mouse click. A new TwoPointObject object is created, with the tool variable and the position of the mouse click as its arguments. The newly created object is assigned to the current variable, and the newObject flag is set to true.

The mouseReleased() method is used to handle the event that is generated when the user releases the left mouse button. This action marks the completion of the drawing of an object. The event is handled by adding the object referenced by the current variable to the objects vector. The newObject flag is then set to False. The object referenced by the current variable is updated with its ending position during the processing of the mouseDragged() event-handling method. The newObject flag is checked to make sure that the mouse was not clicked outside of the current window and then released.

The mouseDragged() method performs somewhat more sophisticated event-handling than the mousePressed() and mouseReleased() methods. It checks the newObject flag to make sure that an object is currently being drawn. It then sets the oldX and oldY variables to the ending position of the object being drawn. These variables will be used to determine which portion of the canvas needs to be repainted. Repainting of the entire canvas is not visually appealing because it causes previously drawn objects to flicker.

If the current drawing tool is not a line, then an oval or a rectangle is the object being drawn by the user. The x,y coordinates of the mouse motion are provided via the MouseEvent argument to the mouseDragged() method. These coordinates are checked to determine whether the mouse was dragged below and to the right of the object being drawn. If this is the case, the ending position of the current object is updated. If the mouse is dragged to the left or above the starting point of the object, the current position of the mouse is ignored. This is to ensure that the starting position of the oval or rectangle is indeed its upper-left corner. The new width and height of the area to be repainted are calculated as the maximum area covered by the previous ending position and the current object ending position. This is to ensure that the repaint operation will erase any previous boundaries of the object being drawn. The max() method of the java.lang.Math class is used to determine this maximum area. The repaint() method of the Component class is then used to repaint the area updated as the result of the mouse drag. This version of the repaint() method takes as its parameters the x,y coordinate of the upper-left corner of the area to be redrawn and the width and height of this area.

Line drawing is not restricted in the same manner as oval and rectangle drawing. If it were, you would not be able to draw lines that go up and to the right or down and to the left. The else part of the if statement updates the starting position of the area to be repainted as the upper-leftmost point of the line being redrawn. It then updates the ending position of the area to be repainted as the lower-rightmost point of the line. The canvas is then repainted using the starting coordinates and the updated width and height of the repaint area.

To get a better feel for the process of local screen repainting, try experimenting with the way the repaint() method is used to update the canvas display.

TwoPointObject

The TwoPointObject class is used to keep track of the objects drawn by the user. It records the type of object and its starting and ending coordinates. It also draws the objects on a Graphics object passed as a parameter.

TwoPointObject defines the LINE, OVAL, and RECTANGLE constants, which are also used by the MyCanvas class. The type variable is used to record the type of object being drawn. The startX, startY, endX, and endY variables identify the starting and ending coordinates of the object.

Three TwoPointObject constructors are declared. The first constructor takes as its parameters the type of object being drawn and its starting and ending coordinates. The second constructor leaves out the ending coordinate and sets them to be the same as the starting coordinate. The last constructor takes no parameters and creates a line at the coordinate 0,0.

The draw() method checks the type variable to determine which type of object is to be drawn. If the object is a line, it uses the drawLine() method of the Graphics class to draw a line from its starting to ending coordinate. If the object is an oval or a line, the w and 1 variables are assigned the width and length of the object to be drawn. The drawOval() and drawRect() methods are used to draw an oval or rectangle, respectively.

DRAWING TEXT

The Font class of java.awt provides a platform-independent method of specifying and using fonts. The Font class constructor creates Font objects using the font's name, style (PLAIN, BOLD, ITALIC, or BOLD + ITALIC), and point size. Java's fonts are named in a platform-independent manner and then mapped to local fonts that are supported by the operating system on which it executes. The getName() method returns the logical Java font name of a particular font, and the getFamily() method returns the operating system-specific name of the font. You'll learn the name of the standard Java fonts in the next programming example of this chapter.

The FontMetrics class is used to return the specific parameters for a particular Font object. An object of this class is created using the getFontMetrics() methods supported by the Component class and other classes, such as the Graphics class. The FontMetrics class provides access to the details of the implementation of a Font object.

When text characters are displayed, they are displayed relative to a baseline. The *baseline* is the line drawn through the bottom of non-descending characters. For example, if you drew a line at the bottom of most text displayed on this line, you would get the text's baseline. Some characters, such as *g* and *y*, descend below the baseline. The number of pixels that the characters of a font descend below the baseline is known as the font's *descent*. The number of pixels that the characters of a font extend above the baseline is known as the font's *ascent*.

FIGURE 14.5
Font parameters.

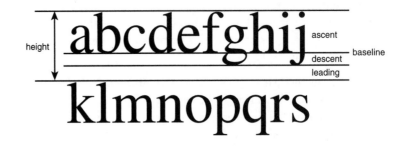

In addition to a font's ascent and descent, a third parameter, referred to as the font's *leading*, is used to describe the amount of vertical spacing, in pixels, used between the descent of a line of text and the ascent of the line of text below it. The overall height of a font is the sum of its leading, ascent, and descent, and is equal to the distance between baselines (in pixels) of vertically adjacent lines of text. The `getLeading()`, `getAscent()`, `getDescent()`, and `getHeight()` methods of the `FontMetrics` class are used to access these important font-related parameters. Figure 14.5 provides a graphical description of these parameters.

The `getMaxAdvance()`, `getMaxAscent()`, and `getMaxDescent()` methods are provided for backward-compatibility with earlier Java versions.

The `FontApp` Program

The `FontApp` program illustrates the use of the `Font` and `FontMetrics` classes and shows how to draw text on a `Graphics` object. Its source code is shown in Listing 14.2.

LISTING 14.2

THE SOURCE CODE OF THE `FontApp` PROGRAM

```
import java.awt.*;
import java.awt.event.*;

public class FontApp extends Frame {
  int screenWidth = 400;
  int screenHeight = 400;
  Font defaultFont;
  // Declare & create FontCanvas object
  FontCanvas fontCanvas = new FontCanvas();
```

```
String fontNames[];
int fontIndex = 0;
public static void main(String[] args) {
 FontApp app = new FontApp();
}
public FontApp() {
 super("FontApp");
 setupFontNames();
 Button nextButton = new Button("Next Font");
 nextButton.addActionListener(new ButtonHandler());
 Panel panel = new Panel();
 panel.add(nextButton);
 add("North",panel);
 add("Center",fontCanvas);
 addWindowListener(new WindowEventHandler());
 pack();
 setSize(screenWidth,screenHeight);
 show();
}
void setupFontNames() {
 // Get font names from local graphics environment
 GraphicsEnvironment ge =
  GraphicsEnvironment.getLocalGraphicsEnvironment();
 fontNames = ge.getAvailableFontFamilyNames();
}
class ButtonHandler implements ActionListener {
 public void actionPerformed(ActionEvent ev){
  // Switch fonts
  int numFonts = fontNames.length;
  if(numFonts > 1) fontIndex = (fontIndex + 1) % numFonts;
  fontCanvas.repaint();
 }
}
class WindowEventHandler extends WindowAdapter{
 public void windowClosing(WindowEvent e) {
  System.exit(0);
 }
}
class FontCanvas extends Canvas {
 // Extend Canvas to display fonts
 public int displayFontName(Graphics g) {
  String text = fontNames[fontIndex];
  if(defaultFont == null) defaultFont = getFont();
  FontMetrics fm = g.getFontMetrics(defaultFont);
  int x = (screenWidth - fm.stringWidth(text))/2;
  int y = 10 + fm.getLeading()+fm.getAscent();
  g.setFont(defaultFont);
  g.drawString(text,x,y);
  return y+fm.getHeight();
 }
 public void paint(Graphics g) {
  // Display U.S. alphabet
  String text = "abcdefghijklmnopqrstuvwxyz";
  int sizes[] = {12,14,18,24};
```

continues

LISTING 14.2 | *continued*

THE SOURCE CODE OF THE FontApp PROGRAM

```
int y = displayFontName(g);
for(int i=0;i<sizes.length;++i) {
 Font currentFont =
  new Font(fontNames[fontIndex],Font.PLAIN,sizes[i]);
 g.setFont(currentFont);
 FontMetrics fm = g.getFontMetrics(currentFont);
 int x = (screenWidth - fm.stringWidth(text))/2;
 g.drawString(text,x,y+fm.getLeading()+fm.getAscent());
 y += fm.getHeight();
 }
 }
 }
}
```

The FontApp program enables you to display a sample of the fonts that are available on your system. Figure 14.6 shows a possible display output. The program displays the name of a font and then a sample of how the font renders the lowercase letters a-z in 12, 14, 18, and 24 point sizes. Click the Next Font button and the next font supported by your system is displayed.

The FontApp class declares a number of field variables. The defaultFont variable identifies the default font used by the program. The fontNames[] array is used to store the names of the fonts that are accessible to Java.

The setupFonts() method obtains the local GraphicsEnvironment object using the static getLocalGraphicsEnvironment() method of the GraphicsEnvironment class. It then uses the getAvailableFontFamilyNames() method to obtain the names of all the fonts supported by the system.

The paint() method of the FontCanvas class is where the primary processing of interest takes place. It invokes the displayFontName() method to display the name of the next font to be displayed. The displayFontName() method returns the vertical offset where the next text line should be displayed. The paint() method uses a for statement to loop through the sizes array and display a line at each point size. Note how the getLeading(), getAscent(), and getHeight() methods are used to determine the vertical position of the text.

FIGURE 14.6
The FontApp program's output.

DISPLAYING BITMAPPED IMAGES

The drawImage() method of the Graphics class is used to display bitmapped images. It has a number of forms that take various arguments. In its simplest form, it takes as its arguments an object of the Image class, an object that implements the ImageObserver interface, the x,y-coordinate where the image is to be displayed.

The Image class is an abstract class that provides format-independent access to graphical images. Image objects are created by invoking methods of other classes that create images. Examples of these image-creating methods are the createImage() methods of the Component and Toolkit classes and the getImage() methods of the Toolkit and Applet classes. The getImage() methods are best methods for retrieving an image that is stored in a disk file or at a URL. Java currently supports GIF- and JPEG-formatted images through these methods.

The ImageObserver interface is defined in the java.awt.image package. This interface provides a set of constants and methods that support the creation and loading of images. The Component class implements the ImageObserver interface; and in most cases, the ImageObserver object used as the parameter to the drawImage() method can be supplied using the this identifier to reference the current Canvas or Frame object being painted.

The ImageApp Program

The ImageApp program shows how bitmapped images can be drawn in a program window using the drawImage() method of the Graphics class. Its source code is shown in Listing 14.3.

LISTING 14.3

THE ImageApp PROGRAM

```
import java.awt.*;
import java.awt.event.*;

public class ImageApp extends Frame {
  Image image;
```

continues

LISTING 14.3 | *continued*

THE ImageApp PROGRAM

```
public static void main(String[] args) {
 ImageApp app = new ImageApp();
}
public ImageApp() {
 super("ImageApp");
 setBackground(Color.white);
 // Use Toolkit to load image file
 Toolkit toolkit = Toolkit.getDefaultToolkit();
 image = toolkit.getImage("test.gif");
 addWindowListener(new WindowEventHandler());
 pack();
 setSize(400,400);
 show();
}
public void paint(Graphics g) {
 g.drawImage(image,0,0,this);
}
class WindowEventHandler extends WindowAdapter{
 public void windowClosing(WindowEvent e) {
  System.exit(0);
 }
}
}
```

Before running the ImageApp program, copy the test.gif image from the \jc2\ch14 directory of the CD-ROM to your jc2\ch07 directory. The ImageApp program displays the image in the test.gif file.

When you run the ImageApp program, it will display the bitmapped image shown in Figure 14.7.

The functionality of the ImageApp program isn't all that astounding. Its purpose is to illustrate the use of the methods involved in loading and displaying image files. You can easily upgrade the program to display arbitrary GIF or JPEG files by passing the image file name as a program argument.

The setBackground() method of the Component class sets the program background to white. The getImage() method of the Toolkit class is used to load the image in the test.gif file and assign it to the image variable.

FIGURE 14.7
The ImageApp program.

The paint() method draws the image referenced by the image variable on the default Graphics object of the program window. It accomplishes this using the drawImage() method of the Graphics class. The arguments to drawImage() include the image to be displayed, the x,y coordinate where the image is to be drawn, and the object implementing the ImageObserver interface associated with the image. The this identifier is used to indicate that the program window is the ImageObserver.

CLIPPING

The AWT supports a painting feature known as *clipping*. Clipping enables you to restrict painting (or drawing) operations to a particular shape. The Shape interface is implemented by classes that define geometric shapes, such as Rectangle and Polygon. The setClip() method of the Graphics class is used to specify a clipping region. It takes a Shape object as an argument. (Another version of the setClip() method takes x, y, width, and height arguments.) When a clipping region is specified, painting of a Graphics object is limited to the clipping region. The ClipApp program of Listing 14.4 shows how clipping works. This program creates a Rectangle object that is set as the clipping area. It is located at (100,100) and is 200 pixels wide and high. Figure 14.8 shows the image displayed as the result of clipping.

> **NOTE**
>
> **Clipping and Repainting** When the AWT background thread invokes the paint() methods of GUI objects to support repainting, it sets the clipping region to the limited area of the applet or application window that requires repainting. This speeds up the repaint operation and conserves processing resources.

LISTING 14.4

THE ClipApp PROGRAM

```java
import java.awt.*;
import java.awt.event.*;

public class ClipApp extends Frame {
 Image image;
 public static void main(String[] args) {
  ClipApp app = new ClipApp();
 }
 public ClipApp() {
  super("ClipApp");
  setBackground(Color.white);
```

continues

FIGURE 14.8
The ClipApp program limits the painting area.

| **LISTING 14.4** | *continued* |

THE ClipApp PROGRAM

```
Toolkit toolkit = Toolkit.getDefaultToolkit();
image = toolkit.getImage("test.gif");
addWindowListener(new WindowEventHandler());
pack();
setSize(400,400);
show();
}
public void paint(Graphics g) {
 // Set clipping region
 g.setClip(new Rectangle(100,100,200,200));
 g.drawImage(image,0,0,this);
}
class WindowEventHandler extends WindowAdapter{
 public void windowClosing(WindowEvent e) {
  System.exit(0);
 }
 }
}
```

CHAPTER SUMMARY

KEY TERMS

- Painting
- Repainting
- Drawing
- Clipping

This chapter covered the classes and interfaces of java.awt that are used to implement drawing and painting. You were introduced to the Canvas, Graphics, Image, and Font classes and learned how they are used in conjunction with the paint() method. You also built several small Java applications that provided concrete painting examples. You should now be prepared to test your knowledge of these topics. The following review questions and exam questions will let you know how well you understand this material and will give you an idea of how you'll do in related exam questions. They'll also indicate which material you need to study further.

APPLY YOUR KNOWLEDGE

Review Questions

1. What is the relationship between the Canvas class and the Graphics class?

2. Name three Component subclasses that support painting.

3. What is the difference between the paint() and repaint() methods?

4. What is the difference between the Font and FontMetrics classes?

5. What is clipping?

6. What is the relationship between clipping and repainting?

Exam Questions

1. Which of the following are passed as an argument to the paint() method?

    A. A Canvas object

    B. A Graphics object

    C. An Image object

    D. A Paint object

2. Which of the following methods are invoked by the AWT to support paint and repaint operations?

    A. paint()

    B. repaint()

    C. draw()

    D. redraw()

3. Which of the following classes have a paint() method?

    A. Canvas

    B. Image

    C. Frame

    D. Graphics

4. Which of the following are methods of the Graphics class?

    A. drawRect()

    B. drawImage()

    C. drawPoint()

    D. drawString()

5. Which Font attributes are available through the FontMetrics class?

    A. ascent

    B. leading

    C. case

    D. height

6. Which of the following are valid forms of the drawImage() method of the Graphics class?

    A. drawImage(Image image, int x, int y, ImageObserver observer)

    B. drawImage(Image image)

    C. drawImage(Image image, int x, int y)

    D. drawImage()

7. When the clipping region is set for a Graphics object, which of the following are true?

    A. Painting is restricted to the clipping region.

    B. Painting is excluded from the clipping region.

    C. All painting is prohibited.

    D. Painting takes place inside of and outside of the clipping region.

APPLY YOUR KNOWLEDGE

8. Which of the following are true?

    A. The AWT automatically causes a window to be repainted when a portion of a window has been minimized and then maximized.

    B. The AWT automatically causes a window to be repainted when a portion of a window has been covered and then uncovered.

    C. The AWT automatically causes a window to be repainted when application data is changed.

    D. The AWT does not support repainting operations.

Answers to Review Questions

1. A Canvas object provides access to a Graphics object via its paint() method.

2. The Canvas, Frame, Panel, and Applet classes support painting.

3. The paint() method supports painting via a Graphics object. The repaint() method is used to cause paint() to be invoked by the AWT painting thread.

4. The FontMetrics class is used to define implementation-specific properties, such as ascent and descent, of a Font object.

5. Clipping is the process of confining paint operations to a limited area or shape.

6. When a window is repainted by the AWT painting thread, it sets the clipping regions to the area of the window that requires repainting.

Answers to Exam Questions

1. B   The paint() method has a Graphics argument.

2. A   The AWT causes the paint() method to be invoked.

3. A and C   The Canvas and Frame classes inherit paint() from Component.

4. A, B, and D   The Graphics class supports all the methods except drawPoint().

5. A, B, and D   Ascent, leading, and height are available through FontMetrics.

6. A   The first form is the simplest form of drawImage().

7. A   The purpose of clipping is to restrict painting operations to the clipping region.

8. A and B   The AWT automatically repaints portions of a window that require repainting as the result of window movement and resizing operations.

Suggested Readings and Resources

The JDK 1.2 java.awt package API description.

This chapter helps you to prepare for the exam by covering the following objectives:

Know how the `java.io` package supports stream-based input and output.

▶ A general knowledge of how Java supports I/O operations is required to develop programs that are able to save and reuse their results.

Know how the `java.io` input and output class hierarchy is structured.

▶ The `java.io` package supports a large number of classes and interfaces. Familiarity with these classes and interfaces is required to answer some certification exam questions.

Know how the `File` class is used to access the directories and files of the local system.

▶ The `File` class enables programs to access the local file system. For this reason, it is an important class for many I/O operations. The certification exam contains questions that require familiarity with this class.

Know how I/O filters are used.

▶ The I/O filter classes combine the capabilities of different input or output streams. This enables you to incorporate features, such as buffering, in your programs. I/O filtering is a topic for the certification exam.

Know how character I/O is supported by the `Reader` and `Writer` classes.

▶ The `Reader` and `Writer` classes support character-based I/O using different character encodings. These capabilities are required to develop programs that support international character sets.

CHAPTER 15

The `java.io` Package

As you read through this chapter, you should concentrate on the following key items:

▶ How I/O is accomplished using input stream, output stream, Reader and Writer classes

▶ How the classes of the java.io package are structured

▶ How the File object is used to access the local file system

▶ How I/O filters are used

▶ How international text is supported

Chapter Introduction

The capability to perform input and output is key to saving and reusing a program's results. Because input and output are fundamental to programming, you may see a few exam questions related to the `java.io` package. In this chapter, you'll learn to use Java streams to perform sophisticated input and output, using standard I/O, memory buffers, and files. You'll explore the input and output class hierarchy and learn to use stream filters to simplify I/O processing. You'll also learn how to perform random-access I/O and access character encodings. By studying the class descriptions of this chapter and working the programming examples, you should be able to do well on related exam questions.

Streams

Java input and output are based on the use of *streams*, which are sequences of bytes or characters that travel from a source to a destination over a communication path. If your program is writing to a stream, that program is the stream's *source*. If your program is reading from a stream, it is the stream's *destination*. The communication path is dependent on the type of I/Os being performed. It can consist of memory-to-memory transfers, a file system, a network, and other forms of I/O.

Streams are not complicated. They are powerful because they abstract the details of the communication path from input and output operations. This enables all I/Os to be performed using a common set of methods. These methods can be tailored and extended to provide higher-level, custom I/O capabilities.

Java defines two major classes of byte streams: `InputStream` and `OutputStream`. These streams are subclassed to provide a variety of I/O capabilities. Java 1.1 introduced the `Reader` and `Writer` classes to provide the foundation for 16-bit Unicode character-oriented I/O. These classes support internationalization of Java I/O, allowing text to be stored using international character encodings.

THE java.io CLASS HIERARCHY

Figure 15.1 identifies the java.io class hierarchy. As described in the previous section, the InputStream, OutputStream, Reader, and Writer classes are the major components of this hierarchy. Other high-level classes include the File, FileDescriptor, RandomAccessFile, ObjectStreamClass, and StreamTokenizer classes.

The InputStream and OutputStream classes have complementary subclasses. For example, both have subclasses for performing I/O via memory buffers, files, and pipes. The InputStream subclasses perform the input, and the OutputStream classes perform the output.

The InputStream class has several direct subclasses. The ByteArrayInputStream class is used to convert an array into an input stream. The StringBufferInputStream class uses a StringBuffer as an input stream. The FileInputStream class enables files to be used as input streams. The ObjectInputStream class is used to read primitive types and objects that have been previously written to a stream. The PipedInputStream class allows a pipe to be constructed between two threads and supports input through the pipe. It is used in conjunction with the PipedOutputStream class. The SequenceInputStream class enables two or more streams to be concatenated into a single stream. The FilterInputStream class is an abstract class from which other input-filtering classes are constructed.

Filters are objects that read from one stream and write to another, usually altering the data in some way as they pass it from one stream to another. Filters can be used to buffer data, read and write objects, keep track of line numbers, and perform other operations on the data they move. Filters can be combined, with one filter using the output of another as its input. You can create custom filters by combining existing filters.

FilterInputStream has a number of filtering subclasses. The BufferedInputStream class maintains a buffer of the input data that it receives. This eliminates the need to read from the stream's source every time an input byte is needed. The DataInputStream class implements the DataInput interface, a set of methods that enable String objects and primitive data types to be read from a stream. The LineNumberInputStream is used to keep track of input line numbers. The PushbackInputStream provides the capability to push data back onto the stream that it is read from so that it can be read again.

```
java.io
    InputStream
        FilterInputStream
            BufferedInputStream
            DataInputStream
            LineNumberInputStream
            PushbackInputStream
        ByteArrayInputStream
        FileInputStream
        ObjectInputStream
            ObjectInputStreamGetField (nested)
        PipedInputStream
        SequenceInputStream
        StringBufferInputStream
    OutputStream
        FilterOutputStream
            BufferedOutputStream
            DataOutputStream
            PrintStream
        ByteArrayOutputStream
        FileOutputStream
        ObjectOutputStream
            ObjectOutputStreamPutField (nested)
        PipedOutputStream
    Reader
        BufferedReader
            LineNumberReader
        CharArrayReader
        FilterReader
            PushbackReader
        InputStreamReader
            FileReader
        PipedReader
        StringReader
    Writer
        BufferedWriter
        CharArrayWriter
        FilterWriter
        OutputStreamWriter
            FileWriter
        PipedWriter
        PrintWriter
        StringWriter
    File
    RandomAccessFile
    FileDescriptor
    FilePermission
    ObjectStreamClass
    ObjectStreamField
    SerializablePermission
    StreamTokenizer
```

FIGURE 15.1

The classes of the java.io hierarchy.

NOTE

Other Stream Classes Other Java API packages, such as `java.util.zip` and `java.util.jar`, contain classes and interfaces that extend those of `java.io`. These packages define input and output stream classes that can be used to support file and stream compression.

The `OutputStream` class hierarchy consists of five direct subclasses. The `ByteArrayOutputStream`, `FileOutputStream`, `ObjectOutputStream`, and `PipedOutputStream` classes are the output complements to the `ByteArrayInputStream`, `FileInputStream`, `ObjectInputStream`, and `PipedInputStream` classes. The `FilterOutputStream` class provides subclasses that complement the `FilterInputStream` classes.

The `BufferedOutputStream` class is the output analog to the `BufferedInputStream` class. It buffers output so that output bytes can be written to devices in larger groups. The `DataOutputStream` class implements the `DataOutput` interface. This interface complements the `DataInput` interface. It provides methods that write `String` objects and primitive data types to streams so that they can be read by the `DataInput` interface methods. The `PrintStream` class provides the familiar `print()` and `println()` methods used to display output to the console window. `PrintStream` provides a number of over-loaded methods that simplify data output.

The `Reader` class is similar to the `InputStream` class because it is the root of an input class hierarchy. `Reader` supports 16-bit Unicode character input, whereas `InputStream` supports 8-bit byte input. The `Reader` class has six direct subclasses.

◆ The `BufferedReader` class supports buffered character input. Its `LineNumberReader` subclass supports buffered input and keeps track of line numbers.

◆ The `CharArrayReader` class provides the capability to read a character input stream from a character buffer.

◆ The `FilterReader` class is an abstract class that provides the basis for filtering character input streams. Its `PushbackReader` subclass provides a filter that allows characters to be pushed back onto the input stream.

◆ The `InputStreamReader` class is used to convert byte input streams to character input streams. Its `FileReader` subclass is used to read character files.

◆ The `PipedReader` class is used to read characters from a pipe.

◆ The `StringReader` class is used to read characters from a `String`.

The Writer class is the output analog of the Reader class. It supports
16-bit Unicode character output. It has seven direct subclasses:

◆ The BufferedWriter class supports buffered character output.

◆ The CharArrayWriter class supports output to a character
   array.

◆ The FilterWriter class is an abstract class that supports character output filtering.

◆ The OutputStreamWriter class enables a character stream to be
   converted to a byte stream. Its FileWriter subclass is used to
   perform character output to files.

◆ The PipedWriter class supports character output to pipes.

◆ The PrintWriter class supports platform-independent character printing.

◆ The StringWriter class supports character output to String
   objects.

The File class is used to access the files and directories of the local
file system. The FileDescriptor class is an encapsulation of the
information used by the host system to track files that are being
accessed. The RandomAccessFile class provides the capabilities needed
to directly access data contained in a file. The ObjectStreamClass
class is used to describe classes whose objects can be written (serialized) to a stream. The StreamTokenizer class is used to create parsers
that operate on stream data.

New classes introduced with Java 2 include the
ObjectInputStream.GetField, ObjectOutputStream.PutField, and
ObjectStreamField classes, which support object stream I/O. The
FilePermission and SerializablePermission classes support security
access controls.

NOTE **Serialization** The process of converting objects to a format that is suitable
for stream input and output is
referred to as *serialization*.
Deserialization is the process of converting a serialized object back to an
object instance. In order for an object
to be serialized, it must implement
the java.io.Serializable interface.

THE java.io INTERFACES

The java.io package declares ten interfaces. The DataInput and
DataOutput interfaces provide methods that support machine-
independent I/O. The ObjectInput and ObjectOutput interfaces
extend DataInput and DataOutput to work with objects. The

NOTE **Other Input/Output Classes** Other
packages, such as java.util.zip,
provide classes that extend the
java.io class hierarchy shown in
Figure 15.1.

ObjectInputValidation interface supports the validation of objects that are read from a stream. The Serializable and Externalizable interfaces support the serialized writing of objects to streams. The FilenameFilter and FileFilter interfaces are used to select filenames from a list. The ObjectStreamConstants interface defines constants that serialize objects to and from streams.

THE InputStream CLASS

The InputStream class is an abstract class that lays the foundation for the Java byte-input class hierarchy. As such, it provides methods that are inherited by all InputStream classes.

The read() Method

The read() method is the most important method of the InputStream class hierarchy. It reads a byte of data from an input stream and blocks if no data is available. When a method *blocks*, it causes the thread in which it is executing to wait until data becomes available. This is not a problem in multithreaded programs. The read() method takes on several overloaded forms. It can read a single byte or an array of bytes, depending upon what form is used. If it reads a single byte then it returns the byte that is read. If it reads an array of bytes it returns the number of bytes read. In both cases it returns -1 if an end of file is encountered with no bytes read.

The read() method is overridden and overloaded by subclasses to provide custom-read capabilities.

The available() Method

The available() method returns the number of bytes that are available to be read without blocking. It is used to peek into the input stream to see how much data is available. However, depending on the input stream, it might not be accurate or useful. Some input streams on some operating systems may always report 0 available bytes when data is available from a stream. In general, it is not a good idea to blindly rely on this method to perform input processing.

The close() Method

The close() method closes an input stream and releases resources associated with the stream. It is always a good idea to close a stream to ensure that the stream processing is correctly terminated.

Markable Streams

Java supports *markable streams*. These are streams that provide the capability to mark a position in the stream and then later reset the stream so that it can be reread from the marked position. If a stream can be marked, it must contain some memory to keep track of the data between the mark and the current position of the stream. When this buffering capability is exceeded, the mark becomes invalidated.

The markSupported() method returns a boolean value that identifies whether a stream supports mark and reset capabilities. The mark() method marks a position in the stream. It takes an integer parameter that identifies the number of bytes that can be read before the mark becomes invalid. This is used to set the buffering capacity of the stream. The reset() method simply repositions the stream to its last marked position.

The skip() Method

The skip() method skips over a specified number of input bytes. It takes a long value as a parameter. You can use the skip() method to move to a specific position within an input stream.

THE OutputStream CLASS

The OutputStream class is an abstract class that lays the foundation for the byte output stream hierarchy. It provides a set of methods that are the output analog to the InputStream methods.

NOTE

Overloading   The `OutputStream` class defines three overloaded forms for the `write()` method. These forms allow you to write an integer, an array of bytes, or a subarray of bytes to an `OutputStream` object. You will often see several overloaded forms for methods that perform the same operation using different types of data.

The `write()` Method

The `write()` method enables bytes to be written to the output stream. It provides three overloaded forms to write a single byte, an array of bytes, or a segment of an array. The `write()` method, like the `read()` method, may block when it tries to write to a stream. The blocking causes the thread executing the `write()` method to wait until the write operation has been completed.

The `flush()` Method

The `flush()` method causes any buffered data to be immediately written to the output stream. Some subclasses of `OutputStream` support buffering and override this method to clean out their buffers and to write all buffered data to the output stream. They must override the `OutputStream flush()` method because, by default, it does not perform any operations and is used as a placeholder.

The `close()` Method

It is generally more important to `close()` output streams than input streams, so that any data written to the stream is stored before the stream is deallocated and lost. The `close()` method of `OutputStream` is used in the same manner as that of `InputStream`.

BYTE ARRAY I/O

Java supports byte array input and output via the `ByteArrayInputStream` and `ByteArrayOutputStream` classes. These classes use memory buffers (arrays) as the source and destination of the input and output streams. The contents of the memory buffers are written and read from the streams. The `StringBufferInputStream` class is similar to the `ByteArrayInput` class, but was deprecated in JDK 1.1. The `StringReader` class is now the preferred class for `String`-based input.

The `CharArrayReader`, `CharArrayWriter`, `StringReader`, and `StringWriter` classes support character-based I/O in a manner similar to the `ByteArrayInputStream`, `ByteArrayOutputStream`, and

`StringBufferInputStream` classes. They are covered later in this chapter.

The `ByteArrayInputStream` Class

The `ByteArrayInputStream` class creates an input stream from a memory buffer. The buffer is an array of bytes. It provides two constructors that use a byte array argument to create the input stream. The class does not support any new methods, but overrides the `read()`, `skip()`, `available()`, and `reset()` methods of `InputStream`.

The `read()` and `skip()` methods are implemented as specified for `InputStream`. The `available()` method is reliable and can be used to check on the number of available bytes in the buffer. The `reset()` method resets the stream to a marked position.

The `ByteArrayOutputStream` Class

The `ByteArrayOutputStream` class is a little more sophisticated than its input complement. It creates an output stream on a byte array, but provides additional capabilities to enable the output array to grow to accommodate new data that is written to it. It also provides the `toByteArray()` and `toString()` methods for converting the stream data to a byte array or `String` object.

`ByteArrayOutputStream` provides some additional methods not declared for `OutputStream`. The `reset()` method resets the output buffer to allow writing to restart at the beginning of the buffer. The `size()` method returns the current number of bytes that have been written to the buffer. The `writeTo()` method takes an object of class `OutputStream` as an argument and writes the contents of the output buffer to the specified output stream. The `write()` methods override those of `OutputStream` to support array output.

FILE I/O

Java supports stream-based file input and output through the `File`, `FileDescriptor`, `FileInputStream`, and `FileOutputStream` classes. It supports direct or random access I/O using the `File`,

FileDescriptor, and RandomAccessFile classes. Random access I/O is covered later in this chapter. The FileReader and FileWriter classes support Unicode-based file I/O. These classes are also covered later in this chapter.

The File class provides access to file and directory objects and supports a number of operations on files and directories. The FileDescriptor class encapsulates the information used by the host system to track files that are being accessed. The FileInputStream and FileOutputStream classes provide the capability to read and write to file streams.

The File Class

The File class is used to access file and directory objects. It uses the file-naming conventions of the host operating system. The File class encapsulates these conventions using the File class constants.

File provides constructors for creating files and directories. These constructors take absolute and relative file paths, filenames, and directory names.

The File class provides numerous access methods that can be used to perform all common file and directory operations. File methods enable files to be created, deleted, and renamed. They provide access to a file's pathname and determine whether a File object is a file or directory. These methods also check read and write access permissions.

Directory-oriented methods enable directories to be created, deleted, renamed, and listed. Directory methods also allow directory trees to be traversed by providing access to the parent and sibling directories.

The FileApp program, shown in Listing 15.1, shows how the File class can be used to traverse a system's directory structure. Figure 15.2 shows the program's opening display. It lists directories in the top of the window and files in the bottom. Double-click a directory name, and that directory's contents are listed as shown in Figure 15.3.

NOTE

Listing the Current Directory You can list the contents of the current directory by creating a File object using new File(".") and then invoking its listFiles() method. However, the File class does not provide any method to change the current directory.

FIGURE 15.2
The FileApp program's opening display.

FIGURE 15.3
Listing the contents of a directory.

You should note the following points about how FileApp uses the File class:

◆ The listRoots() method is used to access an array of File objects that represent your system's root directories. The root directories are represented by ---roots--- in the program.

◆ The getAbsolutePath() method returns the full pathname of a file or directory.

◆ The getParent() method returns the name of a directory's parent directory or null if it is a system root.

◆ The listFiles() method returns an array of File objects corresponding to all directories and files in a directory.

◆ The isDirectory() and isFile() methods identify a File object as a directory or a file.

◆ The getName() method returns the name of a file or directory.

LISTING 15.1

THE FileApp PROGRAM

```java
import java.awt.*;
import java.awt.event.*;
import java.io.*;

public class FileApp extends Frame {
 List list = new List(5);
 TextArea textArea = new TextArea(10,80);
 File[] roots = File.listRoots();
 public static void main(String[] args) {
  FileApp app = new FileApp();
 }
 public FileApp() {
  super("FileApp");
  setup();
  addWindowListener(new WindowEventHandler());
  pack();
  setSize(450,450);
  show();
 }
 public void setup() {
  setFont(new Font("Courier",Font.BOLD,12));
  setLayout(new GridLayout(2,1));
  for(int i=0;i<roots.length;++i)
   list.add(roots[i].getAbsolutePath());
  list.addActionListener(new ListHandler());
  add(list);
  add(textArea);
 }
 void updateWindow(File file) {
  File[] contents = file.listFiles();
  list.removeAll();
  String parent = file.getParent();
  if(parent == null) list.add("---roots---");
  else list.add(parent);
```

```
 String text = "Files:\n";
 for(int i=0;i<contents.length;++i) {
  if(contents[i].isDirectory())
   list.add(contents[i].getAbsolutePath());
  if(contents[i].isFile())
   text += "\n" + contents[i].getName();
 }
 textArea.setText(text);
}
class ListHandler implements ActionListener {
 public void actionPerformed(ActionEvent e) {
  String item = (String) e.getActionCommand();
  if(item.equals("---roots---")) {
   list.removeAll();
   for(int i=0;i<roots.length;++i)
    list.add(roots[i].getAbsolutePath());
   textArea.setText("");
  }else updateWindow(new File(item));
  validate();
 }
}
class WindowEventHandler extends WindowAdapter{
 public void windowClosing(WindowEvent e) {
  System.exit(0);
 }
}
}
```

The FileDescriptor Class

The FileDescriptor class provides access to the file descriptors maintained by operating systems when files and directories are being accessed. This class is *opaque* in that it does not provide visibility into the specific information maintained by the operating system.

The FileInputStream Class

The FileInputStream class enables input to be read from a file in the form of a stream. Objects of class FileInputStream are created using a filename string or a File or FileDescriptor object as an argument. FileInputStream overrides the methods of the InputStream class and provides two new methods, finalize() and getFD(). The finalize() method closes a stream when it is processed by the Java garbage collector. The getFD() method is used to obtain access to the FileDescriptor associated with the input stream.

The FileOutputStream Class

The FileOutputStream class enables output to be written to a file stream. Objects of class FileOutputStream are created in the same way as objects of class FileInputStream, using a filename string, File object, or FileDescriptor object as an argument. FileOutputStream overrides the methods of the OutputStream class and supports the finalize() and getFD() methods described for the FileInputStream class.

The FileIOApp Program

The program in Listing 15.2 illustrates the use of the FileInputStream, FileOutputStream, and File classes. It writes a string to an output file and then reads the file to verify that the output was written correctly. The file used for the I/O is then deleted.

LISTING 15.2

THE SOURCE CODE OF THE FileIOApp PROGRAM

```
import java.io.*;

public class FileIOApp {
 public static void main(String args[]) throws IOException {
  // Create output file test.txt
  FileOutputStream outStream = new
  ➥FileOutputStream("test.txt");
  String s = "This is a test.";
  for(int i=0;i<s.length();++i)
   outStream.write(s.charAt(i));
  outStream.close();
  // Open test.txt for input
  FileInputStream inStream = new FileInputStream("test.txt");
  int inBytes = inStream.available();
  System.out.println("inStream has "+inBytes+" available
  ➥bytes");
  byte inBuf[] = new byte[inBytes];
  int bytesRead = inStream.read(inBuf,0,inBytes);
  System.out.println(bytesRead+" bytes were read");
  System.out.println("They are: "+new String(inBuf));
  inStream.close();
  File f = new File("test.txt");
  f.delete();
 }
}
```

The `FileOutputStream` constructor creates an output stream on the file `test.txt`. The file is automatically created in the current working directory. It then writes the string `"This is a test."` to the output file stream. The output stream is closed to make sure that all the data is written to the file. The file is then reopened as an input file by creating an object of class `FileInputStream`. The program determines the number of available bytes in the file and reads these bytes into a byte array. The number of bytes read is displayed along with the characters corresponding to those bytes.

The program's output follows:

```
inStream has 15 available bytes
15 bytes were read
They are: This is a test.
```

THE `SequenceInputStream` CLASS

The `SequenceInputStream` class is used to combine two or more input streams into a single input stream. The input streams are concatenated, which allows the individual streams to be treated as a single, logical stream. The `SequenceInputStream` class does not introduce any new access methods. Its power is derived from the two constructors that it provides. One constructor takes two `InputStream` objects as arguments. The other takes an `Enumeration` of `InputStream` objects.

FILTERED I/O

The filtered input and output stream classes provide the capability to filter I/O in a number of useful ways. I/O filters adapt streams to specific program needs. These filters sit between an input stream and an output stream and perform special processing on the bytes they transfer from input to output. You can combine filters to perform a sequence of filtering operations, where one filter acts on the output of another, as shown in Figure 15.4.

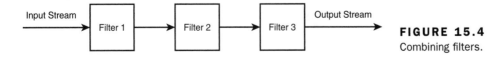

FIGURE 15.4
Combining filters.

The `FilterInputStream` Class

The `FilterInputStream` class is an abstract class that is the parent of all filtered input stream classes. The `FilterInputStream` class provides the basic capability to create one stream from another. It allows one stream to be read and provided as output as another stream. This is accomplished through the use of the in variable, which is used to maintain a separate object of class `InputStream`. The design of the `FilterInputStream` class enables multiple chained filters to be created using several layers of nesting. Each subsequent class accesses the output of the previous class through the in variable. Because the in variable is an object of class `InputStream`, arbitrary `InputStream` objects can be filtered.

The `FilterOutputStream` Class

The `FilterOutputStream` class is the complement to the `FilterInputStream` class. It is an abstract class that is the parent of all filtered output stream classes. It is similar to the `FilterInputStream` class because it maintains an object of class `OutputStream` as an out variable. Data written to an object of `FilterOutputStream` can be modified as needed to perform filtering operations and then forwarded to the out `OutputStream` object. Because out is declared to be of class `OutputStream`, arbitrary output streams can be filtered. Multiple `FilterOutputStream` objects can be combined in a manner that is analogous to `FilterInputStream` objects. The input of subsequent `FilterOutputStream` objects is linked to the output of preceding objects.

Buffered I/O

Buffered input and output is used to temporarily cache data that is read from or written to a stream. This enables programs to read and write small amounts of data without adversely affecting system performance. When buffered input is performed, a large number of bytes are read at a single time and stored in an input buffer. When a program reads from the input stream, the input bytes are read from the input buffer. Several reads may be performed before the buffer needs to refilled. Input buffering is used to speed up overall stream input processing.

Output buffering is performed in a manner similar to input buffering. When a program writes to a stream, the output data is stored in an output buffer until the buffer becomes full or the output stream is flushed. Only then is the buffered output actually forwarded to the output stream's destination.

Java implements buffered I/O as filters. The filters maintain and operate the buffer that sits between the program and the source or destination of a buffered stream.

The `BufferedInputStream` Class

The `BufferedInputStream` class supports input buffering by automatically creating and maintaining a buffer for a designated input stream. This enables programs to read data from the stream one byte at a time without degrading system performance. Because the `BufferedInputStream` class is a filter, it can be applied to arbitrary objects of class `InputStream` and combined with other input filters.

`BufferedInputStream` defines two constructors. One allows the size of an input buffer to be specified, and the other does not. Both constructors take an object of class `InputStream` as an argument. It is usually better to let `BufferedInputStream` select the best size for the input buffer than to specify a size yourself, unless you have specific knowledge that one buffer size is better than another.

`BufferedInputStream` overrides the access methods provided by `InputStream` and does not introduce any new methods of its own.

The `BufferedOutputStream` Class

The `BufferedOutputStream` class performs output buffering in a manner that is analogous to `BufferedInputStream`. It enables you to specify the size of the output buffer in a constructor. It also provides for a default buffer size. It overrides the methods of the `OutputStream` class and does not introduce any new methods of its own.

`PushbackInputStream`

`PushbackInputStream` is a filter that lets you push a byte that was previously read back onto the input stream so that it can be reread. This type of filter is commonly used with parsers. When a character indicating a new input token is read, it is pushed back onto the input stream until the current input token is processed. It is then reread when processing of the next input token is initiated. PushbackInputStream allows only a single byte to be pushed back. This is generally enough for most applications.

The pushback character is stored in a variable named pushBack.

The unread() method is the only new method introduced by this class. It is used to push a specified character back onto the input stream.

The LineNumberInputStream Class

The LineNumberInputStream class provides a handy capability for keeping track of input line numbers. It is also a subclass of FilterInputStream. This class provides two new methods to support line number processing. The setLineNumber() method is used to set the current line number to a particular value. The getLineNumber() method is used to obtain the value of the current line number.

Up until Java 1.1, the LineNumberInputStream class was the preferred class for tracking input line numbers. In Java 1.1, significant support was added for internationalization. As a result, the LineNumberInputStream class has been deprecated. The LineNumberReader class (covered later in this chapter) is now the preferred class for tracking input line numbers.

Data I/O

The DataInputStream and DataOutputStream classes implement the DataInput and DataOutput interfaces. These interfaces identify methods that enable primitive data types to be read from and written to a stream. By implementing these interfaces, the DataInputStream and DataOutputStream classes provide the basis for implementing portable input and output streams.

The DataInputStream Class

The DataInputStream class provides the capability to read String objects and primitive types from an input stream. It implements the methods of the DataInput interface. These methods provide a full range of input capabilities:

◆ readBoolean()—Reads a boolean value

◆ readByte()—Reads a byte as an 8-bit, signed value

◆ readChar()—Reads a Unicode character

◆ readDouble()—Reads a double value

◆ readFloat()—Reads a float value

◆ readFully()—Reads an array of bytes

◆ readInt()—Reads an int value

◆ readLine()—Reads a line of text (deprecated)

◆ readLong()—Reads a long value

◆ readShort()—Reads a short value

◆ readUnsignedByte()—Reads a byte as an 8-bit, unsigned value

◆ readUnsignedShort()—Reads an unsigned 16-bit value

◆ readUTF()—Reads a string that is in the UTF-8 format

◆ skipBytes()—Skips over a specified number of input bytes

Note that most, but not all, of these methods raise the EOFException when an end of file is encountered. The readLine() method returns a null value to signify a read past the end of a file. This method was deprecated in Java 1.1. The readLine() method of the BufferedReader class should be used instead. BufferedReader provides better support for internationalization. Its readLine() method corrects errors that exist in the readLine() method of DataInputStream.

NOTE **UTF-8** The UTF-8 character encoding is covered later in this chapter in the section, "Character Sets and Codings."

The **DataOutputStream** Class

The DataOutputStream class provides an output complement to DataInputStream. It enables String objects and primitive data types to be written to an output stream. It also keeps track of the number of bytes written to the output stream. It is an output filter and can be combined with any output-filtering streams.

The `PrintStream` Class

The `PrintStream` class should be no stranger to you. The `System.out` object that you have been using for many of the console programs in this book is an instance of the `PrintStream` class. It is used to write output to the Java console window.

`PrintStream`'s power lies in the fact that it provides two methods, `print()` and `println()`, that are overloaded to print any primitive data type or object. Objects are printed by first converting them to strings using their `toString()` method, inherited from the `Object` class. To provide custom printing for any class, all you have to do is override the `toString()` method for that class.

`PrintStream` provides the capability to automatically flush all output bytes in the stream when a new line character is written to the stream. This feature can be enabled or disabled when the stream is created.

Because `PrintStream` is a filter, it takes an instance of `OutputStream` as an argument to its constructor. A second constructor adds the capability to use the autoflushing feature.

`PrintStream` introduces only one new method besides the extensively overloaded `print()` and `println()` methods. The `checkError()` method is used to flush stream output and determine whether an error occurred on the output stream. This capability is useful for printing output to devices, such as printers, where error status is needed to notify the user of any changes to the device state.

PIPED I/O

Piped I/O provides the capability for threads to communicate via streams. A thread sends data to another thread by creating an object of `PipedOutputStream` that it connects to an object of `PipedInputStream`. The output data written by one thread is read by another thread using the `PipedInputStream` object.

The process of connecting piped input and output threads is symmetric. An object of class `PipedInputThread` can also be connected to an existing object of class `PipedOutputThread`.

Java automatically performs synchronization with respect to piped input and output streams. The thread that reads from an input pipe does not have to worry about any conflicts with tasks that are being written to the corresponding output stream thread.

Both PipedInputStream and PipedOutputStream override the standard I/O methods of InputStream and OutputStream. The only new method provided by these classes is the connect() method. Both classes provide the capability to connect piped streams via their constructors.

OBJECT I/O

The ObjectOutputStream and ObjectInputStream classes enable objects and values of primitive types to be written to and read from streams. These classes implement the ObjectOutput and ObjectInput interfaces. Of the methods specified by ObjectOutput, the writeObject() method is the most interesting; it writes objects that implement the Serializable interface to a stream. The ObjectInput interface provides the readObject() method to read the objects written to a stream by the writeObject() method.

When an object is stored in a serialized form, information is stored with the object that identifies the Java class from which the contents of the object were saved and allows the object to be restored as a new instance of that class. In addition, when an object is serialized, all of the non-transient and non-static objects that are reachable from that object are also stored with that object.

The Serializable interfaces are used to identify objects that can be written to a stream. It does not define any constants or methods.

The ObjectIOApp Program

The ObjectIOApp program, Listing 15.3, shows how the ObjectOutputStream and ObjectInputStream classes can be used to write and read objects from streams.

LISTING 15.3

THE SOURCE CODE OF THE ObjectIOApp PROGRAM

```java
import java.io.*;
import java.util.*;

public class ObjectIOApp {
 public static void main(String args[]) throws IOException,
  ClassNotFoundException {
  File file = new File("test.txt");
  FileOutputStream outFile = new FileOutputStream(file);
  ObjectOutputStream outStream = new
  ➡ObjectOutputStream(outFile);
  TestClass1 t1 = new TestClass1(true,9,'A',0.0001,"java");
  TestClass2 t2 = new TestClass2();
  String t3 = "This is a test.";
  Date t4 = new Date();
  // Write objects to stream
  outStream.writeObject(t1);
  outStream.writeObject(t2);
  outStream.writeObject(t3);
  outStream.writeObject(t4);
  outStream.close();
  outFile.close();
  FileInputStream inFile = new FileInputStream(file);
  ObjectInputStream inStream = new ObjectInputStream(inFile);
  // Read objects from stream and display them
  System.out.println(inStream.readObject());
  System.out.println(inStream.readObject());
  System.out.println(inStream.readObject());
  System.out.println(inStream.readObject());
  inStream.close();
  inFile.close();
  file.delete();
 }
}

class TestClass1 implements Serializable {
 boolean b;
 int i;
 char c;
 double d;
 String s;
 TestClass1(boolean b,int i,char c,double d,String s){
  this.b = b;
  this.i = i;
  this.c = c;
  this.d = d;
  this.s = s;
 }
 public String toString(){
  String r = String.valueOf(b)+" ";
  r += String.valueOf(i)+" ";
  r += String.valueOf(c)+" ";
```

```
  r += String.valueOf(d)+" ";
  r += String.valueOf(s);
  return r;
 }
}

class TestClass2 implements Serializable {
 int i;
 TestClass1 tc1;
 TestClass1 tc2;
 TestClass2(){
  i=0;
  tc1 = new TestClass1(true,2,'j',1.234,"Java");
  tc2 = new TestClass1(false,7,'J',2.468,"JAVA");
 }
 public String toString(){
  String r = String.valueOf(i)+" ";
  r += tc1.toString()+" ";
  r += tc2.toString();
  return r;
 }
}
```

ObjectIOApp creates a File object that is used to perform I/O to the test.txt file. The File object is used to create an object of class FileOutputStream. This object is then used to create an object of class ObjectOutputStream, which is assigned to the outStream variable.

Four objects are created and assigned to the t1 through t4 variables. An object of class TestClass1 is assigned to the t1 variable, and an object of class TestClass2 is assigned to the t2 variable. The TestClass1 and TestClass2 classes are declared at the end of Listing 15.3. A String object is assigned to t3, and a Date object is assigned to t4.

The objects referenced by the t1 through t4 variables are written to outStream using the writeObject() method. The stream and file are then closed. The test.txt file is reopened as a FileInputStream object, which is then converted to an ObjectInputStream object and assigned to the inStream variable. Four objects are read from inStream, using the readObject() method; then they are written to standard output. The program's output is as follows:

```
true 9 A 1.0E-4 java
0 true 2 j 1.234 Java false 7 J 2.468 JAVA
This is a test.
Sun Feb 07 02:48:43 PST 1999
```

Note that you'll receive a different date value from this one. TestClass1 and TestClass2 are dummy test classes that are used to make the example work. Their toString() methods are automatically invoked by the println() method to convert objects to string values for printing.

THE Reader AND Writer CLASSES

The Reader and Writer classes are abstract classes, at the top of a class hierarchy, that support the reading and writing of Unicode character streams. These classes were introduced with Java 1.1.

The Reader Class

The Reader class supports the standard read(), reset(), skip(), mark(), markSupported(), and close() methods. In addition to these, the ready() method returns a boolean value that indicates whether the next read operation will succeed without blocking.

The direct subclasses of the Reader class are BufferedReader, CharArrayReader, FilterReader, InputStreamReader, PipedReader, and StringReader.

The Writer Class

The Writer class is the output complement to the Reader class. It declares the write(), flush(), and close() methods. Its direct subclasses are BufferedWriter, CharArrayWriter, FilterWriter, OutputStreamWriter, PipedWriter, StringWriter, and PrintWriter. Each of these subclasses, except PrintWriter, is an output complement to a Reader subclass.

CHARACTER ARRAY AND STRING I/O

The CharArrayReader and CharArrayWriter classes are similar to the ByteArrayInputStream and ByteArrayOutputStream classes in that they support I/O from memory buffers. The difference between these classes is that CharArrayReader and CharArrayWriter support

16-bit character I/O, and `ByteArrayInputStream` and `ByteArrayOutputStream` support 8-bit byte array I/O.

The `CharArrayReader` class does not add any new methods to those provided by `Reader`. The `CharArrayWriter` class adds the following methods to those provided by `Writer`:

◆ `reset()`—Resets the buffer so that it can be read

◆ `size()`—Returns the current size of the buffer

◆ `toCharArray()`—Returns a character array copy of the output buffer

◆ `toString()`—Copies and converts the output buffer to a `String` object

◆ `writeTo()`—Writes the buffer to another output stream (`Writer` object)

These methods are similar to those provided by the `ByteArrayOutputStream` class.

The `StringReader` class provides the capability to read character input from a string. Like `CharArrayReader`, it does not add any additional methods to those provided by `Reader`. The `StringWriter` class is used to write character output to a `StringBuffer` object. It adds the `getBuffer()` and `toString()` methods. The `getBuffer()` method returns the `StringBuffer` object corresponding to the output buffer. The `toString()` method returns a `String` copy of the output buffer.

The `CharArrayIOApp` and `StringIOApp` Programs

The `CharArrayIOApp` program (see Listing 15.4) writes the string `"This is a test."` one character at a time to a `CharArrayWriter` object. It then converts the output buffer to a `CharArrayReader` object. Each character of the input buffer is read and appended to a `StringBuffer` object. The `StringBuffer` object is then converted to a `String` object. The number of characters read and the `String` object are then displayed. The program output follows:

```
outstream: This is a test.
size: 15
15 characters were read
They are: This is a test.
```

The StringIOApp program (see Listing 15.5) is similar to CharArrayIOApp. It writes output to a StringBuffer instead of a character array. It produces the same output as CharArrayIOApp.

LISTING 15.4

THE SOURCE CODE OF THE CharArrayIOApp PROGRAM

```
import java.io.*;

public class CharArrayIOApp {
 public static void main(String args[]) throws IOException {
  CharArrayWriter outStream = new CharArrayWriter();
  String s = "This is a test.";
  for(int i=0;i<s.length();++i)
   outStream.write(s.charAt(i));
  System.out.println("outstream: "+outStream);
  System.out.println("size: "+outStream.size());
  CharArrayReader inStream;
  inStream = new CharArrayReader(outStream.toCharArray());
  int ch=0;
  StringBuffer sb = new StringBuffer("");
  while((ch = inStream.read()) != -1)
   sb.append((char) ch);
  s = sb.toString();
  System.out.println(s.length()+" characters were read");
  System.out.println("They are: "+s);
 }
}
```

LISTING 15.5

THE SOURCE CODE OF THE StringIOApp PROGRAM

```
import java.io.*;

public class StringIOApp {
 public static void main(String args[]) throws IOException {
  StringWriter outStream = new StringWriter();
  String s = "This is a test.";
  for(int i=0;i<s.length();++i)
   outStream.write(s.charAt(i));
  System.out.println("outstream: "+outStream);
  System.out.println("size: "+outStream.toString().length());
  StringReader inStream;
  inStream = new StringReader(outStream.toString());
  int ch=0;
  StringBuffer sb = new StringBuffer("");
  while((ch = inStream.read()) != -1)
   sb.append((char) ch);
```

```
  s = sb.toString();
  System.out.println(s.length()+" characters were read");
  System.out.println("They are: "+s);
 }
}
```

CHARACTER SETS AND CODINGS

Most of us are familiar with the ASCII character set. This 7-bit character set represents the upper and lower case letters a-z, digits 0-9, control characters, and special characters. Although this character set is sufficient for most English-language programs, it is not sufficient for programs in other languages, such as Spanish and German, which require special accent marks, and Japanese, which requires a whole new character set.

Unlike most other programming languages, Java provides comprehensive support for the Unicode 2.0 character set. Unicode is a 16-bit character set, meaning that it is capable of representing 65,536 characters. This is a large character set and can be used to represent the characters used by many (but not all) of the world's popular languages. The 128 characters of the ASCII character set are the first 128 characters of Unicode.

> **NOTE**
>
> **ASCII**   ASCII stands for American Standard Code for Information Interchange.

> **NOTE**
>
> **Unicode**   More information about the Unicode character set can be found at `http://www.unicode.org`.

UNICODE VARIANTS

Some languages, such as varieties of Japanese, Chinese, and Korean, require more than 16 bits for full representation. These languages use a Unicode variant known as UTF-16. UTF stands for UCS Transformation Format and UCS stands for Universal Character Set. That's quite an acronym! In addition to UTF-16, there is a UTF-8. UTF-8 is a multi-byte representation of Unicode. It enables ASCII characters to be represented using one byte (instead of two) and other Unicode characters using two or three bytes. If your use of Unicode is minimal, then UTF-8 can help to minimize your storage or transmission requirements.

Unicode characters are written in Java using *Unicode escape character sequences*. These sequences are of the form \uxxxx, where the four x's are replaced with hexadecimal digits. Each of the four hexadecimal digits represents four bits of a 16-bit Unicode character.

To display Unicode characters other than ASCII, you need a Unicode font. In the absence of such a font, Java displays Unicode characters using the \u*xxxx* notation. The Bitstream Cyberbit font is an example of a font that supports Unicode. It can be downloaded from the Bitstream Web site at `http://www.bitstream.com/cyberbit/ftpcyber.htm`.

Java represents `char` values as 16-bit Unicode characters and `String` objects are as collections of 16-bit Unicode characters. However, when Unicode data is written to or read from a stream, the stream's data must be associated with a character encoding. A character encoding is a mapping between the way data is represented internally (as Unicode) and externally as binary stream data. Every platform has a default character encoding, and this default encoding works in most cases. For example, the Cp1252 character encoding is used with English-language Windows platforms, and Cp1251 is used with Cyrillic-language platforms. On Solaris and other systems, the English-language encoding may be ISO8859_1.

In most cases, the default character coding is sufficient. However, in some cases, you may want to change the character encoding of a stream in order to communicate with an application that uses a different character encoding. The `InputStreamReader` and `OutputStreamWriter` classes, that are introduced in the next section, enable the default character coding to be changed to an alternate character coding.

THE InputStreamReader AND OutputStreamWriter CLASSES

The `InputStreamReader` and `OutputStreamWriter` classes are used to convert between byte streams and character streams. The `InputStreamReader` class converts an object of an `InputStream` subclass into a character-oriented stream. The `OutputStreamWriter` class converts a character output stream to a byte output stream.

The InputStreamReader Class

The `InputStreamReader()` constructor takes an `InputStream` object as a parameter and creates an `InputStreamReader` object. This provides a bridge between byte-oriented input streams and character-oriented input streams. A second `InputStreamReader` constructor also takes a `String` parameter that identifies the character encoding to be used in byte-to-character conversion. The `getEncoding()` method may be used to retrieve the encoding that is in effect. The `ready()` method is used to determine whether a character can be read without blocking.

The `InputConversionApp` Program

The `InputConversionApp` program, shown in Listing 15.6, converts the standard input stream (`System.in`) from a byte stream to a character stream. The input characters are echoed to standard output. The program also prints out the encoding that is in effect on your system. The following is an example of the output generated when the program is run on my computer:

```
Encoding: Cp1252
>This is a test.
This is a test.
>
```

The `Cp1252` encoding is the MS Windows Latin-1 character encoding. It is used with English and Western European languages.

LISTING 15.6

THE SOURCE CODE OF THE `InputConversionApp` PROGRAM

```java
import java.io.*;

public class InputConversionApp {
 public static void main(String args[]) throws IOException {
  InputStreamReader in = new InputStreamReader(System.in);
  BufferedReader inStream = new BufferedReader(in);
  // Get the encoding that is in use
  System.out.println("Encoding: "+in.getEncoding());
  String inputLine;
  do {
   System.out.print(">");
   System.out.flush();
   inputLine=inStream.readLine();
   System.out.println(inputLine);
  } while (inputLine.length() != 0);
 }
}
```

The `OutputStreamWriter` Class

The `OutputStreamWriter` class enables a character stream to be converted to a byte stream. Its constructor takes the name of an object of an `OutputStream` subclass as a parameter. The characters written to an `OutputStreamWriter` object are translated and written to the `OutputStream` object specified in the `OutputStreamWriter` object's constructor. The translation is performed according to the encoding specified in the `System` property `file.encoding`. A different encoding scheme may be specified by supplying the name of the encoding scheme in the `OutputStreamWriter` constructor. The `getEncoding()` method may be used to retrieve the current character encoding that is in effect.

The `FileReader` and `FileWriter` Classes

The `FileReader` and `FileWriter` classes are subclasses of `InputStreamReader` and `OutputStreamWriter` that are used to perform character-based file I/O. These classes do not provide any additional access methods. However, their constructors provide the capability to create input and output character streams using `String` objects that represent filenames, `File` objects, and `FileDescriptor` objects.

The `CharFileIOApp` Program

Listing 15.7 demonstrates the use of the `FileReader` and `FileWriter` classes. It converts the `FileIOApp` program that was introduced earlier in the chapter (Listing 15.2) to character-oriented I/O and produces the following output:

```
15 characters were read
They are: This is a test.
```

The main difference between `CharFileIOApp` and `FileIOApp` is that `FileReader` and `FileWriter` classes are used instead of the `FileInputStream` and `FileOutputStream` classes. The other difference is the use of a `StringBuffer` object (instead of a `byte` array) to capture the characters read from the input file stream.

LISTING 15.7

THE SOURCE CODE OF THE CHARFILEIOAPP PROGRAM

```java
import java.io.*;

public class CharFileIOApp {
 public static void main(String args[]) throws IOException {
  FileWriter outStream = new FileWriter("test.txt");
  String s = "This is a test.";
  for(int i=0;i<s.length();++i)
   outStream.write(s.charAt(i));
  outStream.close();
  FileReader inStream = new FileReader("test.txt");
  StringBuffer sb = new StringBuffer("");
  int ch=0;
  while((ch = inStream.read()) != -1)
   sb.append((char) ch);
  s = sb.toString();
  System.out.println(s.length()+" characters were read");
  System.out.println("They are: "+s);
  inStream.close();
  File f = new File("test.txt");
  f.delete();
 }
}
```

BUFFERED CHARACTER I/O

Buffered character I/O is supported by the `BufferedReader` and `BufferedWriter` classes. These classes are character-based analogs to the `BufferedInputStream` and `BufferedOutputStream` classes. In Java 1.1, the `readLine()` method of the `BuffereddReader` class replaced the `readLine()` method of the `DataInputStream` class for reading lines of text from the console, a file, or other character-oriented input streams.

The `BufferedWriter` class provides the capability to write buffered data to character-based output streams. It adds the `newLine()` method to the methods that it inherits (and overrides) from the `Writer` class. The `newLine()` method enables new line characters to be written in a system-independent manner. Using this method is preferable to simply writing an \n character to the output stream. The `line.separator` system property defines the system-specific new line character.

The `LineNumberReader` Class

The `LineNumberReader` class is a subclass of the `BufferedReader` class that is used to associate line numbers with each line of text that is read from a stream. Lines are terminated by a new line character (\n), a carriage return (\r), or a carriage return-new line combination (\r\n).

In addition to the methods that it inherits from `BufferedReader`, the `LineNumberReader` class declares the `getLineNumber()` and `setLineNumber()` methods. The `getLineNumber()` method returns the current line number. The `setLineNumber()` method sets the current line number to an integer value.

FILTERED CHARACTER I/O

The `FilterReader` and `FilterWriter` classes are character-oriented analogs of the `FilterInputStream` and `FilterOutputStream` classes. The `FilterReader` class uses the `in` variable for input filtering and `FilterWriter` class uses the `out` variable for output filtering. Consult the section "Filtered I/O" earlier in this chapter for a description of I/O filtering.

The `PushbackReader` Class

The `PushbackReader` class is a subclass of `FilterReader` that provides the capability to push a character that was previously read back onto the input stream so that it can be read again. It is the character-oriented analog of the `PushbackInputStream` class that you studied earlier in the chapter.

THE `PipedReader` AND `PipedWriter` CLASSES

The `PipedReader` and `PipedWriter` classes support character-oriented piped I/O in the same way that `PipedInputStream` and `PipedOutputStream` support byte-oriented piped I/O. Consult the section "Piped I/O," earlier in this chapter, for a description of piped input and output.

THE PrintWriter CLASS

The PrintWriter class is the character-oriented replacement for the PrintStream class. PrintWriter is now the preferred class for character printing. The PrintWriter class improves PrintStream by using a platform-dependent line separator to print lines instead of the new line (\n) character. The System line.separator property identifies the system unique line separator. PrintWriter also provides better support for Unicode characters than PrintStream. The checkError() method is used to flush printed output and test for an error condition. The setError() method is used to set an error condition. PrintWriter provides support for printing primitive data types, character arrays, strings, and general objects. Objects are converted to a string (via the inherited or overridden toString() method) before being printed.

THE RandomAccessFile CLASS

The RandomAccessFile class provides the capability to perform I/O directly to specific locations within a file. The name *random access* comes from the fact that data can be read from or written to random locations within a file rather than as a continuous stream of information. Random access is supported through the seek() method, which allows the pointer corresponding to the current file position to be set to arbitrary locations within the file.

RandomAccessFile implements both the DataInput and DataOuput interfaces. This provides the capability to perform I/O using primitive data types.

RandomAccessFile also supports basic file read/write permissions, enabling files to be accessed in read-only or read-write modes. A mode stream argument is passed to the RandomAccessFile constructor as r or rw, indicating read-only and read-write file access. The read-only access attribute may be used to prevent a file from being inadvertently modified.

RandomAccessFile introduces several new methods besides those inherited from Object and implemented from DataInput and DataOutput. These methods include seek(), getFilePointer(), and length(). The seek() method sets the file pointer to a particular location within the file. The getFilePointer() method returns the current location of the file pointer. The length() method returns the length of the file in bytes.

The RandomIOApp Program

The RandomIOApp program provides a simple demonstration of the capabilities of random-access I/O. It writes a boolean, int, char, and double value to a file and then uses the seek() method to seek to offset location 1 within the file. This is the position after the first byte in the file. It then reads the int, char, and double values from the file and displays them to the console window. Next, it moves the file pointer to the beginning of the file and reads the boolean value that was first written to the file. This value is also written to the console window. The source code of the RandomIOApp program is shown in Listing 15.8.

LISTING 15.8

THE SOURCE CODE OF THE RandomIOApp PROGRAM

```
import java.io.*;

public class RandomIOApp {
 public static void main(String args[]) throws IOException {
  RandomAccessFile file = new
  ➥RandomAccessFile("test.txt","rw");
  file.writeBoolean(true);
  file.writeInt(123456);
  file.writeChar('j');
  file.writeDouble(1234.56);
  // Use seek() to move to a specific file location
  file.seek(1);
  System.out.println(file.readInt());
  System.out.println(file.readChar());
  System.out.println(file.readDouble());
  file.seek(0);
  System.out.println(file.readBoolean());
  file.close();
 }
}
```

Although the processing performed by RandomIOApp is quite simple, it illustrates how random I/O enables you to move the file pointer to various locations within a file to directly access values and objects contained within the file.

The program's output is as follows:

```
123456
j
1234.56
true
```

THE StreamTokenizer CLASS

The StreamTokenizer class is used by parsers to convert an input character stream into a stream of lexical tokens. It uses special methods to identify parser parameters, such as ordinary, whitespace, quote, and comment characters. These methods also enable and disable number and end-of-line parsing.

Several variables are defined for the StreamTokenizer class, four of which are constant class variables. The TT_EOF, TT_EOL, TT_NUMBER, and TT_WORD constants are used to identify the type of input token encountered when parsing the input stream. The ttype variable is set either to one of these constants or to a single character based on the kind of token that is read from the input stream. The TT_ constants are used to indicate a number, word, end of line, or end of file. When a word token is read, the actual word is stored in the sval variable and ttype is set to TT_WORD. When a number token is read, its value is stored in the nval variable and ttype is set to TT_NUMBER. When other special characters, such as @ or *, are read from the input stream, they are assigned directly to the ttype variable.

The StreamTokenizer constructor takes a Reader object as an argument and generates a StreamTokenizer object. The StreamTokenizer access methods can be divided into two groups: parser parameter-definition methods and stream-processing methods.

The parser parameter-definition methods are used to control the operation of the parser. The commentChar(),slashSlashComments(), and slashStarComments() methods are used to define comments. Comments are ignored by the parser. The whitespaceChars(),wordChars(),quoteChar(),ordinaryChar(), and ordinaryChars() methods are used to set the parser's token-generation parameters. The parseNumbers() and eolIsSignificant() methods toggle number and end-of-line parsing. The lowerCaseMode() method controls whether input words are converted to lowercase, and the resetSyntax() method is used to reset the syntax table, causing all characters to be treated as special characters.

The stream-processing methods are used to read tokens from the input stream, push tokens back out onto the input stream, and return the current line number associated with the input stream. The nextToken() method is used to get the next token from the input stream. The pushBack() method pushes the current token back out onto the input stream. The lineno() method returns the current line number associated with the input stream. The toString() method of class Object is overwritten to allow printing of the current token.

CHAPTER SUMMARY

KEY TERMS

- Stream

- Filter

- Reader

- Writer

- Unicode

- Character encoding

- Serialization

This chapter covered the classes and interfaces of java.io that are used to perform input and output. You explored the input and output class hierarchy and learned how to use stream filters to simplify I/O processing. You learned how the Reader and Writer classes support character-oriented I/O. You also learned how to perform random-access I/O and how to access a stream's character encoding. The following review questions and exam questions will let you know how well you understand this material and will give you an idea of how you'll do in related exam questions. They'll also indicate which material you need to study further.

APPLY YOUR KNOWLEDGE

Review Questions

1. What is the difference between the Reader/Writer class hierarchy and the InputStream/OutputStream class hierarchy?

2. What an I/O filter?

3. What is the purpose of the File class?

4. What interface must an object implement before it can be written to a stream as an object?

5. What is the difference between the File and RandomAccessFile classes?

6. What class allows you to read objects directly from a stream?

7. What value does read() return when it has reached the end of a file?

8. What value does readLine() return when it has reached the end of a file?

9. How many bits are used to represent Unicode, ASCII, UTF-16, and UTF-8 characters?

10. What is your platform's default character encoding?

Exam Questions

1. Which of the following are true?

   A. The InputStream and OutputStream classes are byte-oriented.

   B. The ObjectInputStream and ObjectOutputStream classes do not support serialized object input and output.

   C. The Reader and Writer classes are character-oriented.

   D. The Reader and Writer classes are the preferred solution to serialized object output.

2. How many bytes does the following program write to temp.txt?

```
import java.io.*;

public class TestIOApp {
 public static void main(String args[])
 ➥throws IOException {
  FileOutputStream outStream = new
  ➥FileOutputStream("test.txt");
  String s = "test";
  for(int i=0;i<s.length();++i)
   outStream.write(s.charAt(i));
  outStream.close();
 }
}
```

   A. 2 bytes

   B. 4 bytes

   C. 8 bytes

   D. 16 bytes

3. Which of the following are true about I/O filters?

   A. Filters are supported on input, but not on output.

   B. Filters are supported by the InputStream/OutputStream class hierarchy, but not by the Reader/Writer class hierarchy.

   C. Filters read from one stream and write to another.

   D. A filter may alter data that is read from one stream and written to another.

APPLY YOUR KNOWLEDGE

4. Which of the following are true?

   A. Any Unicode character is represented using 16 bits.

   B. Seven bits are needed to represent any ASCII character.

   C. UTF-8 characters are represented using only eight bits.

   D. UTF-16 characters are represented using only 16 bits.

5. Which of the following are true?

   A. The Serializable interface is used to identify objects that may be written to an output stream.

   B. The Externalizable interface is implemented by classes that control the way in which their objects are serialized.

   C. The Serializable interface extends the Externalizable interface.

   D. The Externalizable interface extends the Serializable interface.

6. Which of the following are true about the File class?

   A. A File object can be used to change the current working directory.

   B. A File object can be used to access the files in the current working directory.

   C. When a File object is created, a corresponding directory or file is created in the local file system.

   D. File objects are used to access files and directories on the local file system.

E. File objects can be garbage collected.

F. When a File object is garbage collected, the corresponding file or directory is deleted.

7. What output is displayed by the following program?

```
import java.io.*;

public class TestIOApp {
 public static void main(String args[])
 ➥throws IOException {
  StringReader stringin = new
  ➥StringReader("test");
  LineNumberReader in = new
  ➥LineNumberReader(stringin);
  PrintWriter out = new
  ➥PrintWriter(System.out);
  out.println(in.readLine());
  out.flush();
 }
}
```

   A. test

   B. 1. test

   C. 1: test

   D. 1 test

8. What output is displayed by the following program?

```
import java.io.*;

public class TestIOApp {
 public static void main(String args[])
 ➥throws IOException {
  RandomAccessFile file = new
  ➥RandomAccessFile("test.txt","rw");
  file.writeBoolean(true);
  file.writeInt(123456);
  file.writeInt(7890);
  file.writeLong(1000000);
  file.writeInt(777);
  file.writeFloat(.0001f);
  file.seek(5);
  System.out.println(file.readInt());
  file.close();
 }
}
```

APPLY YOUR KNOWLEDGE

A. `123456`

B. `7890`

C. `1000000`

D. `777`

E. `.0001`

9. How do you create a `Reader` object from an `InputStream` object?

   A. Use the `static createReader()` method of the `InputStream` class.

   B. Use the `static createReader()` method of the `Reader` class.

   C. Create an `InputStreamReader` object, passing the `InputStream` object as an argument to the `InputStreamReader` constructor.

   D. Create an `OutputStreamReader` object, passing the `InputStream` object as an argument to the `OutputStreamReader` constructor.

10. Which of the following are true?

    A. `Writer` classes can be used to write characters to output streams using different character encodings.

    B. `Writer` classes can be used to write Unicode characters to output streams?

    C. `Writer` classes have methods that support the writing of the values of any Java primitive type to output streams.

    D. `Writer` classes have methods that support the writing of objects to output streams.

Answers to Review Questions

1. The `Reader/Writer` class hierarchy is character-oriented, and the `InputStream/OutputStream` class hierarchy is byte-oriented.

2. An I/O filter is an object that reads from one stream and writes to another, usually altering the data in some way as it is passed from one stream to another.

3. The `File` class is used to create objects that provide access to the files and directories of a local file system.

4. An object must implement the `Serializable` or `Externalizable` interface before it can be written to a stream as an object.

5. The `File` class encapsulates the files and directories of the local file system. The `RandomAccessFile` class provides the methods needed to directly access data contained in any part of a file.

6. The `ObjectInputStream` class supports the reading of objects from input streams.

7. The `read()` method returns `-1` when it has reached the end of a file.

8. The `readLine()` method returns `null` when it has reached the end of a file.

9. Unicode requires 16 bits and ASCII require 7 bits. Although the ASCII character set uses only 7 bits, it is usually represented as 8 bits. UTF-8 represents characters using 8, 16, and 18 bit patterns. UTF-16 uses 16-bit and larger bit patterns.

10. If you are running Java on English Windows platforms, it is probably `Cp1252`. If you are running Java on English Solaris platforms, it is most likely `8859_1`.

APPLY YOUR KNOWLEDGE

Answers to Exam Questions

1. A and C   The `ObjectInputStream` and `ObjectOutputStream` classes are the preferred classes for performing serialized object I/O.

2. B   The `"test"` string is written as 4 bytes.

3. C and D   Filters are supported on both input and output and by the `InputStream/OutputStream` and `Reader/Writer` class hierarchies.

4. A and B   UTF-8 and UTF-16 are multi-byte formats of variable length.

5. A, B and D   `Externalizable` extends `Serializable`.

6. B, D, and E   `File` does not provide any methods to change the current working directory. The creation of a `File` object does not result in the creation of a corresponding directory of file in the local file system. The garbage collection of a `File` object does not normally have any effect on the local file system.

7. A   `LineNumberReader` does not add line numbers to the input content. It makes them available through its `getLineNumber()` method.

8. B   The number `7890` is stored at file location 5 because the previously written `boolean` and `int` values occupy 5 bytes.

9. C   The `InputStreamReader` class provides a constructor for creating `Reader` objects from `InputStream` objects.

10. A and B   `Writer` classes are character-oriented and do not support other primitive types or objects.

Suggested Readings and Resources

The JDK 1.2 `java.io` package API description.

BECOMING A SUN CERTIFIED JAVA 2 ARCHITECT

This chapter helps you to prepare for the exam by covering the following objectives:

Know what topics are covered in the certification exam and what technologies are addressed by these topics.

▶ The skills required of a Java architect are many. An architect must be adept at object-oriented systems design, networking, database and transaction processing, system security, and performance assessment, just to name a few. By knowing the topics and technology areas covered by the exam, you'll be able to focus on acquiring the knowledge you need to pass the exam.

Know how the exam is given.

▶ The more information that you have about the certification exam before going in to take it, the fewer surprises you'll have, and the better off you'll be.

Know how to prepare for the certification exam.

▶ Given limited time and resources, you'll want to get the best return for the time that you put into studying. This chapter will give you study tips that can help you maximize the benefits of your study efforts.

Know how to take the certification exam.

▶ Some people take tests better than others. This doesn't necessarily mean that they are smarter or better prepared. Sometimes it means that they use a better test taking approach. This chapter covers a test taking approach that could help you to improve your overall score.

C H A P T E R 16

Overview of the Java Architect Exam

OUTLINE

CHAPTER INTRODUCTION

This chapter introduces you to the Sun Certified Architect for Java 2 Technology Examination. It identifies the topics that the exam covers, discusses how the exam is given, and provides you with tips and other information on how to take the exam.

This chapter kicks off Part II of this book. Part II prepares you with all the technical information that you need to pass the Java 2 Architect certification exam. Although all the information is covered, some information is more important than the rest. By reading this chapter carefully before going on to other chapters in Part II, you'll have a better feel for the information to focus on in order to successfully pass the exam.

WHAT THE EXAM COVERS

The Java Architect exam covers a wide range of topics related to the development of Java-based architectures for enterprise systems. It contains questions on typical activities, technologies, and design decisions of a Java architect. These questions are organized according to the following topics:

- ◆ Introduction to the Architect Process using Java technology— This objective requires you to be familiar with the duties performed by a Java architect, the relationship between the architecture process and the application lifecycle, the benefits of a distributed-object architecture, and the advantages of Java-based architecture solutions over C++-based solutions.

- ◆ Designing a Java technology architecture—This objective requires you to be able to evaluate alternative solutions based on application requirements, to perform architectural tradeoffs, and to design a basic three-tier architecture based on identified requirements. Sun also mentions that you should be familiar with the advantages of Java servlets over CGI scripts.

- ◆ Java technology architecture details—This objective requires you to be able to design a 3-tier (or n-tier) object-oriented application architecture based on a set of defined requirements. To do this, you'll must be able to incorporate applets and application servers into the architecture and trade off among Java RMI, CORBA, and COM/DCOM design elements. You will also be required to identify the pros and cons of a specific architecture with respect to customer requirements.

◆ Integrations with existing applications and databases—To meet this objective, you'll be required to design a 3-tier (or n-tier) architecture where one tier is based on a legacy system (application, file, or database). You should be familiar with the advantages and disadvantages of technologies for integrating existing applications, such as screen scrapers and legacy object mapping.

◆ Architecting new applications—This objective requires that you recommend strategies for migrating existing applications, design architectures using Enterprise JavaBeans, use Java for transaction processing, and be familiar with the publish/subscribe architecture. You must also be able to evaluate the advantages and disadvantages of partial migration using Java applets and applications.

◆ Designing a secure Java technology architecture—To meet this objective, you should be able to come up with application architectures that are secured (even over the Internet) using available Java security features: firewalls, virtual private networks, and other security technologies. You must also be able to identify security constraints and make security tradeoffs that affect the application architecture. You'll also need to be able to design secure application architectures for extranet applications.

◆ Designing an architecture for performance—This objective requires you to be able to evaluate an architecture, identify potential performance issues, and make recommendations that improve performance. You must also be able to design architectures that meet minimal performance levels and are scalable to larger user bases.

◆ The Java technology architecture in production—This objective requires you to be able to develop architectures that can be more easily moved into production environments. You should be able to assess pilot and prototype projects and make recommendations that enable the project to proceed into production.

You must also be able recommend approaches to deploying and distributing Java solutions.

To be able to successfully meet the above objectives, become familiar with a number of technologies that are used by Java architects:

◆ Object-oriented design—Basic object-oriented design concepts, UML, and the object-oriented design lifecycle process

◆ Enterprise JavaBeans and supporting technologies— Components, containers, servers, JNDI, and transaction-processing support

◆ Web technologies—Applets, Web servers, HTTP 1.1, CGI, servlets, and Web-based, 3-tier architectures

◆ Database technologies—JDBC, JavaBlend, SQL, OQL, and relational, object-oriented, and hierarchical databases

◆ Application architectures—Three-tier architectures, publish/subscribe architectures, synchronous and asynchronous architectures, extranet architectures, and transaction processing architectures

◆ Distributed systems technologies—Java RMI, CORBA, JIDL, COM/DCOM, and TCP sockets

◆ Security technologies—Firewalls, HTTP tunneling, VPNs, SSL, message digests, digital certificates, applet security, browser-based security controls, and the Java Security API

◆ Technologies for working with legacy systems—Screen scrapers, object mapping, and middleware

◆ Java 2 API—AWT, Applets, Internationalization, JNI, and other APIs

While the exam objectives are very high-level and all encompassing, the above technology list is concrete and something that you can easily study for and be tested upon. Most of the exam questions test your ability to act as a Java architect by asking questions that require you to solve application architecture problems using the above technologies. Consequently, the chapters of this part expand your knowledge of the above technologies, and then you are given the change to apply this knowledge in a chapter devoted to Java architecture design.

HOW THE EXAM IS GIVEN

The exam consists of a computer-based test consisting of 60 multiple-choice and short-answer questions. The tests are given at Sylvan Prometric Testing Centers. You'll have two hours to take the test.

The multiple choice questions are either single-answer questions or multiple-answer questions. Single-answer questions are indicated by radio buttons. Multiple-answer questions have check boxes. Most of the multiple-answer questions ask you to select exactly two answers. Pay attention to these cues. Every bit of information helps.

The short-answer questions ask you to enter a word or line of text. These questions comprise less than 10% of the exam questions. The short-answer questions are usually very succinct, because the answer verification software cannot handle a large number of alternative answers.

The exam questions appear on the computer screen one at a time. You can skip a question and return to it later. You can move backward and forward between the questions you've answered and those you have yet to answer.

NOTE

The Java 2 Architect Exam   The URL http://suned.sun.com/usa/cert_progs.html?content= scajtdetails12 is the place to start if you want to sign up for the Java 2 Architect exam.

HOW TO PREPARE FOR THE EXAM

By deciding to study this part of the book, you've taken the best first step to preparing for the exam. The chapters in this part will provide you with the background information that you need to take the test. Read each chapter thoroughly, even if you think that you know the material cold. Sometimes an additional bit of information or a different slant on how a technology is used can make the difference in selecting the correct answer.

After reading through each chapter, answer the review and exam questions. These questions will test your knowledge of the material covered and give you an idea of what you can expect on the exam.

After completing all the chapters of this part, use the exam preparation and simulation programs contained on this book's CD to test and retest your knowledge. The tests are randomized, so they'll be different each time you take them. When you answer a test question incorrectly, go back and restudy the material. Keep on doing this until your exam scores are in the high 90s. At this point, you should be able to easily pass the Java 2 Architect certification exam.

HOW TO TAKE THE EXAM

By working through the approach described in the previous section, you'll have the knowledge required to pass the certification exam. However, by adopting the right test-taking approach, you should be able to improve your test score even more.

The way that test questions are scored is simple. You receive one point for each correct answer. You need 45 correct answers to pass the test. Based on this, your test taking strategy should aim at getting the most correct answers. I suggest that you go through the exam and answer all the questions you are reasonably sure that you can answer correctly. DON'T WASTE TIME DWELLING ON QUESTIONS THAT YOU ARE HAVING A HARD TIME ANSWERING.

After you've made a first pass through the questions, go back and try to answer the questions that you were stuck on. At this point, you should try to answer all the exam questions. If you don't know the answer to a question, take your best guess. You won't be penalized for wrong answers, and any correct guess will improve your overall score.

If, after answering all the exam questions, you have time left, go back and check your answers. However, don't try to second guess yourself. Instead, reread each question and each answer to make sure that you haven't misunderstood any questions or incorrectly read an answer.

CHAPTER SUMMARY

This chapter introduced you to the Sun Certified Architect for Java 2 Technology Examination. It identified the topics that the exam covers, discussed how the exam is given, and provided you with tips and other information on how to take the exam. You should now be able to study the remaining chapters of Part II. But before going on, take a look at the following exam questions. These questions are provided by Sun to give you an idea of the kinds of questions to expect in the certification exam. Don't worry if you don't know the answers to these questions. The information will be presented in the remaining chapters of Part II.

Exam Questions (from Sun)

1. What type of diagram does a Java Architect frequently produce?

    A. Attribute diagram

    B. Property diagram

    C. Constraint diagram

    D. Package dependency diagram

2. What protocol(s) do ORBs from different vendors use to communicate?

    A. XML

    B. IIOP

    C. CORBA

    D. TCP/IP

3. Which Java benchmark measures applet performance?

    A. TPC

    B. Jstone

    C. SpecWeb

    D. JavaPerf

4. Which two functions may be provided by the client tier of a Java application architecture?

    A. Java applet

    B. applet viewer

    C. user interface

    D. database access

    E. input validation

5. What is the purpose of a layout manager?

    A. to manage the interaction of JavaBeans

    B. to provide an area to display AWT components

    C. to display information about the coordinates of components in an applet

    D. to control the arrangement of components within the display area of a container

6. What is the difference between an Enterprise JavaBeans container and an Enterprise JavaBeans server?

    A. Containers run within servers.

    B. Servers run within containers.

    C. Only one server can run in a container.

    D. Only one container can run in a server.

    E. Containers and servers have the same function.

Answers to Exam Questions

1. The package dependency diagram shows the relationship between the packages which comprise an application system.

2. Object request brokers communicate via the Internet Inter-Orb Protocol.

3. The JavaPerf is a measure of an applet's performance.

4. The client tier of an architecture provides a user interface and input validation functions.

APPLY YOUR KNOWLEDGE

5. As you learned in Chapter 12, "The `java.awt` Package: Layout," layout managers are used to arrange the display of components within containers.

6. Enterprise JavaBeans containers run within the context of servers.

Suggested Readings and Resources

Details of the Sun Certified Architect for Java Technologies (`http://suned.sun.com/usa/cert_progs.html?content=scajtdetails12`).

This chapter helps you to prepare for the exam by covering the following objectives:

Be able to describe the duties performed by a Java Architect.

Be able to state how Java architecture design fits into the application development lifecycle.

Be able to state the major architectural issues and trade-offs faced when designing a distributed Java solution.

Know how to design a basic three-tier architecture for a set of customer requirements.

Be able to discuss alternative Java architectures, for example, publish/subscribe.

Know how to design a Java architecture that can be easily moved into production.

Given a Java prototype or pilot application solution, be able to advise on how it can be effectively moved to production status.

Be able to recommend solutions for efficiently deploying and distributing Java solutions in production.

C H A P T E R 17

Java Applications Architecture

OUTLINE

STUDY STRATEGIES

As you read through this chapter, you should concentrate on the following key items:

▶ What does a Java architect do?

▶ How does a Java architecture fit into the application development lifecycle?

▶ What are the advantages of three-tiered architectures?

▶ What is the publish/subscribe model?

▶ What are the differences between synchronous and asynchronous architectures?

▶ What are the differences between Internet, intranet, and extranet architectures?

Chapter Introduction

The first set of questions that you'll see on the exam will test you on the basics of what a Java architect is, what an architect does, what an architecture is, and how an architecture fits into the application development lifecycle. These questions may seem pretty easy. However, the term "Java architect" is relatively new and you may not be familiar with all the roles and responsibilities that it carries. In addition, there is a difference in focus between a Java-based application architecture and other architectures that are based on legacy technologies. This chapter will get you up to speed on what a Java architect is and how a Java-based application architecture is developed.

The Role of the Java Architect

The first questions that you'll encounter on the certification exam are likely to be about the role of the Java architect. Sun has defined what it means to be a Java architect on the certification exam Web site. A Java architect is someone who

- ◆ Advises on the use of Java for maximizing business benefits

- ◆ Recognizes the major architectural issues and trade-offs faced when designing Java solutions

- ◆ Evaluates the advantages and disadvantages of using Java technology for enterprise applications

- ◆ Designs distributed object architectures to a given set of business requirements

- ◆ Designs three- or n-tier architectures for key business scenarios

- ◆ Can compare object-oriented architectures based on Java technology with CORBA and DCOM alternatives per customer requirements

- ◆ Evaluates proposed Java technology architectures and makes recommendations to increase performance and security

- ◆ Integrates security constraints into a Java application architecture

◆ Recommends techniques for effectively deploying and distributing Java technology solutions in production

◆ Can advise on ways Java technology prototypes or pilot applications can effectively be moved to production status

This definition is somewhat long, so I'll break it down point by point.

Advises on Using Java for Maximizing Business Benefits

The first characteristic of a Java architect is that he provides advice on the use of Java. In order to do this, the Java architect must have a breadth of knowledge about how Java works, what capabilities it supports, the Java APIs and products that are currently available, and the advantages and disadvantages of Java-based solutions.

The Java architect advises customers and other members of the application development team on how the benefits of how Java can be used to maximize business benefits. This point is important. The Java architect is more than a Java evangelist. He must be able to determine how Java can be used to maximize the benefits of Java to meet a customer's business needs. Java isn't used just because it is a cool technology. It is used to solve existing business problems in a measurable way. In cases where a non–Java-based technology provides a greater overall benefit, the Java architect must be prepared to recommend the alternative technology.

Recognizes Major Architectural Issues and Trade-Offs

In order to develop Java-based solutions, especially Java-based application architectures, the Java architect must be familiar with the architectural issues and trade-offs related to these solutions. For example, a particular application design may pose issues associated with security. A more secure solution may pose performance problems. The Java architect must first recognize the architectural issues (such as security and performance) and then resolve them by selecting a solution that trades off between conflicting issues in a way that is consistent with customer needs, requirements, and direction.

Evaluates the Use of Java Technology

In order to perform tradeoffs between different architectures, the Java architect must be capable of evaluating Java technologies to determine their advantages and disadvantages. For example, suppose an architect is tasked with developing a distributed Java-based application. The architect must decide whether to use Java RMI or CORBA for distributed object communication. The architect must evaluate Java RMI and Java IDL to determine their advantages and disadvantages in supporting this application. The architect must also be able to design candidate architectures using these technologies and determine how the identified advantages and disadvantages come into play with these architectures. The architect must also be able to adjust the architectures so that the advantages are maximized and the disadvantages are minimized. Finally, the architect must be able to make tradeoffs based on this evaluation.

Designs Distributed Object Architectures

Again, the focus of the Java architect is the customer's business requirements. It is possible to design a technically-superior distributed object architecture that fails to meet customer requirements. It is also possible to design a middle-of-the-road architecture that meets or exceeds customer requirements. The important point is that the customer's requirements are satisfied and not that Java technology is used in new and exciting ways. However, you are often required do both.

Designs Three- or N-Tier Architectures

The use of a multitier architecture for implementing business information systems provides a number of benefits (which you'll study later in this chapter). The Java architect must understand these benefits and must be able to develop architectures which take advantage of these benefits in meeting customer requirements.

Compares Architectures with CORBA and DCOM

Java RMI, CORBA, and DCOM are the three preeminent technologies for building distributed object-oriented architectures. Java can be used with all three technologies. However, its benefits are more strongly realized with Java RMI and, to a lesser extent, with CORBA. However, the Java architect must have a detailed understanding of how each technology can be best applied to solve a set of customer requirements. The Java architect must also know the advantages and disadvantages of each technology so that he can select an approach that is most appropriate for his customer's needs.

Makes Recommendations to Increase Performance

Performance and security are two key characteristics that determine the success or failure of an application architecture. Applications that do not perform well cannot be expected to meet customer expectations and needs. Applications that have exploitable security vulnerabilities may pose significant risks to the customer. These risks may negate all the benefits provided by the application. In order to design a sound architecture for a given set of business requirements, the Java architect must be able to evaluate proposed architectures and identify potential performance and security problems. The architect must also be able to develop design solutions that resolve these problems.

Integrates Security Constraints

In order to develop an application architecture that provides required levels of security, a Java architect must be capable of integrating security countermeasures into the overall application architecture. The countermeasures may range from architectural components (such as firewalls, VPNs, and SSL) to practices (such as the use of signed applets, strong authentication, and security auditing).

Recommends Techniques for Deploying Solutions

Designing and developing a distributed application is only half of the battle. A Java technology solution is not complete until it is deployed in a production environment, distributed to users, and operating in a way that meets customer needs. For a system to be deployed and distributed most efficiently and effectively, the system must be designed with that final goal in mind. The Java architect must be able to design systems that take advantage of technologies, such as Java applets, that facilitate system deployment, distribution, and maintenance.

Advises on Moving Applications to Production Status

After a Java-based application has been successfully developed (with deployment in mind), the application must be deployed to a production environment in a way that minimizes the impact on ongoing operations. In some cases, this might mean that the new application must coexist with any legacy applications that it replaces. In other cases, it might mean that current applications be brought down and cut over to the new application. The Java architect must coordinate with the customer to develop a deployment strategy well in advance of the system's actual deployment date, preferably during the architecture design process.

THE APPLICATION LIFECYCLE

The process of developing a Java-based application architecture is an important step in the overall application lifecycle. Refer to Figure 17.1. It cuts across the requirements analysis, design, and implementation phases and has a significant impact on the validation, deployment, operation, and maintenance phases.

FIGURE 17.1
The application lifecycle.

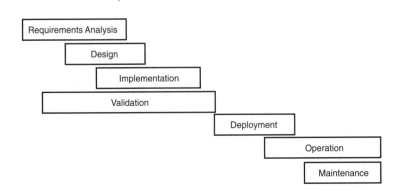

The lifecycle phases shown in Figure 17.1 occur in a particular order. However, they are overlapping and iterating. For example, some design occurs while requirements are being identified and analyzed. Design insights may be fed back into the requirements analysis so that previously ignored requirements may be specified or fuzzy requirements may be cleared up.

Requirements Analysis

During requirements analysis, the Java architect works with the customer to identify the customer's needs and to specify a set of application requirements that, when satisfied, will fulfill those needs. This process involves identifying the problems or opportunities addressed by the application, identifying requirements for the application to solve the problem (or realize the opportunity), and elaborating on the requirements so that they may be sufficiently detailed to enable design decisions to take place. The requirements are analyzed to determine their impact on the application and whether they are at the proper level of detail. Requirements that are specified at too high a level may fail to capture the customer's needs and expectations. Requirements that are too detailed may preclude valid design alternatives.

During the requirements and analysis phase, the Java architect may develop several prototype architectures that capture customer requirements and point out areas for further definition of requirements. For example, a high-level application architecture may provide a solution path that points out areas where performance and security requirements need to be specified.

Design

The design phase is where the Java architect earns his keep. The architect must come up with an overall application design that provides a framework in which all requirements can be satisfied. The architecture must address the client, application business logic, and data storage tiers of the application design. It identifies application internal and external interfaces and addresses performance, security, and other issues. The architecture must be flexible, scalable, upgradable, and manageable. It must also address issues related to deployment, distribution, operation, and maintenance.

Special views of the architecture may be needed for different development specialists. A good example is security. An application security architecture may need to be developed that highlights security-specific elements of the overall architecture. Analysis of the security architecture may identify additional security countermeasures, such as firewalls, VPNs, or certificate servers, that need to be added to the overall application architecture.

The Java architect must work with the customer and other members of the development team to extend and elaborate the architecture to flesh it out to the detailed design level. This involves selecting commercial products to realize different components of the architecture, identifying reuse of legacy components, and determining software that must be developed.

Whenever possible, commercial products should be used in the application's design. If a commercial product can meet a customer requirement, it is usually much more cost-effective to purchase and use the product than it is to develop the equivalent software.

The application architecture may make use of legacy components whenever this is practical. By doing so, the system can be deployed using proven software at a lower cost. The Java architect must determine which legacy components to reuse and what changes are required to support reuse.

The Java architect must determine which software needs to be developed to support the application architecture. This software should be designed in an object-oriented manner. The architect identifies the software packages to be developed as well as the existing packages (including those of the Java 2 Platform and extension APIs) that will be used by the development software. The important classes and interfaces of the developmental packages should be identified, as well as interactions between these classes and interfaces and other components of the application architecture. Chapter 17, "Object-Oriented Architecture Design," describes how the Universal Modeling Language may be used to document an object-oriented software architecture.

Implementation

The application architecture and detailed design should drive the application's implementation. The object-oriented software architecture is fleshed out and code is written to define interfaces and classes and to implement class methods. During the implementation phase, insights may be gained that suggest changes to the design and the application architecture. These delayed insights are common. Sometimes design issues are not thought through to their conclusions. Sometimes opportunities are discovered during implementation that can make the overall architecture more performance efficient, secure, or better able to satisfy customer needs.

Validation

The validation phase consists of independent analysis and testing that verifies that the system meets its requirements. This phase begins with the requirements analysis and extends to deployment. During requirements analysis, requirements are assessed to determine their completeness and sufficiency in meeting customer needs. The application architecture is validated against these requirements. Lower level architectures and the application detailed design are validated against higher level architectures and requirements. During implementation, any code that is developed is validated against its design. Vendor products and legacy components are validated against their allocated requirements. Testing is initiated to determine the extent to which customer requirements are satisfied.

After an application's implementation has reached an initial baseline, validation testing attempts to demonstrate that the application meets all customer requirements. Interface and performance requirements are usually stressed. Any shortcomings are written up, and the system's implementation is modified. These could also lead to modification of the system's design or architecture.

Validation and testing also take place in the production environment. Although it is highly desirable to eliminate any shortcomings before a system is deployed, there are inevitably some problems that are not discovered until the application reaches its target environment and is in the hands of the customer.

Deployment

Deployment occurs when a system is taken out of its developmental environment and put into production. At this time, all architectural and design issues should be resolved, and except for a few undiscovered bugs, implementation should be completed. However, this is not always the case. In some cases, assumptions are made about the production environment that are not debunked until the application is ready to be put into the operation. These failed assumptions can be costly and embarrassing. Examples of these types of problems are failure to plan for production environment upgrades (such as firewalls) and failure to plan for worst-case environments (such as bandwidth or space limitations or special environmental conditions).

The Java architect can help to avoid deployment problems by verifying all assumptions about the production environment as early in the application lifecycle as possible and by continuing to monitor changes to the production environment throughout the application's development. In the case of any deployment glitches, the Java architect can also develop any architectural or design changes that are needed to enable the application to work as intended.

Operation and Maintenance

During operation, the application is put in the hands of its users, who discover bugs and potential application improvements. In addition, new technologies are introduced that may be used to enhance the performance, security, responsiveness, or user satisfaction with the application. Some of these changes will be handled as application maintenance. Others may require the application to be rearchitected, redesigned, or reimplemented. The Java architect may be called upon to support this process or to pass on any insights that will enable the system caretakers to take over in his or her absence.

JAVA-BASED APPLICATION ARCHITECTURES

So far, I've talked a lot about architecting and architectures. Now it's time to look at a few. In this section, I'll cover some of the different types of architectures that may be used in different situations depending on user and application requirements.

One- and Two-Tier Architectures

Legacy applications are generally organized into one or two tiers, as shown in Figure 17.2. Single-tier systems are not distributed. They consist of one system or a set of disconnected systems that interface with the user, implement business logic, and provide storage for the application. Small PC-based systems are typical of a single-tier system. They work well for one-person applications in which application data can be shared in an asynchronous manner by simply passing it between system users. Single-tier systems are limited in terms of scalability and their inability to be integrated with and communicate with other enterprise applications. Their advantage is, because of their limited interfaces, they can more easily be secured. In some cases, this can be accomplished using simple physical access controls.

Single Tier Application

Two Tier Application

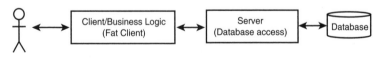

FIGURE 17.2
One-tier and two-tier architectures.

Two-tier systems are typical of legacy client/server applications. The client software provides the user interface, the application business logic, and database access software. The server (usually a database server) provides access to data stored in databases. These systems are typically referred to as fat client systems because the bulk of the application resides on the client. Two-tier systems are often difficult to upgrade, maintain, and usually carry significant lifecycle costs. These systems do not take advantage of the Web paradigm, which distributes the application among clients, Web servers, application servers, and back-end databases.

Three-Tier to N-Tier Architectures

Distributed Java-based applications take advantage of the power provided by Web browsers to separate the client interface, business logic, and data storage functions into multiple application tiers, as shown in Figure 17.3. The client tier is typically provided by a Web browser. Interface functionality is implemented using HTML, JavaScript, and Java applets. The application business logic is implemented on a separate server. For example, Figure 17.3 shows the business logic being implemented by servlets that execute on the Web server. The third tier of the application typically consists of a database server that stores data in a relational database.

The simple three-tier architecture shown in Figure 17.3 may easily be extended to an n-tier architecture. Multiple servers can be used to implement different levels of the application business logic and data storage. For example, one or more application servers might provide support services using Enterprise JavaBeans. A database middleware server can be used to synchronize application data across multiple databases and isolate data access logic from other application tiers.

Three Tier Application

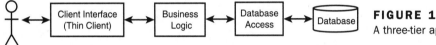

FIGURE 17.3
A three-tier application architecture.

The advantage of three-tier (and higher) architecture is that it is easier and cheaper to deploy, upgrade, scale, and maintain. By using a browser-based interface the client interface can be modified on the Web server and instantly distributed to all clients. The application administrator doesn't have to visit individual user machines to deploy application upgrades. In large organizations, this can represent tremendous cost savings.

Because the application's business logic is separate from the client and data storage tiers, it can be upgraded and improved with less impact on the other tiers. The application can be scaled from few to many users by adding more processing power in the business logic tier (and also the data storage tier). The business logic tier can be spread across several levels of application servers that utilize Java-based enterprise technologies, such as servlets, Enterprise JavaBeans, Java Transaction Service, Java Naming and Directory Interface, Remote Method Invocation, and Java IDL. The data storage tier can be upgraded to use larger, faster, and more efficient database servers, and technologies, such as OQL, JavaBlend, and JavaSpaces.

Publish/Subscribe Architectures

The Web and many other client/server applications use a request/reply model for client/server communication. Browsers make URL requests of servers. Servers retrieve the documents at the requested URL and send the documents to the browsers as replies to the browser's requests.

TIBCO, Inc. (http://www.tibco.com) developed a protocol, referred to as publish/subscribe, to overcome a basic limitation in the request/reply model. This limitation is the fact that the client must know the location of the server from which information is to be requested. Without this knowledge, a client cannot proceed to obtain the information it needs unless it obtains the server's location from a separate search service.

In the publish/subscribe model, publishers publish information anonymously without any connection to or knowledge of the subscribers of the information. Subscribers subscribe to information of a certain type (without knowledge of the publisher) and are notified when the information becomes available. The publishers and subscribers use subject-based addressing in order to identify the information that is published and subscribed to. A publisher publishes information to an address of a particular subject name. Subscribers that subscribe to the subject name receive the information when it becomes available. Refer to Figure 17.4. As an example, a weather service may publish information to a subject name, "Weather Report—San Diego." Any subscriber that subscribes to this subject name would receive a copy of published weather reports.

The publish/subscribe model has the benefit of scalability and location independence. Any number of publishers and subscribers can coexist in the model. The load on each publisher and subscriber is only dependent on the information that it publishes or consumes. Publishers only publish information once. Subscribers may subscribe or renew subscriptions as often as desired. Location independence enables publishers to be mobile and subscribers to obtain the information they need without having to start with the publisher's address.

The publish/subscribe model lends itself to the development of multitier architectures. Individual components within the architecture subscribe to subjects related to the services they provide and publish information related to the results of their services.

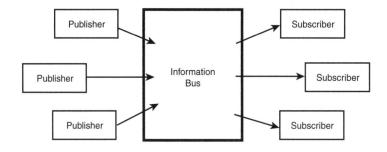

FIGURE 17.4
A publish/subscribe architecture.

Synchronous and Asynchronous Architectures

Distributed application architectures can be characterized by the types of communication they support. Asynchronous architectures are those in which components of the architecture communicate by sending messages in such a way that the sender and receiver do not have to simultaneously support message transmission. The postal system (snail mail) is a good example of asynchronous communication. The sender of a letter mails it to the recipient at one point in time, and the recipient receives it at a later point in time when it is delivered.

Synchronous architectures require the sender and receiver to collaborate on the transmission of a message. A good example is the telephone system. The caller and receiver must simultaneously take part in a phone conversation in order for it to take place.

Asynchronous applications have a number of advantages. Because the sender sends information at its own discretion, it can overcome the limitations of low bandwidth communication channels by sending messages throughout the course of a day. This evens out the traffic load. On the receiving side, the receiver can even out its processing load by processing each message as it can get to it. Because the receiver does not need to respond to the message within the context of an established connection, it can handle the message as time permits. Asynchronous architectures are more scalable because of the decoupling of the sender and receiver. Multiple receivers may be incrementally added to accommodate increasing message loads.

Synchronous systems are appropriate to applications where the receiver must respond to the sender in a timely manner. This is typically accomplished within the context of a single TCP connection. Because the sender and receiver must make themselves available to each other during the course of the connection, they are able to focus on completing a transaction before moving on. The Web is an example of a synchronous architecture. Browsers and servers sync up via the duration of a TCP connection to support the requesting and delivery of documents addressed by URLs.

Internet, Intranet, and Extranet Architectures

Application architectures can also be organized according to whether they support Internet applications, intranet applications, or extranet applications. Internet applications, in general, are designed to support a very large user base. They must be scalable, secure, and available at all times.

Intranet applications are limited to an organization's internal network. The user base is typically much smaller than Internet applications, but it can be sizable in large organizations. Intranet applications must be secured from the Internet. This is typically accomplished via a firewall. Intranet applications may also be secured so that applications are limited to authorized individuals within the organization. The availability of intranet applications depends on the application. Most must be available during normal business hours. However, some may be required to be available at all times.

Extranet applications are applications that are designed for use by external organizations (such as buyers, vendors, suppliers, and financial institutions) and that must take place securely over the Internet.

Access to extranet applications is limited to trusted organizations that require access to such services. Strong authentication, encryption, and access controls may be used to control access to extranet applications. Extranet applications tend to be limited to a small, trusted user base. Availability varies between business hours and 24 hours a day, 7 days a week.

CHAPTER SUMMARY

KEY TERMS

- Java architect
- Requirements analysis
- Design
- Implementation
- Validation
- Deployment
- Operation and maintenance
- Publish/subscribe architecture
- Asynchronous architecture
- Synchronous architecture
- Extranet

In this chapter, you learned the basics about what being a Java architect is all about. You covered the role of the Java architect, the application development lifecycle, and the role of an architecture in the development lifecycle. You also looked at several different architecture types. The following review and exam questions will test your knowledge of these topics and will help you to determine whether your knowledge of Java architect fundamentals is sufficient to answer the questions you'll encounter in the certification exam.

Review Questions

1. What is the overall goal of a Java architect?

2. In which application lifecycle phases is an application architecture produced?

3. What are the three tiers of a three-tiered architecture?

4. What are the advantages of thin clients?

5. What is the publish/subscribe model?

6. What are the advantages of asynchronous architectures?

7. In what cases are synchronous architectures more appropriate than asynchronous architectures?

8. What are extranet applications?

Exam Questions

1. Which of the following are not a role of the Java architect?

   A. Evaluating the advantages and disadvantages of using Java technology for enterprise applications

   B. Designing distributed object architectures to a given set of business requirements

   C. Training users on how to operate a Java-based application

   D. Evaluating proposed Java technology architectures and making recommendations to increase performance and security

2. Which of the following are key skills of a Java architect?

   A. The ability to identify issues associated with Java-based technologies, perform tradeoffs, and make recommendations on how to maximize the use of these technologies in satisfying user requirements.

   B. The ability to convince customers that only pure Java solutions can meet their needs.

   C. The ability to work with customers, help them to identify their needs, and capture their requirements in terms of a requirements specification.

   D. The ability to design an application architecture that satisfies identified customer requirements.

3. What is the primary criterion for success of a Java-based architecture?

   A. Whether it maximizes the use of Java technology.

   B. Whether it maximizes system performance.

   C. Whether it maximizes satisfaction of customer requirements.

   D. Whether it maximizes security.

4. Which are not phases of the application lifecycle?

   A. Requirements analysis

   B. Negotiation

   C. Design

   D. Documentation

APPLY YOUR KNOWLEDGE

5. In which two phases is the application architecture initially defined?

   A. Requirements analysis

   B. Design

   C. Implementation

   D. Deployment

6. Which lifecycle phase determines whether an architecture meets its requirements?

   A. Deployment

   B. Validation

   C. Implementation

   D. Operation

7. Which of the following is a potential advantage of a one-tier application architecture?

   A. Security

   B. Interoperability

   C. Scalability

   D. Manageability

8. Which of the following are characteristics of a two-tier architecture?

   A. Fat clients

   B. Enterprise JavaBeans

   C. Multiple application servers

   D. Servers which tend to be limited to data access

9. Which of the following are tiers of a three-tier architecture?

   A. Client interface

   B. Business logic

   C. Security

   D. Data storage

10. Which of the following are characteristics of an n-tier architecture?

    A. Virtual private networks

    B. Multiple layers of application servers

    C. The use of database middleware

    D. Fat clients

11. Which of the following are characteristics of a publish/subscribe architecture?

    A. Reliance on the use of URLs to identify publishers

    B. Subject-based addressing

    C. Location-independent publishers

    D. Synchronous communication between publishers and subscribers

12. Which of the following are advantages of an asynchronous architecture?

    A. Makes better use of communication bandwidth

    B. Supports leveling of processing loads

    C. Provides senders with instant response

    D. Scalability

APPLY YOUR KNOWLEDGE

Answers to Review Questions

1. The overall goal of a Java architect is to satisfy customer requirements.

2. Application architectures may be produced during requirements analysis. However, an application's architecture is not formalized until design. An architecture may be updated based on problems or opportunities that are encountered in subsequent lifecycle phases.

3. The tiers of a three-tiered system consist of the client (user interface) tier, business logic tier, and data storage tier.

4. Thin clients separate the client tier from the business logic and data storage tiers. This enables applications to be distributed, scaled, upgraded, managed, and maintained more easily.

5. The publish/subscribe model is an approach to distributed system communication in which publishers publish information to a subject address and subscribers subscribe to information at a subject address. The publish/subscribe model has the benefit of making publishers independent of location. This enables subscribers to subscribe to information without having to know the location of a publisher.

6. Asynchronous architectures decouple senders and receivers. This brings about performance advantages for both the sender and the receiver. The sender is able to even out his communication traffic over the course of a day. This is helpful in cases where sender and receiver communicate over low-bandwidth lengths. The receiver can even out its processing load by processing the sender's message as time permits.

7. Synchronous architectures are more appropriate than asynchronous architectures in applications where the sender and receiver must participate in a message exchange, and the sender must respond to the receiver in a limited time frame. An example of this is credit card authorization. The sender needs a response within a short time to complete a electronic commerce transaction and to notify a user that his purchase has been completed.

8. Extranet applications are applications that are designed for use by external organizations (such as buyers, vendors, suppliers, and financial institutions) and that take place securely over the Internet.

Answers to Exam Questions

1. C   Training users is not a role of the Java architect.

2. A, C, and D   Although a Java architect is typically a Java evangelist, the architect should recommend whatever technology (Java or non-Java) best satisfies a customer's needs, requirements, and expectations.

3. C   The primary criterion for success of a Java-based architecture is whether it maximizes satisfaction of customer requirements.

4. B and D   Negotiation and documentation are not phases of the application lifecycle.

5. A and B   An application architecture is initially defined during requirements analysis and design.

6. B   The validation phase determines whether an architecture meets its requirements.

APPLY YOUR KNOWLEDGE

7. A   Because a one-tier application architecture has limited connectivity, it may be more easily secured.

8. A and D   Two-tier architectures are characterized by fat clients and servers that are limited to providing database access.

9. A, B, and D   Security is not a tier of a three-tiered architecture.

10. B and C   An n-tier architecture typically contains multiple layers of application servers and the use of database middleware.

11. B and C   Publish/subscribe architectures are characterized by subject-based addressing and location-independent publishers.

12. A, B, and D   Asynchronous architectures make better use of communication bandwidth, support leveling of processing loads, and are more scalable.

Suggested Readings and Resources

Enterprise JavaBeans Technology, a white paper by Sun Microsystems, `http://java.sun.com/products/ejb/white_paper.html`, December 1998.

This chapter helps you to prepare for the exam by covering the following objectives:

- **Be able to state how Java architecture design fits into the application development lifecycle.**

- **Know how to evaluate the applicability of a Java solution for a given customer-application requirement.**

- **Be able to state the major architectural issues and trade-offs faced when designing a distributed Java solution.**

- **Be able to recommend Java application development techniques, Java reusability techniques, and project management techniques.**

CHAPTER 18

Object-Oriented Architecture Design

STUDY STRATEGIES

As you read through this chapter, you should concentrate on the following key items:

▶ The primary objectives of object-oriented programming

▶ The features of object-oriented programming that promote software reuse

▶ The object-oriented development approaches that led to the development of UML

▶ The types of diagrams used by UML

▶ The notation used by UML to represent classes and objects

▶ The object-oriented development phases

CHAPTER INTRODUCTION

A Java architect designs object-oriented Java-based distributed applications. In this chapter, we focus on the object-oriented aspect of these applications. You'll review the basics of object-oriented analysis, cover object-oriented design approaches, and learn about the Universal Modeling Language. When you finish this chapter, you'll be able to answer certification exam questions concerning the object-oriented nature of distributed applications.

BASIC OBJECT-ORIENTED DESIGN CONCEPTS

The primary objective of object-oriented programming is to simplify software development through the reuse of objects that have already developed. This results in software that may be developed more quickly, reliably, and at lower costs. This objective is achieved through features of classes and objects that allow objects to be instantiated, inherited, and composed:

◆ Instantiation—Classes serve as templates from which objects may be created through instantiation. For example, to create a GUI component, in most cases, you just create an instance of the GUI component's class.

◆ Inheritance—Higher-level classes may be subclassed by lower-level classes to refine and extend the capabilities provided by the higher-level class. The non-private field variables and methods of a class are inherited by its subclasses. This enables you to reuse the capabilities of a class in the development of its subclasses. For example, you typically extend the `java.awt.Frame` class by a class that implements the functionality of a Java window application.

◆ Composition—Lower-level classes of the Java API (and other APIs) may be used to build higher-level classes that can be instantiated as higher-level objects. For example, you can use the socket classes of `java.net` and the `Thread` class of `java.lang` to create a multithreaded Web server. The Web server may be instantiated or inherited to build custom Web server objects.

Instantiation, inheritance, and composition are three important ways in which object-oriented programming simplifies software development and encourages software reuse. However, there are a number of additional capabilities that are provided by Java that provide additional support for simplification and reuse:

◆ Packages—Java's package construct enables collections of related classes and interfaces to be organized into packages. Packages provide separate name spaces for classes and interfaces and allow them to be distributed as separate APIs. Packages provide a means to organize and distribute classes and interfaces in support of reuse.

◆ Interfaces—An interface defines a collection of methods that must be provided by any class that is designated as implementing the interface. Interfaces enable objects from classes of different branches of the class hierarchy to be accessed in the same way. This simplifies the reuse of these objects by allowing them to be handled in a standard way, regardless of their implementation. Interfaces also separate an object's use from its implementation. This enables new versions of an object to be developed and deployed with minimal impact on the objects that use that object. Interfaces are supported during program execution through late binding. Late binding (or dynamic binding) is the capability to defer until runtime decisions about the class to which an object belongs.

◆ Encapsulation—Java classes and interfaces support an object-oriented programming feature, referred to as encapsulation. Encapsulation (which is not unique to Java) refers to the control of access to the details of an object's implementation. The use of Java's access modifiers enables you to limit access to objects of a class to well-defined, controlled interfaces. This enables objects to be self-contained and protects them from accidental misuse, two features which are important to reliable software design. When a class is fully encapsulated, it is possible to change the class's implementation without impacting other objects that use the class. A fully encapsulated class declares all its variables as private and provides methods for getting and setting the properties represented by field variables. Java interfaces also support encapsulation by enabling objects to be accessed in terms of their interface methods and providing even more separation between their design (and use) and their implementation.

◆ Polymorphism—Polymorphism is a helpful feature of object-oriented programming (not just Java) that applies more to method reuse than object reuse. It is covered in Chapter 6, "Overloading, Overriding, Runtime Type, and Object Orientation," but I'll mention it here for the sake of completeness. Polymorphism means the capability of several methods to share the same name, but have different forms. For example, the `print()` and `println()` methods of the `java.io.PrintStream` class contain many overloaded forms (i.e., forms with different parameter lists) that may be used to print objects and values of primitive types. Polymorphism contributes to the simplification of software design and promotes the reuse of methods with common names.

◆ Distributed objects—The Java Platform's support of RMI and CORBA provide the opportunity for objects to be reused in a production environment as well as a development environment. After a distributed object is made available in a development environment, it may be reused by any applications that access that object (after considering security access controls). This enables you to reuse objects from existing applications in new ways to support new and upgraded applications.

◆ Components—Java supports both client and server components through JavaBeans and Enterprise JavaBeans. JavaBeans are objects whose properties may be set at design time, serialized, and reused in a number of different applets and applications. They are typically used to implement custom GUI components, but also may be used to implement non-visible components such as sorting, financial, and cryptographic algorithms. Enterprise JavaBeans function in the same manner as JavaBeans, except they are used as components of application servers. Refer to Chapter 19, "Distributed Application Technologies," for more information on Enterprise JavaBeans. Components extend the capabilities of objects by enabling object instances to be created, tailored, saved, and reused. This is typically accomplished through the use of visual design tools, such as Symantec's Visual Cafe.

◆ The Java 2 Platform and other APIs—Although RMI, Java IDL, and JavaBeans, are specific APIs that support object reuse, the entire Java 2 Platform provides a powerful base of classes and interfaces that can be reused to simplify the design

N O T E

Object-Oriented Programming
Chapter 6 covers the basic concepts
of object-oriented programming.

and development of object-oriented applications. In addition to the rich set of APIs contained in the Java 2 Platform, there are numerous other APIs, such as the Java Media Framework, the Servlet API, and the Java Naming and Directory Interface (JNDI). These can be used to simplify the development of a wide range of Java-based, object-oriented applications.

OBJECT-ORIENTED ANALYSIS AND DESIGN APPROACHES

There are a number of approaches to object-oriented analysis and design. However, three of these approaches stand out from the rest:

◆ Object Modeling Technique (OMT)—OMT was developed by James Rumbaugh at General Electric in the early 1990s. OMT consists of an object model, dynamic model, and functional mode. The object model is used to describe the objects that comprise a system and their relationships with each other. The dynamic model describes the dynamic behavior of the objects, such as state changes, events, and flow of control. The functional model describes a system from a data flow perspective. The models are related to one another in the description of a system's requirements and design. An excellent description of OMT is available online at `http://www.aut.ee.ethz.ch/edu/ciat2-SS98/OMT.html`.

◆ Object-Oriented Analysis and Design (OOAD or The Booch Method)—Grady Booch developed a method (that bears his name) for analyzing and designing object-oriented systems. This method uses a number of graphical symbols to document design decisions. Class and object diagrams are the principle starting point for analysis. The class diagram is used to develop a static model of a system. It is used to identify the classes that comprise a system and describe interactions between classes. The object diagram is used to identify objects, object relationships, and object behavior. Other diagrams supported by the Booch Method are state-event diagrams, module diagrams, process diagrams, and interaction diagrams. These diagrams are used to refine the results of analysis to the point where implementation takes place. A good online description of the Booch

Method is at `http://www.hsr.ch/div/Booch/BoochReference/reference.html`.

◆ Object-Oriented Software Engineering (OOSE)—Ivar Jacobson developed an approach to object-oriented software engineering that is known as OOSE or Objectory. Objectory is the name of an object-oriented software engineering environment developed by Jacobson. This approach is based upon use cases, which focus on user interactions with a system.

The approaches developed by Rumbaugh, Booch, and Jacobson dominated the object-oriented software engineering field of the 1990s and earned them the nickname of the "Three Amigos." The Three Amigos joined forces in Rational Software Corporation, a company that specializes in object-oriented software development. The trio developed an approach that fuses each of their individual approaches. This approach is referred to as the Unified Modeling Language (UML) and is covered in the next section.

THE UNIFIED MODELING LANGUAGE

The Unified Modeling Language (UML) is the unification of the object-oriented development methodologies of James Rumbaugh (OMT), Grady Booch (the Booch Method), and Ivar Jacobson (Objectory). It represents the current standard in designing and documenting object-oriented systems. UML is used to model systems from the point of conception (problem statement) through implementation (object generation). It is organized around the use of the following set of ten diagrams:

◆ Use Case—Describes the users of a system and the functions that are provided to the users.

◆ Package—Package diagrams are used to identify collections of classes and relationships between packages.

◆ Class—Identifies classes, relationships between classes, attributes, and methods.

◆ Object—Describes the state of a system at a particular point in time in terms of objects and relationships between the objects.

- Sequence—Identifies interactions between classes in terms of the exchange of messages.

- Collaboration—Describes interactions between classes and associations. Associations are special classes that model relationships between classes.

- State—Identifies the states of a class and the transitions between states that occur as the result of external influences.

- Activity—Describes the state transitions that occur internal to a class.

- Component—Identifies the components of a system and the dependencies between the components.

- Deployment—Identifies the physical elements of a system and the mapping of software components to these elements.

> **NOTE**
>
> **UML Resource Center** Rational Software, Inc. has a UML Resource Center on their Web site (http://www.rational.com) that provides access to UML specifications and other information about UML.

> **EXAM TIP**
>
> **Knowing Your Diagrams** For the purposes of the certification exam, it is more important to know the purpose of a diagram than to be familiar with its graphical syntax.

The above diagrams are used to capture requirements, identify the application architecture, describe its design, and document implementation decisions. A complete description of UML, its diagrams, and its application is a book in itself. However, the following paragraphs contain a summary description which will give you enough of a background to get you through the certification exam. If you already know UML, it can help you to fill in any gaps in your knowledge.

The Use Case Diagram

The use case diagram identifies the users' view of the system. It identifies actors, use cases, and relationships between them. Use case diagrams may be used to identify ways in which users and other external objects interact with a system. Figure 18.1 provides an example of a use case diagram.

The actors are either human (drawn with stick figures) or system elements (drawn with boxes and labeled with <<actor>>). The use cases are represented using ovals. They represent system functions and services. Lines are drawn between actors and use cases to indicate relations between them. Relationships are also indicated between use cases using lines. The lines may be labeled with <<extends>> to indicate that one use case extends another or with <<uses>> to indicate that one use case uses another.

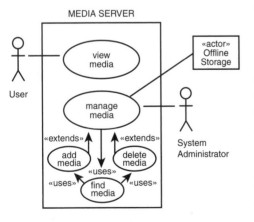

FIGURE 18.1

The use case diagram describes use cases, actors, and their relationships.

The Package Diagram

The package diagram identifies the packages that comprise a system and dependencies between the packages. For example, you can use package diagrams to define the dependencies between a custom API and the Java 2 API. Arrows between packages indicate that the classes of one package (indicated by the arrow head) depend on the classes of another (indicated by the arrow tail). Figure 18.2 provides an example of a package diagram.

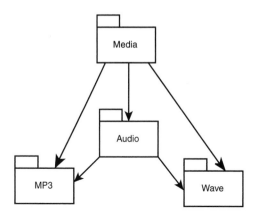

FIGURE 18.2
The package diagram shows the dependencies between packages.

The Class Diagram

The class diagram is used to identify the classes of a system, the attributes (i.e., properties) and methods of a class, and relationships between classes. A class diagram might also contain associations, which are special classes that are used to indicate relationships between other classes. A class diagram serves as the basic blueprint for a system's object-oriented software architecture. Refer to Figure 18.3.

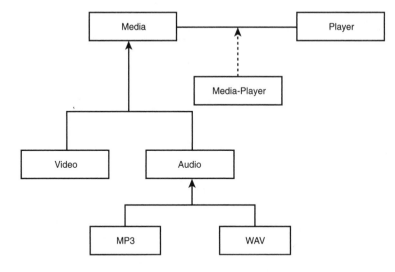

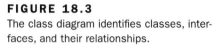

FIGURE 18.3
The class diagram identifies classes, interfaces, and their relationships.

The lines connecting classes may be labeled to indicate the type of relationships between the classes. Some examples of labels are

◆ diamond outline—The class nearest the diamond is composed of the class furthest from the diamond.

◆ solid diamond—The class nearest the diamond is an aggregation (collection) of classes that are further from the diamond.

◆ triangle outline—The class pointed to by the triangle is a superclass of the other class or classes.

◆ solid triangle—Used to indicate an association between classes. A dotted line identifies the class that describes the association.

The individual classes of the class diagram may be specified in terms of their attributes and methods, as shown in Figure 18.4. The attributes appear in the top half and the methods in the bottom. The `create()` method identifies a constructor and the `destroy()` method identifies a destructor (not needed for Java classes). Accessibility is indicated using an – (private), + (public), or # (protected).

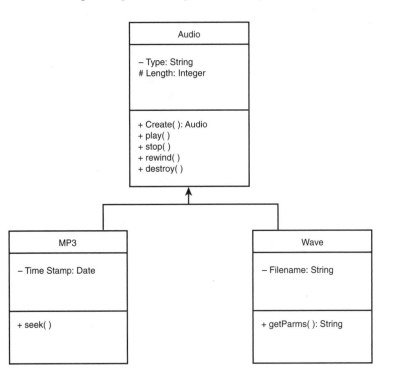

FIGURE 18.4

The detailed class diagram adds information about class members.

The Object Diagram

Object diagrams are snapshots of the objects of a system at a given instant. They are similar to class diagrams in notation and are often used to validate class diagrams for particular sets of object instances. The values of the object's attributes are indicated. Refer to Figure 18.5.

Each object is identified using the notation name:class notation where name is the object's name and class is the object's class. Anonymous objects are objects whose names are left blank (for example, :class). However, their class must be specified.

EXAM TIP	**Object Naming Convention** Make sure that you remember the `name:class object` naming convention. There is at least one exam question that requires you to know it.

The Sequence Diagram

Sequence diagrams are used to describe interactions between classes. They identify class roles, lifelines, activations, and messages. Roles identify the roles of a class and interactions between classes. Lifelines specify the existence of a class over time. Activations indicate the active state of a class role. Messages are used to identify information that is exchanged between classes. Sequence diagrams capture dynamic views of a system. Figure 18.6 provides an example of a sequence diagram.

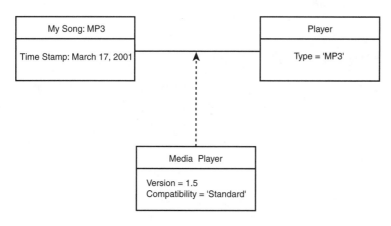

FIGURE 18.5
The object diagram identifies objects and their relationships.

FIGURE 18.6
The sequence diagram describes interactions between classes using messages.

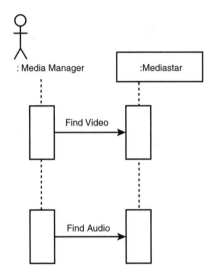

The Collaboration Diagram

Collaboration diagrams are like sequence diagrams in that they are used to describe interactions between classes. They model class roles, association roles, and messages. The focus of a collaboration diagram is on the associations between classes that are involved in the collaboration. Collaboration and sequence diagrams can usually be converted to and from each other. Figure 18.7 provides an example.

The State Diagram

State diagrams (also referred to as statechart diagrams) identify the allowed states of a class and transitions between those states. States are identified as rounded rectangles, and transitions are identified as arrows between states. State diagrams describe finite state machines. Refer to Figure 18.8.

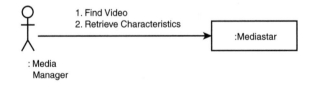

FIGURE 18.7
The collaboration diagram describes both object interaction and structure.

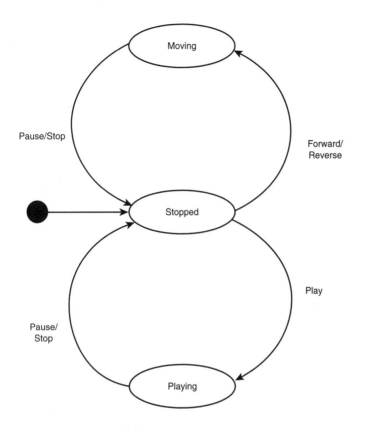

FIGURE 18.8
The state diagram describes a finite state machine.

The Activity Diagram

Activity diagrams are used to describe state changes that occur internally to a class. They are more algorithmic than descriptive in their presentation. They model action states (algorithm steps), action flows (conditional algorithm paths), object flows (object utilization by algorithms), and swim lanes. Swim lanes are lines that are used to identify object boundaries of responsibility in the implementation of an algorithm. Figure 18.9 provides an example.

FIGURE 18.9
The activity diagram shows flows of control between objects.

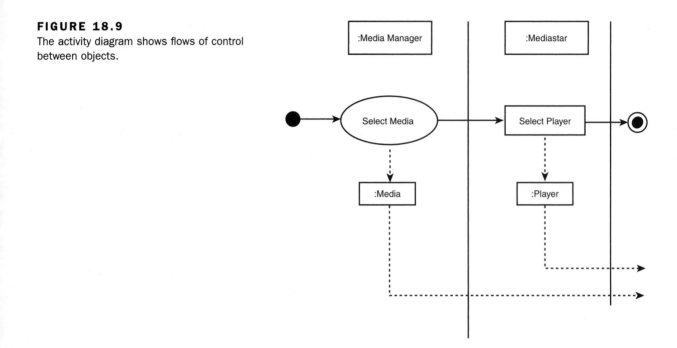

The Component Diagram

Component diagrams identify software components and their dependencies. Components are units of code (source, byte code, or machine-native executable). Dependencies are indicated by arrows between the components. For example, a JIT compiler may generate machine code which is dependent upon Java byte code, which is dependent upon Java source code. Refer to Figure 18.10.

The Deployment Diagram

Deployment diagrams specify the environment in which software components reside. They consist of processing nodes and software components. The components are identified within the nodes in which they reside/execute. Lines are used to indicate communication paths between nodes. 18.11 provides an example.

FIGURE 18.10
The component diagram shows the static relationships between system components.

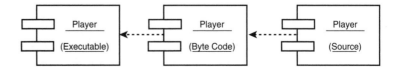

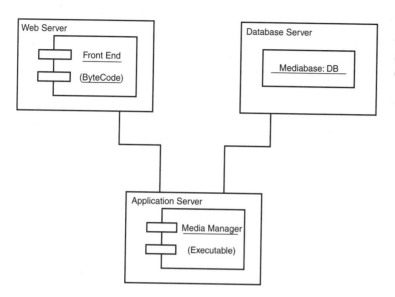

FIGURE 18.11
The deployment diagram provides a static description of a system architecture and its environment.

ARCHITECTING OBJECT-ORIENTED APPLICATIONS

A Java architect takes advantage of the object-oriented features that are covered in the previous section to simplify the process of designing and developing object-oriented applications.

On the certification exam, you'll see questions about the phases of the object-oriented development lifecycle. These phases are a cross-section of the application development lifecycle as it applies to software development. These phases consist of the following:

◆ Problem Statement

◆ Object-Oriented Analysis

◆ Java Architecture Design

◆ Object-Oriented Design

◆ Object Generation

Figure 18.12 shows the relationship between these development phases.

FIGURE 18.12
Object-oriented development phases.

Problem Statement

Applications are upgraded or new applications are deployed primarily for the following two reasons:

◆ Problems are identified with an existing application.

◆ Opportunities are identified that require a new application to be deployed or an existing application to be upgraded.

The problem statement identifies the problem or opportunity that is to be addressed by an application development. It initiates the requirements analysis phase.

Object-Oriented Analysis

Object-oriented analysis is a way of identifying application software requirements using object-oriented techniques.

Use class diagrams form the basis for identifying the user's view of an application. They also provide visibility into the system's business logic.

Classes are identified that represent the types of objects that occur in the application. Hierarchical relationships between classes are specified. The attributes (properties) and methods of the classes are described. Interfaces are also identified.

Classes and interfaces are organized into packages, and relationships between packages are diagrammed. Relationships between individual classes and interfaces are also identified. Object diagrams may be used to specify the relationships between specific instances of the classes being modeled.

Class and object behavior may be modeled using sequence diagrams, state diagrams, and other UML modeling techniques.

Java Architecture Design

A Java-based architecture flows out of the object-oriented analysis. The architecture identifies the allocation of Java classes and interfaces to components of the overall application architecture. As customer needs are assessed and requirements are identified, these needs are often graphically depicted as a high-level application architecture.

The high-level architecture is often used to identify application requirements. For example, the high-level architecture may contain connections to legacy systems, databases, and the Internet. Based on these connections, requirements are identified that specify what information is to be exchanged between the application and application-external objects.

By presenting a visual description of the target application, the high-level architecture may be used as a basis for describing requirements about application performance, determining security requirements, or addressing reliability concerns. For example, if a low-bandwidth communication line appears on the architecture diagram, it may spur a requirement to constrain the application to function correctly over 56Kbps lines (or it may bring about a requirement to upgrade communication bandwidth to support a more media-rich application).

As another example, suppose an unprotected path is found from an application server to the Internet. Security requirements for a VPN or firewall may be identified. In addition, requirements for remote user authentication may also be developed.

As a final example, the presence of a single Web server in the system architecture may give rise to concerns that it may be a single point of failure, and that may result in requirements being identified to cover application reliability.

Requirements analysis tends to work in a hierarchical fashion. High-level application requirements are identified. These requirements are elaborated and refined, and lower-level requirements are identified.

The application architecture is also elaborated and refined in concert with the object-oriented analysis. The components of the high-level architecture are analyzed, and objects that are resident on these components are identified. For example, a high-level architecture may identify a Web server. Upon further analysis, the architecture may be expanded to show servlets, applets, HTML pages, and other objects. These objects are then further refined at subsequent analysis stages. Deployment diagrams may be used to identify software allocation to processing nodes and communication links between those nodes.

When identifying requirements, it is important to organize those requirements according to the application tiers to which they apply. User interface requirements should be separated from the business logic and data storage requirements that they imply. In this way, the application's client tier may be designed and validated with less dependency on the other application tiers. Similarly, the requirements of the data storage tier should be separated from other tiers to allow for a more loosely coupled application architecture. Finally, the requirements for the application business logic should be organized to take advantage of enterprise application technologies, such as those offered by servlets and Enterprise JavaBeans.

Object-Oriented Design

Although requirements analysis and design are separate life-cycle phases, they interact closely with each other. Requirements obviously precede design. You have to know what you want before you can design it. However, design decisions can also lead to requirements. For example, a decision to provide an applet-based interface may lead to requirements for signed applets.

The purpose of the system design is to identify a solution to the customer's requirements. The application architecture depicts the overall design solution. It is refined into lower-level designs that are comprised of three types of components:

- ◆ legacy components
- ◆ vendor products
- ◆ new software

These components are allocated requirements from the higher-level components from which they are derived.

Legacy Components

Customers may vary between two extremes in their desire to reuse legacy components in new or upgraded applications. This decision may depend on how satisfied they are with the application that is being upgraded. Management directives or edicts also have an influence.

Some customers want maximum reuse of legacy components, assuming this will save them money. However, in some cases, it may be more cost-effective to build a new Java-based enterprise application, rather than trying to retrofit an old system based on the constraints of a legacy Windows application. Other customers may take a scrap-it-and-start-again attitude toward their legacy systems. However, in some cases, it may be more prudent to augment the current legacy application rather than to throw it away and start from scratch. This is especially true if the customer's dissatisfaction with the application is confined to a particular area.

For example, if the legacy application suffers from an outmoded client interface, a new browser-based interface may be deployed while retaining the tried-and-true business logic and data storage tiers of the legacy application.

The Java architect needs to work with the customer in making trade-offs concerning whether a legacy component should be augmented or replaced. In general, if a legacy component can satisfy (or be made to satisfy) the requirements that are allocated to it, it is a candidate solution to that requirement. Otherwise, it should be scrapped. The architect must also consider whether reuse of the legacy component has positive or negative effects on the application development schedule and cost.

Vendor Products

In most cases, if a vendor product satisfies the requirements that are allocated to it, it is almost always more cost efficient to buy the product than to develop the equivalent software.

One problem that the system designer is often confronted with is that of vapor products. Vendors announce their intent to provide products that will satisfy your requirements, make your design more efficient and secure, and dramatically lower your development costs. The problem is that the products do not exist—but they will soon.

There are significant tradeoffs in deciding to base a design on a future product. On one hand, the product may arrive on time and result in a better and cheaper application. On the other hand, the product may be delayed, have serious shortcomings, and be unusable.

The maxim, "Hope for the best, but plan for the worst," applies here. This implies the need for a backup solution that can replace the product in the design, in case the vapor product is delayed or fails to match up to its marketing hype.

Developmental Software

Although it is desirable (for cost and schedule reasons) to minimize the amount of software that needs to be developed, in most cases, the unique requirements of your customer will necessitate that some code be written. The requirements for each software component are allocated from the overall application requirements. These requirements form the basis for developing the software's object-oriented design.

The software's design consists of taking the structural (class and object) and behavioral (sequence, collaboration, state, and activity) and refining and extending them to the point where all classes and interfaces are defined along with their interactions. Class behaviors are specified in detail, and the algorithms for implementing methods are selected and documented. The design continues until sufficient information is available from which code can be generated.

Object Generation

Given a thorough analysis and design effort, actual implementation is vastly simplified. Object generation consists of translating package, class, and interface descriptions into Java code. The field variables and methods of each class are defined using class diagrams. Method algorithms are coded using activity, state, sequence, and collaboration diagrams. Object diagrams may be used to support object creation and initialization.

The source code is compiled and Java bytecode files are produced, executed, and tested. Component diagrams may be used to document code dependencies.

CHAPTER SUMMARY

In this chapter, you reviewed the basics of object-oriented analysis, covered object-oriented design approaches, and learned about the Universal Modeling Language. The following review and exam questions will test your knowledge of these topics and will help you to determine whether your knowledge of them is sufficient to answer the questions you'll encounter in the certification exam.

KEY TERMS

- Instantiation
- Inheritance
- Composition
- Encapsulation
- Polymorphism
- Components
- OMT
- The Booch Method
- Objectory
- UML
- Problem Statement
- Object-Oriented Analysis
- Java Architecture Design
- Object-Oriented Design
- Object Generation

APPLY YOUR KNOWLEDGE

Review Questions

1. What are the advantages of encapsulation in object-oriented software development.

2. What is the difference between a component and an object?

3. What is the origin of UML?

4. What is the purpose of a use case diagram?

5. What is the purpose of a class diagram?

6. What does a deployment diagram specify?

7. What are the phases of the object-oriented development lifecycle?

8. What three types of components comprise an application design?

Exam Questions

1. Which of the following support object reuse?

    A. Class inheritance

    B. Object composition

    C. JavaBeans

    D. Attributes

2. Which of the following methodologies were unified by UML?

    A. Structured Programming

    B. Object-Oriented Software Engineering

    C. The Booch Method

    D. OMT

3. Which of the following diagrams are supported by UML?

    A. Use Case diagram

    B. Data Flow diagram

    C. Class diagram

    D. Object diagram

4. If the term name1:name2 appeared at the top of an object diagram, which of the following would name1 and name2 identify?

    A. name1 is the object's name and name2 is the object's class.

    B. name1 is the object's class and name2 is the object's name.

    C. name1 is the class's name and name2 is the class's superclass.

    D. name1 is the class's superclass and name2 is the class's name.

5. Which of the following diagrams map software components to processing nodes?

    A. Component diagram

    B. Collaboration diagram

    C. Deployment diagram

    D. Object diagram

6. Which of the following are phases of the object-oriented development cycle?

    A. Object-oriented analysis

    B. Object generation

    C. Problem statement

    D. Development testing

APPLY YOUR KNOWLEDGE

7. Which of the following occur first in the object-oriented development cycle?

    A. Object-oriented analysis

    B. Object generation

    C. Problem statement

    D. Development testing

8. Which of the following may be specified in a class diagram?

    A. Composition

    B. Aggregation

    C. Inheritance

    D. State transition

Answers to Review Questions

1. Encapsulation hides the private details of a class's implementation. This provides protection from accidental misuse. It also allows a class's design to be separated from its implementation. Changes to a class's implementation can be made with minimal impact on classes that depend on the class.

2. A component is an object that has been created, initialized, and serialized. A component may be used by deserializing it.

3. UML is the unification of OMT (James Rumbaugh), the Booch Method (Grady Booch), and object-oriented software engineering (Ivar Jacobson).

4. A use case diagram describes the users of a system and the functions and services that are provided to the users.

5. A class diagram identifies classes, relationships between classes, attributes, and methods.

6. A deployment diagram identifies the physical elements (processing nodes) of a system, communication links between nodes, and the mapping of software components to these elements.

7. The phases of the object-oriented development lifecycle are problem statement, object-oriented analysis, Java architecture design, object-oriented design, and object generation.

8. An application design is comprised of legacy components, vendor products, and developmental software.

Answers to Exam Questions

1. A, B, and C   Attributes do not support object reuse.

2. B, C, and D   Structured programming was not an input to UML.

3. A, C, and D   UML does not support data flow diagrams.

4. A   The notation is of the form `object name:object class`.

5. C   Deployment diagrams map software components to processing nodes.

6. A, B, and C   Development testing is not a phase of the object-oriented development cycle.

7. C   Problem statement is the first phase of the object-oriented development cycle.

8. A, B, and C   State transitions are not specified in a class diagram.

APPLY YOUR KNOWLEDGE

Suggested Readings and Resources

1. *Object-Oriented Software Development Using Object Modeling Technique (OMT)*, Xiaobing Qiu, `http://www.aut.ee.ethz.ch/edu/ciat2-SS98/OMT.html`.

2. *Object Oriented Modeling and Design*, James Rumbaugh, Prentice Hall, 1991.

3. *Object-oriented Analysis and Design with Applications*, Grady Booch, 2nd edition, Addison-Wesley, 1994.

4. *Object-Oriented Software Engineering*, Ivar Jacobson, Addison-Wesley, 1994.

5. *UML in a Nutshell*, Sinan Si Alhir, O'Reilly & Associates, 1998.

This chapter helps you to prepare for the exam by covering the following objectives:

- **Be able to discuss the advantages of Java servlets compared to CGI scripts.**

- **Know how to design a detailed architecture including Java applet and application server design.**

- **Know how to compare a distributed Java architecture with the OMG CORBA and Microsoft alternatives.**

- **Know how to design a detailed architecture for integrating Java with existing databases and applications.**

- **Know how to design a three-tier (or n-tier) architecture using Enterprise JavaBeans.**

- **Be able to describe how Java can be used for transaction processing.**

CHAPTER 19

Distributed Applications Technologies

STUDY STRATEGIES

As you read through this chapter, you should concentrate on the following key items:

▶ The advantages that Java servlets provide over traditional CGI programs

▶ How JDBC provides database connectivity to Java applications

▶ How RMI, CORBA, and DCOM support communication between distributed objects

▶ How Java supports transaction management

▶ How Enterprise JavaBeans can be used to develop and deploy platform-independent application components

▶ How JNDI supports access to naming and directory services

▶ How JMAPI supports the management of enterprise applications, systems, and networks

CHAPTER INTRODUCTION

To be a Java architect, you must have a commanding knowledge of Java technology. This is necessary so you can select the most appropriate technology solution for a particular application development. In this chapter, you'll review those technologies that are essential to designing distributed, Web-based applications using Java. You'll cover technologies related to the Web, database, distributed objects, transaction processing, application servers, naming and directory services, and system management. While detailed coverage of each of these areas would require a library of technical books, you'll cover enough of each area to give you a basic understanding of how the technology fits into Java application design.

WEB TECHNOLOGIES

You'll start by reviewing some of the basic technologies involved in building Web-based applications. You will probably be familiar with most of these technologies. However, it's a good idea to read through this section to reinforce what you currently know and to fill in any gaps in your knowledge.

HTML

HTML is the language in which Web pages are written. It consists of ASCII text that is marked up using tags. Tags specify how text is to be displayed. For example, the tags <H1> and </H1> are used to identify text that is to be displayed as a level-one heading. HTML provides a rich set of markup tags that can be used to specify a wide variety of text elements, ranging from bulleted lists to tables. Tags can be used to include images, sounds, and other forms of multimedia in Web pages. Tags may also be used to include executable content, such as Java applets and JavaScript scripts in Web pages. One of the most useful features of HTML is the capability to include hyperlinks in Web pages. Hyperlinks are a defining characteristic of the Web.

Universal Resource Locators

HTML links are specified using Universal Resource Locators (URLs). URLs are addresses for Internet-accessible resources, such as Web pages, downloadable files, news groups, and mail. Examples of URLs include the following:

◆ `http://www.courseone.com`—A Web site that specializes in online courses.

◆ `ftp://ftp.cdrom.com`—An FTP site that contains archives of freeware and shareware programs.

◆ `mailto:support@jaworski.com`—A URL that you can use to get email support for this book.

URLs consist of a protocol (for example, `http:`, `ftp:`, or `mail:`) followed by protocol-specific address information. For more information on URLs and their syntax, check out the World Wide Web Consortium Web page at `http://www.w3.org/Addressing/URL/`.

Just about anything that's on the Internet can be located using a URL of one kind or another.

HTTP

While Web pages are created and referenced using HTML and URLs, they are communicated via the hypertext transfer protocol (HTTP). HTTP is the protocol used for communication between Web browsers and Web servers. It specifies a request-response form of communication that is based on the Transmission Control Protocol (TCP).

Web browsers connect to Web servers on TCP port 80. They send requests for URLs to Web servers. The servers receive these requests, process them, and send responses that contain the results of the requests back to the browsers.

Requests consist of a request method, the URL being requested, the version of HTTP supported by the browser, and other information related to the capabilities of the browser. The GET, HEAD, and POST

NOTE

HTTP Basics Make sure that you know the basics of HTTP that are presented in this section. There are a few exam questions that require you to be familiar with its operation and characteristics.

NOTE

TCP Ports For more information on TCP and port numbers, check out the TCP/IP FAQ at `http://www.cis.ohio-state.edu/hypertext/faq/bngusenet/comp/protocols/tcp-ip/top.html`.

methods are the most common request methods. A GET request is used to retrieve information from the specified URL. It is also used to submit HTML form data or invoke and pass data to a CGI program.

Server responses begin with an HTTP header that provides information about the server, errors encountered in processing the request, and MIME type information about the data that is being returned in the response. MIME types are used to specify the type of content contained in a response. For example, the text/html MIME type specifies a Web document and the image/jpeg MIME type specifies an image file type.

The HEAD method is used by browsers to obtain information about a URL instead of retrieving the URL's contents. It is processed by Web servers in the same way as the GET method, except that only the HTTP header data (and no content data) is returned.

The POST method is used to send information to a URL. It is typically used by browsers to send form data to the URL of a CGI program. Web servers handle POST requests by returning an answer to the requesting browser. The answer consists of an HTTP header followed by any information generated by the CGI program as the result of processing the request.

The POST method differs from the GET method in the way data sent from the browser is furnished to a CGI program. The POST method causes data to be sent via a stream, while the GET method sends data via environment variables.

The current version of HTTP supported by most browsers and servers is HTTP 1.1. It incorporates performance, security, and other improvements to the original HTTP 1.0. One of these improvements is the capability to maintain the TCP connection between a browser and a Web server. This capability is known as *keep alive*. Keep alive enables a browser to make several HTTP requests and receive multiple HTTP responses without having to establish a new TCP connection for each request-response pair. This capability provides a significant performance improvement over HTTP 1.0 and can be used to implement more advanced client-server communication using HTTP.

NOTE **The New HTTP** The next generation of HTTP, referred to as HTTP-NG, is currently being standardized. HTTP-NG will simplify HTTP 1.1 and make it more extensible to provide more advanced browser-server communication. Refer to http://www.w3.org/Protocols/HTTP-NG/ for more information on HTTP-NG.

Applets

Applets are Java programs that execute within the context of a Web page. They are included in Web pages via the <APPLET> tag and are restricted in their operation according to the browser security policy. The capabilities afforded to applets by browsers are controlled by the applet sandbox. Chapter 20, "Securing Distributed Applications," discusses the operation of the sandbox, its security aspects, and the evolution of the sandbox from JDK 1.02 through JDK 1.1 to the current Java 2 platform.

The general operation of applets is as follows:

1. A browser requests and receives a Web page that contains a reference to a Java applet (via the <APPLET> tag).

2. The browser requests and receives the applet code from the Web server.

3. The browser allocates a fixed area of the browser window, based on the WIDTH and HEIGHT attributes of the <APPLET> tag. All applet operations are confined to this area of the window. However, the applet is free to open windows of its own.

4. The applet performs its processing by interacting with the user. This interaction is limited by the sandbox and applet security policy, as discussed in Chapter 20.

Netscape Navigator 2.0 and 3.0 and Microsoft Internet Explorer 3.0 support JDK 1.02 applets. Navigator 4.0 through 4.5 and Internet Explorer 4.0 through 5.0 support JDK 1.1 applets. However, these browsers also support some applets that are compiled under the Java 2 platform. In order to ensure the fullest degree of support for Java 2 applets, Sun provides the Java Plug-In (developed under Project Activator) that provides complete Java 2 support for versions 4.0 or later of Navigator and Internet Explorer. In order to use the plug-in, Java applets are included in Web pages as embedded objects. Sun provides tools for converting existing Web pages to use the Java Plug-In.

Other Executable Content

Other forms of executable content may be embedded in Web pages beside applets. JavaScript scripts and ActiveX components are principal among these.

Although JavaScript contains Java in its name, it is an altogether different language. JavaScript is a scripting language that is used to create more dynamic and interactive Web pages. JavaScript scripts are embedded in HTML pages via the <SCRIPT> tag and special event-handling attributes. They enable HTML to be dynamically generated and provide the capability to handle events that occur during user interaction with a Web page, such as clicking on a form button or moving the mouse over an image.

ActiveX is Microsoft's solution to including executable content within Web pages. ActiveX components are Component Object Model (COM) objects that can be downloaded and executed by Internet Explorer. COM is Microsoft's legacy object technology. It dates back to Windows 3.1.

ActiveX enables you to use legacy Windows software in Internet Explorer. However, ActiveX suffers from the fact that it is only natively supported by Internet Explorer. This severely limits its use with general Web-based applications. ActiveX also suffers from poor security. ActiveX components are not restricted in the accesses that they may make. A rogue ActiveX component may easily carry out a wide spectrum of attacks on systems that execute these components.

The Common Gateway Interface

The Common Gateway Interface is a Web standard that specifies how external programs may be interfaced with Web servers. CGI programs are programs that adhere to this standard. They are typically used to process data that is submitted by HTML forms, perform database searches, and implement Web applications (such as online stores).

CGI programs are executed when a browser requests the CGI program's URL. When a Web server receives the browser's request, the Web server executes the CGI program and also passes it any data that was submitted by the browser. After the CGI program completes its processing, it usually generates data in the form of a Web page, which it returns via the Web server to the requesting browser.

The CGI standard specifies how data may be passed from Web servers to CGI programs and how data should be returned from CGI programs to the Web server. This communication consists of the following:

Web server to CGI program:

◆ Command-line arguments—A Web server may pass data to a CGI program via the command line used to execute the program. This command line may specify arguments that are passed to the program upon invocation.

◆ Environment variables—A Web server may pass data to a CGI program by setting environment variables, which are made available to the CGI program via its execution environment.

◆ Standard input stream—A Web server may pass data to a CGI program by sending the data to the standard character input stream associated with the CGI program. The CGI program reads the data as if it were manually entered by a user at a character terminal.

CGI program to Web server:

◆ Standard output stream—A CGI program passes data back to a Web server by writing it to its standard output stream. The Web server reads this data and sends it back to the browser that made the CGI request.

Servlets

While the CGI provides a well-used, standard method for interfacing external programs to Web applications, it has several drawbacks:

◆ CGI programs run as separate operating system processes. This incurs significant overhead in the setup and teardown of each CGI program instance.

◆ The security of CGI programs rests predominantly with the CGI program. If just one CGI program contains an

exploitable security vulnerability, the security of the entire Web
site may be compromised.

◆ CGI programs may not be portable across Web server platforms. If a set of CGI programs are developed for a particular
Web server, and the server platform is changed as the result of
a system upgrade, the CGI programs may need to be rewritten
to work on the new server.

Java servlets retain the benefits of CGI programs and provide a solution to the problems faced by CGI programs. Servlets are the server-
side analog to Java applets. They are small Java programs that
execute in the context of a Web server. The Java Servlet API provides
standardization of the server to servlet interface. This provides the
same benefit as the CGI standard.

Because servlets are Java programs, they run in a JVM. Most servlet
implementations enble servlets to be preloaded to increase servlet
performance. The security features of the JVM, Java runtime system
and Java language all contribute to reducing the security risks faced
by servlets. Because servlets are written in Java, they may be instantly
ported to any other Web server that supports the servlet API.

From the perspective of the Web server, servlets are implemented as
server extensions that are associated with particular URLs. When a
request for the URL of a servlet is received from a Web browser, the
Web server invokes the servlet to process the request. The Web
server provides the servlet with all the information it needs to
process the request. It also provides a mechanism for the servlet to
send response information back to the Web browser. Servlets are
more efficient than CGI programs in that they are invoked as a separate thread and not as a separate process.

DATABASE TECHNOLOGIES

Distributed applications make use of database management systems
to provide their storage layer. These database systems serve as reposi-
tories for large amounts of information that is collected and used by
the application. For example, search sites maintain database information about the URLs that are searched. Online employee directories

use databases to store contact information about employees. Web-based product catalogs maintain product descriptions and sales information in the form of a database. In this section, you'll learn the fundamentals of database programming. You'll learn how relational databases work and how SQL is used to update and retrieve data from relational databases. You'll also cover JDBC, JavaBlend, and Object Query Language (OQL) technologies.

Database Basics

A *database* is a collection of data that is organized so that it can be easily searched and updated. The most important feature of a database is its organization, which supports both ease of use and efficient data retrieval.

Consider an office that is organized with numbered file cabinets containing carefully labeled folders. Office information is stored by subject in specific folders that are kept in designated file cabinets. In such a system, every folder has its place, and it is easy to find a particular folder.

Now consider a different environment where information is stored in folders, but the folders are haphazardly stored in boxes that are placed at seemingly random locations throughout an office building. How do you find a particular folder in such an environment? Where do you store a folder when you're finished with it?

The well-organized environment is analogous to a database. Information that is entered into a database is stored in specific locations within it. Because of the database's structure and organization (assuming the database is well designed), information can be easily retrieved. The database can be accessed remotely and is shared between many users.

The unorganized environment is analogous to a situation where information is stored in files on various user's computers. In such an environment, it is very hard to locate specific information. What file contains the information you need? Whose computer contains that file? Where is the computer located? Where is the file located in the user's file system?

A *database server* is a software program that manages databases, keeps them organized, and provides shared access to them. Database servers manage and organize databases at both a physical level and at a logical level. At a *physical level,* database servers store database information in specific locations within the particular files, directories, and disk volumes used by the server. The server keeps track of what information goes where so that you don't have to. The server is like a trusty office assistant whom you can turn to and say, "Get me the file on…" and the assistant immediately retrieves the information you need and places it on your desk.

As previously mentioned, database servers also manage and organize information at a *logical level.* This logical level corresponds to the type of information that you store in a database. For example, you may have a database that stores the names, companies, email addresses, and phone numbers of your business contacts. The logical organization of the database might consist of a `Contacts` table with five columns: `LastName`, `FirstName`, `Company`, `Email`, and `Phone`.

Relational Databases

Although there are a number of different ways that databases can be logically organized, one particular organization, called the *relational model,* is the predominant method. The relational model was developed by E.F. Codd, a mathematician at IBM, during the late 1960s. Databases that adhere to the relational model are referred to as *relational databases.*

Relational databases are organized into tables that consist of rows and columns. The columns of the table identify what type of information is contained in each row. The rows of the table contain specific records that have been entered in the database.

Working with Keys

Access to information contained within tables is organized by keys. A *key* is a column or group of columns that uniquely identifies a row of a table. Keys are used to find a particular row within a table and to determine whether a new row is to be added to a table or to replace an existing row.

Structured Query Language

The *Structured Query Language,* or *SQL* (pronounced "sequel"), is a language for interacting with relational databases. It was developed by IBM during the '70s and '80s and standardized in the late '80s. The SQL standard has been updated over the years, and several versions currently exist. In addition, several database vendors have added product-specific extensions and variations to the language. The JDBC requires JDBC-compliant drivers to support the American National Standards Institute (ANSI) SQL-92 Entry Level version of the standard that was adopted in 1992.

SQL has many uses. When SQL is used to create or design a database, it is a *data definition language.* When it's used to update the data contained in a database, it is a *data maintenance language.* When it's used to retrieve information from a database, it is a *data query language.*

N O T E

More SQL For more information on SQL, check out the Yahoo! Web page on SQL at http://dir.yahoo.com/ Computers_and_Internet/ Programming_Languages/SQL/.

Remote Database Access

Most useful databases are accessed remotely. In this way, shared access to the database can be provided to multiple users at the same time. For example, you can have a single database server that is used by all employees in the accounting department.

In order to access databases remotely, users need a *database client.* A database client communicates to the database server on the user's behalf. It provides the user with the capability to update the database with new information or to retrieve information from the database. In designing Java-based distributed applications, you will use Java applications and applets as database clients. These clients talk to database servers using SQL statements. (See Figure 19.1.)

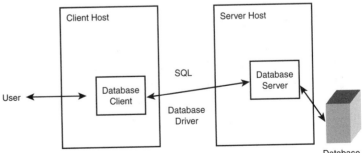

FIGURE 19.1
A database client talks to a database server on the user's behalf.

ODBC and JDBC Drivers

Database clients use database drivers to send SQL statements to database servers and to receive result sets and other responses from the servers. JDBC drivers are used by Java applications and applets to communicate with database servers. Officially, Sun says that JDBC is an acronym that does not stand for anything. However, it is associated with "Java database connectivity."

Microsoft's ODBC

Many database servers use vendor-specific protocols. This means that a database client has to learn a new language to talk to a different database server. However, Microsoft established a common standard for communicating with databases, called *Open Database Connectivity (ODBC)*. Until ODBC, most database clients were server-specific. ODBC drivers provide a common application programming interface to database clients. By writing your database clients to the ODBC API, you enable your programs to access more database servers. (See Figure 19.2.)

Enter JDBC

So where does JDBC fit into this picture? JDBC provides a common database-programming API for Java programs. JDBC drivers do not yet directly communicate with as many database products as ODBC drivers. Instead, many JDBC drivers communicate with databases using ODBC. In fact, one of the first JDBC drivers was the JDBC-ODBC bridge driver developed by JavaSoft and Intersolv.

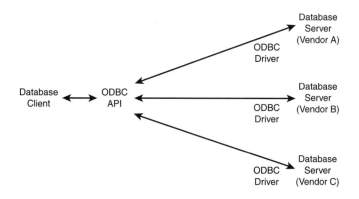

FIGURE 19.2

A database client can talk to many database servers via ODBC drivers.

Why did JavaSoft create JDBC? What was wrong with ODBC? There are a number of reasons why JDBC was needed, which boil down to the simple fact that JDBC is a better solution for Java applications and applets:

◆ ODBC is a C language Windows API, not a Java API. Java is object-oriented and C is not. C uses pointers and other "dangerous" programming constructs that Java does not support. A Java version of ODBC would require a significant rewrite of the ODBC API.

◆ ODBC drivers must be installed on client machines. This means that applet access to databases would be constrained by the requirement to download and install an ODBC driver. A pure Java solution enables JDBC drivers to be automatically downloaded and installed along with the applet. This greatly simplifies database access for applet users.

JavaSoft created the Java-ODBC bridge driver as a temporary solution to database connectivity until suitable JDBC drivers were developed. The JDBC-ODBC bridge driver translates the JDBC API into the ODBC API and is used with an ODBC driver. The JDBC-ODBC bridge driver is not an elegant solution, but it enables Java developers to use existing ODBC drivers. (See Figure 19.3.)

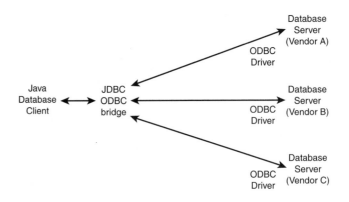

FIGURE 19.3
The JDBC-ODBC bridge lets Java database clients talk to databases via ODBC drivers.

JavaBlend

JavaBlend is a product that simplifies the process of building database applications using JDBC. JavaBlend automatically maps Java objects to information that is stored in databases. All operations on those objects result in automatic querying and updating of the corresponding information stored in the databases.

After a Java object-to-database mapping is constructed, JavaBlend frees Java programmers from having to deal with the execution of SQL statements and the processing of result sets. JavaBlend automatically generates, executes, and processes SQL statements corresponding to the methods that are invoked on Java objects. This enables JDBC and SQL programming to be abstracted out of database application development.

JavaBlend is not included in JDK 1.2. It is a separate product that is available from Sun. The reason that I mention JavaBlend is that it appears as an answer on at least one certification exam question.

OQL

OQL is a query language that has been standardized by the Object Database Management Group (ODMG). OQL is based on SQL and provides object-oriented extensions that support object database management systems.

OQL is a functional language that supports object manipulation. It can be used to search databases for objects of particular types, retrieve objects from databases, or add objects to databases. OQL can also be used to invoke the methods of objects that are stored in databases. A Java binding for OQL is supported. OQL is also intended for use with object databases that provide object persistence in CORBA applications. For more information on object-oriented databases and OQL, check out the Object Data Management Group Web site at http://www.odmg.org.

DISTRIBUTED COMMUNICATION TECHNOLOGIES

A *distributed application* is an application whose processing is distributed across multiple networked computers. Distributed applications are able to concurrently serve multiple users and, depending on their design, make more optimal use of processing resources.

Distributed applications are typically implemented as client/server systems that are organized according to the user interface, business, and data storage tiers. This is shown in Figure 19.4.

The user interface tier is implemented by an application client. Email programs and Web browsers are examples of the user-interface component of distributed applications.

The business logic tier may be implemented on an application client, a Web server, a dedicated application server, or application support servers. For example, an electronic commerce application may utilize an applet to perform local computations, a servlet to communicate with the applet and forward transaction data to back-end servers, and a dedicated application server to process customer orders, accept electronic payments, and interface with inventory control systems.

The data storage tier is implemented by database servers, Web servers, FTP servers, file servers, and any other servers whose purpose is to store and retrieve information.

FIGURE 19.4

The organization of distributed systems into user interface, business logic, and data storage tiers.

Distributed Applications on the Internet

The popularity of the Internet and the Web has resulted in an almost fully networked world. Computers on opposite ends of the world are directly accessible to each other via the TCP/IP protocol suite. This worldwide connectivity has given rise to distributed applications that run within the Internet's client/server framework. These first-generation applications support client/server communication using application-specific protocols such as HTTP, FTP, and SQL*NET. Figure 19.5 illustrates a typical Internet application.

Typically, a client program is executed on multiple host computers. The client uses TCP to connect to a server that listens on a well-known port. The client makes one or more requests of the server. The server processes the client's requests, possibly using gateway programs or back-end servers, and forwards the response to the client.

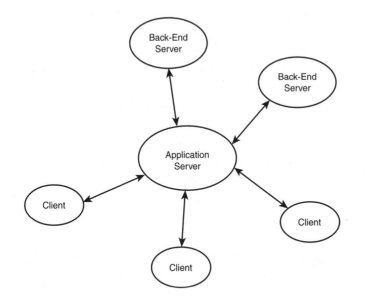

FIGURE 19.5
A distributed Internet application showing multiple clients and back-end servers.

Applets on an Intranet

In an intranet environment, corporate information systems support services that are tailored to the organizational needs of the company. These services consist of applications that support business areas such as management, accounting, marketing, manufacturing, customer support, vendor interface, shipping and receiving, and so on. These intranet services can be implemented using client/server services, such as a company-internal Web. Java applets provide the capability to implement the client interface and part of the business logic of business applications within the context of a Web browser. Figure 19.6 shows an approach to implementing corporate information services using the applet paradigm. Applets are represented by the small, filled-in squares within browsers.

The approach shown in Figure 19.6 is essentially the Internet client/server approach shown in Figure 19.5, but applied to an intranet, using Java applets to program client information system interfaces. This approach is popular for developing distributed intranet applications, and it can also be used with Internet applications. It enables business applications to be distributed among browsers, Web servers, and other back-end servers.

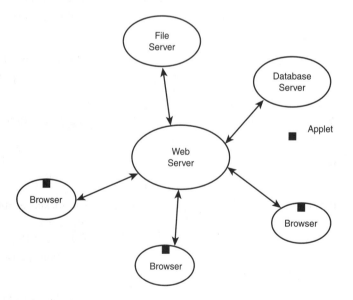

FIGURE 19.6
Implementing intranet services using applets.

The Distributed Computing Environment

The *Distributed Computing Environment (DCE)* is another approach to building distributed applications. DCE was developed by the Open Software Foundation, now referred to as the Open Group. DCE integrates a variety of fundamental services and technologies to build distributed applications. Distributed systems are organized into *cells*, which are groups of processing resources, services, and users that support a common function and share a common set of DCE services. For example, cells can be organized according to company functions. In this case, you may have separate cells for your finance, manufacturing, and marketing departments.

The DCE services of a cell are used to implement distributed applications that serve the users of the cell and interface with the applications implemented by other cells. The services and technologies used within a DCE cell consist of the following:

◆ Directory Services—Store the names of resources that are available within the distributed environment. The Cell Directory Service (CDS) supports naming within a cell, and the Global Directory Service (GDS) supports naming across all cells within an enterprise. GDS implements the X.500 directory service standard.

◆ Distributed File Service (DFS)—An optional DCE service that provides a seamless file system that operates across all computers contained within a cell.

◆ Distributed Time Service (DTS)—Used to synchronize time across all computers within a cell.

◆ Security Service—Used to authenticate cell users and control access to the resources that are available within a cell.

◆ Remote Procedure Calls (RPCs)—Replace TCP sockets as the basic mechanism for client/server communication. RPCs are implemented as a layer that is built on top of the TCP/IP transport layer and transparently manages connection management and protocol-specific concerns.

◆ DCE Threads—Similar to Java threads. They are lightweight processes that simplify the design of client/server applications.

DCE is referred to as *middleware* because it is not a standalone product, but rather a bundle of services that are integrated into an operating system or operating environment. These services are used as an alternative approach to constructing distributed applications. They are used to build the same kinds of applications as the Web-based example covered in the previous section, but they go about it in a different manner.

The Distributed Component Object Model

The *Distributed Component Object Model*, or *DCOM*, is Microsoft's approach to developing distributed systems. DCOM is based on COM, which is the heart of Microsoft's object-oriented development strategy. Because DCOM is essentially a distributed system extension to COM, understanding COM is essential to understanding DCOM.

Understanding COM

COM is an outgrowth of Microsoft's *Object Linking and Embedding* technology, or *OLE*. OLE was used in early versions of windows to support *compound documents*, or documents that are the product of multiple applications. COM was a solution to early problems in OLE, and like most great solutions, it solved a much more fundamental problem—how general objects should interact with and provide services to each other.

COM objects are instances of classes and are organized into interfaces. Interfaces are simply collections of methods. COM objects can only be accessed via their methods, and every COM object is implemented inside a server. A server may be implemented as a dynamic-link library, independent process, or an operating service. COM abstracts away the implementation details and presents a single uniform interface to all objects, no matter how each object is implemented.

The COM library is key to implementing this common interface between objects. It is present on any system that supports COM and provides a directory to all classes that are available on that system. The COM library maintains information about available classes in the system registry. When one COM object accesses another, it first invokes functions in the COM library. These functions can be used to create a COM object from its class or obtain a pointer to its interfaces.

The COM runtime is a process that supports the COM library in implementing its functions. It is supported by the Service Control Manager. The invoking object uses interface pointers to invoke the methods of the object that it accesses through the COM library. The pointers used by COM objects can be used by objects written in any programming language.

The interface definition language used to define COM interfaces and methods is borrowed from DCE. COM also defines a binary interface standard. This standard helps to promote language-independence.

From COM to DCOM

DCOM is essentially COM distributed over multiple computers. DCOM allows COM objects executing on one computer to create COM objects on other computers and access their methods. The location of the remote object is transparent. Using DCOM, remote objects are accessed in exactly the same manner as local objects.

In order for an object on a local system to access the methods of an object on a remote system, the local system must have the remote object's class registered in its local registry. The local object, oblivious of the location of the object that it is accessing, creates the remote object and/or obtains a pointer to its methods by invoking the functions of its local COM library.

The COM library processes the function calls using its local COM runtime. The COM runtime checks the system registry for the class of the object being accessed. If the registry indicates that the class is defined in the registry of a remote machine, the local COM runtime contacts the COM runtime on the remote machine and requests that it perform the creation of the remote object or invocation of its methods.

The remote COM runtime carries out the request if the request is allowed by the system's security policy. This policy typically defaults to the Windows NT security policy, but may be tailored and made more restrictive for a particular application. Figure 19.7 summarizes

DCOM's operation. Note that the Service Control Manager (SCM) is an element of the COM runtime that supports the location and execution of COM servers.

The COM runtime processes on separate machines communicate with each other using an RPC mechanism referred to as *Object RPC* or *ORPC*. ORPC is based on Microsoft RPC, which is essentially DCE RPC. ORPC may be configured to use a number of transport protocols, but works best with UDP. Because most firewalls block UDP, it is necessary to use TCP with ORPC to build distributed applications that work over the Internet.

Although DCOM is a Microsoft product, it is an open standard and has been ported to other platforms, such as UNIX. Microsoft intends DCOM to be a cross-platform solution for distributed application development. So far it has received a high level of acceptance by Windows users, but it has had only mediocre popularity among users of cross-platform applications.

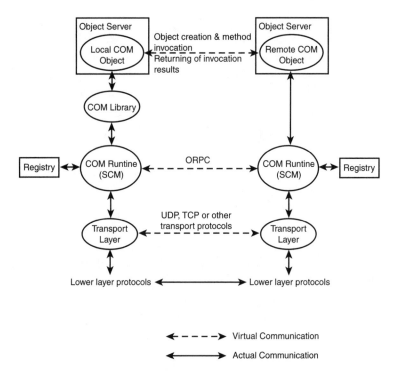

FIGURE 19.7

DCOM enables COM objects to be used as building blocks of distributed systems.

One of the prominent features of DCOM is its application support. DCOM security integrates with and extends the Windows NT security model. It allows access control decisions to be made with a fine level of granularity. For example, it is possible to specify whether one object is allowed to create or invoke the methods of another.

DCOM also provides strong and flexible communication security. A variety of encryption mechanisms may be used to protect information as it is transmitted from one COM object to another. Windows 2000 extends these encryption capabilities to Kerberos-based authentication, encryption, and access control. Kerberos is a very strong security protection mechanism developed at the Massachusetts Institute of Technology. Information on Kerberos may be found at `http://www.ov.com/misc/krb-faq.html`.

The Common Object Request Broker Architecture (CORBA)

The *Common Object Request Broker Architecture (CORBA)* provides another approach to building distributed systems. CORBA, like DCOM but unlike DCE, is object-oriented. It allows objects on one computer to invoke the methods of objects on other computers. CORBA, unlike DCOM, is an open standards solution and is not tied to any particular operating system vendor. Because of this, CORBA is a great choice for building distributed object-oriented applications.

CORBA makes use of objects that are accessible via *Object Request Brokers (ORBs)*. ORBs are used to connect objects to one another across a network. An object on one computer (client object) invokes the methods of an object on another computer (server object) via an ORB.

The client's interface to the ORB is a stub that is written in the *Interface Definition Language (IDL)*. The stub is a local proxy for a remote object. The IDL provides a programming language-independent mechanism for describing the methods of an object.

The ORB's interface to the server is through an IDL skeleton. The skeleton provides the ORB with a language-independent mechanism for accessing the remote object.

Remote method invocation under CORBA takes place as follows: The client object invokes the methods of the IDL stub corresponding to a remote object. The IDL stub communicates the method invocations to the ORB. The ORB invokes the corresponding methods of the IDL skeleton. The IDL skeleton invokes the methods of the remote server object implementation. The server object returns the result of the method invocation via the IDL skeleton, which passes the result back to the ORB. The ORB passes the result back to the IDL stub, and the IDL stub returns the result back to the client object. Figure 19.8 summarizes this process.

Figure 19.8 shows the ORB as being a single layer across the client and server hosts. This is the standard way in which the ORB is viewed. A number of possible ORB implementations are possible. For example, peer ORBs could be implemented on the client and server hosts, or a central system ORB could be implemented on a local server. Other ORB implementations are also possible.

Now that you know how CORBA works, you may be wondering how it is used to develop distributed applications. The answer is that CORBA provides a flexible approach to distributed application development. It provides a finer level of granularity in the implementation of client/server systems. Instead of relying on monolithic clients and servers (as is the case of the browsers and servers of the Web), both clients and servers can be distributed over several hosts.

The advantages of CORBA over other distributed application integration approaches are significant:

◆ It provides a true object-oriented approach to developing distributed applications.

◆ It is language-independent. It can be used to connect objects that are developed in any programming language, as long as an IDL stub for the objects can be furnished.

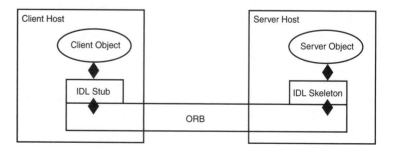

FIGURE 19.8

The CORBA ORB provides connectivity between client and server objects.

◆ It is recognized as an international standard and is supported by nearly all major software vendors.

Interoperability Between ORBs

There may be multiple ORB implementations from different vendors within the same network that are used in the same distributed application. A client may simultaneously use two different ORBs to access multiple objects, or one ORB to access an object that is serviced by another ORB. Because multiple ORBs may exist within the same application, it is necessary that the ORBs be able to communicate with each other.

The *General Inter-ORB Protocol (GIOP)* is the common interface that is used to support communication between ORBs. The GIOP specifies a syntax and a set of message formats for inter-ORB communication. Because ORBs may be implemented on networks that use a variety of transport protocols, such as TCP/IP, IPX, or SNA, the protocol used to transport information between ORBs is not specified in GIOP.

The *Internet Inter-ORB Protocol (IIOP)* is used to map the GIOP to the TCP/IP protocol suite. Different ORBs can communicate with each other across TCP/IP networks using GIOP and IIOP, as shown in Figure 19.9.

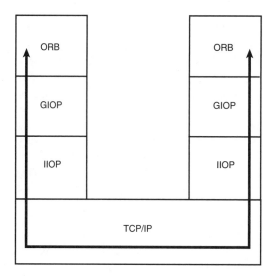

FIGURE 19.9

Different ORBs communicate using GIOP and IIOP across TCP/IP networks.

In addition to GIOP and IIOP, CORBA also provides *Environment-Specific Inter-ORB Protocols (ESIOPs)*, which are used to connect legacy applications to distributed applications that are CORBA-compliant. Legacy systems use ESIOPs to communicate with ORBs. ESIOPs, like the GIOP, need to be tailored to their networking environment. The *DCE Common Inter-ORB Protocol (DCE-CIOP)* is used with ESIOP to integrate DCE applications with CORBA applications.

Java Remote Method Invocation

Java RMI enables objects that execute in one JVM to invoke the methods of objects that execute in other JVMs. These other JVMs may execute as a separate process on the same computer or on other remote computers. The object making the method invocation is referred to as the *client object*. The object whose methods are being invoked is referred to as the *server object*. The client object is also referred to as the *local object* and is said to execute locally. The server object is also referred to as the *remote object* and is said to execute remotely.

In Java RMI, a client object never references a remote object directly. Instead, it references a remote interface that is implemented by the remote object. The use of remote interfaces enables server objects to differentiate between their local and remote interfaces.

For example, an object could provide methods to objects that execute within the same JVM that are in addition to those that it provides via its remote interface. The use of remote interfaces also allows server objects to present different types of remote access services. For example, a server object can provide both a remote administration interface and a remote user interface.

Finally, the use of remote interfaces allows the server object's position within its class hierarchy to be abstracted away from the manner in which it is used. This enables client objects to be compiled using the remote interface alone, eliminating the need for server class files to be locally present during the compilation process.

In addition to remote interfaces, the model makes use of stub and skeleton classes in much the same way as CORBA. *Stub classes* serve as local proxies for the remote objects. *Skeleton classes* act as remote

proxies. Both stub and skeleton classes implement the remote interface of the server object. The client interface invokes the methods of
the local stub object. The local stub communicates these method
invocations to the remote skeleton, and the remote skeleton invokes
the methods of the server object. The server object returns a value to
the skeleton object. The skeleton object returns the value to the stub
object, and the stub object returns the value to the client. Figure
19.10 summarizes the use of stubs and skeletons.

If you are a CORBA programmer, you'll notice the conspicuous
absence of IDL and ORBs in Figure 19.10. (IDL and ORBs are
required by CORBA because it is language-neutral.) The stub and
skeleton classes used by Java RMI are automatically generated by the
rmic compiler from the server object. (The rmic compiler is a standard JDK tool.) These classes are true Java classes and do not rely on
an external IDL. No ORB is required because the Java RMI is a pure
Java solution. The client object and stub communicate using normal
Java method invocations, and so do the skeleton and the server
object. The stub and the skeleton communicate via a remote reference layer.

The remote reference layer supports communication between the
stub and the skeleton. If the stub communicates with more than one
skeleton instance (not currently supported), the stub object communicates with the multiple skeletons in a multicast fashion. The RMI
API currently only defines classes that support unicast communication between a stub and a single skeleton. The remote reference layer
may also be used to activate server objects when they are invoked
remotely.

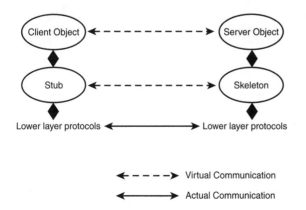

FIGURE 19.10

The use of stubs and skeletons in the Java distributed object model.

The remote reference layer on the local host communicates with the remote reference layer on the remote host via the RMI transport layer. The transport layer sets up and manages connections between the address spaces of the local and remote hosts, keeps track of objects that can be accessed remotely, and determines when connections have timed out and become inoperable. The transport layer uses TCP sockets, by default, to communicate between the local and remote hosts. However, other transport layer protocols, such as SSL and UDP, may also be used.

Figure 19.11 illustrates the layering used to implement Java RMI. In this expanded view of the model, the client object invokes the methods of the local stub of the server object. The local stub uses the remote reference layer to communicate with the server skeleton. The remote reference layer uses the transport layer to set up a connection between the local and remote address spaces and to obtain a reference to the skeleton object.

In order for a server object to be accessed remotely, it must register itself with the remote registry. It does this by associating its object instance with a name. The remote registry is a process that runs on the server host and is created by running the rmiregistry program, another JDK tool.

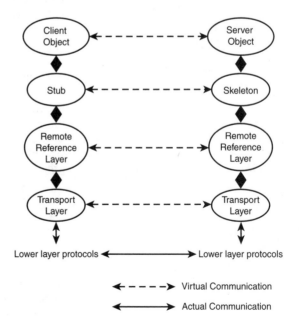

FIGURE 19.11
Java RMI uses a layered approach to supporting distributed object communication.

The remote registry maintains a database of server objects and the names by which these objects can be referenced. When a client creates an instance of a server object's interface (that is, its local stub), the transport layer on the local host communicates with the transport layer on the remote host to determine if the referenced object exists and to find out the type of interface the referenced object implements. The server-side transport layer uses the remote registry to access this information. A separate process, referred to as the Java RMI Activation System Daemon, supports the activation of remote objects. The Java RMI Activation System Daemon is run by executing the `rmid` program of the JDK on the remote system.

Passing Arguments and Returning Values

In order for a client object to pass an argument as part of a remote method invocation, the type of the argument must be *serializable*. A serializable type is a primitive or reference type that can be written to and read from a stream. In practice, all Java primitive types are serializable, and so are all classes and interfaces that implement or extend the `Serializable` interface. The `Serializable` interface is defined in the `java.io` package.

Object references are used within the JVM that contains the object. When a local object is passed as an argument to a remote method invocation, the local object is copied from the local JVM to the remote JVM. Only non-static and non-transient field variables are copied.

When a remote object is passed via a remote method invocation within the JVM that contains the object, a reference to the remote object is passed.

When an object is returned by a server object as the result of a remote method invocation, the object is copied from the remote JVM to the local JVM.

> **NOTE**
>
> **Marshaling** The process of serializing and passing objects used as arguments to a remote method invocation is referred to as *marshaling*.

TRANSACTION PROCESSING

A transaction is a group of related operations that are to be performed as a single unit. A transaction is an all-or-nothing occurrence. Either all operations in a transaction are successfully performed or all the operations are aborted. Transaction processing is the process of implementing transactions in a system context.

Transactions are important in many distributed applications. They ensure that critical sets of operations are performed in a reliable manner, support coordination and synchronization among distributed objects, and enable systems to recover from partial or total failures.

Consider an electronic commerce transaction in which a person orders and purchases a product over the Web. Several things must happen before the transaction is completed:

◆ The customer must select a product or set of products.

◆ The customer must identify his or her shipping address.

◆ The customer must pay for the products via credit card.

◆ The customer's payment must be authorized by the customer's credit card company.

If any of the above operations are not performed, the transaction is aborted.

Transactions processing is supported by transaction monitors, which are programs that monitor transactions to ensure that they are completed in a successful manner. Successful transactions are committed or rolled forward by the transaction monitor. Unsuccessful transactions are aborted or rolled backward.

The JTA is an API that specifies the interfaces between the objects involved in a distributed transaction and a *transaction manager*. The transaction manager provides services for identifying transactions, managing resources used in transactions, coordinating between the objects involved in a transaction, and managing the context of a transaction. The transaction manager interfaces with an application server, resource manager, communication resource manager, and application program. The application server provides the services used by the application and transaction monitoring support. The resource manager provides resources used by the transaction, such as database services. The communication resource manager manages incoming and outgoing transaction requests. The application program is the client or server program on whose behalf the transaction is performed.

The JTS is an implementation of a JTS transaction manager. It provides transaction management services to application managers, resource managers, communication resource managers, and application programs. The JTS also implements the Object Transaction Service (OTS) version 1.1 of the Object Management Group. The OTS provides transaction services in support of CORBA objects.

ENTERPRISE JAVABEANS

Enterprise JavaBeans provides an infrastructure for deploying server-side components. These components are JavaBeans that have been extended to support distributed enterprise applications. They are used as platform-independent building blocks for developing application services.

One or more components run in an application server. The application server provides services that are used by the components to provide their applications. These services are supplied in different ways by different application server products (for example, IBM TXSeries, and BEA Tuxedo). Enterprise JavaBeans provides a common set of Java interfaces for accessing the services provided by vendor-specific products. It enables server components that are written in Java to be portable across application servers. The EJB environment provides a common platform for developing beans that takes care of mapping EJB services to those provided by different vendor products.

The EJB platform provides a standard set of APIs (from the Java 2 platform and extension APIs) for developing server-side distributed application components. These APIs include the following:

◆ EJB API—Provides access to the EJB platform and supports the EJB component model.

◆ Java IDL—Supports CORBA objects.

◆ Java Server Pages—Supports dynamic HTML generation.

◆ JDBC—Provides database access.

◆ JMS—Supports asynchronous messaging services.

◆ JNDI—Provides access to naming and directory services.

◆ JTA—Provides a standard API for implementing transaction management services.

◆ JTS—Supports distributed transaction management.

◆ RMI—Provides remote method invocation between distributed objects.

◆ Servlets—Supports HTTP session management.

The EJB platform and the above services enable application components to be developed in Java to work in distributed environments as diverse as DCE, CORBA, DCOM, and Java RMI.

The EJB component model is a server-side extension of the client-side JavaBeans component model. In the EJB model, components execute within containers. Components are an encapsulated application software building blocks that are the server-side analog of JavaBeans. Containers provide an execution context for combining one or more components into an application. Containers also support the management of the components that they contain. Figure 19.12 shows the relationship between components, containers, the EJB platform, and application servers.

Components have properties which can be used to tailor and customize them for different applications. These properties are the server-side analog of those supported by client-side JavaBeans. For example, a credit card authorization component may have properties that allow it to be tailored for use with different credit card systems.

Containers provide components with basic execution services:

◆ Thread creation and management

◆ Object activation, persistence, access, and destruction

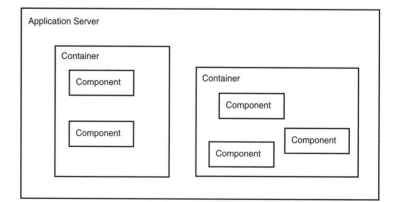

FIGURE 19.12

The relationship between components, containers, and their surrounding environment.

◆ Security

◆ Resource management

◆ Connection management

◆ Transaction support

Because containers depend on application servers to provide these services, application servers must provide a minimal standard set of services to these components. This minimal standard set of services is embodied in the EJB platform. Application servers that support the EJB platform are referred to as EJB servers.

EJB components are also referred to as enterprise beans. Beans come in two basic flavors: entity beans and session beans. Entity beans are beans that are persistent (in other words, retain state) across multiple client sessions. Session beans are beans that are limited to a single client session. Session beans are also referred to as transient beans. For example, in a Web-based application, a session bean would provide services to a browser client throughout the duration of an HTTP connection. An entity bean would retain information that persists across HTTP connections.

All client interaction with a bean is mediated by the bean's container. Containers provide two interfaces, EJB Home and EJB Object, through which clients access beans. These interfaces are referred to as bean wrapper interfaces.

The EJB Home interface enables beans to be created, accessed, and destroyed. The EJB Home interface is made available to clients via a naming and directory service. Containers automatically register EJB Home interfaces with naming and directory services using JNDI. Clients find EJB Home interfaces using JNDI location services. The client then uses the EJB Home interface to create or find an EJB Object interface.

The EJB Object interface provides access to the application-specific methods of the enterprise bean. Other bean methods, such as those used by EJB Home to manage the bean, are hidden. The EJB Object acts as a wrapper for the enterprise bean and mediates all application-specific method invocations. When a method is invoked via the EJB Object interface, the method invocation is passed to the bean's container to determine what security, transaction, resource, or other services need to be provided to support the method invocation.

Access to EJB Objects is supported through RMI. Secure access may be accomplished by using RMI with SSL. Support for CORBA, DCOM, and other distributed object protocols may also be provided via protocol bridges.

NAMING SERVICES

Naming services map names to network objects and are essential to network communication. Imagine using the phone without a phone book or a directory information service. Or worse, imagine using the Internet without the Domain Name Service (DNS). The phone book is an example of a naming service. It maps people's names and addresses to their phone numbers. DNS is another name service. It maps computer names to their IP addresses. Other naming services are used with distributed objects, such as those provided with Jini, Java Remote Method Invocation (RMI), and CORBA.

Naming services are said to *bind* an object name with the object being named. A *context* is a set of name-to-object bindings. This terminology is commonly used in the DNS, RMI, and CORBA naming services, but not in naming services such as the phone book. A naming service *lookup* results in the named object being retrieved based on its name. The process of using a name to look up a named object is *name resolution*.

Names may be atomic, compound, or composite. *Atomic* names are indivisible names that identify an object. For example, the name index.html names a file on my Web server. *Compound* names are names that consist of one or more atomic names. For example, the relative path /java/certification/index.html names a file on my Web server. *Composite* names are names that are composed of multiple naming services. For example, the URL http:// www.jaworski.com/java/certification/index.html consists of a protocol identifier (http), a DNS name (www.jaworski.com), and a file system path (/java/certification/index.html).

Directory services build upon and extend naming services. Directory services usually organize name spaces in a hierarchical fashion and include attributes that provide additional information about named objects. For example, consider the DOS and UNIX file systems. File and directory names are mapped to file and directory objects. These objects are organized in a hierarchical fashion, with subdirectories and files extending the directories in which they are contained. Size, date, and access attributes provide additional information about the files and directories of the file system.

Network directory services provide information about the enterprise network, computers, devices (such as printers), network services and applications, users, security information, and other objects. Examples of directory services include the International Standards Organization's X.500 directory service, the Novell NetWare Directory Service (NDS), and Sun's Network Information Service Plus (NIS+). NDS and NIS+ are both proprietary protocols.

Lightweight Directory Access Protocol

The *Lightweight Directory Access Protocol (LDAP)* is a popular protocol for accessing directory services. It was developed at the University of Michigan as a front end for the X.500 directory service, but it has grown to replace X.500 servers with its own directory servers. Its principal advantages are that it is non-proprietary, runs over TCP/IP networks, and is a manageable subset of the X.500 international standard. LDAP version 3 is the current version and is described in RFC 2251.

LDAP's popularity stems from X.500's shortcomings. X.500 provides the basis for large directory services that are distributed over wide-area networks; LDAP scales X.500 services to the needs of large enterprises. X.500 requires the use of the higher-level OSI protocol layers; LDAP works over TCP/IP. LDAP simplifies the management of X.500 directories, making these directories globally accessible via the Internet.

LDAP directories consist of individual *entries* that contain information about an object, such as a person. Each entry consists of a set of attributes. Each attribute consists of a type and a value. Figure 19.13 provides an example of an LDAP entry.

LDAP entries are organized in a hierarchical fashion. For example, an LDAP server could contain information about the Federal Government, one part of which is the Department of Defense (DOD). DOD directories can be organized into the Army, Navy, and Air Force, as shown in Figure 19.14. These directories are refined into smaller organizational units until all Federal Government employees are included in the directory name space.

FIGURE 19.13

An LDAP entry describes an object.

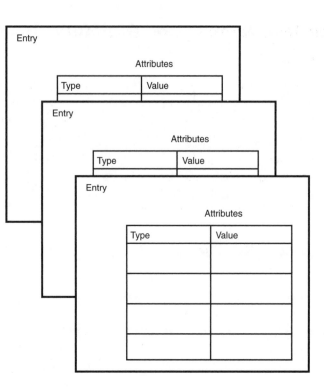

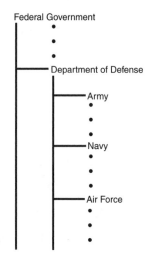

FIGURE 19.14

LDAP directories are organized in a hierarchical structure.

The Java Naming and Directory Interface

The Java Naming and Directory Interface (JNDI) is an API for developing naming and directory service clients that work with multiple naming and directory services. These services are implemented by specific service providers, such as LDAP or NIS+. Figure 19.15 shows how the JNDI API fits into this architecture. A Java application uses the classes and interfaces of the JNDI API to access local naming and directory service capabilities, which are provided through a *naming manager*. The naming manager provides access to locally installed service provider implementations through the JNDI Service Provider Interface. These service provider implementations, such as LDAP and NDS, provide access to enterprise naming services.

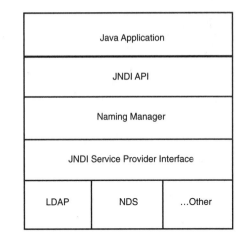

FIGURE 19.15
The JNDI architecture is built upon existing naming and directory services.

THE JAVA MANAGEMENT API

With the growing reliance by companies and other organizations on their enterprise networks, the management of these networks and the systems and services they support has become critical. Network administrators use a wide array of system monitoring and management tools to ensure continuous reliable operation. These tools are designed to detect and respond to potential problems that could affect service continuity. However, with the heterogeneous nature of modern networks, these tools run on a variety of operating system platforms, do not operate well together, and sometimes conflict.

The Java Management API (JMAPI) provides an integrated solution for system, network, and service management. Because of Java's platform-independent nature, it eliminates the need to use several nonintegrated, platform-specific system and network management tools to manage the diverse computing resources that are common to medium-to-large-sized enterprise networks.

Overview of System, Network, and Service Management

Imagine that you are responsible for the management of a medium-to-large-scale enterprise network. Your primary responsibilities are to keep the network up and running, keep its systems operational, make sure that its services are available, and keep its users happy. Your users demand the latest Internet and intranet services from the moment that they read about them on a Web page or in a magazine. Continuous, reliable operation is expected 24 hours a day, seven days a week.

In a typical medium-to-large-scale enterprise network, you'll find thousands of users, some quite sophisticated and some not. These users will have workstations, PCs, Macintoshes, X terminals, and dumb terminals. They will use several flavors of UNIX, all versions of Windows and MacOS, Netware, Linux, DOS, and anything else that's available. Your networks will run TCP/IP, IPX, NetBEUI, AppleTalk, and other protocols. Your enterprise will maintain legacy systems that run on DEC VAXes and IBM minicomputers and mainframes. You will interface with customers, vendors, and suppliers via the Internet, dedicated lines, and dial-up connections. You'll have one or more firewalls, several routers, a slew of network hubs, and all sorts of system, network, and service management tools.

The tools that you'll use to manage your network will run on a variety of platforms, mostly UNIX and Windows. These tools will be independent. They will not know about or interoperate with each other, and will sometimes conflict when run concurrently.

Some of these tools will be system-specific. They'll let you manage the legacy applications that you have running on DEC and IBM minicomputers and mainframes. They'll tell you that you need to change disk volumes, do a backup, or perform some application-specific maintenance.

Some tools will be protocol- and service-specific. You'll use them to manage specific protocols, such as TCP/IP, IPX, and SNA. They'll tell you what your network traffic load is like, when you have interruptions in service, and what network components are malfunctioning. You'll also have a sniffer or two to tell you what these other tools can't. Service-specific tools will tell you what types of hits your Web and FTP servers are taking, what your email situation looks like, and how file and print servers are behaving.

Some tools try to be integrated network management solutions, at least from the vendor's viewpoint. You'll run HP OpenView, Microsoft's System Management Server, and possibly one or two other management tools. In the end, you'll need a chair that rolls easily in order to move between the computers that run each of your system management tools.

The JMAPI Solution

The goal of JMAPI is to leverage Java's platform independence to provide a set of system management building blocks that can be used to integrate a diverse set of system and network management tools under a common look and feel.

JMAPI enables you to run all management applications from a Java-enabled browser. Not only do you have a common, cross-platform user interface, but the organization of this interface is governed by the recommendations and standards of the JMAPI User Interface Guide. This guide describes a standard approach to developing browser-based interfaces for use with JMAPI.

JMAPI also provides a common architecture for managing systems, networks, and services. This architecture, referred to as the Java management architecture, is shown in Figure 19.16.

Administrators use Java-enabled Web browsers to manage the systems, networks, and services of a network. The browsers interface with managed object servers that manage one or more appliances within their domain. An appliance is any system that is to be managed. It can be a network computer, PC, workstation, or any other type of computer or device that is capable of running the JVM.

Agents are objects that execute on appliances and communicate with managed object servers. Agent objects maintain information about the configuration and status of the appliances they manage, and they report this information to managed object servers. The agent objects provide methods that allow managed object servers to control and reconfigure their appliances. The agent software can be dynamically updated and is installed on appliances as Java classes that are loaded from Web servers.

FIGURE 19.16
The Java management architecture ties
together all of the elements of a modern
enterprise.

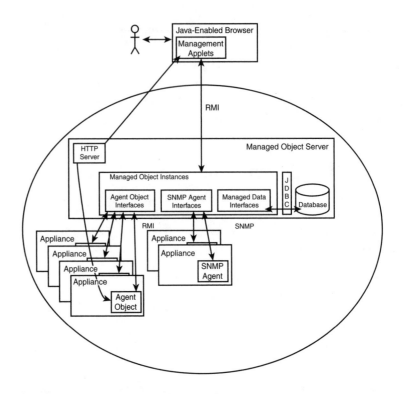

Managed object servers are the link between the browser interface
and the managed appliances of an enterprise. They consist of Java
applications that provide the following capabilities:

◆ Appliance configuration and status reporting—Appliance configuration and status information that was retrieved from agent
objects are both available as managed objects that can be
browsed by administrators.

◆ Control and configuration of appliances—The managed
objects provide methods that can be used to control the appliances or modify their configuration data.

◆ SNMP agent interfaces—These interfaces are presented to
administrators as browsable, managed objects.

◆ Managed data interfaces—These data interfaces enable management information to be maintained by relational database
servers.

◆ Database connectivity through JDBC—Managed object servers use JDBC to interface with relational database servers.

◆ A Web server—HTTP servers make management applets available to the browsers used by administrators. These applets provide GUI controls that are used to browse and display managed objects. The HTTP servers are also used to distribute agent objects throughout the domains of the managed object servers.

The Java Management API and architecture help system and network administrators solve the problem of managing multiple heterogeneous components. By leveraging Java's platform-independence and the classes and interfaces of JMAPI, agent software can be quickly developed and deployed to any appliance that is capable of running the JVM. New and updated software can be easily distributed via the Web server components of the managed object servers. These same Web servers provide the management applets that are used by administrators to monitor and control network resources as managed objects.

The managed object servers create managed object abstractions that enable resources to be managed without knowing the details of the object's implementation. This separation between management and implementation allows administrators to concentrate on the problem at hand. Resources can be monitored, reconfigured, and controlled independently of the protocols, vendor packages, or hardware and software platforms used to provide these resources.

By using a common browser interface, administrators are able to take advantage of consistent, intuitive GUI controls for managing all system and network resources. By providing access to all managed resources as managed objects, administrators can use the single browser interface for all management functions. Administrators no longer have to move from station to station to use the tools that are independently implemented at each one. In addition, the single browser interface can be accessed via any computer that supports a Java-enabled Web browser. When an administrator is paged in the middle of the night, he can securely access the managed object server by launching his browser from home, a hotel, a coffee shop, or anywhere.

CHAPTER SUMMARY

KEY TERMS

- HTML
- URL
- HTTP
- Keep-alive
- CGI
- Servlet
- SQL
- JDBC
- JavaBlend
- OQL
- DCE
- COM
- DCOM
- ActiveX
- RMI
- CORBA
- IIOP
- Stub
- Skeleton
- Transaction
- Transaction Processing
- Transaction Monitor
- Application Server
- Enterprise Bean
- Directory Service
- LDAP
- JMAPI

This chapter covered the use of technologies that are used to build distributed applications. Knowledge of these technologies is required to design distributed Java applications. The certification exam expects you to be familiar with these technologies and contains a number of questions that require you to make design decisions based on this knowledge. The following review and exam questions will test your knowledge of these technologies and will help you to determine whether your knowledge of them is sufficient to answer the questions you'll encounter in the certification exam.

APPLY YOUR KNOWLEDGE

Review Questions

1. What is the connection keep-alive feature of HTTP 1.1?

2. What is the Common Gateway Interface?

3. What advantages do servlets have over CGI programs?

4. What is the purpose of SQL?

5. How does JDBC differ from ODBC?

6. What is OQL?

7. What are the primary differences between RMI and CORBA?

8. What is IIOP used for?

9. What is the difference between a stub and a skeleton?

10. What is the purpose of a transaction monitor?

11. What is the relationship between an EJB component, EJB container, and an application server?

12. What is the purpose of JNDI?

Exam Questions

1. Which of the following may be found in a Web page?

    A. HTML

    B. HTTP

    C. URL

    D. JavaScript

2. What is the well-known port of HTTP?

    A. 21

    B. 25

    C. 80

    D. 137

3. One of the restrictions of the applet sandbox is that an applet is not allowed to make a network connection to a host other than the one from which it was loaded. Which of the following may be used to allow an applet to connect to other network hosts?

    A. A servlet that runs on the applet host and proxies connections to other network hosts.

    B. A signed applet that may be trusted to establish network connections to other hosts.

    C. The applet run as an enterprise bean.

    D. HTTP 1.1-compatible Web server.

4. Suppose that you use an applet that uses a large number of classes. What can you do to shorten the time it takes for Web browsers to load your applet?

    A. Compile the applet using a Java 2 compiler.

    B. Package the applet's classes in a JAR file.

    C. Package the applet's classes as a ZIP file.

    D. Use an HTTP 1.1-compatible Web server.

APPLY YOUR KNOWLEDGE

5. Suppose that a database server does not support a pure JDBC driver, but it does support an ODBC driver. How can you access the database server using JDBC?

   A. Use SQL.

   B. Use JNDI.

   C. Use the JDBC-ODBC bridge driver.

   D. Use Java RMI.

6. Which distributed object technology is most appropriate for systems that consist entirely of Java objects?

   A. RMI

   B. CORBA

   C. DCOM

   D. DCE

7. Which distributed object technology is most appropriate for systems that consist of objects written in different languages and that execute on different operating system platforms?

   A. RMI

   B. CORBA

   C. DCOM

   D. DCE

8. Which of the following are used by Java RMI?

   A. stubs

   B. skeletons

   C. ORBs

   D. IIOP

9. Which of the following Java technologies support transaction processing?

   A. RMI

   B. JTS

   C. JMAPI

   D. JTA

10. Which of the following are true about EJB components, containers, and application servers?

    A. Components run in containers.

    B. Containers are hosted by application servers.

    C. Containers run in components.

    D. Application servers run in containers.

11. Which objects would you find in a directory service?

    A. An EJB Home interface

    B. An EJB component

    C. The EJB API

    D. An EJB Object interface

12. Which of the following is a Java API for managing enterprise services, systems, and networks.

    A. JTA

    B. Java Server Pages

    C. JMAPI

    D. JDBC

APPLY YOUR KNOWLEDGE

Answers to Review Questions

1. HTTP 1.1's connection keep-alive feature allows the TCP connection between a browser and a Web server to remain open throughout multiple HTTP requests and responses. This significantly improves the overall performance of browser-server communication.

2. The Common Gateway Interface is a standard for communication between Web servers and external programs.

3. Servlets are written in Java and are platform-independent. Servlets run under the JVM and may be secured using the Java sandbox. Servlets run as threads and may be preloaded to improve their performance.

4. SQL is used to define the structure of relational databases, update their contents, and perform queries that retrieve data from the databases.

5. ODBC is the industry-standard interface by which database clients connect to database servers. JDBC is a pure Java solution that does not follow the ODBC standard. However, there is a bridge between JDBC and ODBC that allows JDBC to access databases that support ODBC.

6. OQL is a database query language that is based on SQL and supports the adding, retrieving, querying, and invocation of objects.

7. RMI and CORBA are both distributed object technologies that support the creation, activation, and invocation of objects. CORBA supports a language-independent approach to developing and deploying distributed objects. RMI is a Java-specific approach.

8. IIOP is used to support communication between object request brokers via TCP/IP.

9. A stub is a proxy for a remote object that runs on the client computer. A skeleton is a proxy for a remote object that runs on the server. Stubs forward a client's remote method invocations (and their associated arguments) to skeletons, which forward them on to the appropriate server objects. Skeletons return the results of server method invocations to clients via stubs.

10. Transaction monitors are programs that monitor transactions to ensure that they are completed in a successful manner. They ensure that successful transactions are committed and that unsuccessful transactions are aborted.

11. An EJB component is an enterprise bean that runs in a container. The container provides a platform-independent execution environment for the bean. Containers are hosted on EJB-compliant application servers. The vendor-specific application servers provide a common set of services to the containers via the EJB framework.

12. JNDI provides a platform-independent Java interface to naming and directory services, such as LDAP, NDS, and Active Directory.

Answers to Exam Questions

1. A, C, and D   HTTP is a protocol that supports the request and transfer of Web pages.

2. C   HTTP uses port 80 as a default.

3. A and B   A server-side proxy will work with all Java-enabled Web browsers. Signed applets will only work with JDK 1.1-capable Web browsers.

APPLY YOUR KNOWLEDGE

4. B and D   The use of JAR files and HTTP 1.1 can speed up applet delivery and loading.

5. C   The JDBC-ODBC bridge driver provides connectivity between JDBC and ODBC.

6. A   RMI is the most appropriate distributed object technology for pure Java applications.

7. B   CORBA is the most appropriate object technology for systems that use objects written in different languages and support a variety of operating system platforms.

8. A and B   RMI makes use of stubs and skeletons. ORBs and IIOP are used with CORBA.

9. B and D   JTA defines an API for transaction management. JTS provides an implementation of this API.

10. A and B   Components run in containers which are hosted by application servers.

11. A   EJB Home interfaces are placed in a directory service to facilitate access to an EJB component. The EJB Home interface is used to obtain access to an EJB Object interface. EJB components are never accessed directly, but only through their EJB Home and EJB Object interfaces.

12. A   JMAPI is a Java API for managing enterprise services, systems, and networks.

Suggested Readings and Resources

Java Unleashed 1.2 by Jamie Jaworski (Sams, 1998).

This chapter helps you to prepare for the exam by covering the following objectives:

Be able to state the security constraints and trade-offs that affect a Java application architecture.

Know how to use available Java technologies design a three (or *n*) tier Java architecture for use over an unsecured public network such as the Internet.

Be able to evaluate a proposed (or existing) Java solution architecture and make recommendations (based on Java 2 security features) to provide or increase security.

Know how to use Java 2 distributed object technologies to design a three (or *n*) tier architecture for an extranet application.

CHAPTER 20

Securing Distributed Applications

STUDY STRATEGIES

As you read through this chapter, you should concentrate on the following key items:

▶ How the applet sandbox works and how its security approach has changed in Java 2

▶ How message digests, digital signatures, and digital certificates are used to support authentication

▶ How SSL is used to improve the security of TCP/IP-based applications

▶ How firewalls work

▶ How HTTP tunneling is used to pass other protocols through a firewall

▶ How virtual private networks allow geographically-dispersed sites to communicate securely through the Internet

CHAPTER INTRODUCTION

Security is important in almost any application—especially in those that are accessible to the Internet. You must have a basic understanding of Java's security capabilities to design Java-based applications. You must also be able to work with other non-Java security technologies, such as firewalls and virtual private networks. The certification exam recognizes the importance of security and contains a number of security-related questions. This chapter reviews the basics of Java security and covers non-Java security technologies, such as SSL, firewalls, and virtual private networks. Although it doesn't address all of the security considerations faced by a system architect (that's a book in itself), it does address the security issues that are covered by the certification exam.

JAVA SECURITY AND THE SANDBOX

One of the most appealing features of Java in its debut as a Web programming language was the comprehensive security built into the Java runtime environment. The Java sandbox provided a mechanism for untrusted code to be downloaded from the Web and executed in a secure manner. The sandboxes of JDK 1.0 and 1.1 had some holes, but Sun encouraged the Internet community to find those holes and then quickly fixed them. The security model implemented by the Java sandbox has been strengthened and at the same time made more flexible from JDK 1.0 to Java 2. In addition, Java 2 provides a number of security mechanisms that can be used within the sandbox.

Java 2 provides the capability to specify a security policy for both applets and applications. This capability gives software developers a great deal of flexibility in the functionality that they can incorporate into their applets and applications. At the same time, it provides users with total control over the access they allow to these programs. The configurable security policy of Java 2 allows Java software developers to provide the capabilities their users want, and enables users to limit those capabilities based on their degree of trust in the source of the Java software they execute.

The Evolution of the Sandbox

To understand how the configurable security policy works and why it is useful, it is helpful to trace the evolution of Java security. JDK 1.0 introduced the *sandbox* approach to applet security. In this approach, all standalone Java applications are trusted by default and are allowed unrestricted access to your system resources (file system, network, and other programs). Applets that are loaded over the network are, by default, untrusted and prevented from accessing your local file system and other programs. In addition, applets are only allowed to make network connections to the host from which they are loaded.

The objective of the JDK 1.0 sandbox is to protect users from malicious applets that are downloaded from the Web. With the exception of a few security holes (which were subsequently corrected) the JDK 1.0 sandbox met this objective. However, in blocking potentially hostile applet accesses, the 1.0 sandbox also removed useful applet capabilities. Figure 20.1 summarizes the operation of the JDK 1.0 sandbox.

In addition to extending the sandbox for signed applets, JDK 1.1 also allows the SecurityManager class to be subclassed to implement a custom security policy for standalone Java applications, such as those that load applets. If SecurityManager is overridden, the capabilities of standalone applications can be restricted. The capability to implement a custom SecurityManager is provided for software developers, but not for users. If a user runs a standalone Java application, it is executed with unrestricted privileges unless the application polices itself. The SecurityManager class is also the key to securing applets that are loaded by browsers. However, both Navigator (4.5 and earlier) and Internet Explorer (5 and earlier) provide a fixed, default SecurityManager. Signed applets may be given additional privileges based on user approval.

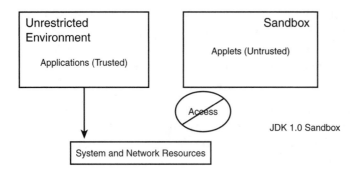

FIGURE 20.1

The JDK 1.0 sandbox.

The JDK 1.1 sandbox is designed to maintain the security of the JDK 1.0 approach while allowing certain applets to be designated as *trusted*. Trusted applets are allowed to perform accesses that exceed the bounds of the sandbox. The Security API of JDK 1.1 provides the capability to digitally sign an applet and then verify that signature before an applet is loaded and executed. This capability enables browsers to authenticate that an applet is signed by a trusted party and that it has not been modified since the time of its signature. Given this additional level of security assurance, signed applets are considered to be as trustworthy as standalone application programs (or more so). Figure 20.2 shows how the JDK 1.1 sandbox extends the JDK 1.0 sandbox.

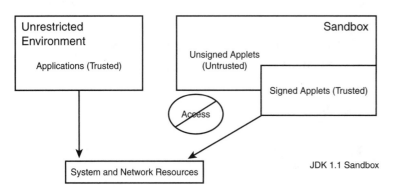

FIGURE 20.2

Security is improved and extended in JDK 1.1.

The JDK 1.1 security approach is a significant improvement to the JDK 1.0 approach because it enables applet designers to add useful capabilities such as reading from and writing to the local file system, launching programs, and advanced networking.

The problem with the JDK 1.1 approach is that it violates the security principle of *least privilege*. This principle states that an application should be given only those privileges that it needs to carry out its function and no more. According to least privilege, trusted applets and applications should be limited in the privileges they are allowed. Least privilege may be implemented in JDK 1.1, but it is the exception and not the norm. This is due to the fact that the JDK 1.1 security approach does not allow users to easily "fine tune" their security policies to give applications and applets only those privileges they require.

Java 2 introduced a security architecture for implementing least privilege. This architecture is based on the capability to specify a security policy that determines what accesses an applet or application is allowed, based on its source and on the identities of those who have signed the applet on application code.

The security policy feature of Java 2 enables users to specify the following types of policies easily by simply editing their local security policy files:

◆ Grant all applets from http://www.trusted.com/ permission to read files in the c:\tmp directory.

◆ Grant all applets (from any host) permission to listen on TCP ports greater than 1023.

◆ Grant all applets signed by Mary and Ted (hypothetical Java programmers) that are from http://www.trusted.com permission to read and write to files in the c:\tmp directory.

◆ Grant all applications loaded from the c:\trusted directory permission to set security properties.

The above policies are specified in a local security policy configuration file. Figure 20.3 shows how Java 2 extends the JDK 1.0 and 1.1 sandboxes using a configurable security policy.

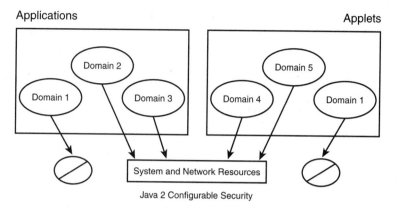

FIGURE 20.3
In Java 2, security policies can be configured by the user to implement least privilege.

The Contents of the Security Policy File

The policy file (system or user) consists of a series of statements, referred to as *grant entries*, that identify the permissions granted to code (applet or application) based on the location from which it is loaded and any signers of the code.

In Java 2, all code, whether it is an applet that is loaded from a remote host or an application from the local file system, is associated with a *code source*. This code source is defined by the URL from which the code is loaded and a list of signers of the code. These signers are identified by the names associated with the signer's public keys. These names are referred to as *aliases*. The aliases and keys are stored in a user's keystore, as shown in Figure 20.4.

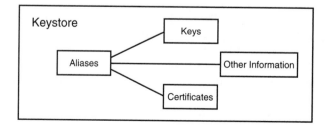

FIGURE 20.4
The keystore stores aliases, keys, certificates, and other information about entities.

A `keystore` is a repository for the aliases, certificates, public keys, and other information about the entities (organizations and individuals) that are recognized by a user. A user's `keystore` resides in the `.keystore` file located in the user's home directory.

The grant entries of the security policy identify a code source (URL and list of signers), followed by the permissions granted to that code source. The permissions (also referred to as *permission entries*) specify the actions that a code source may take with respect to a protected resource.

CRYPTOGRAPHY AND THE JAVA SECURITY API

The JDK 1.1 expands the security capabilities of JDK 1.02 to support application-level security. This new security support is provided by the Security API of the `java.security` packages and includes support for message digests, digital signatures, digital certificates, and key management. Java 2 extends the capabilities provided by JDK 1.1 to include support for X.509 version 3 certificates and added new tools for working with certificates. The *Java Cryptography Extension (JCE)* is a separate add-on to the Security API that implements cryptographic algorithms that are subject to U.S. export controls.

The application-level security controls provided by the Security API can be used to protect information from unauthorized modification and disclosure as it traverses the Internet. They can also be used to authenticate the contents of messages and files and the identities of applications and individuals.

Overview of Cryptography

Cryptography is the study of algorithms and protocols for securing messages during transmission and storage. However, cryptographic techniques can be applied to other applications, such as identity verification and data authentication.

One of the most fundamental applications of cryptography is to disguise a message so that it can only be read by those who know how to recover the original message content. *Encryption* is the process of disguising a message, and *decryption* is the process of recovering the original message. An encrypted message is referred to as *ciphertext*, and an unencrypted or decrypted message is referred to as *plaintext*. Figure 20.5 provides an overview of these concepts.

Although a number of approaches to encryption have been developed over the years, most current encryption algorithms are based on the use of secret keys. A *key* is a sequence of binary digits that are used to encrypt or decrypt data. In key-based cryptography, the encryption and decryption algorithms are publicly known. Data is encrypted using one key and decrypted using another (possibly the same) key. Figure 20.6 provides an overview of key-based encryption. It is important that the decryption key be kept secret, or else anyone will be able to use it to decrypt messages.

In some encryption algorithms, the encryption and decryption keys are the same, or the decryption key can be calculated from the encryption key within a useful time frame. These algorithms are known as *secret-key algorithms* or *symmetric algorithms*. Secret-key algorithms require the encryption key to be kept secret and require the sender and receiver to coordinate the use of their secret keys. The *Data Encryption Standard (DES)* is an example of a secret-key algorithm.

> **NOTE**
>
> **Applications of Cyptographic Techniques**   Cryptographic techniques are oriented toward the protection of messages. However, these techniques can be used to protect other forms of data, such as files, database records, and Java byte-codes.

FIGURE 20.5
Encryption and decryption.

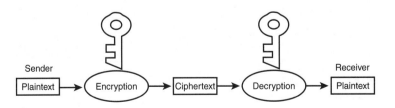

FIGURE 20.6
Key-based encryption.

Other encryption algorithms, known as *public-key algorithms* or *asymmetric algorithms*, are based on the use of separate encryption and decryption keys. Public-key algorithms require that it be computationally infeasible to calculate the decryption key from the encryption key. Because of this requirement, the encryption key can be made public without affecting the security of the encryption algorithm. Figure 20.7 shows how public-key cryptography works.

In public-key cryptosystems, each communicating entity (individual, organization, software program, and so on) is assigned a public key and a private key. Entities encrypt messages using the public key of the receiver. The receiver decrypts messages using his, her, or its private key. The public key cannot be used to determine the private key, so it does not need to be kept secret and can be openly published. Because of this feature and others, public-key encryption is very popular in open communication environments, such as the Internet. The RSA (Rivest, Shamir, Adelman) encryption algorithm is an example of a public-key algorithm.

Cryptographic techniques are not limited to preserving the secrecy of messages. They are also used to maintain message integrity and to verify the authenticity of a message. *One-way functions* are used in these applications. A one-way function is one that is easy to compute, but computationally infeasible to reverse. A real-life example of a one-way function is a shredding machine. It is easy to put a document in a shredder and produce paper strips, but it is very difficult to reverse the process. *Message digest functions* are also one-way functions. They compute values, referred to as *message digests* or *hash values*, that are used as fingerprints for messages. Good message digest functions have the following properties:

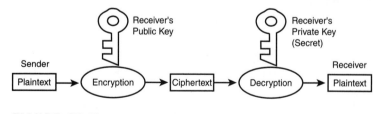

FIGURE 20.7
Public-key cryptography.

◆ Given a particular message digest value, it is computationally infeasible to compute a message that will produce that value under the message digest function.

◆ It is computationally infeasible to find two messages that yield the same message digest value under the message digest function.

Figure 20.8 illustrates the use of message digest functions. Note that there is nothing secret about a message digest function—it is publicly available and uses no keys. The MD5 and MD4 algorithms are examples of message digest algorithms.

A *digital signature* is a value that is computed from a message using a secret key. It indicates that the person who holds the secret key has verified that the contents of the message are correct and authentic. Digital signatures often use public-key encryption algorithms with a slight twist—a private key is used for encryption, and a public key is used for decryption. This approach is often implemented as follows:

Signature generation:

1. A message digest is computed.

2. The message digest is encrypted using the private key of a public/private key pair, producing the message's digital signature.

Signature verification:

1. The signature is decrypted using the public key of a public/private key pair, producing a message digest value.

2. The message digest value is compared with the message digest calculated from the original message.

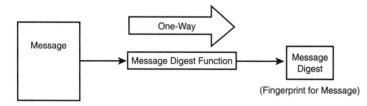

FIGURE 20.8
Message digest functions.

3. If both digest values match, the signature is authentic. Otherwise, either the signature or the message has been tampered with.

The preceding approach to signature generation/verification has the following features of real-world signatures, as well as other features that provide additional benefits:

◆ Unforgeability—Because the signer uses his private key and the private key is secret, only he can sign messages with that key.

◆ Verifiability—Because the signer's public key is openly available, anyone with access to the message and signature can verify that the message was signed by the signer and that neither the message nor signature have been altered.

◆ Single use—A signature is unique to a particular message. It is computationally infeasible to use a signature with another message.

◆ Non-repudiation—After a signer has signed a message and the message and signature have been sent to others, the signer cannot claim that he didn't sign the message. (Unless the signer can prove that his private key was stolen.)

◆ Sealing—A signed message is digitally sealed—it cannot be altered without invalidating the signature.

Figure 20.9 summarizes the mechanics of using digital signatures. An example of a digital signature algorithm is the National Institute of Standards and Technology's (NIST) Digital Signature Algorithm (DSA).

Digital certificates, based on digital signatures, are messages signed by a *certification authority* that certify the value of an entity's public key. The X.509 certificates of the International Standards Organization are a popular digital certificate format. Figure 20.10 illustrates the use of digital certificates.

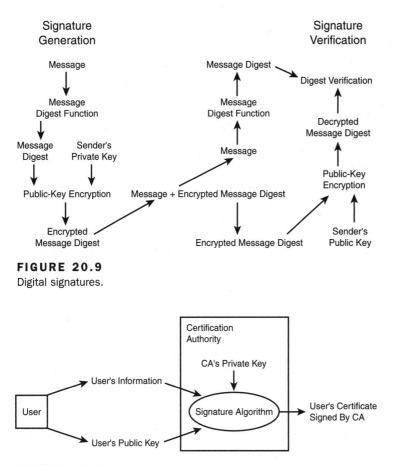

FIGURE 20.9
Digital signatures.

FIGURE 20.10
Digital certificates.

Central to the use of digital certificates is the notion of a *certification authority (CA)*. A certification authority is an entity that is trusted to verify that other entities are who they claim to be and that they use a particular public key with a particular public-key encryption algorithm. To obtain a certificate from a CA, you usually have to submit documentation that proves your identity or that of your organization. For example, the certification process helps prevent unauthorized individuals from setting up business on the Web using the identity of Microsoft or Bank of America.

EXAM TIP

Digital Certificates Make sure that you know what certificates are and how they are used. You can expect to see several questions about certificates on the certification exam.

In a large networking environment, such as the Internet, multiple levels of CAs may be required. In this case a high-level CA, such as Verisign, Inc., the U.S. Post Office, or the National Security Agency, may provide certificates for second-level CAs. These second-level CAs may then provide certificates for other organizations. Individual companies may themselves act as a certification authority for their employees. A hierarchical certification structure, like that shown in Figure 20.11, is the result. Certification of an entity at the leaves and branches of this hierarchy depends on the certification of entities at higher levels within the hierarchy. These hierarchical certification relationships are referred to as *certification chains*.

The Java 2 Cryptographic Architecture

The Java Security API provides a flexible framework for implementing cryptographic functions and other security controls. It contains the *hooks* for message digest and digital signature computation, key generation and management, and certificate processing. It includes standard algorithms (such as MD5 and DSA) that support these security functions, but leaves out encryption algorithms (because of the restrictions of U.S. export controls). Instead of promoting a small set of cryptographic algorithms, the Java Security API implements an approach where different cryptographic packages may be provided by vendors and then be plugged in and installed within the common Security API framework.

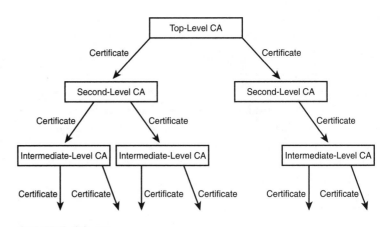

FIGURE 20.11
Certification authorities form a tree-like hierarchy.

Package Providers

The `Provider` class of `java.security` lays the foundation for using pluggable packages of cryptographic algorithms that support common functions such as message digest computation, digital signing, certificate processing, and key generation. The `Provider` class is a subclass of the `Properties` class of `java.util`. It encapsulates the notion of a cryptographic provider in terms of a provider name, version number, and information about the services provided by the provider.

The rationale for the `Provider` class is that it can be used to separate specific implementations of a cryptographic function (such as Company A's implementation of MD5, Company B's implementation of SHA-1, and Company C's implementation of MD5) from their provider-specific implementation. For example, several DSA packages may be available—some faster than others, some approved by the U.S. Department of Defense, and others supported by Internet standards.

> **NOTE**
>
> **A Default Provider**   Java 2 comes with a default provider, named "SUN," that includes an implementation of the MD5 and SHA-1 message digest algorithms, the DSA, and a DSA key generation capability.

The `Security` Class

The `Security` class provides a set of `static` methods that are used to manage providers. Providers are ranked in order of preference, with the most preferred provider receiving a rank of 1 and less preferred providers receiving a larger number. The methods of the `Security` class can be used to install providers, adjust their preference ranking, and retrieve information about the providers that are installed.

Cryptographic Engines

The Security API supports the notion of *cryptographic engines*. These engines are generic algorithm types, such as message digest, digital signature, and key generation, that support common cryptographic functions. The engines of the Security API include the `MessageDigest`, `Signature`, `KeyPairGenerator`, `KeyFactory` `AlgorithmParameters`, and `AlgorithmParameterGenerator` classes.

The `MessageDigest` class, as you would expect, supports the computation of a message digest. The `Signature` class is an engine for calculating digital signatures based on provider-furnished digital signature algorithms. The `Signature` class supports both the creation and verification of a digital signature.

The KeyPairGenerator class is an engine that provides a mechanism by which provider-furnished key generation algorithms may be accessed. Unlike MessageDigest and Signature, key generation is difficult to implement in an algorithm-independent manner. Because of this, KeyPairGenerator supports both algorithm-independent and algorithm-specific key generation—the difference being in the way that the algorithms are initialized. The KeyFactory class is used to translate algorithm-specific keys into objects that can be handled in a generic fashion.

The AlgorithmParameters class is used to manage the parameters of cryptographic algorithms, and the AlgorithmParameterGenerator class is used to generate parameters for algorithms. Specific implementations of the engine classes are provided by cryptographic package providers.

In addition to the engine classes described in the previous paragraphs, Java 2 introduces the java.security.cert package to support the processing of digital certificates. The Certificate class provides an abstract class for managing certificates. It is extended by the X509Certificate, which supports X.509 certificate processing. The X509Extension interface is provided to support the extensions of X.509 version 3. The java.security.cert package also provides classes for working with revoked certificates.

Using Certificates

X.509 identifies a particular format and content for digital certificates. This format has been popularized by Netscape's Secure Sockets Layer (SSL), the Java Archive (JAR) file format, and Privacy Enhanced Mail (PEM), as well as other emerging Internet security standards. X.509 certificates contain the following information:

◆ The version of X.509 being used with the certificate (1, 2, or 3)

◆ The entity's name and public key

◆ A range of dates for which the certificate is valid

◆ A serial number assigned by the CA

◆ The name of the CA

◆ A digital signature created by the CA

The current version of X.509 is 3, although version 1 certificates are still in use. Version 3 provides the capability to add custom extensions to certificates, such as email and IP addresses.

With respect to Java, the primary use for digital certificates is to support code authentication, as shown in Figure 20.12. Developers of Java code can digitally sign their code using their private keys. Users of the code verify the developers' signatures using the developers' public keys. Developers use digital certificates as a secure way to inform users of their public keys. Users manage developer certificates, identities, and public keys using the keytool, and they establish developer-specific policies using the policytool.

SECURE SOCKETS LAYER

The Secure Sockets Layer (SSL) protocol was developed by Netscape to overcome security deficiencies in the TCP/IP protocol suite. SSL is a protocol layer that runs between TCP/IP and application-layer protocols as shown in Figure 20.13.

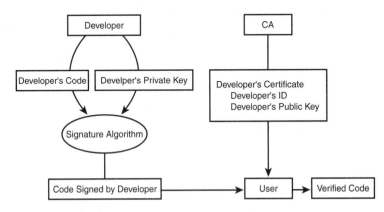

FIGURE 20.12
Certificates are used to support code authentication.

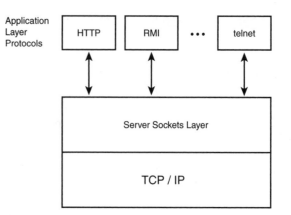

FIGURE 20.13
The Secure Sockets Layer.

SSL provides secure TCP services to higher-level protocols. These services include authentication of client to server, authentication of server to client, and encrypted transmission of data.

Figure 20.14 illustrates these SSL services.

Server authentication enables a user to determine that a server is, in fact, the server that it purports to be. Public-key encryption is used to authenticate that a server's certificate is valid and signed by a trusted certification authority. After a server's certificate is authenticated, the public key contained in the certificate can be used to setup a trusted client-to-server connection. This connection is typically used to support electronic commerce applications. However, it may be used to support a wide range of Internet services.

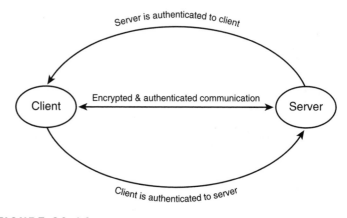

FIGURE 20.14
SSL services.

Client authentication allows a server to positively identify a user. It is performed in the same manner as server authentication, but in the opposite direction. For example, a server verifies that a user possesses a valid certificate that is signed by a trusted certification authority and then uses the public key information in that certificate to determine if the user possesses the required private key.

SSL is also used to ensure the confidentiality of all information that is transmitted between client and server (in both directions) by encrypting this information by a selectable encryption algorithm. SSL can be configured to use a wide range of encryption algorithms including the following:

◆ Data Encryption Standard—A U.S. Government standard private-key encryption algorithm

◆ Rivest Cipher 2 (RC2) and Rivest Cipher 4 (RC4)—Private-key encryption algorithms developed by Ronald Rivest for RSA Data Security

◆ Rivest, Shamir, and Adleman (RSA)—A public-key encryption developed at the Massachusetts Institute of Technology

◆ Skipjack—A U.S. Government-classified private-key encryption algorithm

◆ Triple-DES—Triple-DES encryption

Encryption SSL connections also support the detection of any data that is modified in transit between client and server or data that is falsely inserted between client and server by a third party. SSL can also be configured to run without encryption. In this case, message authentication (MD5) may be used to authenticate data transmitted between client and server and to detect an adversary tampering with the communication stream.

The important point about SSL is that it can be used to secure application protocols that run over TCP/IP. For example, it is used in the Secure Hypertext Transfer Protocol by providing a secure layer between HTTP and TCP as shown in Figure 20.15.

SSL is used to encrypt browser HTTP requests and server HTTP responses. HTTPS uses TCP port 443 instead of the port 80 used by HTTP. Other protocols, such as telnet, FTP, CORBA's IIOP, and Java RMI, may also be secured using SSL. In these cases, SSL is placed between the application protocol and TCP.

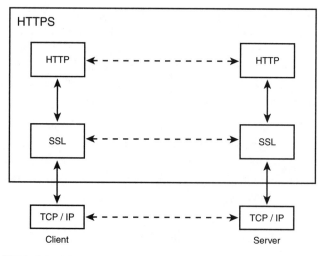

FIGURE 20.15
HTTPS = HTTP + SSL.

SSL 3.0 is the current version of SSL.

FIREWALLS AND NETWORK SECURITY

The Transmission Control Protocol/Internet Protocol (TCP/IP) suite was designed to support flexible, reliable, and survivable communications. Security labeling is factored into the design of the IP and TCP protocols. However, security protection mechanisms are not incorporated into the protocol design. As a result, any security countermeasures in the TCP/IP protocols are usually inadvertent and result from other protocol design considerations. Because of the lack of deliberate security features incorporated into the TCP/IP protocols, these protocols, and the protocol suite as a whole, suffer from several serious security vulnerabilities.

◆ IP datagrams are not authenticated—Any host receiving an IP datagram cannot trust that the datagram is, in fact, from the identified source or that its contents are unaltered.

◆ IP datagrams are not encrypted—IP datagrams that are sent out over the Internet may be observed in their transit from source to destination.

◆ The User Datagram Protocol (UDP) is vulnerable to attacks aimed at disclosing, modifying, inserting, or deleting UDP datagrams.

◆ TCP connections are subject to eavesdropping.

◆ TCP connections are subject to spoofing, masquerading, false packet insertion, and packet modification.

◆ IP, UDP, and TCP are vulnerable to denial of service attacks.

In addition to the fundamental vulnerabilities in the TCP/IP protocol suite, application-level protocols introduce their own vulnerabilities which allow sensitive data to be disclosed over the Internet, integrity-critical data to be modified in an unauthorized manner, false data to be inserted into network applications, and unauthorized individuals to obtain control over systems to which they are not permitted access.

Although these vulnerabilities may seem ominous, there are security countermeasures that enable an organization to connect to the Internet in a secure manner. Firewalls are a prominent Internet security countermeasure that protect an organization's sites from Internet-based attacks. Firewalls are used to physically and logically isolate a site's networks from the Internet and control access between the Internet and the site. Refer to Figure 20.16.

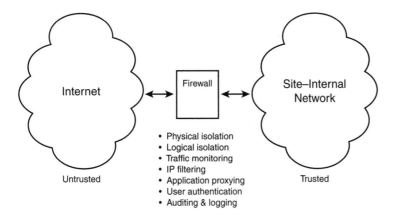

FIGURE 20.16
Firewalls isolate site-internal networks from the Internet.

NOTE

Firewalls The fact that a firewall may act as a choke point through which all Internet traffic passes is a double-edged sword. On one side, it enables all Internet traffic to be closely controlled. On the other side, it makes the firewall a single point of failure for a site's Internet connectivity.

NOTE

Firewalls' Other Uses Firewalls are not limited to the Internet. They may also be used to isolate security-sensitive segments of a site's internal networks.

EXAM TIP

Firewalls Although firewalls are not a Java technology, questions about firewalls appear on the certification exam.

Firewalls limit Internet access to a single point (or a few points) where all traffic between the Internet and a site must pass. By limiting access to Internet traffic, firewalls provide the capability to monitor and control how a site communicates with the Internet.

Firewall monitoring and access control capabilities include the capability to examine every IP datagram coming from or going to the Internet and determine which datagrams will be allowed to pass based upon an explicit firewall security policy. Firewalls also provide the capability to log selected Internet traffic and to trigger alarms based on the occurrence of suspicious events.

Firewalls can operate on protocol levels above the IP layer. For example, most firewalls provide the capability to block all or selected UDP datagrams or to only allow TCP segments to a particular destination host and port. Firewalls can limit UDP or TCP traffic based on the source host name or the IP address from which it is sent.

More advanced firewalls simultaneously provide security at the network, transport, and application layers. These firewalls use application proxies to restrict the Internet service that may pass through the firewall. Proxies communicate at the application layer with both internal and external clients and servers. They isolate lower-level protocols that enter and exit the firewall, and limit the vulnerability of the site to IP and TCP-level attacks. By using application layer protocols to communicate with clients and servers, proxies are able to implement countermeasures that limit the vulnerabilities of the application-layer protocols. The proxies also support auditing, logging, and application-specific user authentication. Refer to Figure 20.17.

Firewalls are configured to permit or deny traffic entering or leaving a site based on the firewall's security policy. This policy makes access control decisions about which application layer protocols are supported by the firewall, what connections may be made between the Internet and site-internal systems, and what controls are placed on these connections based upon protocol characteristics, source and destination addresses, authentication results, and other factors. Firewalls implement their policy to mediate and control all traffic between a site and the Internet. Most firewalls implement a default deny policy which denies all communication that is not specifically permitted by the firewall policy.

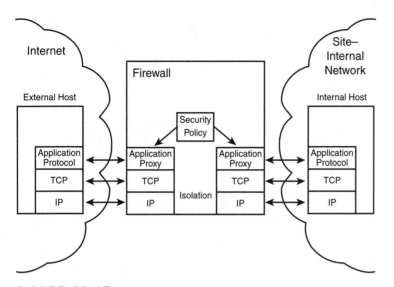

FIGURE 20.17
Application proxies provide security at the application protocol layer.

Because any traffic that is allowed to enter a site from the Internet may pose a potential security risk, many organizations place systems which are accessible to the general public (such as public Web servers and FTP servers) outside the firewall in an area that is often referred to as the DMZ (named in analogy to the demilitarized zone that separates North and South Korea). The DMZ is a subnet that is outside the firewall's protection. The reason that publicly-accessible Web and FTP servers are placed in the DMZ is to keep the public out of the site's internal networks. Because the systems that are placed in the DMZ are not protected by the firewall, they are subject to direct attacks by hackers and others. Because of this, systems that are placed in the DMZ are often referred to as victim hosts. Victim hosts provide services that are publicly accessible, difficult to provide securely, or have unknown security implications. To reduce the risks of attack, victim hosts should not contain sensitive information and should run the absolute minimum services necessary. Refer to Figure 20.18.

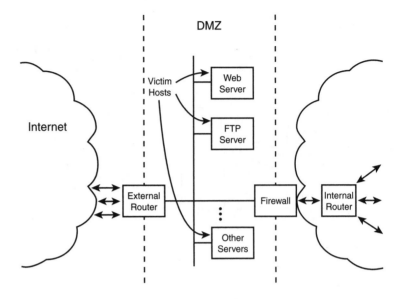

FIGURE 20.18
Victim hosts are placed in the DMZ.

HTTP TUNNELING

Firewalls are a great way to control access between a site and external networks such as the Internet. However, in some cases, firewalls may do too good a job. Suppose that you intend to deploy a new multi-site, distributed application that makes use of CORBA, IIOP, and Java RMI. If a site's firewall does not provide proxies for these protocols, you're out of luck. One or more of your deployment sites may be cut off from your application.

The obvious solution is to go to the firewall administrator and ask him to allow the required protocols to pass through the firewall. However, your request may be denied for a number of reasons:

◆ The protocols may not be secure and may introduce unnecessary risks.

◆ The protocols may be prohibited by the organization's security policy.

◆ The firewall may not support the protocols.

◆ The administrator may not know how or care to configure the firewall to support the protocols.

At this point, you probably wish you had designed your application based on the protocols supported by the firewall and the firewall's security policy. However, there are still a few available options. One of these options is to tunnel your application's protocols through the firewall using a protocol that the firewall supports. *Tunneling* is the process of encapsulating a protocol under another protocol. Refer to Figure 20.19. Because most firewalls are designed to support the Web's Hypertext Transfer Protocol, HTTP tunneling is a common method of passing application protocols, that would otherwise be stopped by the firewall, through it. The intent of HTTP tunneling is not to circumvent the firewall's security, but to enable otherwise nonsecurable protocols to pass through the firewall in a controlled manner.

In many cases, Secure HTTP (HTTPS) is used (instead of HTTP) to support tunneling. The advantage of HTTPS is that it uses SSL to support encryption and authentication of information that is tunneled through the firewall.

E X A M T I P

HTTP Tunneling   Questions related to HTTP tunneling appear on the certification exam.

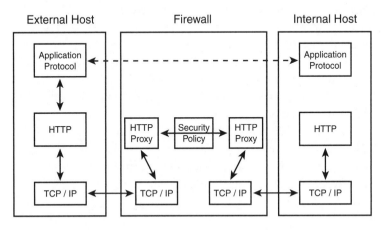

FIGURE 20.19
HTTP tunneling may be used to pass other protocols through a firewall.

VIRTUAL PRIVATE NETWORKS

Given a large organization with multiple Internet sites, it is often highly desirable to use the Internet to support communication between these sites. The advantages of using the Internet are convenience and lower communication costs. The disadvantages are that anything that is sent across the Internet may be disclosed, modified, or deleted by hackers or other threat agents. Although it is possible for an organization to purchase dedicated communication links to connect its geographically-dispersed sites, this often comes at great costs. Virtual private networks (VPNs) use encryption technologies to provide secure communication between sites over the Internet. As their name implies, VPNs are like private networks except that they are implemented in a virtual manner using public networks, such as the Internet. Refer to Figure 20.20.

A VPN uses data encryption and strong authentication mechanisms to create a secure virtual connection between network subscribers (sites or hosts). This is accomplished using regular Internet connections. All communication between subscribers is encrypted to prevent unauthorized disclosure and authenticated to ensure data integrity.

Over the past several years, many vendors have integrated VPN technology into their products, including firewalls and routers. However, until recently, the VPN technology used in these products has often been proprietary. As a result, the VPN products of different vendors often didn't work together. In order to solve this problem, the Internet Engineering Task Force (IETF) established a standard set of IP extensions that provide security services at the network level. This new standard, referred to as the IP Security (IPSec) protocol, adds authentication, encryption, and data integrity services to the IP layer in a manner that is compatible with both the existing IP version 4 standard and the upcoming IP version 6 standard.

EXAM TIP

Virtual Private Networks You can expect to see a handful of questions on the certification exam that require you to be familiar with the basics of VPNs.

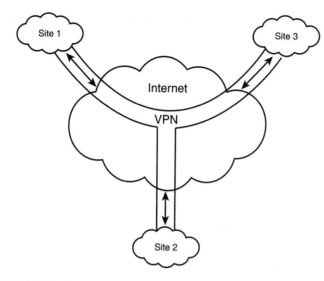

FIGURE 20.20
A VPN may be used to securely connect an organization's sites over the Internet.

CHAPTER SUMMARY

This chapter covered the basics of Java security. You learned about the applet sandbox and the new security features of the Java 2 Security API. You were also introduced to non-Java security technologies, such as SSL, firewalls, and virtual private networks. The following review and exam questions will test your knowledge of these topics and will help you to determine whether your knowledge of security is sufficient to answer the questions you'll encounter in the certification exam.

KEY TERMS
- firewall
- SSL
- Java sandbox
- message digest
- digital signature
- digital certificate
- public-key encryption
- private-key encryption
- HTTP tunneling
- virtual private network

APPLY YOUR KNOWLEDGE

Review Questions

1. What is the applet sandbox?

2. How has the sandbox changed with Java 2?

3. What is the principle of least privilege?

4. What is the content of the Java 2 security policy file?

5. What is the keystore?

6. What is the difference between public-key encryption (asymmetric) and private-key (symmetric) encryption?

7. What is a message digest?

8. What is a digital signature?

9. What is a digital certificate?

10. What is a certification authority?

11. What is Secure Sockets Layer (SSL)?

12. What is the purpose of a firewall?

13. What is the purpose of HTTP tunneling?

14. What is a virtual private network?

15. What is IPSec?

Exam Questions

1. Which of the following security features were introduced with Java 2?

    A. The capability to sign JAR files.

    B. The applet sandbox.

    C. The capability to specify an applet security policy.

    D. Support for X.509 version 3 certificates.

2. Which of the following are contained in a Java security policy file?

    A. grant entries

    B. trusted code

    C. aliases and their public keys

    D. digital certificates

3. Which of the following are contained in a keystore?

    A. grant entries

    B. trusted code

    C. aliases and their public keys

    D. digital certificates

4. Which of the following are true about the Java Cryptography Extension (JCE)?

    A. It is included with the Java 2 platform.

    B. It implements cryptographic algorithms.

    C. It is subject to U.S. export controls.

    D. It contains the Java Security API.

5. Which of the following are true about message digests?

    A. They are calculated using an encryption algorithm.

    B. They are used as a digital fingerprint for messages and files.

    C. They summarize the content of a message.

    D. They are computed using one-way functions.

APPLY YOUR KNOWLEDGE

6. Which of the following are true about digital signatures?

   A. They are created by encrypting a message digest with the signer's private key.

   B. They are created by encrypting a message digest with the signer's public key.

   C. They are created by passing a message digest through a hash function.

   D. They are verified by decrypting them with the signer's public key.

7. Which of the following security features are provided by digital signatures?

   A. Confidentiality

   B. Non-repudiation

   C. Verifiability

   D. Sealing

8. X.509 version 3 specifies which of the following?

   A. A format and content for digital certificates

   B. The IPSec standard

   C. The Secure Sockets Layer

   D. The Data Encryption Standard

9. Which of the following capabilities are provided by SSL?

   A. The capability for a client to authenticate a server.

   B. The capability for a server to authenticate a client.

   C. The capability to mediate and control all communication between an internal (trusted) network and an external (untrusted) network.

   D. The capability for a client and a server to encrypt their communication using a selectable encryption algorithm.

10. Where are victim hosts located with respect to a firewall?

    A. In the external untrusted network

    B. In the internal trusted network

    C. In the DMZ

    D. In an application proxy

11. Which of the following are characteristics of HTTP tunneling?

    A. It uses the Hypertext Transfer Protocol.

    B. It is used to pass other protocols through a firewall.

    C. It is part of the Java 2 API.

    D. It is used to sign JAR files.

12. What are the advantages of virtual private networks?

    A. Their costs are lower than dedicated networks.

    B. They may make use of existing Internet connectivity.

    C. They support data encryption, data integrity, and authentication.

    D. They are a Java-based security solution.

APPLY YOUR KNOWLEDGE

Answers to Review Questions

1. The applet sandbox is a mechanism by which all applets that are loaded over a network are prevented from accessing security-sensitive resources, such as the local file system and networking resources.

2. Java 2 provides the capability to specify a security policy that determines the accesses that an applet or application is allowed based on its source and the identities of those who have signed the code.

3. The principle of least privilege requires that an application be given only those privileges that it needs to carry out its function and no more.

4. The security policy file contains a series of grant entries that identify the permissions granted to an applet or application based on its source and signatures.

5. The keystore is a database of identities and their aliases, public keys, and certificates.

6. Public-key encryption makes use of a pair of public and private keys. The public key is used to encrypt data and the private key is used to decrypt it. In private-key encryption the encryption and decryption keys are usually the same. Both keys must be kept secret to maintain the security of encrypted information.

7. A message digest is a value that is computed from a message, file, or other byte stream that serves as a digital fingerprint for the byte stream. Message digests are computed using one-way functions.

8. A digital signature consists of text that is encrypted using the private key of a public key/private key pair. The public key is used to decrypt the signature to verify its authenticity.

9. A digital certificate is a message that is signed by a certification authority that certifies the value of a person or organization's public key.

10. A certification authority is an organization that is trusted to verify the public keys of other organizations and individuals. Certification authorities issue digital certificates that verify the public keys of these entities.

11. SSL is a protocol that sits between the Transmission Control Protocol and application layer protocols. It provides authentication and encryption services to the application layer protocols.

12. Firewalls are used to mediate and control all information that is communicated between an external (untrusted) network and an internal (trusted) network. Firewalls make use of IP filtering and application proxies to implement firewall security policies.

13. HTTP tunneling is used to encapsulate other protocols within the HTTP or HTTPS protocols. It is typically used to pass protocols that would normally be blocked by a firewall through the firewall in a controlled manner.

14. A virtual private network is a network between geographically-dispersed sites that takes place over an untrusted network. Encryption and authentication mechanisms are used to secure data that is transmitted over the untrusted network.

15. IPSec is a set of IP extensions that provide security services, such as encryption, authentication, and data integrity. IPSec is typically used with a VPN.

APPLY YOUR KNOWLEDGE

Answers to Exam Questions

1. C and D   The capability to specify an applet security policy and support for X.509 version 3 digital certificates are new to Java 2.

2. A   A Java security policy file is made up of grant entries.

3. C and D   A keystore contains aliases, public keys, and digital certificates; but it does not contain grant entries or trusted code.

4. B and C   The JCE implements cryptographic algorithms that are subject to U.S. export controls. It is not included with the Java 2 platform.

5. B and D   Message digests are digital fingerprints of messages and files that are computed using one-way functions. They generally do not use encryption.

6. A and D   Digital signatures are created by encrypting a message digest with the signer's private key. They are verified by decrypting them with the signer's public key.

7. B, C, and D   Digital signatures do not encrypt the objects they sign and do not directly support confidentiality.

8. A   X.509 version 3 specifies a format and content for digital certificates.

9. A, B, and D   The capability to mediate and control traffic between two networks is provided by a firewall.

10. C   Victim hosts are placed in the DMZ.

11. A and B   HTTP tunneling uses the Hypertext Transfer Protocol to encapsulate other protocols so that they may be passed through a firewall.

12. A, B, and C   VPNs are lower in cost than dedicated private networks because they make use of existing Internet connectivity. They also provide encryption, data integrity, and authentication services. However, VPNs are not a Java technology.

Suggested Readings and Resources

The Java Security Web page at (`http://www.javasoft.com/security/index.html`).

This chapter helps you to prepare for the exam by covering the following objectives:

Know how to design a three- (or n-) tier Java architecture where the third tier is an existing application, file, or database.

Know how to design a detailed architecture for integrating Java with existing databases and applications.

Be able to state the advantages and disadvantages of using screen scrapers to access applications at tier three.

Be able to state the advantages and disadvantages of object mapping for legacy system access.

Be able to recommend a migration strategy for an existing application.

Be able to state the advantages and disadvantages of partial migration using Java applets and applications.

Know how to explain the advantages of such a Java solution compared to alternative solution technologies such as C++.

CHAPTER 21

Working with Legacy Systems

STUDY STRATEGIES

As you read through this chapter, you should concentrate on the following key items:

▶ What issues do legacy systems pose when upgraded to Java-based distributed applications?

▶ What issues are involved in upgrading the client tier of legacy systems?

▶ What issues are involved in upgrading the application business logic tier of legacy systems?

▶ What issues are involved in upgrading the data storage tier of legacy systems?

▶ How are legacy system components secured?

CHAPTER INTRODUCTION

As a Java architect, you must be capable of designing new Java-based applications that take advantage of existing application components. These existing application components consist of legacy systems that range from custom mainframe applications to legacy Windows-based COM objects. You must be able to determine which components to keep, which to replace, and which to upgrade. You must also develop a strategy for integrating the remaining and upgraded legacy components into a Java-based architecture. This chapter will examine some of the issues involved with legacy systems and describe some common strategies for addressing these issues.

ISSUES WITH LEGACY SYSTEMS

Few of you have the luxury of designing enterprise applications from scratch. Most of you have to deal with legacy databases, legacy services, and legacy interfaces. Rather than replacing existing applications, you are often required to keep what works well, eliminate what doesn't, and augment what's left over with new and promising technologies, such as those supported by Java. These legacy constraints shape the way in which you apply Java technologies.

Legacy systems aren't necessarily problematic. They perform a particular set of functions and meet an established set of requirements. In some cases, their worst sin is that they are old. However, they may pose a number of issues in moving toward a distributed Java-based architecture:

◆ Legacy systems may not provide a clean separation between the client, business logic, and data storage tiers. This is one of the most frustrating problems in trying to upgrade legacy systems to new technologies. Some systems not only ignore object-oriented design approaches, they seem to be designed with a total disregard for any design principles, whatsoever. In these systems, you'll find that the user interface, business logic, and data storage layers are so intertwined that it is nearly impossible to separate them. You'll find some systems where the data storage layer is implemented on the client or is distributed across a thousand application-specific files that are used by a wide range of barely compatible application programs. You'll find systems where the business logic is distributed between client-side macros and sets of SQL statements that are stored across several databases. You'll also see systems where the user interface is dynamically generated by application business logic that is dispersed between several application servers and database management programs. Not all legacy systems are this bad. However, some are even worse.

◆ Legacy systems may not adhere to open standards. Although it is highly desirable to build systems that adhere to open standards, this is not always done. Sometimes sexier proprietary products are substituted for products that follow open standards. The legacy systems that you'll inherit are likely to be loaded with proprietary products or home-grown software that doesn't comply with any standards other than its own. This includes non-standard communication protocols, custom-built, flat-file databases, and proprietary file formats. To make matters worse, these products will perform system-critical functions, and the vendor or developer of the proprietary product will either be long gone or will no longer support the product.

◆ Legacy systems may make use of outdated hardware. If a legacy system has a heavy investment in outdated hardware, such as old VAX minicomputers and character-based VT220 terminals, moving to a Java-based architecture will present some challenges. The legacy hardware/software platforms might not support a JVM. The client machines might not support Java-capable browsers. The hardware might be limited to low-bandwidth communication. The hardware might not be able to scale to support the thousands of users that are typical of Web-based applications.

◆ Legacy systems might not be secure. One common problem found with legacy systems is that they are designed to operate using proprietary closed networks in a restricted user environment. Computer and network security measures that are designed for this environment are not sufficient to protect against Internet-based attacks. Under pressure to utilize the communications resources and services of the Internet, these systems and their networks evolve into an environment where they are accessible from the Internet, often without the protection of a firewall. Upgrading systems like these to play into distributed applications often presents a number of security challenges. The legacy systems must be secured to be protected from Internet-based attacks and to integrate into the security policy and architecture of the overall distributed application.

The four issues identified in the previous list are typical of those faced by architects when developing new applications that interface with legacy systems. However, a Java architect may face numerous other difficulties, some that are related to these issues, as well as other application-specific problems.

WORKING WITH LEGACY SYSTEMS

Building a three-tiered or n-tiered, distributed, Java-based application that uses legacy systems may seem to be a formidable challenge. However, there are a number of approaches that can be used to solve these problems.

As a Java architect, you will be required to develop a system architecture that takes advantage of the new features of Java while preserving the capabilities that are provided by legacy systems. In some cases, you will be able to decide whether a legacy system should be preserved or replaced. In other cases, you will have to live with someone else's decision. The architecture that you develop will have to reflect tradeoffs between a number of factors including cost, schedule, and functionality.

In deciding how to develop an architecture that utilizes legacy systems, it is important to assess the role of each system in terms of its support for the client, business logic, and data storage tiers. Most system upgrades tend to focus on the client tier. This is especially true of applications that are transitioning from older, character-based or Windows-based GUIs to take advantage of the features provided by Web browsers, HTML, XML, Java, and JavaScript. In these cases, the Java architect needs to determine whether the business logic embodied by legacy systems will be reengineered and reimplemented in Java or whether Web-based GUIs will be integrated with existing business logic. The Java architect will also have to determine whether existing data storage capabilities will be preserved or replaced.

UPGRADING CLIENT-TIER GUIS

The benefits of using a browser-based interface are almost self-evident: rich graphical content, full multimedia support, executable content, thin client paradigm, cutting-edge technologies, and so on. However, even with all that browser-based GUIs have to offer, there is not always a pressing business case for moving existing client interfaces to the browser. For example, there are systems that use character-based terminals that enable users to interact with applications, enter data, and quickly extract the information they need. If the system continues to satisfy user needs, there is no need to upgrade it to a browser-based interface.

When upgrading a non-browser interface to a browser-based interface, the degree of integration of the current interface with the application business logic and data storage tiers must be assessed. In cases where the client interface is loosely coupled with the other tiers, the interface can probably be replaced along the current boundary between the client interface tier and other tiers as shown in Figure 21.1.

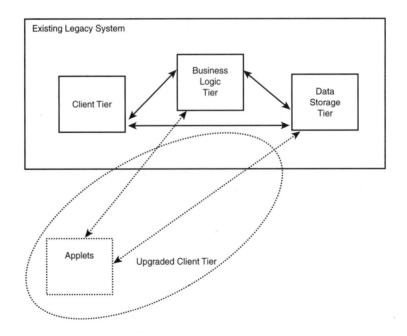

FIGURE 21.1

Upgrading well-defined client interfaces.

In ideal situations, such as these, applets or small client-side applications can be used to upgrade the current user interface by providing a GUI to replace existing interface functionality and communicating with application business logic and application storage tiers. Applets are the preferable solution because they are easier to deploy, upgrade, and maintain. The following options apply to their use:

◆ TCP sockets—If the business logic and data storage tiers of the legacy system interface with the existing GUI via TCP sockets, applets can be deployed that utilize these communication interfaces. These applets can either be signed and trusted (in order to open up separate network connections) or can make use of TCP proxies provided by the Web server from which they are loaded.

◆ COM—If the non-client tiers of the legacy system are implemented as COM objects, the applets can communicate with these objects by taking advantage of Java-to-COM bridging technologies that enable COM objects to be accessed as Java classes. RMI may be used to support communication between applets and remote Java code that supports Java to COM bridging.

◆ CORBA—If the non-client tiers of the legacy systems are implemented as CORBA objects, applets may take advantage of Java IDL to communicate directly with these objects.

◆ JDBC—If portions of the current interface communicate directly with the data storage tier, this communication may be replaced by applets that use JDBC (and possibly the JDBC-ODBC) bridge to communicate with the data storage tier.

◆ Custom interfaces—In some cases, there may be a clean, well-defined interface between the existing client tier and other system tiers. However, the interface may use custom, non-standard communication mechanisms. In these cases, the Java Native Interface can be used to create native methods that implement these mechanisms.

In applications where the client interface is tightly coupled with the business logic and data storage of the existing legacy system, providing an applet-based interface becomes more complicated. In situations like these, *screen scraper* technology may be used to integrate an applet interface with the existing system. A screen scraper is a software application that translates an existing client interface into a set of objects that can be used to build new client software. Refer to Figure 21.2. The MozNet product of the Mozart Corporation is an example of a Java-compatible screen scraper (http://www.mozart.com/Documents/Products/moznet/index.htm).

In most cases, screen scrapers function as a terminal emulator on one end and an object interface on the other. The screen scraper is configured to read data from terminal fields that are displayed on the screen and make that data available as a property of the object interface. The object interface provides methods for getting or setting these properties and for entering commands (as if they were implemented by a terminal user).

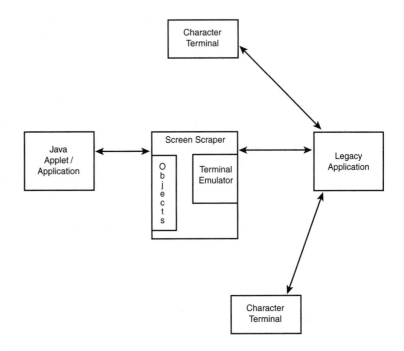

FIGURE 21.2
How screen scrapers work.

The primary advantage of a screen scraper is that it provides a low-level, object-based interface to the application. By doing so, it enables you to build a new GUI by laying it over the existing client interface. The disadvantage of screen scrapers is that they are a fundamentally a kludge. Any changes to the interface of the existing application can break the new GUI. In addition, GUIs that are built upon screen scrapers are prone to errors resulting from unexpected outputs generated by the legacy interface. They are also prone to interface freezes that occur when the legacy interface is awaiting input from the screen scraper that the screen scraper is unaware of. When using screen scraper technology, it is important that the user be provided with a capability to reset the new GUI, screen scraper, and legacy interface to a known, well-defined state. This can help to ameliorate the difficulties presented by interface errors.

In some cases, it may be easier to ignore the existing legacy system interface and access elements of legacy system business logic and database tiers directly. These software elements might not be implemented as objects. However, it might be possible to model these software elements as objects and access them directly. Special tools, referred to as object mapping tools, may be used to facilitate this kind of approach. These tools are used to create proxy objects that access legacy system functions and make them available in an object-oriented manner. Refer to Figure 21.3.

The Legacy Object Framework of the Yrrid Corporation (`http://www.yrrid.com/lof/lof.htm`) is an example of a legacy object mapping solution.

Object mapping tools are usually more effective than screen scrapers in that they are not as dependent on the format of the output generated by the existing user interface. The objects produced by object mappers do not "read the screen." Instead, they access application data directly. This makes them less prone to interface anomalies.

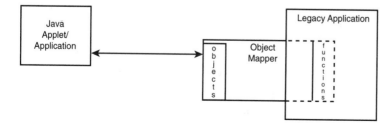

FIGURE 21.3
Using legacy object mapping.

Object mapping is not limited to user-interface upgrades. It may also be used to upgrade application business logic and data storage tiers.

UPGRADING APPLICATION BUSINESS LOGIC

Most system upgrades aren't limited to the client interface. Instead, they are the result of an organization reengineering its business practices to make it more competitive in a changing business environment. A common example of this is a company that upgrades its current business logic to make it work in a Web and Internet-based environment. It typically starts out by deploying a company Web site and after a few months realizes the benefits of conducting business on the Internet. The company then wants to upgrade its existing systems to support electronic commerce, product distribution, vendor communication, or to satisfy other business objectives. To do this, the company must redesign the way it does business to support a new Internet-centric business model.

In most cases, a company will not want to start from scratch and deploy entirely new business applications. Instead, it will opt to extend its current business information systems to take advantage of the opportunities provided by the Internet. Some core business logic may be rewritten. However, some will remain. In situations like these, the Java architect must carve out the legacy system elements that are to be replaced, upgraded, and maintained. The challenge will be to do this in such a way that new application components can communicate with those that remain using established interfaces.

Java servlets provide a capability to make existing enterprise applications available through the Internet or available in Web form over the company's intranet. Applets executing within the context of a user's browser access servlets via HTTP, HTTPS, and other Internet protocols. The servlets take the browser requests and communicate with application and database servers to process these requests. The application and database servers provide access to the business logic and database tiers of a company's intranet. Refer to Figure 21.4.

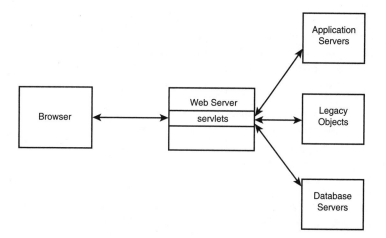

FIGURE 21.4
Using servlets to connect legacy systems to the Web.

The intranet applications consist of legacy system components that are upgraded to implement new business rules and to support access to the servlets. Enterprise JavaBeans (EJB) provide a component-oriented approach (refer to Chapter 18, "Distributed Applications Technologies") to upgrading these legacy applications. EJB makes use of existing application servers and services and enables these services to be integrated with application components that are written in Java. EJB-compliant application servers provide an environment in which enterprise beans can be plugged into containers and integrated with existing application components. Refer to Figure 21.5.

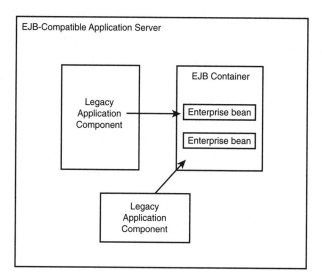

FIGURE 21.5
Using Enterprise JavaBeans to upgrade legacy application services.

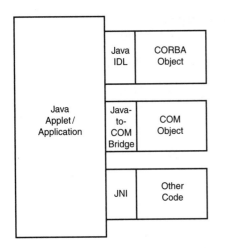

FIGURE 21.6
Upgrading legacy systems using CORBA, DCOM, and JNI.

Java's support for CORBA enables CORBA objects to be accessed from Java and Java objects to be accessed as CORBA objects. These capabilities simplify the process by which Java can be used to upgrade existing CORBA-based systems.

Microsoft's JVM provides a bridge between Java and COM objects. It allows COM objects to be accessed as COM classes and Java objects to be accessed as COM objects. These capabilities enable existing legacy Window applications to be reused within applications that are upgraded to Java.

When all else fails, JNI may be used to write custom code to interface new business logic, encapsulated as Java objects, to be integrated with existing legacy software. Refer to Figure 21.6.

UPGRADING THE DATA STORAGE TIER

In many cases, the data storage tier of existing systems is the easiest to transition to a Java-based architecture. If the data storage tier of a legacy system utilizes a relational database system, JDBC may be used to provide connectivity to legacy databases. In most cases, legacy databases will not support a pure JDBC driver. If the existing system provides ODBC support, the JDBC-ODBC bridge can be used. If the legacy database uses custom drivers, it might be possible to find database middleware that supports the custom driver and either an ODBC or JDBC interface. The middleware is used to translate between JDBC and the custom database driver as shown in Figure 21.7. If this option does not work, the contents of the database may be exported in such a way that they can be imported into a more compatible RDBMS.

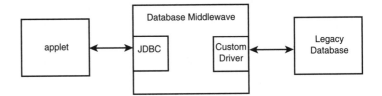

FIGURE 21.7
Using database middleware.

If the existing database system is a hierarchical or flat-file database, in many cases, the database may be exported and imported into an RDBMS. If the existing application stores data in an unorganized manner, strewn over multiple files, conversion may still be possible, although it is likely to be a complicated and error-prone effort.

A significant problem occurs when the existing database system makes use of non-standard SQL or a custom, non-standard database query language. In cases like these, the portions of existing applications that are implemented in the non-standard language must be ported to SQL.

In addition to accessing legacy databases using JDBC, other more object-oriented approaches may be used. Sun's Java Blend product provides the capability to access SQL-compatible databases as collections of objects. (Refer to Chapter 18.) OQL-compatible databases provide the capability to store objects in databases and query databases in an object-oriented manner.

SECURING LEGACY SYSTEM COMPONENTS

If an existing legacy system is not secure, its security probably cannot be easily increased. Retrofitting a system with security is generally more expensive and less productive than redesigning and redeveloping the system to operate in a secure manner. However, few of us have the budget to replace existing systems solely for security purposes.

The good news is there are some general steps that you can take to minimizing the risks associated with operating legacy systems in an Internet environment. These steps involve isolation, access control, auditing, and surveillance.

Legacy systems may be isolated from Internet-based threats by placing them behind a firewall. Intranet firewalls can also be used to isolate legacy systems from threats that might occur within the intranet environment. Access to legacy systems can be controlled by requiring

NOTE **Security** Chapter 19, "Securing Distributed Applications," covers technologies that are used to secure Java-based distributed applications.

users and external applications to authenticate themselves with the firewall before access is granted to the legacy systems. Auditing features of the legacy systems should be utilized whenever possible. In addition, firewall auditing capabilities can be used to determine when legacy systems are accessed and by whom. Network monitoring tools can be used to monitor all network traffic that passes to and from the legacy systems to detect any outside tampering or unauthorized access. Finally, if significant risks still exist, virtual private networks may be used to secure all communication with legacy systems.

Moving C/C++ Legacy Code to Java

Java is a powerful language that provides many useful features to the software developer. However, if your software organization is typical, you will have to trade off moving to Java with the constraints imposed by a dependency on in-place legacy code. This section summarizes the pros and cons of moving existing legacy code to Java. It identifies a spectrum of approaches for accomplishing software transition and discusses the issues involved with each approach. It also covers approaches to translating C and C++ code to Java. This section assumes that the transition of C/C++ code to Java is being performed by a moderately large software organization. Some of the software porting issues become insignificant if only a few small programs are translated into Java.

Why Move to Java?

When you're deciding whether to move existing applications to Java, you must consider the trade-off between the advantages and disadvantages of such a move. This section identifies many of the advantages of Java programs over C-based and C++-based applications. The following section considers some disadvantages of using Java and identifies roadblocks to any software-transition effort.

Platform Independence

One of the most compelling reasons to move to Java is its platform-independence. Java runs on most major hardware and software platforms, including Windows 98, 95, and NT, Linux, Macintosh, and several varieties of UNIX. Java applets are supported by Java-compatible browsers, such as Netscape Navigator and Internet Explorer. By moving existing software to Java, you can make it instantly compatible with these software platforms. Your programs become more portable, and any hardware and operating-system dependencies are removed.

Although C and C++ are supported on all platforms that support Java, these languages are not supported in a platform-independent manner. C and C++ applications that are implemented on one operating system platform are usually severely intertwined with the native windowing system and OS-specific networking capabilities. Moving between OS platforms requires recompilation, at a minimum, and significant redesign in most cases.

Object-Orientation

Java is a true object-oriented language. It does not merely provide the capability to implement object-oriented principles; it enforces those principles. You can develop object-oriented programs in C++, but you are not required to do so; you can use C++ to write C programs as well. Java does not allow you to slip outside the object-oriented framework. You either adhere to Java's object-oriented development approach, or you do not program in Java.

Security

Java is one of the first programming languages to consider security as part of its design. The Java language, compiler, interpreter, and run-time environment were each developed with security in mind. The compiler, interpreter, API, and Java-compatible browsers all contain several levels of security measures that are designed to reduce the risk of security compromise, loss of data, and program integrity, and damage to system users. Considering the enormous security problems associated with executing potentially untrusted code in a secure manner and across multiple execution environments, Java's security measures are far ahead of even those developed to secure military systems. C and C++ do not have any intrinsic security capabilities. Can you download an arbitrary untrusted C or C++ program and execute it in a secure manner without a high-security operating system?

Reliability

Security and reliability go hand in hand. Security measures cannot be implemented with any degree of assurance without a reliable framework for program execution. Java provides multiple levels of reliability measures, beginning with the Java language itself. Many of the features of C and C++ that are detrimental to program reliability, such as pointers and automatic type conversion, are avoided in Java. The Java compiler provides several levels of additional checks to identify type mismatches and other inconsistencies. The Java run-time system duplicates many of the checks performed by the compiler, and it performs additional checks to verify that the executable bytecode forms a valid Java program.

Simplicity

The Java language was designed to be a simple language to learn, building on the syntax and many of the features of C++. However, in order to promote security, reliability, and simplicity, Java has left out those elements of C and C++ that contribute to errors and program complexity. In addition, Java provides automated garbage collection, freeing you from having to manage memory deallocation in your programs. The end result of Java's focus on simplicity is that it is easy to learn how to write Java programs if you have programmed in C or C++. Java programs are also less complex than C and C++ programs, because many of the language elements that lead to program complexity have been removed.

Language Features

The Java language provides many language features that make it preferable to C or C++ for modern software development. At the top of this list is Java's intrinsic support for multithreading, which is lacking in both C and C++. Other features are its exception handling capabilities (which were recently introduced into C++), its strict adherence to class and object-oriented software development, and its automated garbage-collection support. In addition to these features, Java enforces a common programming style by removing the capability to slip outside of the class- and object-oriented programming paradigm to develop C-style, function-oriented programs.

Standardization

Although C and C++ have been standardized by the American National Standards Institute (ANSI), many C and C++ compilers provide custom enhancements to the language, usually through additional preprocessor directives. These enhancements usually make their way into source code programs, resulting in a general lack of standardization. Since C and C++ are not controlled by a single organization, they allow for non-standard extensions. Java does not yet suffer from any standardization problems because its syntax and semantics are controlled by a single organization.

The Java API

The predefined classes of the Java API provide a comprehensive, platform-independent foundation for program development. These classes provide the capability to develop window and network programs that execute on a wide range of hosts. The Java API's support of remote method invocation, database connectivity, and security are unmatched by the API of any other language. In addition, no other language provides as much platform-independent power as Java's API. Consider C and C++, for example. Only a very tiny standard API is common to all C/C++ implementations. Third-party developers provide their own APIs. However, these APIs are usually incompatible and rarely cross-platform.

Transition to Distributed Computing

Sun has taken important steps to support fully distributed computing with its support of RMI, CORBA, and JDBC. These APIs provide the capability to develop and integrate remote objects into standalone programs and applet-based Web applications.

Rapid Code Generation

Because Java is an interpreted language, it can be used to rapidly prototype applications that would require considerably more base software support in languages such as C or C++. The Java API also contributes to the capability to support rapid code generation. The classes of the Java API provide an integrated, easy-to-use repository for the development of application-specific software. Because the Java API provides high-level windows, networking, and database support, custom application prototypes can be constructed more quickly using these classes as a foundation.

Ease of Documentation and Maintenance

Java software is essentially self-documenting when doc comments and the javadoc tool are used to generate software documentation. The Java API documentation is an example of the superior documentation capabilities provided by Java. Because Java software is inherently structured and documented better than C or C++ software, it is generally easier to maintain. In addition, the package orientation of Java software provides considerable modularity in software design, development, documentation, and maintenance.

Reasons Against Moving to Java

Java's many benefits make it an attractive language for developing new applications and porting existing legacy code. The previous section discussed some of the advantages of porting existing code to Java. This section identifies some of the disadvantages of any migration from C or C++ to Java.

Compatibility

Although Java is supported on many platforms, it is not supported on all of them. If your target hardware or software platform does not support Java, you are out of luck. Your alternatives are to switch to a different platform or to wait for Java to be ported to your existing software platform.

Also, your operating system or browser platform may not support the latest version of Java. For example, Netscape Communicator 4.0 supports JDK 1.1, but Microsoft Internet Explorer supports *most* of JDK 1.1 but not *all* of it. Earlier browsers support JDK 1.02. In order to develop Java software that is compatible with a wide range of users, you must ensure that your users are upgraded to an execution platform that runs the version of Java required by your software. The Java Plug-In may be used to ensure compatibility with the Java 2 platform.

Compatibility may also be a problem at the design level. Suppose that your target software platform does support the latest version of Java. If your legacy code is unstructured and incompatible with a class- and object-oriented model, the effort required to migrate the software may be prohibitive.

Performance

Java is interpreted, and although its execution is efficient, it might not meet the performance demands of applications in which execution speed is of paramount importance. Examples of these types of applications include numerical, "number crunching" programs, real-time control processes, language compilers, and modeling and simulation software.

Just because your application fits into one of these categories does not necessarily rule out Java. For example, the Java compiler is written in Java and performs admirably for small programs. However, its performance is greatly enhanced when it is compiled into native machine code instructions. Java-to-C translators allow programs to be developed in Java and translated into C for native machine code compilation. The translation process generally improves the performance of Java programs. Some Java development tools, such as Symantec Visual Café, provide the capability to create native binary code executable files (.exe) directly from Java code.

Probably the biggest boost to Java's performance is the HotSpot technology from JavaSoft. HotSpot allows Java programs to execute as fast as or faster than compiled programs. HotSpot increases execution performance by integrating a just-in-time compiler and a code optimizer with the Java interpreter.

Retraining

Although Java is simple, easy to learn, and based on C++, some training will be required to get programmers up and running with it. This is especially true if the programmers haven't been using C++ in a structured, object-oriented fashion. I never really appreciated the object-oriented programming features provided by C++ before I began programming in Java. Until I had adopted the Java program-development mindset, I was trying to apply my outdated and inefficient C++ programming techniques to Java software development. After I had made the mental transition to the Java object-oriented programming model, I became much more comfortable and efficient in writing Java programs.

Impact on Existing Operations

Moving legacy code to Java can adversely affect company operations that are supported with legacy software. This is especially true when the legacy code is implemented in the poorly structured, convoluted manner that typically evolves from extensive software patches and upgrades. When existing system software is tightly coupled and fragile, a transition to Java (or any other language) may break the software application and require a complete software redevelopment.

Cost, Schedule, and Level of Effort

Any software transition effort is subject to cost and schedule constraints. Moving current legacy software to Java might not be cost-effective, given the current software investment and its expected operational life. The software transition may also have a significant impact on system availability and prior scheduled activities. Transition from C or C++ to Java might also require a significant level of effort that would exceed the expected budget for the maintenance of the legacy code.

Transition Approaches and Issues

There are many ways to integrate Java into existing software applications. This section identifies some of these approaches and explores the issues involved in making the transition to a Java-based software environment.

Interfacing with Existing Legacy Code

One of the easiest ways to introduce Java to an operational environment is to use it to add functionality to existing legacy code. Java programs do not replace existing legacy software; they merely enhance it to support new applications. This approach involves minimal impact to existing software, but introduces a potentially thorny maintenance issue because Java is added to the current list of languages that must be used to maintain the system.

Incremental Re-implementation of Legacy Code

You can re-implement legacy code in Java in increments, moving over to a Java-based software-development approach while minimizing the impact on existing legacy software. This approach assumes that the legacy software is developed in a modular fashion and can be replaced in an incremental manner. If this is the case, legacy software can be migrated to Java on a module-by-module basis, with the legacy code ultimately replaced by new Java software.

Off-Boarding Access to Legacy Objects

If in-place legacy code can be upgraded using Java software that is implemented on separate hardware platforms, Java can be used to *off-board* many of the functions performed by the legacy code. The use of off-board server software preserves the investment in legacy code, while expanding the services provided by the system as a whole.

Full-Scale Redevelopment

In some cases, it is more cost-effective to keep legacy code in place while completely redeveloping system software from scratch. This is typically the case when the system is subject to large-scale reengineering, or when it is so fragile that it breaks as the result of the simplest upgrades. If full-scale system redevelopment is necessary, this is actually an advantage to Java software development because the developed software is under no legacy compatibility constraints and can take full advantage of Java's capabilities.

Translation Approaches and Issues

Translation of existing C and C++ code into Java can be performed in several different ways, depending upon the compatibility of the existing software with Java. This section describes some of the different approaches to software translation.

Automated Translation

Tools and utilities have been developed that enable Java source code and bytecode to be translated into C to support native machine code compilation. Future Java integrated software-development environments are planned, where either Java or C++ code may be generated based on the configuration of the development software. These development tools will enable easy movement between C++ and Java and require a common set of libraries that can be used by either Java or C++ programs. Automated translation between these two languages will be supported to some extent.

The degree to which C++ programs can be automatically translated into Java will depend on the planning and effort put into the code's design. Factors to be considered include compatible libraries, the use of single inheritance, the use of object-oriented programming capabilities, and the minimization of the use of incompatible language features.

Manual Translation

Manual translation of C and C++ to Java will probably be the most common approach to moving C and C++ legacy programs to Java. This approach requires you to use two editor windows—one for the legacy C++ code being translated, and the other for the Java program being created. Some of the translation is accomplished by cutting and pasting C++ statements into the Java window, making the corrections necessary to adjust for language differences. Other parts of the translation require that new Java classes, interfaces, variables, and methods be developed to implement C++ functions and data structures that cannot be directly translated from C++ to Java. The effectiveness of the manual translation process will be determined by the degree to which the C++ legacy code meets the compatibility considerations identified at the end of the previous section.

Source-Level Redesign

In many cases, manual translation is hampered because the C++ legacy code is written in a style that renders it impossible to migrate using cut-and-paste translation methods. In these cases, a class- and object-oriented design of the legacy code needs to be extracted from the legacy code and used as the basis for the Java source code development. A two-level approach to software translation is followed. The legacy code is reverse-engineered to an object-oriented design, and the recovered design information is used to develop a Java software design, which is in turn translated into Java source code. Code is not translated from one language to another. Instead, legacy code is translated into general design information that is used to drive the Java design and implementation.

CHAPTER SUMMARY

KEY TERMS

- Screen scrapers
- Legacy object mapping
- Database middleware
- Java Native Interface
- Offboard servers

This chapter covers the issues involved with integrating legacy systems into Java-based distributed applications. It also describes approaches to addressing these issues. It covers strategies for upgrading legacy system client interfaces, business logic, and data storage tiers. It also covers the use of firewalls to secure legacy system components and strategies for porting C and C++ applications to Java. The following review and exam questions will test your knowledge of legacy system issues and solutions and will help you to determine whether your knowledge of them is sufficient to answer the questions you'll encounter in the certification exam.

APPLY YOUR KNOWLEDGE

Review Questions

1. What is a screen scraper?

2. How does legacy object mapping work?

3. What is an off-board server?

4. How is database middleware used to access legacy databases?

5. How is JNI used to access legacy system software?

6. How is Java-to-Com bridging used to access COM objects?

Exam Questions

1. Suppose a small company has a character-terminal–based legacy application that it wants to make available over the Web. However, it does not want to modify the legacy application in order to support Web connectivity. Which technologies are appropriate to accomplishing these goals?

   A. Off-board servers

   B. Screen scrapers

   C. Applets

   D. JNDI

2. Suppose that a legacy application is primarily comprised of COM objects. Which technologies could be used to access these objects from Java?

   A. Java IDL

   B. JDBC

   C. RMI

   D. A Java-to-COM bridge

3. Suppose that an existing legacy database supports ODBC but not JDBC. Which technologies may be used to access the database from a Java applet?

   A. The Java-ODBC bridge driver

   B. JDBC and ODBC-capable database middleware

   C. JNI

   D. JNDI

4. Suppose that the business logic of an existing application is implemented using a set of CGI programs. Which Java technologies can be used to implement the CGI programs as a Java-based solution?

   A. JMAPI

   B. Screen scrapers

   C. Enterprise JavaBeans

   D. Servlets

5. What are the primary differences between the use of object mapping and screen scrapers in providing access to legacy systems?

   A. Object mapping is less prone to fail because of anomalies in the legacy system user interface.

   B. Screen scrapers appear as display terminals to legacy systems and object mappers generally do not.

   C. Screen scrapers execute on character-display terminals and object mapping tools do not.

   D. Screen scrapers are more secure than object mapping tools.

APPLY YOUR KNOWLEDGE

6. Which technologies are effective in securing legacy systems?

    A. Firewalls

    B. Virtual private networks

    C. Screen scrapers

    D. Java RMI

7. Which technologies are effective in accessing legacy systems that are implemented as CORBA objects?

    A. Java IDL

    B. JNI

    C. A Java-to-COM bridge

    D. JDBC

8. Which of the following are advantages of Java-based solutions over C++-based solutions?

    A. Platform independence

    B. Security

    C. Performance

    D. Automatic garbage collection

Answers to Review Questions

1. A screen scraper is a software application that translates an existing client interface into a set of objects that can be used to build new client software.

2. Legacy object mapping builds object wrappers around legacy system interfaces in order to access elements of legacy system business logic and database tiers directly. Legacy object mapping tools are used to create proxy objects that access legacy system functions and make them available in an object-oriented manner.

3. An off-board server is a server that executes as a proxy for a legacy system. It communicates with the legacy system using the custom protocols supported by the legacy system. It communicates with external applications using industry-standard protocols.

4. Database middleware enables legacy databases to be accessed from Java by translating between JDBC and the drivers that are supported by the legacy databases.

5. JNI is used to write custom code to interface Java objects with legacy software that does not support standard communication interfaces.

6. A Java-to-COM bridge enables COM objects to be accessed as Java classes and Java classes to be accessed as COM objects.

Answers to Exam Questions

1. A, B, and C   JNDI is not appropriate to providing access to character-based applications.

2. D   A Java-to-COM bridge may be used to access COM objects from Java.

3. A and B   Both the JDBC-ODBC bridge driver and database middleware may be used to provide connectivity to ODBC from JDBC.

APPLY YOUR KNOWLEDGE

4. C and D   Both Enterprise JavaBeans and Servlets may be used to upgrade CGI programs to Java-based solutions.

5. A and B   Since object mapping does not depend on "reading the screen," it is less prone to interface anomalies. Object mappers do not generally provide terminal emulation.

6. A and B   Firewalls and VPNs may be used to secure existing legacy systems.

7. A   Java IDL provides the capability to access CORBA objects from Java.

8. A, B, and D   Security, platform independence, and automatic garbage collection are advantages of Java over C++.

Suggested Readings and Resources

Legacy Objects Framework Yrrid Incorporated (`http://www.yrrid.com/lof/lof.htm`).

BECOMING A SUN CERTIFIED JAVA 2 DEVELOPER

This chapter helps you to prepare for the exam by covering the following objectives:

Know how the exam is given.

▶ The more information that you know about the certification exam, before going in to take it, the fewer surprises you'll have and the better off you'll be.

Know how to prepare for the certification exam.

▶ Given limited time and resources, you want to get the best return for the time that you put into studying. This chapter will give you study tips that can help you to maximize the benefits of your study efforts.

Know how to take the certification exam.

▶ The developer exam consists of two parts. The first part is a programming assignment. The second part is a series of short essay questions. Each of these parts requires a different set of skills. This chapter provides pointers that will help you improve your overall score.

CHAPTER *22*

Overview of the Java Developer Exam

OUTLINE

CHAPTER INTRODUCTION

This chapter introduces you to the Sun Certified Java Developer Exam for the Java 2 Platform. It identifies the topics that the exam covers, discusses how the exam is given, and provides you with tips and other information on how to take the exam.

This chapter kicks off Part III of this book. Part I prepares you with the information that you need to pass the Java 2 programmer certification exam. Part II covers the Java 2 architect certification exam. The Java 2 developer examination is independent of the Java 2 architect examination.

NOTE **Developer Exam Prerequisite** You are required to take and pass the Java 2 programmer examination before taking the Java 2 developer examination.

HOW THE EXAM IS GIVEN

The Java 2 developer examination is unique in that it consists of two parts: a programming assignment and a short essay exam. The programmer and architect exams consist mostly of multiple choice and fill-in-the-blank questions. The developer exam is considered to be the most difficult of the three exams. It is certainly the most time-consuming and the most difficult to prepare for. However, I also found it to be the most challenging and enjoyable of the three examinations.

The Programming Assignment

The programming assignment is referred to as the performance-based part of the examination. It consists of a partial program, a database file, program documentation, and instructions that are either emailed to you or downloaded from Sun's Web site. These files are personalized for each exam candidate in that they contain different programs and assignments. This reduces the benefits of multiple candidates collaborating on their programming assignments. You complete the program according to the instructions and upload it to Sun's Web site.

The assignment is graded in two parts. In the first part, a human examiner tests the functionality of your program to see if it correctly performs all required operations. Because you are given as much

NOTE

Test Harness   The JDK 1.1 developer exam used a test harness to test the functionality of your code. The test harness is not part of the Java 2 developer exam.

NOTE

Grading Information   The numbers in parentheses beside each criterion indicate the number of points available in that area. Note that the number of points adds up to 155 not 100.

time as you need to complete the programming assignment, there is no reason why you should not pass this part of the test. If you fail this part of the test, you fail the examination as a whole, and you'll have to start again with a new programming assignment.

In addition to testing the correct operation of your code, the examiner evaluates your submission according to the following evaluation criteria. Some criteria are general and may have an effect on the marks in other areas. The grading is covered in more detail in Chapter 23, "The Programming Assignment."

General Considerations (72 points total)

◆ Ease of use of, and documentation for, finished programs (15 points)—The overall ease of use and user friendliness of your program. The documentation of non-obvious aspects of source code. The avoidance of excessive commenting of obvious aspects of source code.

◆ Consistent and logical approach to problem solving (20 points)—The degree to which your program exhibits a unified, well thought out solution to its requirements. The use of appropriate coding techniques and the avoidance of complex algorithms when simpler ones can be used.

◆ Adherence to coding standards and readability of code (15 points)—The degree to which your program uses conventional indentation, naming conventions, and consistent coding style.

◆ Clarity and maintainability of the design and implementation (7 points)—The extent to which your source code can be understood from comments, identifiers, and algorithms. The organization of the code in such a way that it may be easily modified without requiring global changes to the software design and implementation.

◆ Consistent and appropriate error handling (10 points)—The use of standard Java exception handling facilities. The ability to communicate errors to the user without having the program abort its execution.

◆ Use of Java core packages rather than reinvention(5 points)— The use of standard classes and interfaces from the Java 2 API, rather than ad-hoc, custom-built ones.

Documentation (10 points total—not broken out)

◆ Documentation of how to use the finished programs—The completed assignment must supply a README file that describes how to execute the programs and that identifies and describes each of the files that were submitted (and their location in the directory structure). This criterion measures how well you followed the instructions for preparing the README file.

◆ Javadoc source documentation—The extent to which you incorporated appropriate javadoc comments in your code. The clarity, consistency, and lack of errors in the javadoc documentation that is generated from your code.

◆ Documentation of non-obvious aspects of the code—Those areas of your code where the software's behavior is not obvious should be commented to describe the code's operation.

◆ Avoidance of excessive commenting of "obvious" aspects of code—Those areas of your code where the software's behavior is obvious should not be commented.

◆ User documentation—The extent to which you satisfied all deliverables identified in your programming assignment.

Object-Oriented Design (6 points total—not broken out)

◆ Appropriate use of member variables, methods, and method automatics—The decision as to which variables should be member variables and which should be local. An appropriate choice of methods, method parameters, and method return types.

◆ Appropriate accessibility and scope of members—The decision as to which access modifiers are used with member variables and methods. The declaration of local variables with an appropriate scope.

User Interface (20 points total—not broken out)

◆ Layout supports required features and extensions—The degree to which the user interface satisfies its requirements.

◆ Layout uses good/accepted Human/Computer Interaction (HCI) principles—The extent to which the user interface follows standard GUI designs. The implementation of proper JDK 1.1 event interfaces/adapters and properly structured event handlers. Avoiding unnecessary components in GUI construction. Avoidance of untidy appearance, in so far as the assignment's specifications allow choice.

Data Conversion Program (10 points total)

◆ The degree to which the data conversion program described in the assignment satisfies its requirements and the overall usability of the program.

Server Design (37 points total)

◆ Appropriate classes are utilized in a thread-safe manner (8 points)—The use of thread-safe programming practices in the server and network interface.

◆ Locking is correctly implemented (15 points)—Record locking is used within the database and correctly implemented.

◆ Error-handling (6 points)—The use of appropriate error-handling techniques.

◆ Search algorithm, clarity, and efficiency (8 points)—The use of a standard, efficient search algorithm implemented in a straightforward manner.

Because the second part of the grading is performed by a person, it may take some time to get the results back. Allow up to 30 days for the grading to be completed.

The Essay Exam

The second part of the developer exam consists of a small number (5–10) of short-answer essay questions. The exam is taken at a Sylvan Authorized Prometric Testing Center in the same manner as the programmer exam. It differs from the programmer exam in that the developer exam questions are short essay questions, and the programmer exam consists of multiple-choice and fill-in-the-blank questions. The questions that are asked of you depend on the specific programming assignment that you were given. The following is a sample question that is provided by Sun:

SAMPLE QUESTION

In various method calls in your assignment submission, you were forced to deal with possible exceptions that could be thrown due to a number of different circumstances.

A. Describe (in not more than four sentences each) two approaches to indicate to the caller of a method that the method has failed its operation. One of these approaches should be the one you implemented in your assignment submission.

B. Which of these approaches did you use in your assignment submission?

C. Describe (in not more than two sentences each) a total of no more than six advantages and disadvantages of these approaches.

D. Describe the design goals you were guided by that led you to implement the approach you selected in your assignment submission.

As you can see from the preceding question, the exam requires careful thought and clear, concise, and well-justified answers. Unlike the programmer and architect exams, you can't simply guess at questions that you do not know. For this reason, the developer exam is considered to be the most difficult of the three Java certification exams.

WHAT THE EXAM COVERS

The Java 2 developer exam covers a wide range of topics related to Java software development. To complete the programming assignment and answer the essay exam questions, you need to be very familiar with the Java language, its use in developing applications, the Java 2 API, and your particular assignment. The following technologies are listed by Sun as being covered by the exam:

- TCP/IP Networking
- I/O Streams
- RMI
- Object Serialization
- JDBC
- Swing
- JDK 1.1 Event Model
- Javadoc
- Multithreading
- Error and Exception Handling
- Client-Server Design
- Interface Design

HOW TO PREPARE FOR THE EXAM

By taking and passing the programmer exam, you are well on your way to taking the developer exam. The developer exam requires additional experience in two areas:

- Hands-on Java programming
- More breadth and depth of knowledge of the Java 2 API

In my opinion, by passing the programmer exam, you've demonstrated your ability to write small Java applications. In addition, you've also demonstrated your ability to read and work with the Java

API documentation in so far as the fundamental API classes are concerned. You simply need to extend your programming skill to an application the size of the developer programming assignment and your API knowledge to the topics listed in the previous section. Depending on your current programming skills, there are two ways to do this.

If you've already written medium-sized, GUI-based, client-server applications in Java as part of a work or school assignment, I urge you to jump right in and download the programming assignment. In that way, you'll be able to determine your strengths and weaknesses.

If you don't feel comfortable in your knowledge of the Java 2 Platform API or writing medium-sized, GUI-based, client-server applications, I suggest that you pick up *Java 2 Platform Unleashed* (Sams Publishing, ISBN: 0-672-31631-5) and work your way through some of the relevant programming examples before downloading the developer programming assignment. You'll know that you're ready for the assignment when your programming confidence and curiosity about the assignment dominate your apprehension about completing the assignment.

The most critical step in the developer exam is getting your code to work correctly and satisfy all requirements specified in the instructions of your assignment. To this end, I suggest that you read the instructions that come with the programming assignment. After you have read the instructions, read them again. After you have read them a second time, take notes on what you have read. There are few things more frustrating than spending time and effort programming the wrong thing or writing a program that overlooks a critical aspect of the assignment. In the end, your program must conform to the instructions.

After you've completed the programming part of the assignment, test your program to make sure that it satisfies all requirements identified in the instructions. When you're satisfied that it does so, have someone else independently test it as a backup check.

Now you're ready to evaluate your code according to the evaluation factors identified earlier in the chapter. When performing a self-evaluation, don't try to justify why you've met each criterion. Instead, try to think of ways that your software can be improved to better satisfy each criterion. After you are satisfied that you've done all you can, have a friend perform an independent evaluation.

> **NOTE**
>
> **Do's and Don'ts** Chapter 23, "The Programming Assignment," provides a detailed list of do's and don'ts that will help you complete the developer assignment.

Preparation for the essay exam should be directed at helping you improve your ability to discuss the programming tradeoffs that were involved in your assignment. This requires thinking and writing skills in addition to your programming skills. I suggest that you write up a summary of all the programming changes that you made in your assignment.

This will help you in two ways. First, it will force you to revisit your assignment and keep it fresh in your mind. Second, it will spur you to think about what you've done, what alternatives were open to you, and why you selected one approach over another. When you've finished, try explaining what you've written to a friend. When you get to the essay exam, this practice will help you better explain different aspects of what you've done.

HOW TO TAKE THE EXAM

There are several areas of preparation that you should address in order to prepare for the developer exam:

◆ Make sure that your code satisfies all of its requirements. This is a must. If you fail to meet a requirement, you will not pass the developer exam.

◆ Make sure that your completed assignment addresses the instructions completely. You should do what you're told—nothing more and nothing less.

◆ Perform a self-evaluation and identify ways that you can improve your code.

After you've uploaded your completed programming assignment, you're ready to take the essay exam. I suggest that you do this as quickly as possible, while the assignment is still fresh in your mind.

When you answer each question, remember the three Cs—clarity, completeness, and conciseness. Clarity is a must. A human has to read your answer. If he or she can't understand what you're talking about, you lose. Completeness is also important. Half-answers get half points. Finally, conciseness is also a factor. Long, rambling answers give the appearance that you are shotgunning your response to increase the likelihood that you'll hit on the important points of the answer. If you don't know how to answer the question, this may be your only alternative. However, if you do know the answer, write it as succinctly as you can. The evaluator will appreciate it and be more inclined to grade you highly.

Here are a few tips on writing style that may help you win some points from the evaluator:

◆ Try to limit your answers to short, declarative sentences that make a point. Don't use long, rambling, run-on sentences.

◆ Make your answers as easy to read as possible. But, don't talk down to the reader.

◆ Don't explain the obvious.

◆ Try to convince the evaluator that you thought through the programming tradeoffs involved with your assignment and selected an approach that is consistent with your thought process.

After you've made a first pass through the questions, go back and try to answer any questions that you had difficulty with. At this point, you should try to answer all the exam questions. If you don't know the answer to a question, take your best guess. Any correct guess will improve your overall score.

If after answering all the exam questions, you have time left, go back and check your answers. However, don't try to second guess yourself. Instead, reread each question and each answer to make sure that you understood each question and provided an appropriate answer to each question.

EXAM TIP **Managing Your Time** Make sure that you budget your test time to allow yourself to answer all the exam questions. Don't waste time dwelling on questions that you're having a hard time answering.

EXAM TIP **Outline Your Answers** Use the blank sheets of paper that are made available to you during the exam to outline your answers to the questions. By doing so, your answers will be better organized, more complete, and more to the point.

CHAPTER SUMMARY

This chapter introduces you to the Sun Certified Java Developer Exam for the Java 2 Platform. It identifies the topics that the exam covers, discusses how the exam is given, and provides you with tips and other information on how to take the exam. You should now be able to go on to study the remaining chapters of Part III. There are no review or exam questions in this chapter.

Suggested Readings and Resources

Details of the Sun Certified Java Developer Program for the Java 2 Platform
(http://suned.sun.com/usa/cert_test.html)

This chapter helps you to prepare for the exam by covering the following objectives:

Know what to expect in the programming assignment.

▶ The more information you know about the programming assignment the more you'll be able to prepare before starting it.

Know the do's and don'ts of completing and submitting your programming assignment.

▶ Although the programming assignment instructions are fairly specific, some of us have a tendency to overlook the obvious. There are a few key do's and don'ts that you should be aware of before completing and submitting your assignment. Following these points will ensure that you don't overlook important points about the assignment or do any extra work that is not required.

Get experience with a sample assignment.

▶ In order to give you a good feel for what to expect on the programming assignment, you'll take a look at a programming assignment that was given to me as part of my Java 2 developer's exam.

CHAPTER 23

The Programming Assignment

OUTLINE

CHAPTER INTRODUCTION

Successful completion of the programming assignment is key to passing the developer exam. If your program doesn't meet its requirements or doesn't meet the evaluation criteria, you don't pass. In this chapter, you'll learn how to get past this critical step in the developer certification process. You'll learn how the programming assignment works, do's and don'ts for completing the assignment, and what a sample assignment is like.

HOW THE PROGRAMMING ASSIGNMENT WORKS

The programming assignment is the core of the developer exam. Successful completion of the assignment is key to passing the exam.

Each person who takes the developer exam is given a unique programming assignment. The assignment consists of a partial set of programs that need to be completed as specified by the instructions that accompany the programming assignment. The instructions are very detailed and provide all the information that is needed to successfully complete the assignment. If you read the instructions and follow them step-by-step, you'll be well on your way to passing this part of the exam.

When you finish the assignment, you package your assignment as a .jar file, according to the instructions, and upload it to the Sun Educational Services Certification Database. It is then evaluated as described in Chapter 22, "Overview of the Java Developer Exam."

DO'S AND DON'TS

It is very tempting to dig into your programming assignment as soon as you download it. After all, to take the developer exam, you are required to be a Certified Java Programmer. This means that you know the Java language inside out and are familiar with the fundamental API packages. After breezing through the instructions, it is tempting to start coding. You might even note some deficiencies in the sample code that is provided and decide to upgrade the programming assignment to make it more efficient, more capable, or more user friendly. The purpose of this section is to help you put the brakes on your ambition and concentrate on what you need to do to pass the exam. The subsections that follow provide simple lists of five do's and five don'ts that will help you avoid costly errors in your programming assignment.

Do's

◆ After you download your programming assignment, make a copy of it, and put the original copy away somewhere safe. Never modify or use the original copy. Make another copy of it when you need access to the original files. You'll need access to these files when you test your program.

◆ Read through the instructions for your programming assignment at least twice before you start your assignment. It's very frustrating to be about to complete your assignment and then find out that you overlooked a critical part of it or have done far more work than you needed to.

◆ Make your code easy to read and easy to understand. Format your code using the same style used in the code that is provided. Comment your code as instructed. Use javadoc comments with your classes and interfaces and the public properties, constructors, and methods of these classes and interfaces. Use comments with any complex or non-standard algorithms where the code does not document itself. But don't over comment. Commenting the obvious will cause you to lose points.

◆ Use the JDK 1.1 event delegation model as opposed to the JDK 1.02 event inheritance model. If you feel more comfortable with the JDK 1.02 model, don't let that sway you. You will lose points if you don't use the JDK 1.1 event delegation model.

◆ Use standard objects and algorithms whenever possible. If you have to lay out a container, use a standard layout manager. If you have to perform a sort, use a standard sort algorithm. Don't create a home-grown solution where a standard one will suffice. Failure to do so will cause you to lose points.

Don'ts

◆ Don't use the programming assignment files of others. It's OK to collaborate with others, just don't mix your files together, even if you think you have the same assignment. Some assignments differ only slightly.

◆ Don't add to your workload by doing things that are not called for by your programming assignment's instructions. Additional bells and whistles will not improve your grade, but they can lower it.

◆ Don't use a complex solution if a simple solution is available. The evaluation criteria stress simplicity and maintainability.

◆ Don't duplicate what's available in the Java 2 API. If the Java 2 API provides a class that you can use, use it. You'll lose points if you don't use the Java 2 API to the maximum extent possible.

◆ Don't submit a 95% solution. If your program does not completely satisfy its requirements or meet the evaluation criteria, don't submit it. Take whatever time is needed to complete the assignment as specified in a way that all requirements are satisfied.

A Sample Assignment

The programming assignment that I received for the Java 2 developer's exam was to complete the development of a database application for "Fly By Night Services," a travel agency. According to the assignment's description, the application was developed by an undergraduate student during his summer break. The application consists of a rudimentary database system. My assignment was to extend the existing application in accordance with a strict set of guidelines.

Project Description and Guidance

The instructions provided an overall description of what I was to do to successfully complete the programming assignment. It began with some background information on the system, which I'll summarize as follows:

◆ The application maintains flight information about airline routes and is used to find and book flights that meet customer requirements.

◆ The database implemented by the student is a flat ASCII file and must be converted for use with a database provided in the suncertify.db package. A conversion program must be written that is easy to use and that can support future conversions.

The instructions then go on to identify what must be accomplished as part of the programming assignment:

◆ Develop a GUI client for viewing flight information and booking flights.

◆ Develop extensions to the database to support flexible searching and record locking.

◆ Implement the database as a multithreaded server on the network.

◆ Provide a communications interface between the GUI client and database server.

◆ Implement the data conversion program used to convert the ASCII text file for use with the database.

In addition, the following requirements were identified:

◆ Clarity and maintainability—A clear, simple design is preferred to a more complex one. The design should be maintainable by junior programmers. Standard algorithms should be used where possible. Poor algorithm design is penalized.

◆ Documentation—The code should be designed so that its processing is as clear as possible. Awkward or complex code should have descriptive comments. Javadoc comments should be used for each part of a class's public interface. Javadoc documentation must be created for all classes of the completed project. User documentation must be provided for both the application (client and server) and the conversion program. The documentation should allow someone who is familiar with travel agency functions to use the application and conversion program. Documentation may be provided on-line, as appropriate.

◆ Correctness—The design used must correctly implement all requirements and pass all tests performed by the examiner.

Architectural Design

The architectural design section of the instructions describes the intended system architecture:

◆ The application consists of three major components: the GUI client, the database server, and a client-side database client that supports communication between the GUI client and database server.

◆ The application must be able to run in either a networked or standalone mode. In the networked mode, the database server executes on a separate computer from the client and client-server communication occurs over a network. In the stand-alone mode, the client and server run in the same JVM. The mode of operation must be user selectable at program startup.

◆ The network connection protocol may be either Java RMI or a custom protocol that uses serialized objects over TCP sockets.

◆ The remote client code must provide an implementation of the `public` methods of `suncertify.db.Data`, a class that's provided with the assignment.

Figure 23.1 summarizes this architecture.

Software Description

The architectural design is followed by a description of the software that comprises the application. This description also includes instructions for what needs to be modified, how the application is to run, and how it is to be submitted.

FIGURE 23.1

Target system architecture.

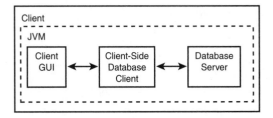

Networked Architecture

Standalone Architecture

◆ The suncertify.db package—The three classes in this package—Data, DataInfo, and FieldInfo—are complete with the exception of three methods that must be supplied for Data. Additional classes and interfaces may be created and added to the suncertify.db package.

◆ Methods to be implemented—A description of the three methods of the Data class that are to be implemented as part of the assignment is provided. The criteriaFind() method is used to perform a database search. The lock() and unlock() methods are used to implement record locking. Record locking allows multiple clients to access the database concurrently.

◆ Database server—The database server must be capable of supporting multiple concurrent network connections and must be implemented in a threadsafe manner. The suncertify.db package also must be made threadsafe.

◆ Database client program—The database client program should implement the same public methods as suncertify.db.Data and support constructors for specifying network connection parameters.

◆ Target Platform—Sun's Java 2 platform (both the Java 2 SDK and JRE 1.2) is the target platform on which the assignment is to be developed and run.

◆ Use of an Integrated Development Environment (IDE)—An IDE may be used to develop the application, however the final software must be independent of the IDE and must be able to run apart from it.

◆ Packaging—The submitted assignment must be packaged in such a way that it is clear how it should be run using the JRE 1.2 on any platform (not just Solaris or Windows). The command lines that run these programs must be documented.

The above requirements provide a framework for completing the database portion of the programming assignment.

User Interface Design

The programming assignment instructions go on to provide an additional description of the user interface. This description greatly simplifies the user-interface development.

◆ Use of Swing components—The client GUI should only use Swing components. The JTable class should be used to provide the core of the user interface.

◆ Interface capabilities—The user should be able to select flights based on origin and destination and book flights seats on a selected flight. The user must be informed about the success or failure of a booking.

◆ Future enhancements—The user interface must be upgradeable to support future enhancements and must minimize operational impacts of an upgrade on its users.

◆ Modes of operation—The user interface must be able to connect to the database server in either a networked or standalone mode, as selected by the user.

Unlike the JDK 1.1 developer assignment, the Java 2 developer assignment provides much more leeway on how the GUI is to be organized.

> **NOTE**
>
> **Use of Java 2 Platform**   Make sure that you use the Java 2 platform to compile and run your code. It won't matter if your code runs under JDK 1.1 or a Java 2 platform supplied by an independent vendor. If your code doesn't run under *Sun's* Java 2 platform, you'll fail your assignment. Also, make sure that your code runs with the Java Runtime Environment (JRE) 1.2, as well as the full-blown Java 2 platform SDK.

> **NOTE**
>
> **Deprecated Methods**   You may notice some deprecated methods when you attempt to compile the code that is provided with your assignment. The deprecated methods must be corrected using non-deprecated alternatives.

Network Protocol

The next major element of the programming assignment instructions is a summary of the protocol between the user interface and the database server. This description identifies the configuration information required to implement the client-server connection:

◆ The use of network or standalone mode

◆ The server's host name or IP address

◆ The server port

◆ Data file names

◆ The RMI code base

◆ The application's security policy file

Even though a security policy file is provided, the application security is minimal. The database server does not authenticate the client, data is not encrypted, and no data integrity measures are used in client-server communication.

The Data Conversion Tool

Requirements for the data conversion tool are specified and the format and contents of the test data set are included.

Deliverables

A description of the deliverables that need to be included with the submission of the programming assignment is identified. These deliverables are as follows:

◆ Source and object code

◆ Javadoc documentation

◆ Database server documentation

◆ User interface

◆ Data conversion tool documentation

◆ README file

The details on what should appear in the README file are covered. However, the details of the database server, user interface, and data conversion tool documentation are not provided.

CHAPTER SUMMARY

In this chapter, you learned how the programming assignment works, do's and don'ts for completing the assignment, and what a sample assignment is like. The following review questions will reinforce important points about what you learned. Because there are no exam questions on the programming assignment, there are no exam questions provided with this chapter.

APPLY YOUR KNOWLEDGE

Review Questions

1. What happens if you submit a programming assignment that does not meet all requirements identified in the instructions?

2. When should comments be used?

3. Is extra credit given for programs that provide additional functionality?

4. Why is it a good idea to make a backup copy of the programming assignment?

Answers to Review Questions

1. You fail the programming assignment. There is no reason to submit a program that doesn't satisfy all identified requirements.

2. Javadoc comments should be used with all classes and interfaces that you develop. They should also be used with public properties (field variables), constructors, and methods. Standard comments should be used to document complex or non-standard code. Comments should not be used to describe what is obvious.

3. No extra credit is given for extra functionality that is not identified in the instructions. You may lose points if you stray too far beyond what is required by the programming assignment instructions.

4. It is a good idea to make a copy of the assignment because some of the files used by the program may be modified. If you don't make a backup copy, you may not be able to recover these files.

Suggested Readings and Resources

Jamie Jaworski, *Java 2 Platform Unleashed*, Sams, 1999.

This chapter helps you to prepare for the exam by covering the following objectives:

Know what to expect in the essay exam.

▶ The more information that you know about the essay exam, the better prepared you'll be.

Know how to write your responses.

▶ Because the essay exam involves writing, the better you write, the better grade you'll get (everything else being equal). With this in mind, there are a few key do's and don'ts that you should keep in mind when you write your essays.

Get experience with some sample questions.

▶ In order to get a good feel for what to expect on the essay exam, you'll take a look at a few sample questions and answers.

CHAPTER 24

The Essay Exam

OUTLINE

CHAPTER INTRODUCTION

After you have successfully completed your programming assignment, the final step in the Developer certification process is to take and pass the essay exam. At this point, you're past the hardest part of the exam. All you have to do is remember what you did in your programming assignment and answer a few questions that test your knowledge of the trade offs involved in your assignment. In this chapter, you'll learn how to prepare for the essay exam. You'll learn how the essay exam works, do's and don'ts for writing your essays, and you'll go over a few sample questions.

HOW THE ESSAY EXAM WORKS

After you have completed and uploaded your programming assignment, you are eligible to take the essay exam. The essay exam is taken at a Sylvan Authorized Prometric Testing Center in the same way as the Programmer and Architect exams. The only difference between these exams and the essay exam is the type of questions (short essay versus multiple choice/fill in). The exam contains between five and ten short essay questions.

I recommend that you take the exam as soon as possible after completing the programming assignment, when it is still fresh in your mind. I also recommend that you follow all the tips in this chapter before you take the test. The following section, "How to Prepare for the Exam," will help you to thoroughly review your programming assignment.

You should be aware of one issue regarding the organization of the Developer exam. The sequence of testing activities is as follows:

1. Obtain voucher ($250) for programming assignment.

2. Receive programming assignment via email or download it.

3. Complete programming assignment.

4. Upload the completed programming assignment to the Sun Educational Services Certification Database.

5. Obtain voucher ($150) for the essay exam (exam number 310-024).

6. Take the essay exam at a Sylvan Authorized Prometric Testing Center.

7. Wait four weeks while your programming assignment and essay exam are graded by an independent, third-party assessor.

The catch in the above process is that you do not know whether you passed or failed your programming assignment before you take the essay exam. You have to shell out an extra $150 not knowing whether the essay exam will make a difference. However, in most cases, the fact that you completed the programming assignment and verified that you have satisfied the requirements in the instructions means that you are on the way to passing the Developer exam. You need a score of 80% to pass the programming assignment, but only a 70% score to pass the essay exam.

HOW TO PREPARE FOR THE EXAM

There are two basic ways to prepare for the essay exam:

1. Study the code you developed in your programming assignment.

2. Study ways to improve your written responses to the essay questions.

Each of these is equally important. You must remember what you did in the programming assignment in order to answer the essay questions. After all, part of the reason for the essay exam is to connect you to your programming assignment. Without the essay exam, you could simply get someone else to do your programming assignment for you. You must also be able to express yourself clearly and concisely in order to get a good grade for your answer.

There are a number of things that you can do to study for your programming assignment. I suggest the following:

◆ Make a list of all the changes that you made in your programming assignment.

◆ Make a list of all the tradeoffs and design decisions involved with these changes.

◆ Describe the thought processes involved in resolving the trade-offs and making the design decisions identified in the previous step. You should document the how and why of your design decisions.

◆ Put yourself in the shoes of the examiner. Try to come up with a list of questions that you would ask, based on the assignment and the information that you came up with in the previous steps.

◆ For each of the questions that you came up with in the previous step, identify the important points that you would look for in answers to these questions.

By following the above steps, you'll have a significant advantage when you take your exam. Not only will you have thoroughly reviewed your programming assignment, you will also have reexamined all your major design decisions from the perspective of the examiner. The next section looks at the second major exam preparation area: improving your writing.

Writing Do's and Don'ts

Having gone through the process of reviewing your programming assignment and looking at it from the perspective of the examiner, you should have the knowledge you need to answer the essay exam questions. To do well on the exam, all you have to do is take that knowledge and express it in a way that is clear, concise, consistent, and that answers the question. For some of you, this is easy to do. For others, it may be the most difficult part of the Developer exam. No matter what the level of your writing skills, the following 10 do's and don'ts can help you to complete the exam essays in an appropriate manner and convince the examiners that you thought through your programming assignment and made reasonable decisions.

Do's:

◆ Think about what you're going to write before you start typing. Use the scratch paper that is provided to you to outline your response. This will go a long way toward making your answer more thoughtful and better organized.

◆ Use short declarative sentences. Keep your sentence structure simple. Avoid complex, run-on sentences. This will make it easier for the reviewer to understand what you have to say.

◆ Get to the point and stick to the point. The exam questions are fairly specific. Focus on answering the question. Don't get into tangential discussions. It's okay to provide background information, as long as it makes your point. Remember the reviewer is looking for specific information that will convince him or her that you understand how to make good design decisions and tradeoffs. Give the reviewer what he needs. However, don't make him wade through a lot of information to find it.

◆ If you don't know the complete answer, provide as much information as you can. For example, if the question asks you to discuss the three alternatives you had in throwing and catching exceptions, and you can only think of two, describe those two. When you finish the other exam questions, you can go back and try to come up with a third alternative. If you absolutely don't know the answer, take your best shot at it. Use your intuition. After all, you are a certified Java programmer. You may get lucky and hit upon the correct answer. You may get partial credit. You may help to identify a bad exam question. Nothing ventured, nothing gained.

◆ When you finish the exam, go back and review your answers. Make whatever changes you can to improve the clarity of your responses. However, don't second guess yourself. Your first instincts are usually correct.

Don'ts:

◆ Avoid ambiguity. If you are referring to the getXYZ() method of the MyException exception, refer to it by name. Reading a description of someone's code can be quite complex. Make it easy as possible for the reviewer.

◆ Don't be stilted, stuffy, or condescending. Write naturally. The reviewer will understand technical programming terms like bubble sort, linked list, etc. You don't have to waste time explaining them. Pretend that the reviewer is a friend who is at the same programming level as you. Write down what you might say to explain your coding decisions to him. However, don't be too chummy.

◆ Don't explain too much. After you've answered the question and made your point, stop. There are two reasons for this: first, if you spend too much time on one question, you might not finish the exam and second, after you've carefully answered the question, any additional information will not help. In fact, it might confuse the reviewer. The reviewer may think, "He answered the question and then provided this additional stuff. Maybe he was shotgunning his answer."

◆ Don't criticize the question. If you don't like the question, keep it to yourself. Don't say, "This is a terrible question" or "Why would anyone want to know that?" However, if you don't understand the question or you think that it is ambiguous, let the reviewer know. For example, if you aren't sure whether a question is asking you to cover X or Y, then state, "I'm not sure whether the question is asking for X or Y, so I'll cover both." The reviewer will take your confusion into account and give you credit for X or Y, whichever is correct.

◆ Don't criticize your code. If a question makes you think that you overlooked a better way to have completed your assignment, don't break down and confess your lack of insight to the reviewer. Stand behind your work. If you are asked a direct question why you didn't follow a seemingly better course, state the advantages of your solution, state the disadvantages of the alternative, and come up with a really good reason for doing things the way you did. The reviewer is more interested in seeing that you thought through your programming assignment and made the proper tradeoffs. Responses such as "I didn't think of that" won't help your grade.

By following the above suggestions, you'll be well on your way to answering the essay questions clearly, concisely, and consistently. This will make it easier for the reviewer to give you a good grade.

SAMPLE ESSAYS

In order to give you an example of how the exam works and how to model your answers, I'll cover three example questions. The first one is from the 1.1 Developer's exam. The other two I made up based upon the Java 2 Developer's exam.

Question 1

In various method calls in your assignment submission, you were forced to deal with possible exceptions that could be thrown due to a number of different circumstances.

A. Describe (in not more than four sentences each) two approaches to indicate to the caller of a method that the method has failed its operation. One of these approaches should be the one you implemented in your assignment submission.

B. Which of these approaches did you use in your assignment submission?

C. Describe (in not more than two sentences each) a total of no more than six advantages and six disadvantages of these approaches.

D. Describe the design goals you were guided by that led you to implement the approach you selected in your assignment submission.

Answers to Question 1

This question is pretty straightforward. The answers ahould be organized according to the four subquestions (A through D). The first answer is limited to four sentences and the third answer is limited to a maximum of twelve sentences (six advantages/disadvantages at two sentences each). The following is a sample response to this question:

A. Two ways to notify a caller of a method that the method has failed its operation are 1) throw an exception that indicates the type of failure that occurred, or 2) return a value that indicates the success or failure of the method.

B. I used the first approach (throwing an exception) in my programming assignment.

C. The advantages of using exceptions are that first, it is the standard way of signaling errors that occur during the execution of a Java program and second, it enables error-handling code to be separated from a program's normal flow of control. The disadvantage of using exceptions is that it requires slightly more code to declare, throw, and catch the exceptions. The advantage of using a return value to indicate an error is that it requires less code to set up. The disadvantage of using an error return value is that it is non-standard and forces the caller to immediately check for an error upon the method's return.

D. My design goals were to use all the features of the programming language and to use them in the standard way that they are intended to be used. That is why I chose to use exceptions rather than error return values.

Question 2

In your assignment, you were required to implement a multi-threaded server.

A. Describe two approaches to implementing your thread classes and identify the approach you selected.

B. Identify the tradeoffs involved and reasons why you selected one approach to implementing your threads over the other.

Answers to Question 2

This question comes in two parts. The answer to the first part requires you to be able to identify two approaches to implementing threads. The answer to the second part requires you to be able to identify the reasoning behind the approach that you selected. The following is a sample answer:

A. The two alternative approaches to implementing my thread classes were first, to extend the `java.lang.Thread` class and second, to implement the `java.lang.Runnable` interface. I opted to extend the `java.lang.Thread` class.

B. The tradeoff involved determining whether it was more appropriate to have my thread class (`ServerThread`) extend `Thread` or be somewhere else in the Java class hierarchy (implement `Runnable`). I decided to extend `Thread` because my `ServerThread` class did not need to extend any other classes in the Java class hierarchy. The reasoning behind the decision was that I could take advantage of the support provided by `Thread` rather than having to provide that support for a class that implements `Runnable`.

Question 3

In your assignment, you were required to organize your application's GUI as shown in the example screen shot.

A. Describe the approach you used to lay out the GUI. If you used a null layout manager (absolute sizing and positioning), explain the reason why you chose to do so. If you used one or more of the standard AWT or Swing layout managers, explain why you selected the layout managers that you used.

B. What are two advantages of using a layout manager rather than absolute positioning?

Answers to Question 3

This question requires three answers. The first requires you to describe your approach to laying out your GUI. (Hopefully, you'll remember it.) The second answer requires you to explain your approach and compare it to using absolute positioning. Here is an example of how the question may be answered.

A. I used a combination of a BorderLayout and a FlowLayout to lay out the GUI as shown in the sample screen shot. I used a BorderLayout as the overall layout for the GUI because it consisted of a large text box in the center of the screen with controls along the bottom border. I used a FlowLayout to lay out the controls because they were organized in a left-to-right manner along the bottom border.

B. Two advantages of using a layout manager instead of absolute positioning are as follows:

1. Layout managers are portable across Java platforms. Absolute positioning runs into problems when dealing with platform-specific component sizes.

2. Layout managers adjust their layout appropriately when a container is resized. Absolute layouts do not change when a container is resized.

CHAPTER SUMMARY

In this chapter, you learned how to prepare for the essay exam. You learned how the essay exam works, how to review your programming assignment, and do's and don'ts for writing your essays. You also covered a few sample questions. The following review and exam questions will test your knowledge of the material that you covered in this chapter and identify areas for further study.

APPLY YOUR KNOWLEDGE

Review Questions

1. Why is it important to review your programming assignment before taking the essay exam?

2. Why is it important to write clearly and concisely when submitting your short essay answers?

Exam Questions

1. Why is it a good idea to review your programming assignment before the essay exam?

   A. The essay exam will ask you questions about tradeoffs and design decisions involved in your programming assignment.

   B. If you find any errors in the programming assignment, you can resubmit the assignment and get a higher grade.

   C. So you can decide which essay exam questions should be answered.

   D. By doing so you may be able to get some insight into the types of questions that you will be asked in the essay exam.

2. Which of the following should you consider when reviewing your programming assignment?

   A. All the code changes that you made in your programming assignment.

   B. The tradeoffs and design decisions involved with completing the assignment.

   C. The number of lines of code that you wrote in each class.

   D. The types of questions that are reasonable for an examiner to ask based upon the code changes that you made.

3. Which of the following will help you in writing your short essays?

   A. Praising the creator of the exam and the questions he or she wrote.

   B. Outlining what you're going to write before you start writing.

   C. Using simple declarative sentences as opposed to more complex sentence structure.

   D. Reviewing and improving your answers after you have answered all questions.

Answers to Review Questions

1. The essay exam will ask questions about the tradeoffs and design decisions involved in your programming assignment. These questions are difficult to answer if you forgot what you did in your assignment.

2. Your objective in answering the essay questions should be to convince the examiner that you understand the tradeoffs involved with your design decisions and made appropriate choices. This is difficult to do if the examiner has trouble understanding your response or must wade through volumes of information to find the answer he is looking for.

Apply Your Knowledge

Answers to Exam Questions

1. A and D　The reasons that you should review your programming assignment are so that you have it fresh in your mind when you go to take the test and so that you can gain some insight into the types of questions that you'll be asked.

2. A, B, and D　Although you want to perform a thorough, thoughtful review of your assignment, you don't have to keep track of the number of lines of code you wrote.

3. B, C, and D　Flattery will not earn you a higher grade.

Suggested Readings and Resources

1. Jamie Jaworski, *Java 2 Platform Unleashed*, Sams, 1999.

2. William Strunk and E. B. White, *The Elements of Style*, Macmillan Publishing Company, 1979.

PART IV

Appendixes

Running the Simulated Exam Program

OBJECTIVES

This appendix shows you how to install and run the simulated exam program. This program provides you with a set of questions that simulate those found on the exam. You can use this program to measure your knowledge of the material covered in each chapter and identify those areas where you need more study.

INSTALLING THE SIMULATED EXAM PROGRAM

The simulated exam program is pre-compiled and can be run directly from the CD. However, it will run faster if you copy it to your hard disk. It requires that the final version of the Java 2 platform (formerly known as JDK 1.2) be installed.

Both the simulated exam program and the exam preparation program are located in the \com\jaworski\quiz directory of the CD. Copy the \com directory and its subdirectories to the base directory in which the Java 2 platform is installed. On Windows systems, this will be the c:\jdk1.2 directory. After copying, the com directory will be a subdirectory of jdk1.2.

The next thing that you should do is set your CLASSPATH to include the c:\jdk1.2 directory. Under Windows 98 and 95, I set my CLASSPATH using the following statement:

```
set CLASSPATH=.;c:\jdk1.2;
```

> **NOTE**
>
> **Setting your CLASSPATH** Always make sure that your CLASSPATH ends with a semi-colon. Otherwise, it may fail to pick up the last element in your CLASSPATH.

RUNNING THE SIMULATED EXAM PROGRAM

To run the simulated exam program, use the following command from within a console window:

```
java com.jaworski.quiz.Quiz
```

This launches the Quiz program as shown in Figure A.1. Select Open from the File menu to launch an Open File dialog box. Navigate to the com\jaworski\quiz directory and load any of the files with the .quiz extension. The part1.quiz file contains all the practice questions for the Java 2 programmer exam, and the part2.quiz file contains all the practice questions for the Java 2 architect exam. In addition, the files of the form `chnn.quiz` contain the questions for each chapter. For example, `ch02.quiz` contains the practice questions for Chapter 2, and `ch21.quiz` contains the practice questions for Chapter 21.

FIGURE A.1
The `Quiz` program opening display.

When you open a quiz file, the program's title bar changes to reflect the file that you loaded. Refer to Figure A.2. You should maximize the program window in order to use it most effectively. The program is designed for an 800x600 size screen. However, it will also work with screens of higher or lower resolution.

The program displays the first question of the practice exam. By default, the program displays the questions in the same order everytime you run it. You can select Randomize from the Questions menu to cause the program to display the questions randomly. Refer to Figure A.3. This randomize setting is not saved when you exit the program.

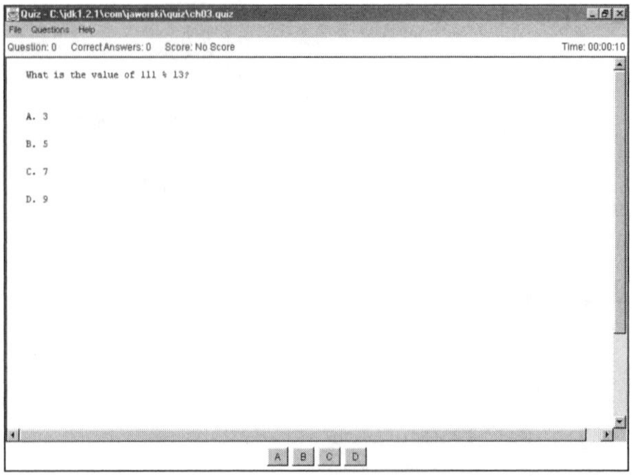

FIGURE A.2
Maximize the program window to increase its usability.

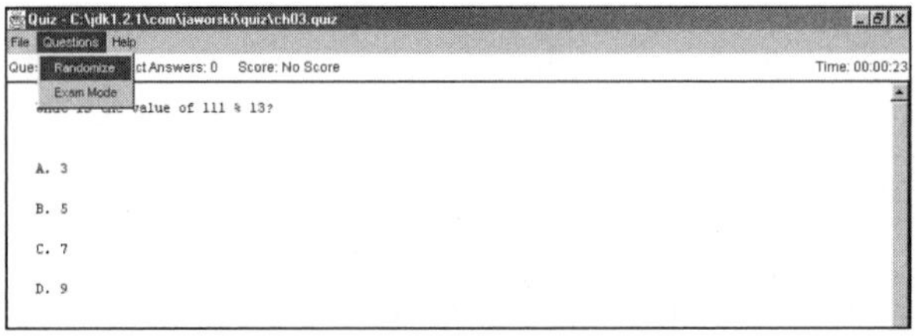

FIGURE A.3
Select Randomize from the Questions menu to randomize the order in which questions are asked.

The program supports both single-answer questions and multiple-answer questions. Figure A.4 shows an example of a single-answer question. The answers to the question are displayed as buttons at the bottom of the program window. To select an answer, simply click on the button that corresponds to that answer.

Figure A.5 provides an example of a multiple-answer question. Multiple-answer questions are answered by clicking the check boxes that correspond to each possible answer. Be sure to check all check boxes that apply to the question. When you have finished checking the check boxes, click on the Check Answer button.

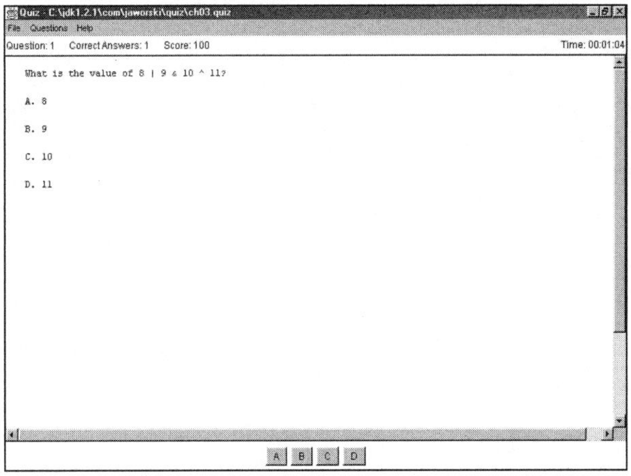

FIGURE A.4
Answer single-answer questions by clicking on the button that corresponds to the answer.

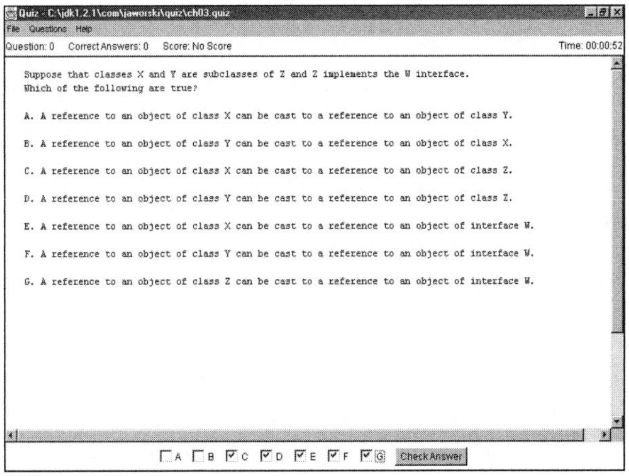

FIGURE A.5
Answer multiple-answer questions by checking all applicable check boxes and clicking on the Check Answer button.

After your have answered a question, the program will immediately check your answer and tell you how you did. If your answer is correct, the pro-

gram will notify you, as shown in Figure A.6. If your answer is incorrect, the program will display the correct answer, as shown in Figure A.7. In either case, the program will provide the rationale behind the correct answer.

> **NOTE**
>
> **Differences with actual exam program** The Quiz program differs from the actual exam program in that it provides you with immediate feedback on whether you answered a question correctly or incorrectly. I've added this feature to help you to learn from your mistakes. The actual exam program does not tell you which questions you've answered correctly or incorrectly.

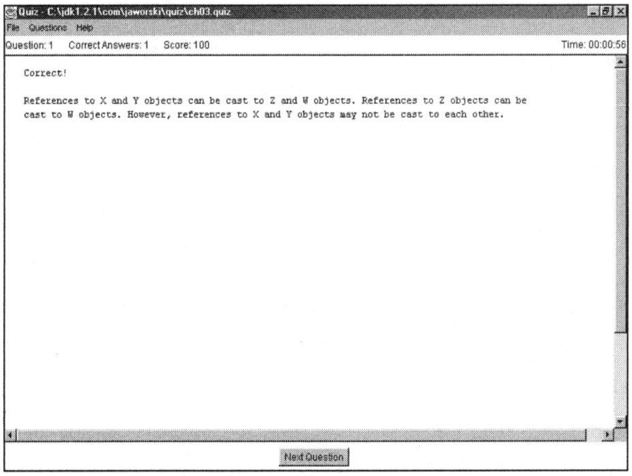

FIGURE A.6
The Quiz program notifies you of a correct answer.

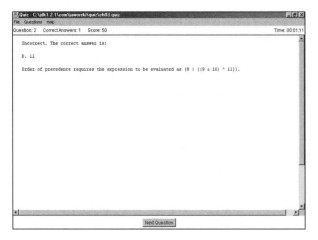

FIGURE A.7.
The `Quiz` program notifies you of an incorrect answer.

When you have finished reviewing the answer, click the Next Question button to go on to the next question.

The top of the program window displays the number of questions that were asked, the number of questions that you answered correctly, and your overall score. The score is calculated as the ratio of correctly answered questions to the number of questions that were asked. The total time that you've been taking the quiz is also displayed.

When you have answered all the questions in the file and reviewed the answer to the last question, the program notifies you that you've completed the quiz, displays your final score, and provides you with suggestions based on your score (see Figure A.8).

At this point, you can click the Restart button to take the quiz over again or open a new quiz file. In either case, your current randomize setting will carry over to the new quiz.

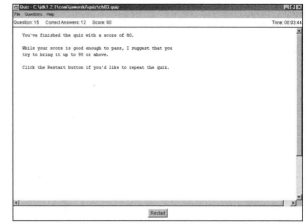

FIGURE A.8
When you finish a quiz, the program tells you your final score and gives you some advice.

The Questions menu also provides the Exam Mode option (see Figure A.9). You can use this option when you are running the part1.quiz or part2.quiz files. Exam mode causes your session to be limited to 2 hours or 59 questions (whichever comes first) just like on the actual exam. When the time or number of questions has expired, the exam will automatically stop and you will be notified of your results.

The File menu also provides the Close and Exit menu items. Selecting Close causes the current quiz to be terminated. Selecting Exit causes the program to terminate.

The About menu item of the Help menu displays the program's copyright notice. Figure A.10 shows this notice.

FIGURE A.9
The Exam Mode option may be used to simulate the actual two-hour exam.

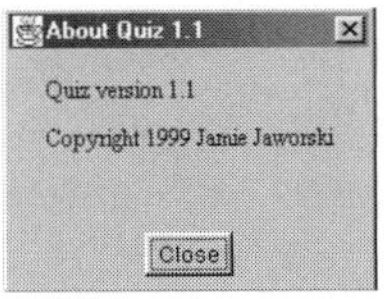

The Quiz program is simple to run and easy to use. Use it to test your knowledge of each chapter and to determine those areas in which you need further study. Check my Web site at http://www.jaworski.com/java/certification/ to download any new and updated quiz files.

FIGURE A.10
Selecting About from the Help menu displays the program's copyright notice.

Running the Simulated Preparation Program

OBJECTIVES

This appendix shows you how to install and run the exam preparation program. This program reviews the information presented in each chapter and presents you with flashcard-like questions that test your knowledge of this material.

INSTALLING THE EXAM PREPARATION PROGRAM

The exam preparation program is installed in the same manner as the Quiz program. Refer to Appendix A, "Running the Simulated Exam Program." It requires that the final version of the Java 2 platform (formerly known as JDK 1.2) be installed.

Both the simulated exam program and the exam preparation program are located in the \com\jaworski\quiz directory of the CD. Copy the \com directory and its subdirectories to the base directory in which the Java 2 platform is installed. On Windows systems, this will be the c:\jdk1.2 directory. After copying, the com directory will be a subdirectory of jdk1.2.

The next thing that you should do is set your CLASSPATH to include the c:\jdk1.2 directory. Under Windows 98 and 95, I set my CLASSPATH using the following statement:

```
set CLASSPATH=.;c:\jdk1.2;
```

> **NOTE**
>
> **Setting Your CLASSPATH** Always make sure that your CLASSPATH ends with a semi-colon. Otherwise, it may fail to pick up the last element in your CLASSPATH.

RUNNING THE EXAM PREPARATION PROGRAM

To run the exam preparation program, use the following command from within a console window:

```
java com.jaworski.quiz.Review
```

This launches the Review program as shown in Figure B.1. Select Open from the File menu to launch an open file dialog box. Navigate to the com\jaworski\quiz directory and load any of the files with the .review extension. The part1.review file contains all the review questions for the Java 2 programmer exam, and the `part2.review` file contains all the review questions for the Java 2 architect exam. In addition, the files of the form `chnn.review` contain the questions for each chapter. For example, `ch02.review` contains the review questions for Chapter 2, and `ch21.review` contains the review questions for Chapter 21.

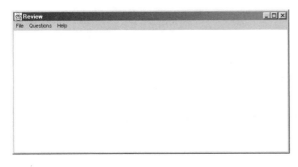

FIGURE B.1
The `Review` program opening display.

When you open a review question file, the program's title bar changes to reflect the file that you loaded. Refer to Figure B.2. Unlike the `Quiz` program, the `Review` program doesn't require much screen real estate and doesn't need to be maximized.

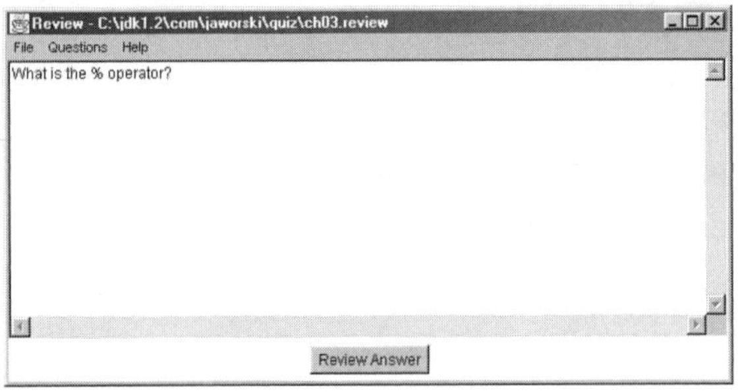

FIGURE B.2
The program's title bar confirms the file that was loaded.

The `Review` program, like the `Quiz` program, displays the questions in the same order every time you run it. You can select Randomize from the Questions menu to cause the program to display the questions randomly. This setting is not saved when the program is terminated.

The `Review` program displays a question which requires some thinking to answer. After you've thought through the answer, click the Review Answer button to see the question's answer. Refer to Figure B.3.

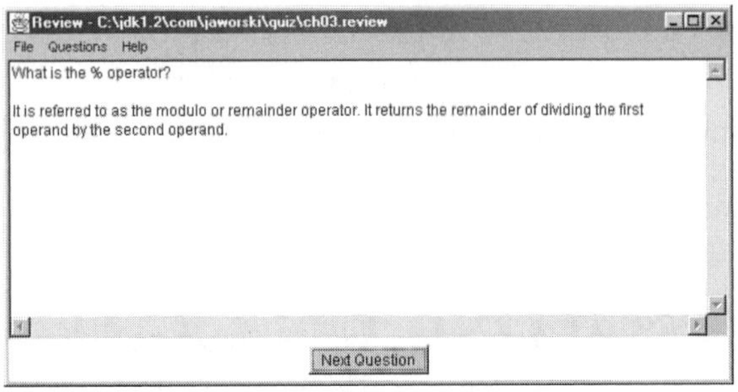

FIGURE B.3
The `Review` program displays the question with the answer.

Continue working through the questions. When you have finished the last question, the program will display the Finish button as shown in Figure B.4. When you click the Finish button, the program will tell you that you've finished the review and will allow you to restart the review questions. Refer to Figure B.5.

At this point, you can click the Restart button to review the questions over again or open a new file. Your current randomize setting will still be in effect.

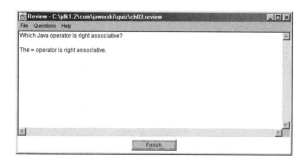

FIGURE B.4
The Review program displays the Finish button when all questions have been asked.

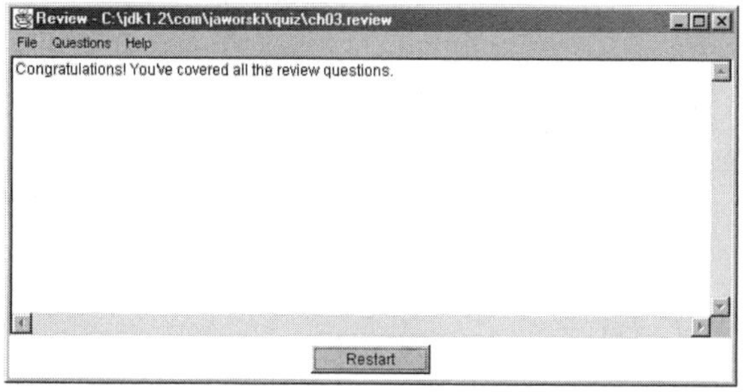

FIGURE B.5
The Restart button allows you to restart the question review.

The File menu also provides the Close and Exit menu items. Selecting Close causes the current file to be closed. Selecting Exit causes the program to terminate.

The About menu item of the Help menu displays the program's copyright notice. Figure B.6 shows this notice.

FIGURE B.6
Selecting About from the Help menu displays the program's copyright notice.

The Review program is simple to run and easy to use. Use it to test your knowledge of each chapter and to determine those areas in which you need further study. Check my Web site at http://www.jaworski.com/j2c/ to download any new and updated review question files.

Index

Q-R

S

New Riders

We Want to Know What You Think

To better serve you, we would like your opinion on the content and quality of this book. Please complete this card and mail it to us or fax it to 317-581-4770.

Name_____

Address _____

City _____ State _____ Zip _____

Phone _____

Email Address _____

Occupation _____

Operating System(s) that you use _____

What influenced your purchase of this book?

❑ Recommendation ❑ Cover Design
❑ Table of Contents ❑ Index
❑ Magazine Review ❑ Advertisement
❑ New Riders' Reputation ❑ Author Name

How would you rate the contents of this book?

❑ Excellent ❑ Very Good
❑ Good ❑ Fair
❑ Below Average ❑ Poor

How do you plan to use this book?

❑ Quick reference ❑ Self-training
❑ Classroom ❑ Other

What do you like most about this book?
Check all that apply.

❑ Content ❑ Writing Style
❑ Accuracy ❑ Examples
❑ Listings ❑ Design
❑ Index ❑ Page Count
❑ Price ❑ Illustrations

What do you like least about this book?
Check all that apply.

❑ Content ❑ Writing Style
❑ Accuracy ❑ Examples
❑ Listings ❑ Design
❑ Index ❑ Page Count
❑ Price ❑ Illustrations

What would be a useful follow-up book to this one for you? _____

Where did you purchase this book? _____

Can you name a similar book that you like better than this one, or one that is as good? Why?

_____

_____

How many New Riders books do you own? _____

What are your favorite computer books? _____

_____

What other titles would you like to see us develop? _____

_____

Any comments for us? _____

_____

_____

_____

Java 2 Certification Training Guide, 0-56205-950-5

Fold here and tape to mail

Java Team
Macmillan Computer Publishing
201 W. 103rd St.
Indianapolis, IN 46290